AN
AFFIRMING
FLAME

AN AFFIRMING FLAME

MEDITATIONS ON LIFE AND POLITICS

ROGER COHEN

ALFRED A. KNOPF

New York

2023

THIS IS A BORZOI BOOK PUBLISHED BY ALFRED A. KNOPF

Copyright © 2023 by Roger Cohen

All rights reserved. Published in the United States by Alfred A. Knopf,
a division of Penguin Random House LLC, New York, and distributed
in Canada by Penguin Random House Canada Limited, Toronto.

www.aaknopf.com

Knopf, Borzoi Books, and the colophon are registered
trademarks of Penguin Random House LLC.

Owing to limitations of space, all acknowledgments to reprint previously
published material appear at the end of the volume.

Library of Congress Cataloging-in-Publication Data
Names: Cohen, Roger, author.
Title: An affirming flame : meditations on life and politics / Roger Cohen.
Other titles: Columns. Selections
Description: First edition. | New York : Alfred A. Knopf, 2023. |
"This is a Borzoi Book published by Alfred A. Knopf."
Identifiers: LCCN 2022027151 (print) | LCCN 2022027152 (ebook) |
ISBN 9780593321522 (hardcover) | ISBN 9780593321539 (ebook)
Subjects: LCSH: World politics—21st century. | Civilization, Modern—21st century. |
Journalism—United States. | American essays—21st century.
Classification: LCC PN4725.C64 2023 (print) | LCC PN4725 (ebook) |
DDC 071/.3—dc23/eng/20220926
LC record available at https://lccn.loc.gov/2022027151
LC ebook record available at https://lccn.loc.gov/2022027152

Jacket photograph by Dmitry Naumov / Shutterstock
Jacket design by John Gall

Manufactured in the United States of America
First Edition

For Sarah Hull Cleveland

As for me, I am tormented with an everlasting itch for things remote. I love to sail forbidden seas, and land on barbarous coasts.

HERMAN MELVILLE, *Moby-Dick*

"Simply because we were licked a hundred years before we started is no reason for us not to try to win."

HARPER LEE, *To Kill a Mockingbird*

May I, composed like them
Of Eros and of dust,
Beleaguered by the same
Negation and despair,
Show an affirming flame.

W. H. AUDEN, "September 1, 1939"

CONTENTS

Contents   xiii

AN
AFFIRMING
FLAME

INTRODUCTION

THE ELIXIR OF HATRED

To underestimate hatred is easy. It was comforting to think that the twentieth century, with its estimated eighty-five million dead in two world wars, its killing fields, its Nazi Holocaust, its Soviet Gulag, its Cambodian and Rwandan genocides, its Hiroshima, its mass transfers of populations, its slaughter of Bosnian Muslims at Srebrenica, its endless lessons in the inhumanity of tyrants, would be sufficient to deter or even eradicate an urge so destructive.

President Bill Clinton suggested in 1997 that great-power territorial politics were over. A new era had dawned, he said, in which "enlightened self-interest, as well as shared values, will compel countries to define their greatness in more constructive ways."

It was not to be. In her poem "Hatred," Wisława Szymborska, the Nobel Prize–winning Polish poet, writes of "How easily it vaults the tallest obstacles. / How rapidly it pounces, tracks us down." "Hatred. / Its face twisted in a grimace / of erotic ecstasy." How listless, how wan, are other feelings!

"Since when does brotherhood draw crowds?" she writes. "Has compassion ever finished first?"

Hatred "Let's face it: / it knows how to make beauty. / The splendid fire-glow in midnight skies. / Magnificent bursting bombs in rosy dawns." People say hatred is blind. No, retorts Szymborska. "It has a sniper's keen sight / and gazes unflinchingly at the future / as only it can."

Clinton was far from alone in his Panglossian view. To think like this on the eve of the millennium was seductive, but it was to succumb to an illusion. The ghosts of repetition that haunt history do not go quietly. Hatred is an elixir, a potent political bomb, a seductive answer to the unbearable banality of life. It ushers the lone individual into a consoling tribe. It brings to tired faces a rictus of arousal at the sight of the savior. Szymborska was right: the Eros of hatred is potent. It replaces pointlessness with purpose. It is always available to the nationalist demagogue ready to identify scapegoats, promise vengeance, and whip a pliant or algorithmic populace into a baying frenzy. It propagates what the poet Paul Celan called the "thousand darknesses of murderous speech."

A year before Hitler and the Nazis came to power in 1933, Kurt Schumacher, a German Social Democrat, noted in a prescient speech to the Reichstag in Berlin that certain politicians make "a continuous appeal to the inner swine" by "ceaselessly mobilizing human stupidity." That inner swine always lurks, smirking, confident of the ultimate depravity of human nature. For decades, Vladimir Putin has nursed a grievance at the breakup of the Soviet empire in 1991. It became devouring, a case of what Friedrich Nietzsche called the "whole tremulous realm of subterranean revenge, inexhaustible and insatiable in outbursts."

Nationalism is not fascism, but it is an essential component of it. Its perennial essence is a promise to change the present in the name of an illusory past in order to create a future vague in all respects except its glory. That is as true in the United States that elected Donald Trump president as it was in Belgrade when, in the last decade of the twentieth century, a surge of Serbian nationalist frenzy ripped Yugoslavia apart.

As I emerged from covering the Bosnian war in 1995—my limbs intact, unlike those of several cherished colleagues—I never thought I might draw some parallel between my own country and the Balkan carnage. But that was in the time before Trump and the turning. That was before Trump brought a European idea pregnant with violence—the mystic pull of blood and soil—into the American political theater.

If I was alive, it was to say something. Otherwise, life was wasted breath. Something about crazed nationalism, how it giddies people with myth, how it affixes the devil's horns to once-beloved neighbors, how it stirs the ghosts of blood feuds, how it frees the restive id to rampage, how it births loony ideas like turning Ukrainians into Russians or the East-West crossroads of Sarajevo into an ethnically pure Serbian preserve, how its end point may be a hundred thousand dead in the rubble and the ashes of Bosnia, or a post-apocalyptic scene in Bucha, Ukraine, with dozens of bodies in black plastic bags laid out beneath weeping birches laden with mistletoe. How nationalist fever quashes tolerance, destroys civilization, builds concentration camps, enables dictators, devours freedom, and erects walls to keep out an entire nation of "rapists."

I was not going to look away, least of all if the pestilence I had witnessed in wars from Lebanon to the former Yugoslavia began eating into the American soul.

Nor was I going to despair. If, as I do, you come from a land like South Africa, where for decades a conflagration seemed inevitable, only to discover that the statesmanship of Nelson Mandela and F. W. de Klerk could avert the inescapable bloodbath and overcome the evil of apartheid by other means, you arrive at a stubborn optimism, W. H. Auden's "affirming flame."

I like to visit the Constitutional Court in Johannesburg, guardian of the progressive 1996 Constitution that is the foundation of the new South Africa. It stands adjacent to the site of the Old Fort, where both Mohandas Gandhi and Nelson Mandela were imprisoned. In the courtroom itself, the eleven judges look out of windows set at the level of the feet of passersby, a reminder that they are there to serve the people. A fire burns outside—the "Flame of Democracy." In front of it, the preamble to the Constitution is engraved:

> We, the people of South Africa, recognize the injustices of our past; honor those who suffered for justice and freedom in our land; respect those who have worked to build and develop our country; and believe that South Africa belongs to all who live in it, united in our diversity.

The road to racial justice in the United States has been equally long. My American patriotism, which is to nationalism as love is to loathing, could only engage me in the same fight for dignity and equality. So does the oath to uphold the Constitution that I made in becoming an American.

An oath to certain foundations of a decent life: that we are a nation of laws, precisely because we know that the hatred lurking in the human heart must be constrained; that all Americans, whatever their beliefs or faith or color, have the same rights and responsibilities under the law; that this law establishes checks and balances designed to safeguard our freedom and our democracy; and that these are the values we carry out into the world in the belief that if they cannot always deliver the best they may at least avert the worst.

As Albert Camus wrote, the plague returns "for the instruction or misfortune of mankind." If the plague is not to cause enduring misfortune, it must be for the instruction of a sufficient number to prevent that.

INWARD

Through the obstacles it threw up and the borders it closed, the coronavirus was an invitation to be still. Forsake the frenetic. Journey inward. Take stock. A warming earth where seas rise and icebergs melt struck back. Exacting breathlessness, the earth asserted its demand to breathe.

So it was that I found myself in southwest Colorado among the luminous aspens, in the vastness and silence of American space, with a big moon swimming up in the sky at night to send its gleam over the untroubled peaks. It seemed implausible that I should be here. My forebears ended their lives on other continents. The friend, my age exactly, who first lured me westward, collapsed and died in 2021 at his house beyond the pasture where elk graze. My Jewish family's twisting path out of Lithuania to South Africa and Britain had no right to lead here. I am a stranger, but perhaps this is my form of belonging, the outsider looking on a little askance. It is the impostor who has no home or quiet.

I retreated to this place where the stars blaze and coyotes howl to look back at all the pieces written from countless datelines in an attempt to get to the nub of things, to connect the points of light.

Gathered in this volume are a selection of the columns I wrote for *The New York Times* over a period of fifteen years, from 2005 to 2020, first for the news pages of the international edition (the former *International Herald Tribune*) and, from 2008, for the op-ed pages of the domestic edition. They address a variety of themes, including the personal and the political.

In them, a growing alarm is discernible. This has been the Age of Undoing—of world order, of international law, of truth, of the ozone layer, of peace. It is a dangerous time. Autocracy feeds on fear and lies. So do pandemics. The plague seeped into a post-truth culture, the perfect medium for its propagation. It fed on inequality bred over decades, taking the weakest and the poorest. It revealed a moral and political vacuum, a world unanchored.

As the pandemic ebbed, President Vladimir Putin of Russia went to war to "de-Nazify" Ukraine, a country led by a Jew. This was something new under the sun. He asserted that Russia's neighbor Ukraine was an invented nation, a fiction, fit only for obliteration. In Putin, the isolation of the COVID-19 pandemic had fed obsession to the point of derangement over the Soviet Union's dissolution.

There is no environment more conducive to the strongman's promises than disorientation. There is no surer prologue to dictatorship than the destruction of truth. Without a concept of truth, there are no facts; and without facts, there is no science or law, only the whirling of conspiracies that sweep people away like moths drawn to an orange flame.

We, ever-unrequited Americans, have "a republic, if you can keep it," as Benjamin Franklin responded in Philadelphia in 1787, when asked what form of government the nascent United States had adopted. Across the world, as autocratic and illiberal models spread, the task of keeping democracies, and reforming them to that end, has been entered upon in earnest.

A CURIOUS COMPANION

A column needs a voice or it is nothing. It requires an idea, and they do not fall to order from trees. The best columns write themselves. They come, all of a piece, a gift from some deep place. They enfold the subject just so, like a halter on a horse's face.

Such inspiration is rare. Most columns resemble exquisite torture. They demand succinctness and pithiness, given their customary eight-hundred-word form, but also live or die on their ability to establish an emotional bond with the reader, despite the space limit on descriptive or narrative writing. Lincoln did all right with 272 words at Gettysburg. When the cutting began, I consoled myself with that.

The head, too dry, withers without the heart. The columnist's bully pulpit may serve to hammer on a cherished theme, at the risk of uninteresting predictability. More important is the view from the ground, the detail hard-earned, the smell of a place, the phrase that jolts. To see, to listen, to remain, to reflect, to report: these are the elements. Think of the columnist as a querulous, curious companion blessed with the curse of complete freedom.

Gathered here are the fruits of a double journey, out into the world and, increasingly, into myself. A naturalized American, raised in the South Africa of my Jewish parents' birth and the Britain they migrated to in 1957, when apartheid became intolerable, I have been concerned with themes of democratic freedom, repression, racism, poverty, displacement, dignity, and belonging. The son of a South African mother who never fully adapted to the dirty-dishwater skies of Britain, I have pondered the pain and dilemmas of the uprooted. Throughout this journey my readers accompanied me, prodding, criticizing, pushing me further.

When I wound up my column for *The Times* on November 20, 2020, with a farewell entitled "Au Revoir but Not Adieu," Lynn Ochberg of Key Largo, Florida, sent a comment thanking me for my "constant reminders of our precious responsibility as citizens." Perhaps, at root, that is what I have been about. I have witnessed in too many wars and too many repressive states how easy it is to extinguish freedom and the small miracle of the ballot box.

Our times feel fragile, bereft of certainties. There is talk of nuclear war, of World War III. There is a rush on bunkers to resist the bomb. Strongmen ride roughshod over borders where too much blood has already been shed in the pursuit of dangerous nationalist illusions.

Vladimir Putin struts his stuff, kills because he can, master of what John le Carré called the "classic, timeless, all-Russian, barefaced whopping lie." He justifies his invasion of Ukraine as a riposte to the "Nazi" rule of Volodymyr Zelensky, who has, with courage and aplomb, resisted in the name of freedom. Russia and China, an alliance of autocracies, proclaim "no limits" to their friendship.

The plague takes many forms.

At the outbreak of COVID-19 the planet went so quiet you could almost hear it whirling around the sun, feel its smallness, picture for once the blue loneliness and tenuousness of life. I was in New York in early 2020. On Front Street in Brooklyn I saw a single rat wandering around as if it owned the city. It stopped beside a garbage bag ripped open by a dog. An apocalyptic vision of filth and vermin on a dying planet overcame me as sirens wailed and choppers circled over triage tents.

Since then, vaccines have tamed the worst of the pandemic's ravages but are not the deliverance they once seemed. The technology that enabled the wealthy to globalize their advantages also created the perfect mechanism for globalizing panic.

The adjective "viral" entered everyday parlance to describe a video, image, or story spreading uncontrollably. Today, "coronavirus" is a long word that rolls off the tongues of small children. For long periods, they were schooled on remote screens. Berserk eight-year-olds, confined in "pods," clutching school-issued iPads (if they were lucky), longing for a "brain break," ordering Amazon's Alexa about, offered a troubling hint of the American future.

The pandemic has become a mirror of our anxiety, our vanity, our bafflement, our out-of-control lives. The monster is many-headed. If it is tamed by science, it is nourished by fear. It will be with us for years, like the shadow of Putin's war.

"Nothing," Victor Hugo wrote, "is more imminent than the impossible."

TAKE THE STRANGER IN

As a columnist I wandered—across the North American continent, in Europe, Africa, and the Middle East, Papua New Guinea, Argentina, China—in search of ways to tell stories that would touch people. Often the news drove me. Just as often I tried to shut out the news to reach something deeper.

To live free and in dignity seemed to me to be the bedrock quest of most of humanity. But when life becomes struggle, the easy answers promised by the nationalist autocrat become seductive. Those answers are generally illusory. The nation, whatever else it may be, is an insufficient framework for the world's shared problems, from rising inequality to rising temperatures. Withering crops and parched riverbeds do not respect borders. Nor does a pandemic. Nor do the global supply chains on which we depend.

My gaze was cast in many directions, but perhaps above all at America in the world, the obsessive way this sprawling, rambunctious nation inhabits people across the globe. As Saul Bellow observes in *Humboldt's Gift*, the United States is "a big operation, very big." Bellow, of course, was from Chicago, that handsome upstart of a city where light and contour exhilarate and the varied faces and physiognomies on the street seem to proclaim America's enduring everyday promise.

At its best, America takes the stranger in. That is what happened to me in New York. I am a New Yorker, because it is the city that took me in. Displacement, which is loss, is a lingering state. Yet home may also sink its roots in little time, as if in a revelation.

The United States is a relatively new nation, coeval with a revolutionary idea from which it is inseparable, a country "conceived in liberty and dedicated to the proposition that all men are created equal." That aspiration—however flawed in execution, however contradicted at the outset by slavery, however battered of late by the rise of xenophobic nationalism and the decline in social mobility—retains its riveting appeal. To be an American, as I have been for seventeen years as I write, is to be part of an experiment in an unattained but liberating idea. We are an unsubtle nation that believes in a fair shake for everyone. Becoming an American is not complicated.

America asks not where you come from, what ancestry you may boast, but what you can *do*. Its gaze is fixed forward. Anyone can dream of becoming an American, as I did, and therein lies part of the country's magnetism.

No other nation exists in such an intense state of churn or offers such a radical and ever-renewed invitation to reinvention; and no other developed country can be so cruel to those outcast from its promise. To what extent its harshness is intrinsic to its creative energy and fierce work ethic is an open question that lurks behind some of America's eternal debates on the nature of liberty and the appropriate role of the state.

Europeanizing America, in the sense of extending social insurance to assure greater protection in something resembling a welfare state, will always be problematic, in that the United States was born in contradistinction to Europe—its monarchies, its hierarchies, the centralized state Napoleon raised to its apotheosis. But obstinate attachment to some rigid notion of "freedom," along with a caricatural portrayal of the menace of European "socialism," tends to produce disasters like the unwieldy, wildly expensive, often dysfunctional American health-care system.

SURE

No word is more essential to American being than "sure," the single-syllable readiness to give it a whirl, because, what the hell, how much of that open sky are you prepared to turn your back on? In France, where I now live and have intermittently throughout my life, no word, by contrast, is more essential than *"terroir,"* the particularity of a fixed place. *"Terroir"* is the land, the special characteristics of one parcel of it, the nature of its soil, its climate, and *the unique enduring human relationship to it.*

American restlessness; French rootedness. New World; old Europe. Yonder or deeper. American reinvention; European fate. The cussedness of the frontier; the culture of the bourgeoisie. American idealism; French realism. Each indelible idea exerts its own degree of magnetism. Each takes half of me. Part of the work of my columns has been an attempt to explain why.

By equality Americans understand equality of opportunity, not of outcome. It's fine to get rich, in a way that it's not fine in France, where wealth is best concealed. Live happy, live hidden, goes the old French saying. To which Americans would retort, make money, become free.

There is a reason you can get a shoeshine all over the United States but nowhere in France, where the conception of equality is irreconcilable with the indignity of working at somebody's feet. There's a reason it's maddeningly difficult to get the check at a French restaurant and maddeningly easy at an American one: France is not bent on the monetization of everything. Scrawled on a wall in Paris I saw this political slogan: "The economy out of our lives!"

At America's core is an idea of openness, the haven of Emma Lazarus's "huddled masses yearning to breathe free." Threatened, assaulted by inward-turning temptations, it is still there. Americans believe in the second act because that is how their forebears' lives in a New World began.

To succumb to morosity is not an option. As Samuel Beckett put it, "Ever tried. Ever failed. No matter. Try again. Fail again. Fail better."

In Alabama, a Chevron gas station in Wilton, an hour south of Birmingham, is run by a Vietnamese immigrant family now renowned for making the best fried chicken for miles around. Huynh Kim left Vietnam in 1980, one of some eight hundred thousand "boat people" fleeing the communist regime after the end of the Vietnamese war in 1975. She and her family spent two years in a refugee camp in Malaysia before reaching the United States. Chance led them to Alabama, where her husband, Hyunh Loan, saw a business opportunity in the gas station the family has now run for more than thirty years.

Long lines of Alabamians waiting to buy chicken and biscuits attest to this small encapsulation of American openness. "Americans are the most generous people in the whole world," her daughter Diana says. "They are good."

Diana's father died of COVID-19 in 2020, at the age of seventy-four.

The American dream persists. The dream is frayed.

AMERICAN SPACE

In its vastness, at its birth, the United States beckoned. It was not empty. Indigenous people were killed or displaced. There was a reason the United States declined for forty years to ratify the U.N. Genocide Convention, only doing so in 1988.

The limitless land unfolded westward; it was populated by migrants who *left everything behind*. To be anti-immigrant in the United States is at some level an act of self-denial. It is to betray a decision taken by some forebear to turn away from cold or famine or hurt, and to embrace America's promise; a decision, in a New World, to live as a free agent on one's own terms.

American space, which in its immensity embodies possibility, is the key to the national psyche most difficult for Europeans, on a densely populated continent, to grasp. On American soil, risk could only be something to be embraced rather than mitigated.

In Colorado, where I write, the grandeur of the state's beauty and space seems to stir some nobler instinct in the name of preserving nature and advancing the common good. It's impossible to drive across the state and not be reminded of the initial boundlessness of American potential. People disagree; they are rarely disagreeable, even if Lauren Boebert, a Glock-wielding, first-term Republican lawmaker from Rifle, Colorado, has become a prominent face of hard-right, take-no-prisoners senti-ment. The state still feels like a place where it's possible to come and be defined by how hard you are willing to work. That's the American way.

There's another American way, of course: a life of harsh struggle. Many people can't easily afford housing, can't easily afford health care, can't easily afford higher education or early-childhood education. In other words, most people cannot afford a middle-class lifestyle. Aspira-tional American ascension is supplanted by American alienation.

Still, in Colorado, the capacity for compromise—as an oil-and-natural-gas state with limited water committed to environmental preservation and an outdoors lifestyle—has not been entirely lost, as it appears to have been in Washington.

Wedge issues like guns, immigration, and abortion tend to obscure the fact that many Americans of whatever political persuasion want the same things: affordable health care, better schools and wages, protec-tion of public lands and water.

In 2018, I met Don Colcord, a pharmacist and one of the rare Democrats in Nucla, Colorado, population seven hundred. The town was founded around 1900 by a utopian socialist group. It lived off ura-nium mining during the Cold War and has now turned to the cultivation of marijuana's cousin, hemp, in a stab at a revival. Colcord believes that

Democrats need to stop alienating small-town America. Environmental concerns are worthy, but what happens when, as in Nucla, they lead to the shutdown of a coal-fired power plant with the loss of dozens of jobs and the tax base that pays for schools?

I went to a funeral service at Nucla's First Baptist Church for Lacie Redd, a thirty-four-year-old divorced mother of two girls who had committed suicide. Redd's mother, Glenna Nix, worked at Colcord's pharmacy. He knows the family. Redd suffered from seizures; her prescription medicine was expensive.

"Thirty tablets cost more than a thousand dollars, and she needed more than one a day, and she was fighting and fighting to get insurance to cover it, and sometimes she'd run out," Colcord recalled.

In the end, this particular American misery was too much for Redd—caring for her girls, coping with seizures, getting her medicine, just plain surviving.

"There are a lot of wonderful things about free enterprise," Colcord reflected. "And a lot of devastating things, too. Good old America."

THE ELEMENTAL

"I'm a writer," James Baldwin wrote. "I like doing things alone."

To be alone on deadline is the journalist's lot, facing the many-faceted world and seeking the means to render it as closely as possible, knowing that something in the quiver of life is always ineffable and will slip through the cracks. These ancient piñon pines on which I gaze, these Jurassic sandstone rocks perhaps 150 million years old, these majestic, snow-capped peaks silhouetted in the dawn as if cut from paper, murmur of the elemental. What do they, or the straight-backed stoical cattle, or the lone fox in the field with eyes aglow, care for our dilemmas?

A human life is nothing. It is all we have.

At the risk of dishonoring ourselves through flight, we must discover and render the elemental in our own lives. Think of life as a corridor with endless doors to left and right, whispering and beckoning: Come hither, go thither. The glimpsed vistas look seductive. They also distract from the challenge of looking deeper and make it impossible to know where a single path leads.

For years you may gaze at the cobwebs dangling from a light fitting. Tomorrow, you say, I will borrow the neighbor's ladder, and then tomorrow you find yourself thinking those cobwebs are not so bad after all, they're inoffensive, they even catch bugs. Until, one day, you do the simple thing that is also the hardest thing and remove the cobwebs of your life.

Patience. It takes time to understand. Listen, touch, smell, feel. The subject will reveal itself to you if you restrain the impulse to impose it. The story must build from the inside out, like the butterfly from the chrysalis with a slow unfolding of wings. Writing begins where the anecdotal stops. Writing dies where the preconceived prevails over the telling detail.

Never in my wandering did the thrill of filling in the blank canvas of a new dateline fade. Jet fuel shimmering through the hot Lagos air and an assignment looming, to deadline. Go until you are stopped. Piece together the details.

In his haunting novel *A Sport and a Pastime,* James Salter writes: "Life is composed of certain basic elements. . . . Of course, there are a lot of impurities, that's what's misleading."

Today, contagious impurities multiply. Life becomes an exercise in serial distraction, yielding to the influence of the influencer. Every singular place, what journalists call a dateline, becomes fungible everywhere. Cross the world, remain in your comfort zone. If great journalism involves immersion in place—and it does—this dateline devaluation is dangerous. If you write from anywhere, you write from nowhere.

It is impossible to bear witness from digital distance, removed from the mire, the tears, the sediment in the syrupy coffee. No search engine gives you the stench of a crime, the tremor in the air, the eyes that smolder, or the cadence of a scream. No miracle of technology renders the lip drying taste of fear. No news aggregator tells of the air reverberating from the shell's blast in the tapering valley. No algorithm captures the hush of dignity, or evokes the adrenaline rush of coalescing courage, or traces the fresh, raw line of a welt.

In war it is the children and the aged who wave, even from the ruins, the innocent and the wise. Look at them. Write them down. Carry them in your heavy heart.

When I was young and in Buenos Aires, fair city, melancholy city, a friend said to me: "Journalism's a cheap shot for you." I never asked what she meant, but I never forgot it either. I think she meant that journalism tends to stop where artistic creation begins, and that is the realm of deeper truths.

Buenos Aires in the mid-1980s was awakening to the scope of a national nightmare. Every conversation seemed to end in tears as parents, haunted by desperate imaginings, recalled their children who had been "disappeared" by the military junta. *Los desaparecidos.* That many of the tens of thousands of corpses were dumped from planes into the South Atlantic between 1976 and 1983 was not yet known.

So did the Argentine military turn "disappear" into a transitive verb.

I sat and listened. That's what journalists do: listen through silence, awaiting a clue, the revealing epiphany, the face that crumples like a dynamited building, the beauty that lingers like the scattered rhododendron blossom half trodden into the pathway.

Students summoned by police for questioning ("shouldn't take more than a half hour"), never to be seen again. Students bundled into Ford Falcons on Avenida Corrientes, never to be seen again. Pregnant women kept alive to give birth before their execution so that childless military couples could take the children and raise them as their own.

Plundered flesh.

Argentina, so rich, so plundered, always plundered, in every way, was haunting. Perhaps because it was depressive, it appealed to me. Buenos Aires, in its elaborate elegance, reminded me of Flaubert's remark that style is the "discharge from a deeper wound." In the most beautiful smiles, painful knowledge hovers. Distance weighed on Argentines, down at the bottom of the world—a form of banishment. It lay at the heart of the strange story of a rich nation's failure, all that impossibly fertile black topsoil of the Pampas yielding a recurrent harvest of blood. Coup after coup and the madness of Peronism.

Grief and mourning twist the mind toward irrational acts. Clawing the earth to demonstrate that the remains of a beloved daughter are not buried there. See, she may still live! The finality of sudden death compounded by disappearance is too much to bear.

Hisham Matar, the Libyan novelist whose father was "disappeared" by Egyptian security agents in 1990, wrote that everything and everyone had become "a possibility for resemblance."

I told the story in the way that seemed most revealing to me: from within the anguish of the people I met. Theirs was the latest inflection of the Argentine tragedy. Recurrent disappearances: of indigenous peoples, of so-called leftists, of the past, all of them feeding the potent ever-ready fuse of suppressed memory.

The intersection of personal and national psyches has always constituted the richest point of journalistic inquiry for me. I wandered the world in search of a "possibility for resemblance."

FACTS AND TRUTH

In June 2009, I walked in silence in Tehran with the protesters against an election stolen by the brutal enforcers of the Islamic Republic. The crowd was immense, later estimated in the millions. It stretched, appropriately enough, from Revolution Square to Liberty Square. I spoke in a whisper to the young woman next to me, and at last I asked her name.

My name is Iran, she said.

A complete story in four words.

I stuck to what I knew. But facts can feel inadequate. A lot of war is waiting around. Defiance lies in small things, waiters folding linen napkins with great care in war-ravaged Beirut in 1983, the stylish women hurling elegance back at the barbarians in the hills in encircled Sarajevo in 1994. *Inat,* the Bosnian women called it, a mixture of stubbornness and spite, as pointed as their high heels.

A young couple seated at a restaurant in Beirut in 1983, cocooned in the world of their love. I wondered how the small magical space of their interlaced fingertips blotted out the shelling. War is one thing, wartime another.

For a writer, *it's all material.* You inhabit the world; you keep a distance as an onlooker and note taker. You are within and without. You write it down, to see how words may change aspect over time, like peonies changing color as they fade.

Amos Oz, the Israeli novelist who became a friend, once said to me, "Facts at times become the dire enemies of the truth." I think Oz, who died in 2018, meant that certain elements of reality yield only to some combination of intuition and imagination, in addition to observation. Another late friend, Ward Just, a journalist turned novelist, put the conundrum this way: "Many of the things that make you a good journalist have to be discarded to make you a good writer. In a novel, every fact is a rock thrown in the hull, and the boat sinks a bit."

Picasso's *Guernica* is a poor factual account of what happened in a Basque village on April 26, 1937, and a magnificent rendering of what happened in every village ever bombed in any war. The painting is perfect journalistic reportage, if measured by how much universal truth it contains.

Speaking of Guernica, on September 25, 2016, François Delattre, then the French ambassador to the United Nations, described Putin's flattening of Aleppo in these terms: "In many ways, Aleppo is to Syria what Sarajevo was to Bosnia or furthermore Guernica to the Spanish civil war."

Nobody listened. So was the flattening of Mariupol in eastern Ukraine foretold.

Journalists must seek specific truth. Stubborn facts, the kind that bring down governments, usher barbarians like that Argentine junta to judgment at last. Facts are the essential ballast of decency.

As the Polish poet Czesław Miłosz has written: "Do not feel safe. The poet remembers. / You may kill him—another will be born. / Deeds and words shall be recorded."

Journalists remember. Record the trail of barbarism, set down the torture, that the perpetrators may not efface their own crimes.

The truth, it is said, will out. But will it in the maelstrom of our days?

"Fake news," "alternative facts," "fact-based journalism" (as if there is any other kind) are the phrases of an era in which velocity trumps veracity. Down the rabbit hole of 2 + 2 = 5 lies dystopia. As the British historian Simon Schama has pointed out, it is "indifference" to the distinction between truth and falsehood that lays the groundwork for despotism.

Behind every bystander to a crime, watching neighbors with their bundles troop off, heads bowed, to their faraway executions, lurks that same word: *indifference.* The Germans have a good word for those who make their quiet accommodations with evil—"*Mitläufer,*" or "fellow traveler." It is they who leave the naked victims clawing at concrete walls to die. How did the executioner feel about the scratch marks in the gas chamber?

Indifference is the enabler of the crime. It is the course a majority of people adopt in the face of evil if that evil poses an immediate threat to their lives. Still, as Hannah Arendt wrote, "Under conditions of terror most people will comply but *some people will not.* . . . Humanly speaking, no more is required, and no more can reasonably be asked, for this planet to remain a place fit for human habitation."

In the disorienting bombardment of social media, when Monday's outrage cannot be recalled because Friday's has supplanted it, indifference spreads.

AMERICAN FRACTURE

Shortly after the chaotic American withdrawal from Afghanistan in August 2021, I found myself in a funky Denver bar with a bunch of Marine vets. Bob Marley blared from the jukebox, craft beer flowed. Opposite me sat Michael Van Duren, a gaunt man with a touch of Forrest Gump about him, his good heart scarred by gore and mayhem.

"Eat, sleep, stay alive," he said. "Look after the guy to your left and the guy to your right." He bit his lip. "Life is simple in war. I often yearn for that simplicity."

These Marines signed up soon after 9/11 because they wanted to serve their country. They felt they owed it something, only to return to an ungrateful land. They trudged their trauma home and nobody seemed to notice. Money rode roughshod over sacrifice.

"How do you make it *personal* to the American public?" Van Duren asks, his face knotted in pained perplexity. "Don't they see they are rely-ing on us to be able to lead the life they lead?" He often feels his neigh-bors don't have a clue. Most Americans, waiting in numbed expectation for their Amazon packages, never saw a buddy blown to pieces in a carmine-tinted sand swirl far from home.

The American wars where everyone served and everyone sacrificed are long gone, along with the wars that ended in victory and ticker-tape parades.

From battlefields without a name, America now slips away in the night like a dying animal.

What was it all for? The Taliban marched into Kabul unopposed as soon as America left in August 2021. Afghans who risked their lives for the American cause were abandoned to their fates. All this gnaws at the Marines, who live by the credo "Leave no one behind."

So—did they change during these past twenty years of war, or did America? Whichever it was, probably both, they don't feel they belong, at least not outside their tribe, where their service in Iraq and Afghani-stan is honored.

Raw anger ricochets around the table. This broken America! Nar-cissism and entitlement and Gender 360 and people complaining their latte is not served right. What were they supposed to do as warriors? Come home, bury everything, and never talk again about the wars that cost $2.3 trillion in national treasure? Or listen to all the pandemic guid-ance, fit for children, about how to wash your hands and how to cock your elbows for a don't-get-too-close greeting?

The exasperated mood around that Denver table tells a familiar story of an America where Americans have lost sight of one another. These Marines feel invisible, their sacrifice taken for granted, just as the labor of American workers with stagnant wages in the postindustrial knowledge-economy—packagers, drivers, cashiers, caregivers—were never really noticed until COVID-19 struck. Suddenly, it was the afflu-ent in their Zoom meetings who were *nonessential*, and the blue-collar workers whose *essential* physical endeavor held some semblance of society together.

The virus exposed a country that could not come together to defeat a pathogen about one-thousandth the width of an eyelash. Far from uniting before a mortal threat, America divided further. Social mobility had lost out to an entrenched caste of the superrich. The highly educated beneficiaries of globalization and the knowledge economy had parted company with its casualties marooned on shoals of stagnant wages across the land. Truth was lost in the howl of social-media noise, its burial led by a president for whom everything equaled ME. Violence was in the air. A neighbor in Colorado told me to gun up before it was too late.

The unity that tragedy forged in the immediate aftermath of 9/11 proved to be an illusion. America's great gift, its breezy individualism, had devolved into the cancer of its devouring self-indulgence. Growing American heedlessness and self-absorption made the 9/11 attack possible in the first place.

A SMALL GIRL DIES

The Marines' frustration reminded me of conversations in Kentucky a few months before the election of Trump in 2016, when I heard a lot about how white lives matter, too, and of how illegal—as in "illegal immigrant"—means *illegal*, just as robbing a bank is.

For anyone used to New York discourse, it was a through-the-looking-glass experience. Something was up; the country was boiling.

There were just as many certainties. They were simply the opposite ones—whether on police violence toward Blacks, the Second Amendment, immigration, or reproductive choice. Guns, God, and abortion divided the land. America's internal split is economic but cultural above all. It is about values: an idea, or mythology, of what the United States *means*. This is not a country that can merely *be*.

As Richard Hofstadter observed, it is the fate of the United States "not to have an ideology but to be one." The question, by 2022, for a growing number of Americans was whether that ideology had ever been credible. How could "the proposition that all men are created equal" coexist with the institution of slavery and the enfranchisement of only a small male and white share of adult Americans? Were life, liberty, and the pursuit of happiness only for these men? The rush to absolutist judgment of the past seemed impervious to the notion that two centuries from now our own mores would appear similarly grotesque. It sometimes appeared that the American idea, still luminous even in its imperfection, had sunk in a morass of inward-turning tribalism and hatred across the abyss of extreme inequality.

The commonwealth had withered and fractured. Dean Sanchez, one of the Marines at my table in Denver, is troubled by "politicians setting our country on fire for their own personal gains. They are *representatives* of us, and they forget that."

Sanchez, all coiled energy, trains Marines. "You lose two rifles at the Camp Lejeune training base and the entire chain of command is relieved," he says. "You are *accountable* for everything you do or say. I beat my guys down when they screw up. But you lose tens of billions of weapons now in the hands of the Taliban, thirteen service members—ten of them Marines—in a terrorist attack at Kabul Airport, and you lose America's longest war, and it looks like there's total impunity."

The fix is in, the same way it was in 2008, when toxic mortgage-backed securities were revealed for what they were, the leverage binge came to an end, and, after 158 years, Lehman Brothers went poof in the night.

The wealthy architects of the newfangled financial instruments that abolished risk long enough for them to make a killing walked away to ensconce themselves with a dozen screens in some mansion. Nobody was convicted for the financial crimes that left millions of Americans homeless.

There were two standards: one for the privileged, one for the Americans they treated as suckers. As Kipling noted, in lines that say much about how rival American tribes now eye one another, "All good people agree, / And all good people say, / All nice people, like Us, are We / And every one else is They."

The Americans beside me risked their lives in Iraq and Afghanistan, but these were unwon wars the nation wants to forget. So the warriors fade from sight even as the scenes they witnessed, the things they did in their patriotic ardor, will not leave *them*. There is less place in the culture for their memories than there is for Kim Kardashian's Instagram influencer account or the alternate reality of the metaverse.

Invisible people, far from the urban hubs of a globalized world, will rise up to be *seen.*

Van Duren is suddenly back in Iraq, entering some dust-blown town. His unit is on edge. Improvised explosive devices known as IEDs are everywhere.

"I was in the point vehicle, they were shooting down on us, bullets whizzing," he says. "We used to ask them how they learned to shoot and they would say Rambo, and a lot of them did shoot from the hip like him. We kept on pushing. And there's a woman coming toward me with a little girl, a two-year-old. All these women and children in the mix, and I'm thinking, *What the fuck are we doing here?"*

He tears up and looks me in the eye. "I'm pretty sure I killed that little girl, and I think about it all the time."

A small girl dissolving in red dust. The blood spilled in faraway wars sticks to these Marines like resin from a tree.

Van Duren also thinks about Lance Corporal Jeremy Burris, who was killed by an IED near the Syrian border on October 8, 2007. Burris is buried in Liberty, Texas. Van Duren finally got to visit the grave in 2021. When he was killed, Van Duren recalls, Sergeant Adam Bosley knelt beside what was left of Burris's body. A couple of years later, Bosley died in a motorbike accident near San Diego. He is buried in Nebraska. Van Duren dressed his corpse for the funeral.

"He was driving at some crazy speed," Van Duren says. "A lot of Marines do that when they come home. We have all had our troubles."

It's tough trying to outrun the past, even at 180 miles per hour.

That image of Van Duren as Forrest Gump comes back to me, and Gump running, running, running. And Gump saying: "Mama always said dying was part of life. I sure wish it wasn't."

EXCAVATION

We all die. My mother gone, my father gone now. There is no preparation for the loneliness of a world from which the two people who put you in it have gone. The death of parents removes the last cushion against contemplation of your own mortality. The cycle of life becomes internal, bone-deep knowledge, a source now of melancholy, now of inspiration.

This above all, to thine own self be true.

My mother often said that.

"What happens to a dream deferred?" asks Langston Hughes in his poem "Harlem." "Does it dry up / like a raisin in the sun?"

Or "Maybe it just sags / like a heavy load. / *Or does it explode?*"

The wick is lit, the clock is ticking, taking you backward, always backward, into the sterile patterns of yourself denied. There is always somebody else. There is always the next distraction or detour; always, also, the debris after the explosion.

No, not that. It is time.

To write is violent combat in search of the irrefutable cadence. There is more to be abjured than added, more truth in distillation than accumulation. To write is loneliness. It is excavation. It is struggle for declarative sentences that hammer out discomforting truths.

Working from a core of pain and melancholy, it is not surprising that I sought out those same emotions. In refugee camps, in war zones, at remote borders, in the shanties and the shebeens, at the face of a South African gold reef one mile down; in Chengdu, where a Chinese woman crushed by the state had self-immolated; among the displaced and the exploited and the terrified—that was my place, that my debt.

Take me home, the outcasts whispered, you who have none.

Why, I wondered, did they look at me with such intensity? Was it recognition I saw in the eyes of the lost of the earth? *"Hypocrite lecteur,— mon semblable,—mon frère!"* Baudelaire's line, taken up by T. S. Eliot in *The Waste Land:* "Hypocrite reader!—My fellow!—My brother!"

"Objectivity" is a fine word, a fine journalistic aspiration even, but it is a dead word, freighted with too many syllables, and we are human. We bring to what we write our own unique sensibilities, our rawness, our sisters and brothers. We bring our hypocrisies too, and if we fail to do so we become uninteresting. If I wanted my readers to accompany me through life, they needed clues.

Halftones interest me more than primary colors. Van Gogh's flowers are always wilting slightly. His lilies have turned from pink to purple and are a little brownish on the edges. The artist is interested in the beauty of the equipoise between life and death—and isn't that where we are all situated without paying much attention to it? Van Gogh is less taken by perfection than by decay.

Ours is a culture of perfection, of all or nothing, of primary colors and primal screams, of presumption of guilt, of unforgiving trial by the mob, proud in its refusal to compromise—and so it is broken.

Florists cut the stamens out of lilies because the pollen stains. But as some lilies wilt, others bloom, with their pale-green-and-crimson stamens. It is important to live with the stains. As Leonard Cohen observed, there's "a crack in everything / That's how the light gets in."

It is the deviation from strict symmetry that imbues the Parthenon with the pulse of life. The folds and pleats of Athenian statuary are supple. That is why they are alive. The human pulse is not a metronome. We are not storage devices. We inhabit the intermediate zones. The human timber is crooked and, as Immanuel Kant observed, "Out of it no straight thing was ever made."

Isaiah Berlin wrote in *The Crooked Timber of Humanity*, "No perfect solution is, not merely in practice, but in principle, possible in human affairs, and any determined attempt to produce it is likely to lead to suffering, disillusionment and failure."

Democracy is imperfect, and in that imperfection lies its distinctive humanity, its beauty, its elasticity, its terrifying fragility: the quality that every quest for utopia ends up crushing on the way to terror.

Sometimes, wandering around the archeological ruins of Greece, I've wondered: Does the caryatid in her stoic grace even know the burden she carries? We might ask the same of democracy and the miracles it undergirds.

A SNAKE'S SKIN

The snake has shed its skin. Silvery-gray, it is coiled around a branch in the wintry light, meeting my gaze each morning, a reminder that as humans we do not get to slither free and hang up an old coat every year to proclaim our renewal. On we go, toward a destination too well known, haunted by memories that expand with the years.

We want to love. We want to be free. We want to belong. I hear the whistle of the freight train, the wind chimes at the Alabama farm, the foghorn of the Staten Island Ferry, the birdsong in the Colorado dawn, the footsteps in the Paris dawn, fading slowly, like memories, like Apollinaire's hunters' horns. These are familiar sounds that comfort me. A single leaf flutters down and lands next to me on a table. I close my eyes, run my finger along its slight undulations, and feel the surface of my father's thumbnail.

Transported by a leaf. The purple liver spots on the back of Sydney's hand as he aged, mold of the years.

My father, a physician, had the hands of the healer. He knew, and was at one with, the natural world. No terrain was so forbidding that he could not conjure a garden from it. His elements were trees, grass, flowers, wind, sky, and water. From them he created patterns and in them he found solace. I see him gazing at the reflection of leaves quivering in a pool, the raindrops making silver circles.

His was a double life of anguish. He strove over forty-nine years of marriage to cope with the mental illness of my mother, June. This was, as he once wrote to me, "the deepest and most sacred element of my life." He was wounded, found somebody else, and, in time, withdrew.

Each of us carries a measure of mystery; each of us faces situations in which there are no good choices; each of us, untying the knot of life, living forward and striving to understand it backward, becomes wary of casting the first stone.

Displacement from the South Africa of her birth, and from the tight-knit Jewish community there, overcame my mother. She first broke down with postpartum depression in London in 1958 and, on July 30 of that year, three days before my third birthday, was treated with electroconvulsive therapy in a Victorian Gothic psychiatric hospital later used as the set for horror movies. It was well suited for that. She remained there for many months.

I see her, strapped down, slight, pale, electrodes clamped to her beautiful curls, shuddering on a table.

Her scream is silent.

Everybody knows that abandonment induces an enduring form of panic, for which there are no words in the muteness of infancy and only pale words ever after.

Later came June's suicide attempts, one of them so determined it took a miracle to save her; the alternating inertia and mania of her bipolar condition; the fiascoes of various kinds; the arrests and near arrests; and at last the cancer that she regarded as welcome deliverance from mental anguish.

My sister, Jenny Walden, writing now:

Your tiny, wasted frame in your pink dressing gown on the sofa, or curled up in bed, Dad's empty one beside you, curtains drawn against the world. How alone you were, how lost and fearful and desperate. How often I went past your house, looked up at your bedroom window nestled amongst the wisteria and drove on, unable to face going inside. The atmosphere as heavy as a morgue, the sham of your marriage, the pain—hot and brutal—engulfing me. I wish that I could have done more.

After my mother's death in 1999, when my father was free at last to live his other life openly, he wrote to me: "I did strive within the feeble limits of my human fallibility to preserve and cherish and sustain her. But alas—for Mama ultimately, death was the only angel that could shield her from despair." He continued: "I hope that before too long the turbulence of your spirit will subside and you will reach to tranquility in your inner self."

This above all, to thine own self be true.

My mother knew she could not do that, after the electricity jolting through her brain, after the pills and the gin, the hectic urges of mania, the being timed and being watched, the lightning overhead, the thunderclaps. She was like a tree hollowed out by lightning. A solitary owl perched on one of its branches hooting into the night. There was no identifiable self left. The love inside her, and it overflowed, could not find full expression. She knew, and that is why she repeated the phrase. *Be true.*

My father could not be true to himself, either. Survival exacted a heavy price. He had to lie to maintain the elaborate balance of his double life. He could not live two lives and two loves and be true to both. I see him at a window gazing out on a wild moor, a ghostly silhouette, a lone and austere figure. Before he draws the curtains.

All that was hidden took its toll in suffering, just as the unacknowledged scars of one war may ignite another, as I saw in Bosnia. My parental reference points were suicide and duplicity: maternal love strangled and paternal love withdrawn.

Time, also, to acknowledge that.

The pinched mask of my dead mother propped at a regal angle, recalling the likeness of some diminutive French monarch in a frosty medieval crypt. Trying to prize her wedding ring off her stiffening finger because my father could not bear to do so. A mistake to attempt that. *Mama, please let go now.* My father turning the ring in his long fingers, unable to stifle a sob, as he says, "I am amazed how grief-stricken I am. It's like falling in love again."

He had waited so long, he was overcome by the chains of his double existence dissolving.

"Only connect!" wrote E. M. Forster. "Live in fragments no longer."

Time to connect the pieces, end the evasions. I have slaked my thirst on adrenaline for too long. The tranquility of your inner self may be reached only at the furthest point of acknowledged melancholy. My father did not tell me that. Nor could my mother.

I left Britain because I had to get away, not because one thing led to another. I found a home in another country, America, that allowed my Jewishness to emerge from a whisper into some form of comfortable expression. I told stories of confused identity and abandonment that ended in tears. In every generation for almost 150 years my family had moved: from Lithuania to South Africa, from South Africa to Britain, from Britain to the United States or Israel. Assuaging the wounds of loss as it went, insofar as it could.

The hammering of the artisan in a Rome backstreet comes to me as the hammering of the craftsman in the Lithuanian shtetl. Words are linear but sensations are not.

I went back to the wars, again and again, not by chance but for a reason. The anticipation of war was always worse than the reality. Still, with every exploding shell the stomach contracts. In war you need not luck but the absence of bad luck. Everyone was laid bare. I could take my scalpel to them.

Life ended suddenly in the lottery of the shrapnel's spray, or over the edge of some muddy, slithering Balkan precipice, the vehicle somersaulting. Eyes suddenly unseeing, pupils dilating into circles of blackness, under the sun.

Through some subterranean yearning, and not from mere nostalgia, I ached for South Africa. I went back. It was the only place I saw my mother happy. There, she was as content as a cat in a shaft of sunlight, far from chilly Britain, where she was a transplant that did not take.

I was double because to be whole was to be vulnerable, all chips on a single number as the roulette wheel spins. I'd lost out early in life with that approach. So I kept drawing new magical circles of protection out of new journalistic adventures. I sometimes extolled moral clarity from within a moral fog.

Perhaps there is nothing more brutal in life than honesty; and the truth is, my choices ran out.

The columns collected here are also the story of my life. There was only so much, in fairness, that I could hide, even in the age of the mask.

"Brave the sunlight in a new coat," that old crinkled snake skin on a tree outside my window whispers.

Perhaps I will remove the translucent snake skin. No, not yet.

DEMOCRATIC ILLUSIONS

On the whole, these columns tell a sobering story. If the first half of my life, from 1955 to 1989, culminated in the liberation of a hundred million Central Europeans from the Soviet imperium, and the spread of freedom and representative government from Chile to South Korea, the last thirty-three years have seen an autocratic counterrevolution. Hatred, implacable, stirred.

The end of the Cold War promised the inevitable spread of liberal-democratic societies, anchored by the rule of law, as the best guarantor of human dignity and freedom. They were the anti-Gulag, the best if imperfect guarantee against the horror of war. Democracy had outlasted fascism and communism, whose end points were totalitarianism. It was the surest foundation for prosperity.

In fact, smug in their certainties, blind to their failings, Western democracies were vulnerable. If they proved to be engines of inequality, exhibits in double standards that favored elites, and promoters of a globalized race to the bottom that left many people jobless in beleaguered communities and medical deserts, they would sooner or later face revolt.

A society where billionaires pay less tax than production-line workers is a society with a problem. No greater spur to uprising exists than feelings of humiliation. Too many people for too long have felt invisible, disposable, and worthless. In the United States, the quest for dignity and a fair wage has often encountered the contempt of the privileged, whose money increasingly sways electoral outcomes through unlimited campaign contributions.

Stephen Heintz, the president of the Rockefeller Brothers Fund, has written persuasively of a crisis "that stems from the growing obsolescence of three core operating systems that have shaped civilization for the past 350 years: capitalism, fueled by carbon since the dawn of the Industrial Age and increasingly driven by global financialization; the nation-state system, formalized by the Treaty of Westphalia in 1648; and representative democracy, a system of self-rule based on Enlightenment ideals of freedom, fairness, justice and equality."

The problem is that "our practice of capitalism is both putting the planetary ecosystem at risk and generating vast economic inequality." The nation-state is "inadequate for managing transnational challenges like global warming." And "representative democracy is neither truly representative nor very democratic as citizens feel that self-rule has given way to rule by corporations, special interests and the wealthy."

A counter-model arose in China, the rising power of the twenty-first century. The democratization of China, as it integrated with the global economy and its wealth and middle class grew, was deemed inevitable. This, too, was wishful thinking.

Market-Leninism, skillfully enforced, proved resilient. President Xi Jinping, emperor for life, has "techtarianism" at his disposal, an autocratic nationalist surveillance state that uses technology to know every movement and inclination of its citizens.

An aggressive, one-party China proved able to pocket what open societies could provide in the way of technology, education, and wealth, while preserving the kind of repressive system that is incapable of admitting fault.

"Hide our capacities and bide our time," advised Deng Xiaoping. President Xi has other ideas. He offers the Chinese model as a global model through the so-called Belt and Road Initiative. He pursues both maritime and territorial expansion. He makes the quest for technological dominance by 2025 explicit.

Wuhan, where the pandemic broke out in late 2019, was China's biological Chernobyl: a disaster compounded by the evasions, ruthlessness, and lies essential to any dictatorial state. The winds that blew radioactive contamination across Europe from the Soviet nuclear plant in 1986 also blew the continent-hopping pathogen from Wuhan across the world in 2019. To be human is to be fallible, but fallibility is incompatible with the party-as-God.

Li Wenliang, a doctor in Wuhan, became a martyr. Before he died of COVID-19, his attempts to warn friends—and by extension the world—of a strange new disease ravaging his hospital were met by official threats. His social-media account has become known as China's "Wailing Wall," a place where people grieve and seek solace for the silence imposed on them and for all that has been lost in a remote world.

RISING HEGEMONS SEIZE ON WEAKNESS

There was only one Cold War. Russian-American confrontation will henceforth be played out in different ways. A hyper-connected world ensures that centers of power have become diffuse. The Chinese and American economies are symbiotic. Putin's hardening dictatorial repression in what amounts to a Mafia state is not Soviet totalitarianism, a closed system based on terror.

The nature of power has been radically reordered. Pax Romana, Pax Britannica, and Pax Americana depended on the military might of sovereign governments. Now national authorities compete for influence with supranational connected platforms and the private corporations behind them. In what Philip Howard, a professor of Internet studies at Oxford, has called "Pax Technica," stability lies in an "empire of connected things." Such stability, like its forebears, is finite, however. President Putin has illustrated that the readiness to use military power can upend every assumption.

An ideological war will determine the course of the twenty-first century. At its most elemental the conflict is between repression and freedom. On one side the autocratic command economy of a risen China and the military might of Russia; on the other the economies of democratic systems based on the rule of law, checks and balances, independent judiciaries, and the sanctity of the individual.

China's harsh repression of Uighurs and other predominantly Muslim ethnic minorities in its northwestern region of Xinjiang, including its use of internment camps and forced sterilization, are ominous warnings of how a China-dominated world might look.

For now, autocrats feel the wind in their sails. Vladimir Putin, having annexed Crimea, wants to redraw the map of Europe to assert a Russian sphere of influence and deny a sovereign country like Ukraine the right to make its own strategic choices, or even exist. He carries the military banner for autocracy; China handles the ideological and economic side. Putin proclaimed liberalism "obsolete" in 2019. He meant it, but his retreat from Kyiv suggests the delusional nature of his own ideas.

Putin could make his outlandish claim because the United States ceased to be the exemplar and underwriter of the liberal-democratic model. It retrenched. President Barack Obama's "slippery-slope" school of foreign policy, which saw potential disaster in any intervention, led the leaders of Russia and China to conclude that no provocative action would bring American reprisal. Endless posing of the question "What if?" in the White House Situation Room would prevent that.

Obama's eleventh-hour decision in 2013 not to bomb Syria after Bashar al-Assad, the Syrian president, had crossed an American "red line" against using chemical weapons marked the moment when America's word wobbled. Later, Obama said of this decision that it was the one that "required the most political courage."

I don't believe the word "courage" should be applied to the American abandonment of people fighting for dignity against a tyrant who has just gassed his people.

The Russian annexation of Crimea, incursion into eastern Ukraine, and takeover of the Syrian endgame ensued. China asserted its sovereignty in the South China Sea; helped itself to Hong Kong, quashing the freedoms of its special status; and later ratcheted up unification demands on Taiwan by dispatching fighter jets over the island.

Rising hegemons seize on weakness when they see it. Autocrats knew they could test a wounded animal called America and it would flinch. A world of great-power rivalry became more dangerous.

The American weakness was internal. Obama sensed some form of national exhaustion. He chose realism. He was done with the chimera of American exceptionalism. He felt he had no choice. The weakness did not stem from a lack of superb military materiel, dedicated officers, or patriotic, brave service members. It stemmed from the fact that the United States had disunited, as those Marines in Denver felt in their bones. It reflected a weakening of the American idea.

HAIL THE SAVIOR

Obama's successor, Trump, was the product of this crack-up. He was a symptom, at most a catalyst, not a cause. What Trump saw was how the anger and mutual incomprehension of Americans cried out for a savior. Therein lay his political genius. He was a thug at a time when part of America was looking for a thug. Therein lay his luck.

As heists go, his was extraordinary. The multimillionaire son of a bigoted real-estate developer from Queens, a man who had spent his life as a flimflam merchant, became the hero of millions of upstanding, churchgoing, rural Americans who grew up with guns and never had it easy.

It did not matter that Trump had no idea how to hold a Bible the right way up. It did not matter that he could not shoot an elk if it stood staring at him on Fifth Avenue. It did not matter that he treated women with "grab-'em-by-the-pussy" disdain. It was okay that he had been born on third base and spent his life as a liar and braggart. A bone-spur coward who liked to stick his chin out à la Mussolini became the heartthrob of the so-called *Real America* of self-reliance and hard work.

History repeats itself, first as tragedy, then as farce—and at last as a Twitter storm.

Trump is a recognizable American character, master of the tall story, spoken in the vernacular of the people—*I am your voice!* His shameless-ness is part of his appeal. He is the great American swindler, relying on the endless expanse of the country to stay just ahead of disaster by con-juring up one more tall story. He belongs to *Huckleberry Finn.*

In the quintessential American story, Mark Twain's king and duke—claiming to be the dauphin of King Louis XVI of France and the usurped Duke of Bridgewater—lie and hoodwink their way down the Mississippi. Their claims are as far-fetched as Trump's regal fan-tasies, but that does not make them any less credible to the audiences scammed along the way.

Trump had learned on TV that cruelty, far from alienating viewers, could provoke in them an addictive frisson. He understood the potency of hatred, always looking for its chance. He deployed his lesson where he could. The main thing was to get the blood up.

Talk of Mexican immigrants being "rapists" delivered that throb of excitement from the start of his presidential campaign in 2015, just like saying, "You're fired!" to some hapless job applicant on *The Apprentice,* his hit TV show. To his votaries this was *telling it like it is,* a form of "hon-esty" that was more important than any fact.

The shiftless savior would make the rich richer. He would protect white, heterosexual, Christian males from the inexorable march of demographic change and the pursuit of racial justice. After the Black presidency, resented by millions of Americans, Trump's would be the white presidency. Trump and his terrorized Cabinet would form a pali-sade against the "great replacement," a phrase generally attributed to a French writer, Renaud Camus, who wrote: "The great replacement is very simple. You have one people, and in the space of a generation, you have a different people."

That, of course, is a good definition of American vitality—one peo-ple becoming another over and over, yet remaining a people bound by an unchanging attachment to the promise of a new nation built on the foundation of freedom protected by laws. Trump turned his back on that idea. America was not for Muslims; it was not for Mexicans; it was threatened by Black demands for racial equality. It was for straight people, "regular folk," not for LGBTQ people. Behind "America First" stood a very un-American credo.

Trump would preserve the God-fearing, business-promoting, straight-talking, gun-toting heart of the American frontier from the Democrats' politically correct, quinoa-eating, gender-transitioning, Black Lives Matter, socialist takeover. His Neediness—he was insatiable in his thirst for praise, playing the imperious master and then the wheedling martyr—would reverse the course of history. He had grasped that nativism and xenophobia were ripe for a rerun.

Demography, science, and reason would be defiled as he restored America to *greatness*. Coal was good; fossil fuels, too. Drill, baby, drill redux!

Nationalism, the most destructive and giddying of ideologies, would be Trump's core America First theme. He offered a dumbed-down knockoff of Ronald Reagan's America as a "shining city on a hill." The Republican Party signed on. One after another, party members genuflected. Their spinal columns disintegrated. Demonstrating all the backbone of amoebas, they kissed the ring.

Trump's supporters never had any illusions about him. They knew he was a lowlife who likes to shoot his mouth off. They knew he might go as far as an *insurrection* and that American democracy meant nothing to him. It was despots Trump envied, after all. The Trump cheerleaders made a bargain with the devil in full knowledge. They did so because they were done with politics as usual, they were done with Clinton-Global Initiative America, the Aspenites, the avocado-toast crowd, the kale-and-grain apostles, the smart people oozing contempt for the unwashed, lining their pockets as they assuaged their Democrat consciences with tax-deductible do-goodism.

The Trump game was clear from the outset: to blind Americans to the fact that the United States is a self-governing enterprise; to say government is evil, government is terrible, bad government is what Democrats do—so just leave it to us! The objective was to eviscerate the institutions conceived to preserve the Republic. It was never to unify; it was to bring America to the breaking point. It was to turn checks-and-balances into a blank check for Trump.

All roads led to the January 6, 2021, mob storming the Capitol and an explicit attempt to "overturn" the election of Joe Biden.

Over two decades, the outside threat of 9/11 morphed into the internal threat of 1/6. This time, the assailants were not jihadi terrorists, most of them Saudi, convinced of America's imperial evil. They were American white supremacists and seditionists, dressed in camouflage and horns and pelts, convinced of American decadence but unable to see that *they personified it* by defiling the sacred chamber of our democracy. President Trump had whipped them into a mob.

A time of reckoning had come. The country that voted Trump into office had experienced a seesawing quarter century of trauma. First there was the giddy all-powerful interlude of the 1990s with its temptations of hubris, after the end of the Cold War in 1989 and the dissolution of the Soviet Union. Then America-the-hyperpower evaporated with the devastation of 9/11, which shattered the idea of American inviolability, turned jihadi Islamist terrorism into every American's new specter, and propelled the nation into its demoralizing wars without victory in Afghanistan and Iraq. The sanctuary of sea to shining sea was no more.

Along came the Great Recession of 2008, with its stench of impunity for the financiers who had developed the notion that debt was desirable, leverage lovely, greed great.

The impact of globalization was felt deep in America. It freed up global trade and investment, and ushered hundreds of millions of people from poverty in the developing world. It also led to lost American jobs, precariousness, and growing income inequality.

With the rapid rise of China, America's relative decline became irrefutable. Optimism and power shifted from the West toward Asia.

All this was accompanied by the growing threat to the planet of global warming and the relentless technology-driven transference of life to an online borderless world, where the winner was the super-educated *Homo technologicus,* and the losers were Joe Sixpack, truth, and downtime.

This buffeting unsettled Americans who were also grappling with hardening conflict over race, gender, guns, identity politics, and even the date of the country's founding—differences that turned the cultural gap between Metropole and Heartland into a chasm and left American democracy hanging by a thread.

WEIMAR AMERICA

Great powers pass from the face of the earth. They tend to die "gradually and then suddenly," as Ernest Hemingway described the onset of bankruptcy. Rome and Vienna are condemned to contemplate the palatial vestiges of their imperial zenith. No might is impermeable to decay; this is the lesson of history. Another is that empires rarely leave the stage without a conflagration.

Writing off America tends to be a fool's errand, however, because the country's core business is reinvention through immigrant churn. Still, by the time Donald Trump descended the escalator at Trump Tower on June 16, 2015, to announce his candidacy for president, the mood in the nation that inherited the earth in the rubble of 1945 was ripe for a dunderhead dedicated to the language of violence.

Six months later, on December 14, 2015, eleven months before the 2016 election, I wrote a column called "Trump's Weimar America":

> Trump is a clown. No, he is not. He is in earnest. And he's onto something. It is foolish not to take him seriously.
>
> A near-perfect storm for his rabble-rousing is upon the United States. China is rising. American power is ebbing. The tectonic plates of global security are shifting. Afghanistan and Iraq have been the graveyards of glory. . . .
>
> Over more than a decade, American blood and treasure have been expended, to little avail. President Obama claims his strategy against Islamist jihadist terrorism, which he often sugarcoats as "violent extremism," is working. There is little or no evidence of that.
>
> A lot of Americans struggle to get by, their pay no match for prices.
>
> Along comes Trump, the high-energy guy. He promises an American revival, a reinvention, even a renaissance. He insults Muslims, Mexicans,

the disabled, women. His words are hateful and scurrilous. They play on fears. They are subjected to horrified analysis. Yet they do not hurt him.

Make America Great Again! Enforce "a total and complete shutdown of Muslims entering the United States!" For many Americans racked by doubt, Trump's MAGAphone answers were irresistible.

They still are. Trumpism persists even after Americans, voting in record numbers, sent him kicking and screaming from the White House to Mar-a-Lago in January 2021.

The Trump bequest to his country was debilitating: an America whose word was no longer trusted, unbound from the principles that had guided it since 1945, unbound from its core values, unbound from simple decency, unbound from the truth.

A razor-thin victory over Hillary Clinton in 2016 was a "massive" triumph for Trump, even if he lost the popular vote to her by some margin. A razor-thin loss to Joe Biden in 2020 was a "stolen" election. The workings of a disturbed mind were never difficult to discern in Trump. He is a man with an ironclad incapacity to accept any truth incompatible with his own omnipotence.

Today, Trumpism endures despite its now demonstrated contempt for the nation's self-rule. Many Americans support Trump *because* he led an insurrection; and most Republicans, college-educated or not, still believe, with no evidence, that the 2016 election was stolen. For them it is the "Great Lie." For the United States, their unfounded conviction is the great threat.

There is only one possible conclusion: many Americans now consider their experiment in democracy dispensable. The Constitution they claim to venerate is the Constitution they are ready to eviscerate.

A two-party system has become a party-cult system. There is one party and one cult. Trumpism has entrenched itself. Gerrymandered district by gerrymandered district, pliant electoral official by pliant electoral official, the cult prepares the ground.

Societies slide into dictatorship. "Just a buffoon," people say, "and vulgar." Until it's too late.

There is a passage in Fred Uhlman's remarkable novella, *Reunion,* in which a proud German Jewish physician, twice wounded in World

War I, and convinced the Nazis are a "temporary illness," lambastes a Zionist for trying to raise funds for a Jewish homeland: "Do you really believe the compatriots of Goethe and Schiller, Kant and Beethoven will fall for this rubbish? How dare you insult the memory of twelve thousand Jews who died for our country?"

Germans fell for the rubbish, Goethe and Beethoven notwithstanding. No Iron Cross bestowed for valor on a German Jew in World War I would save him or his family from the gas in World War II.

Perhaps it's easy to wave away the notion of fascist storm troopers marching on Washington to smash the institutions that "We the people" enshrined in the Constitution more than two hundred years ago; absurd to think a dictatorship where enemies disappear in the night could come to America. It is much less easy, however, to dismiss the possibility of the emergence of an illiberal, authoritarian American system along the lines of Prime Minister Viktor Orbán's in Hungary.

The Orbán template is admired within the cult: Neutralize an independent judiciary. Subjugate much of the media. Demonize migrants, especially Muslims. Create loyal new elites through crony capitalism. Defend the historically dominant white race. Energize a national narrative of victimhood and heroism through the manipulation of historical memory. Claim the "people's will" overrides constitutional checks and balances. Gerrymander accordingly. And, lo, the new Promised Land: a form of American single-party rule that retains a veneer of democracy while skewing the contest sufficiently to ensure it will yield only one result.

Tucker Carlson, the top-rated Fox News host, broadcast from Budapest for a week in the fall of 2021, calling Hungary a place "with a lot of lessons for the rest of us." By early 2022, Orbán, formally endorsed and supported by Trump, had ruled Hungary for fifteen years. Nobody should doubt that if Trump returns to the Oval Office, it will likely be for life.

There's somebody else presiding over a system much like Orbán's: Vladimir Putin, the latest embodiment of what Joseph Conrad called Russian officialdom's "almost sublime disdain for the truth." No wonder Trump was in the Russian leader's thrall.

EUROPEAN UNRAVELING

On June 21, 1944, my uncle Bert Cohen of the Sixth South African Armored Division, Nineteenth Field Ambulance, reached Italy's Monte Cassino, abandoned a few weeks earlier after repeated Allied assaults. He made an entry in his war diary:

> Poor Cassino, horror, wreck and desolation unbelievable, roads smashed and pitted, mines, booby traps and graves everywhere. Huge shell holes, craters filled with stagnant slime, smashed buildings, hardly outlines remaining, a silent sight of ghosts and shadows. Pictures should be taken of this monument to mankind's worst moments and circulated through every schoolroom in the world.

This was the memento mori proposed by my uncle, then aged twenty-five and recently arrived from the bottom of the African continent onto the blood-soaked soil of its longtime colonizer: Europe. Those pictures were not circulated; and today the miracle and fragility of European peace is too often forgotten.

In April of that year, Captain Cohen had sailed from Egypt to Italy. Born in the last year of World War I, he was now thrust into World War II. How strange, he mused, were the "circumstances that should bring me—plain-routine, rut-living Bertie Cohen of Johannesburg—to be driving in a cumbersome truck through a rural part of southern Italy."

Rut-living Bert Cohen had come to help save Europe from its repetitive suicides, although he would not have framed it that way. My father, Sydney, would follow, determined to treat Europe's war-wounded as a recently qualified physician. He would never see his own father, Morris, again.

They were two young Jews summoned from a faraway land to defeat a Nazi ideology bent on the annihilation of the Jews.

I have thought of them often as Europe, cheered on for a while by Trump, fragmented and fell victim to amnesia—until Putin jolted Europeans into pondering the fragility of peace. It should not be so easy to forget that the quest to form homogeneous societies lay behind the twentieth century's worst crimes.

The world was rebuilt after 1945 on something of more substance than British-American lies and bloviation. The European Union, the only institution in the world that can imbue the descriptor "entity" with a certain beauty, played a significant part in that rebuilding. I came to love this borderless thing—today comprising twenty-seven nations and almost 450 million citizens—because it played a critical role in giving my generation a peace denied my forebears, all those young men whose names are engraved on stone memorials in melancholy town squares across Europe. It spared my generation our Cassino.

During the years I spent as the *New York Times* chief correspondent in Berlin, from 1998 to 2001, I never ceased to wonder at the miracle of the near-invisible German-Polish border, crossed with scarcely a thought, although a few decades earlier millions had died at this frontier of the Germanic and Slavic worlds. I would pass from one country to the other and nobody asked me who I was, what papers I bore, or what my intent was. If German-Polish reconciliation was possible, anything is.

To stand at that border is to know that the European Union, in its essence, is a peace magnet.

You feel the same thing in Strasbourg, the city where the French-German enmity that produced three wars between 1870 and 1945 alone finally died. As Jean Monnet, the postwar architect of European unity, wrote: "Nothing is possible without men, but nothing is lasting without institutions." When humankind fails, the best institutions may save it from the brink. That is why Trump wanted to dismantle them.

The union is the great miracle of the second half of the twentieth century.

It could not, however, save Britain from Brexit, an act of folly. The British departure from the European Union, consummated in 2020, felt like the death of hope, a strange self-amputation. A generally prudent people, the British hurled themselves over a cliff. They had been persuaded by a bunch of conviction-free and jingoistic opportunists, led by Boris Johnson, that "liberation" from European shackles would cause money to flow into "Global Britain." The world would become Britain's oyster. In fact, Britain would become Johnson's, which is to say, often a laughingstock, before the prime minister's recklessness cost him his job in the summer of 2022. His was a political shipwreck foretold.

Americans chose to blow up the status quo through Trump. Britain chose Brexit and Johnson. The British, in their majority, did not want to "remain," a passive verb in a time of agitation. They preferred turmoil, the movement of "leave." They preferred anything to stasis. It did not matter that lies, including a supposed windfall of hundreds of millions of pounds a week for the National Health Service, permeated the "leave" campaign. It did not matter that being in Europe had over decades made British lives better.

Inequality, poor infrastructure, low investment, inadequate schools were real British problems, but the take-back-your-country transference of blame for them onto "Brussels bureaucrats" was manipulation. It demonstrated the hold of an Age of Illusion. As in the United States, truth withered and the mob roared. Britain, in a fit of deluded fantasy, opted for littleness.

To be so orphaned was painful. I was raised mostly in London. The forty-seven years of British membership in the European Union covered the entire arc of my adult life. Europa was our dream. I covered Anwar Sadat, the Egyptian president, speaking to the European Parliament about hope and peace in 1981, eight months before his assassination. So much for dreams.

Yet they persist, for otherwise life is unlivable. I wandered from Brussels to Rome to Paris to Berlin to London, and everywhere I lived, I experienced some iteration of Europe's beauty, as a physical thing, as a cultural bond, and as a transformative idea.

The sensation was most acute in Germany, where the idea of the union was an effective escape from postwar shame, a form of atonement. It was much easier, after Auschwitz, to say "I am a European" than "I am a German."

The nascent pride in Europe was broad; this was no mere German salvage operation. Here, rising from the ashes, was the guarantor of deliverance and the symbol of a capacity to reinvent the world and even make it better.

Every European country, through the goal of ever-closer union, changed itself. Member states grew richer, no small thing, but they also reframed their self-image.

Central European countries reinforced their deliverance from the deadening Soviet imperium to which Yalta had confined them. Britain ceased equating Europe with scourges like intellectuals, rabies, and garlic. Hyde Park became a babble of European tongues. The British economy surged. Britain had given up its colonies and found a new identity in association with Europe, or so it seemed, flickeringly.

How important this new "Europa" was became clear when the Berlin Wall fell in 1989. Soon after, war erupted in the Balkans as communist Yugoslavia fell apart. Freedom for the people of this beautiful but perennially fragile country did not mean pluralist democracy; it meant the possibility to assert Serbian or Croatian or Slovenian or Bosnian nationhood, in flames. It was freedom to be free of one another, not to build something together.

So it was that, *nel mezzo del camino,* I found myself in Sarajevo covering the Bosnian war and saw, in inert bodies torn by shrapnel, and in history revived as a galvanizing myth of might and conquest, the horror from which the European Union had saved me and hundreds of millions of others. It had laid bad history to rest. This was enough to be forever a European patriot.

I am a European patriot because I have lived in Germany and seen how the idea of Europe provided salvation to postwar Germans; because I have lived in Italy and seen how the European Union anchored the country in the West when the communist temptation was strong; because I have lived in Belgium and seen what painstaking steps NATO and the European Union took to forge a Europe that is whole and free; because I have lived in France and seen how Europe gave the French, after the shame of Vichy, a new avenue for expressing their universal message of human dignity; because I have lived in Britain and seen how Europe broadened the post-imperial British psyche and, more recently, to what impasse little-England insularity leads; because I have lived in the Balkans and chronicled a European war that took a hundred thousand lives; because "plain-routine, rut-living Bertie Cohen of Johannesburg" and my father came from South Africa to Europe to save the Continent from horror, along with all the young Americans whose graves I have gazed at in Normandy. Not least, I am a European patriot

because I am a Jew. I know where the innuendo about rich "cosmopolitans" from the likes of nationalists like Orbán and Trump can lead. The
Nazis called the Jews "rootless parasites."

I am a European patriot and an American patriot. I am not from one
place but from several. Theresa May, the former British prime minister,
uttered a terrible thing when she said in 2016: "If you believe you are a
citizen of the world, you are a citizen of nowhere." She might have said:
If you are *not* a citizen of the world, you are a citizen of a doomed planet.

The free world is being tested, not for the first time. Yet it is a mistake to underestimate the resilience of democracies, buttressed by the
transatlantic bond. Slow to anger, they are formidable in the breach. A
century ago, in the single Battle of Verdun between France and Germany, three hundred thousand people were killed. Laid side by side,
the corpses would stretch 140 miles from the battlefield to Paris. Such
slaughter now seems unthinkable, thanks to the European Union and
NATO, whatever Putin's explicit nuclear threats.

At Verdun Cemetery, among the rows and rows of dead, a section
is reserved for hundreds of Muslims who fought for France in 1916.
Yet nationalist French politicians now say Islam is incompatible with
France. Unless, I suppose, Muslims are giving their lives for it. Europe is
bigger than such hypocrisy.

The bond of the West is freedom—the cry of revolutions on both
sides of the Atlantic. There is no contradiction in my patriotisms. Patriotism is nationalism tamed, a positive assertion of community in the
place of tribalism directed against the stranger. Nationalism equals war.
Patriotism builds the sense of belonging that we need to live.

DO NO EVIL

In early 2011, I wrote a column with the dateline of Sidi Bouzid, a
hardscrabble patch of nowhere in Tunisia. It told the story of a young
fruit-and-vegetable peddler named Mohamed Bouazizi and a police-
woman much older than him called Faida Hamdy; how an alterca-
tion between them had led to Bouazizi's self-immolation in front of
the modest governor's building, how word of his suicide had spread via

Facebook and stirred a revolution without a leader, and how a seemingly impregnable fifty-four-year-old Arab dictatorship had fallen.

Fidel Castro spent years preparing revolution in the Cuban interior, the Sierra Maestra. Facebook propelled insurrection from the interior to the Tunisian capital in twenty-eight days—and on from there to much of the Arab world.

How, I wrote, "could a spat over pears in Nowheresville turn into a national uprising? No Tunisian newspaper or TV network covered it. The West was busy with Christmas. Tunisia was the Arab world's Luxembourg: Nothing ever happened. Some poor kid's self-immolation could never break a wall of silence. Or so it seemed."

Until the Dignity Revolution gathered pace and spread across the Arab world.

I concluded that Mark Zuckerberg, the founder of Facebook, was the Arab revolution's leader. The youth of Tunisia were able to use Facebook for instant communication and so cyber-inspire their parents. Suddenly, the "*hogra*," or contempt, shown by the dictator's kleptocracy could galvanize an Arab people and kindle an Arab Spring. When Zine el-Abidine Ben Ali, the late dictator, addressed the nation, as he would three times, Facebook-ferried fury was the response. Ben Ali might have 1.5 million members in his puppet party; he soon faced two million Facebook users.

The dictator was doomed. As President Hosni Mubarak in Egypt and Colonel Muammar el-Qaddafi in Libya would be soon after.

What a difference a decade makes. Technology, it transpired, is twin-souled, like Goethe's Faust. It has changed the world for good and ill. It has liberated and it has imprisoned. The organizing tool of the freedom fighter may equally serve the surveillance system of the despot.

Facebook is used by the military in Myanmar to stir a frenzy of hatred against the Muslim Rohingya that leads to the mass expulsion and genocide that began in 2016. It's easy enough to light the kindling: just tell a false story about the rape of a Buddhist woman by a Muslim man.

It was used by Russian intelligence agencies to interfere in the 2016 American election. As Paul Horner, who ran a big Facebook fake-news operation during the election, observed to *The Washington Post*: "Honestly people are definitely dumber. They just keep passing stuff around

Nobody fact-checks anything anymore." It's used by hate groups to recruit and it was used by the backers of Brexit to foster the myths that led Britain to leave the European Union in 2020.

The link between the biggest American social-media platforms and the spread of hatred and bigotry has become so evident as to be irrefutable.

We are corralled into herds by social-media algorithms, trolls, and bots. We forsake community to become tribes with megaphones. We like. We dislike. We follow. We unfollow. We broadcast our lives. We fall silent. Adrenaline rushes. Status anxiety ensues. We turn in circles. Above all, we grow lonelier, caught in a vortex, starved of connective tissue.

In a remote world, people ask who they are, what they have become, and where they are headed. They lose their anchors. Facebook has the effect of consistently blurring the distinction between truth and false-hood for its 2.91 billion active users, about a third of humanity.

This, too, is something new under the sun.

In testimony in 2018 to Congress, Zuckerberg acknowledged, "We didn't do enough to prevent those tools (Facebook's) from being used for harm as well—and that goes for fake news, foreign interference in elections, and hate speech." He said, "it's not enough just to connect people, we have to make sure those connections are positive."

This was largely righteous piety. You can't make everyone happy. You can, however, be more vigilant about having your platform used to organize genocide, without curtailing free expression.

Barring the Myanmar military from using Facebook after the coup in 2021 was one step in that direction, even if it did not change the situa-tion of one million Rohingya refugees. In Myanmar, Facebook is the de-facto Internet, universally used to communicate.

In another, more defensive speech the following year, Zuckerberg said:

> We now have significantly broader power to call out things we feel
> are unjust and share our own personal experiences. Movements like
> #BlackLivesMatter and #MeToo went viral on Facebook—the hashtag
> #BlackLivesMatter was actually first used on Facebook—and this just

wouldn't have been possible in the same way before. One hundred years back, many of the stories people have shared would have been against the law to even write down. And without the internet giving people the power to share them directly, they certainly wouldn't have reached as many people. With Facebook, more than 2 billion people now have a greater opportunity to express themselves and help others.

There *is* hope in the spread of free speech and connectedness. The closed and murderous totalitarian systems of the twentieth century will not be re-created. But it is not the hope I felt a decade ago in Tunisia, sitting under a bare lightbulb in a small house near a trough where sheep were feeding. "Our family can accept anything but not humiliation," Samia Bouazizi, the dead fruit-seller's sister, told me then.

Millions of Arabs who at the turn of the twenty-first century would not have been able to communicate heard that message. Empowered, they took to the streets to claim agency. They wanted to cast off the dead hand of dictatorships that were the incubators of Islamist terrorism in frozen societies. They dreamed of the dignity of self-rule. Autocrats fled or were killed in Egypt, Libya, and Tunisia. The Syrian people rose up. Gulf monarchies shook.

The tide gradually turned. Despots like Syrian president Bashar al-Assad and his ally Putin, along with would-be "saviors" like Trump, learned they could tweak the digital tools of liberation to turn them into potent weapons in the service of disorientation and repression. Freedom of the press is under attack, with 293 journalists imprisoned in 2021, the highest number since 1992, and at least two dozen killed.

The Arab Spring turned arid. Technology was only as good as the human beings who created it. Facebook and Twitter, too, could do good and evil with equal facility. They were force multipliers of humankind's eternal doubleness.

The new means to change everything were also the new means to ensure that everything remained the same. Google removed "Don't be evil," long the core of its ethos, from its code of conduct in 2018. This seemed like an acknowledgment of defeat. It was certainly a form of realism.

Facebook changed its name to "Meta" in 2021. Zuckerberg decided to bet his company on building the metaverse, a 3D-navigable, totally immersive, consuming virtual world. Perhaps he tired of this one. Initial results were so negative they led in early 2022 to a single-day $232-billion stock-market loss for Meta, the largest ever. The associations of the name "Facebook" had changed over a decade, and not for the better.

FREEDOM OR ENSLAVEMENT?

Is the world freer than a half century ago? On paper it certainly is. The totalitarian Soviet imperium is gone. The generals who lorded over Latin America are gone. Much of Asia has overcome paralyzing poverty, unshackled itself, and claims this century as its own. The African continent, whose population will almost double to 2.4 billion by 2050, has the fastest-growing economy in the world, even as overwhelming social problems persist. Through social media the great majority of human beings across the world have a voice. Women have more power. People live longer. They are less poor.

Yet minds feel more crimped, fear seems more pervasive, debate more confined, religion more fanatical, possibility more limited, adventure more choreographed, politics more violent, economies more skewed, conspiracy more rampant, pressure more crushing, escape more elusive.

When I was seventeen, I left London at the wheel of a VW Kombi, bound for New Delhi. This seemed normal enough at the time. With two friends, I drove across Europe, through Turkey, across Iran, and into Afghanistan, arriving there just in time to witness the coup that deposed King Mohammed Zahir Shah on July 17, 1973, and ushered in decades of turmoil. Mayhem, illness, mechanical problems, and the inertia incumbent on any hippie led us to change plans and stay in Afghanistan, rather than drive on to India. We visited the fifteen-hundred-year-old Buddhas of Bamiyan. We sat on their heads in the dusk, in blissful contemplation of the pale poplars tracing golden lines, little imagining that the Taliban would destroy the Buddhas twenty-eight years later in their quest to rid the country of the "gods of the infidels."

I think we were freer then. We were travelers without a map. Nobody could make that journey now. Any foreigner driving from Herat to Kabul, as we did, would be taking a big risk. As for traversing the Ayatollahs' Iran, that would scarcely be possible. The unknown shrinks. Fear grows. "Safetyism" spreads. Experience gets diluted. Tiger moms will not let children stray far, let alone allow a bunch of seventeen-year-olds to embark on a journey of several thousand miles into the perilous unknown. My recollection is that we spoke to our parents a couple of times over several months, no more than that. We did, however, write letters. I celebrated my eighteenth birthday beneath the stars beside the ice-blue lake of Band-e Amir, high in the Hindu Kush.

In 2007, I went back to Bamiyan and gazed at the gashes in the reddish-brown cliff where the two Buddhas had stood. I climbed a steep staircase in the rocks to reach a rickety platform at the level of the vanished smaller Buddha's head. Before me the sacred valley stretched away. Oxen plowed potato fields. A war-blasted bazaar lay in dusty ruin. Mud-colored mountains, their geometric folds and pleats as intricate as robes by Vermeer, rose to snowy peaks. Young girls in white hijabs walked toward a newly built primary school, dust swirling behind them.

Life goes on—that is the sometimes unbearable thing. From the ruins of the old, even from the ashes of barbarism, the new arises.

As to whether technological progress equals expanded freedom, I have my doubts.

Diabolical in their temptations, social media have spread a psychological enslavement whose true cost is not yet known. Connectedness is also loneliness. Civil discourse has receded, disinformation spread. In the world on a portable device, it is impossible not to lament the loss of the lost places, for which there was no "rating."

Technology, like debt, never sleeps. It binds you to your workplace, it deadens you through the cacophony it delivers. It becomes the reflex through which empty moments are filled with diversionary nothingness. It is the pandemic's strange co-conspirator in the isolation it engenders and the remote work it enables.

Bread and circuses to keep the masses happy; the Roman emperors proceeded on that basis. Perhaps they were not wrong.

The eternal puzzles persist because death is terrifying and life is short. The search for happiness and meaning goes on. Scourges are vanquished; others arise.

Dot-com billionaires dream of interplanetary existence, a metaworld, and the reversal of aging. They devote part of their fortunes to such ends. Perhaps the planet, growing warmer and more crowded, will undergo some undreamed-of reinvention. For myself, I prefer not to imagine life without death, the dark mirror of our strivings.

Perhaps my favorite painting is Velázquez's portrait of Pope Innocent X, in Rome's Doria Pamphilj Gallery: the ruddy and weathered face of the pontiff, the shrewd eyes, the expression that sees through all the pomp of his position and suggests awareness that life, even at the summit of power, may be viewed as a cruel joke. *"Troppo vero!"*—"Too true!"—the pope is said to have exclaimed on seeing it.

"So we beat on, boats against the current, borne back ceaselessly into the past." Scott Fitzgerald in *The Great Gatsby* said it all.

Yet we must fight the current or die.

A FOOT ON THE NECK

In South Africa, as a child, I absorbed racism like a twinge, the first hint of a microbe in the blood. Fear was never quite absent from sunlit South African sojourns. The beach at Muizenberg, near Cape Town, was vast and full of white people. The surf leapt. White bathers frolicked. Blacks waded into the filthy harbor at Kalk Bay. They were always walking as our cars purred past. There was no sidewalk for them to walk on.

Black women bathed me as an infant. They touched my white skin. They dangled me from a height. They made me feel loved. They made me feel afraid. Their world was untouchable. They slept, as staff, in concrete-floored outbuildings whose small windows resembled baleful eyes.

Blacks were paid starvation wages for working in the mines that undergirded the growth of apartheid South Africa. They were banished to the "kaffir" townships of dust and dirt and drudgery, where water was drawn from a communal spigot, homes consisted of a single room, and the alleys were full of the stale stench of urine. They were rendered less than human by design.

They were less than human in colonial Africa and less than human in the Americas to which they were shipped. What of Black slaves, their value set in the United States Constitution at 60 percent of free human beings? America's original sin has proved ineradicable.

Throughout American history, white cruelty in keeping Blacks down has been matched only by white ingenuity in finding new ways to do so. Deep and ongoing struggle between embedded racism and the ideal of racial equality in America continues. The images of unruly Black protesters that sustained Jim Crow were the same images used by Trump in 2020 to communicate sotto voce to his fanatical white base that he had their interests at heart.

Ahmaud Arbery, a young Black man killed in Georgia, was hunted down like an animal on February 23, 2020, as he jogged through Satilla Shores, near Brunswick, a coastal neighborhood of pleasant bungalows beneath live oaks garlanded with Spanish moss.

Gregory McMichael and his son Travis, both white, grabbed a revolver and a shotgun, piled into their pickup truck, and pursued Arbery—convinced, they told police, that he looked like a suspect in recent break-ins. In a video that took months to emerge, Travis is seen shooting Arbery, twenty-five, dead at point-blank range as they tussle over his shotgun in the bright sunlight.

No arrest was made at the time. The McMichaels had acted in accordance with Georgia's citizen's-arrest statute! Travis McMichael had fired in self-defense! This was the initial police view. An old story: white connections and impunity denying justice in the good old way of the Deep South.

Four months after the murder, I found a small shrine at the corner of Holmes Road and Satilla Drive, where Arbery was cut down. Flowers half-covered a plaque that reads: "It's hard to forget someone who gave us so much to remember." Yet Arbery was nearly forgotten. He was just another Black man killed by white men in an American subdivision.

I shuddered at the banality and familiarity of the scene.

Progress on race issues is not resolution of race issues, as Derek Chauvin's white knee on George Floyd's black neck for over nine minutes on May 25, 2020, further demonstrated. Police brutality, mass Black incarceration, poor education, redlining of neighborhoods all tell a story so routine as to be invisible: a Black life is worth less than a white life in America. That idea is woven into the psyches even of people loath to admit it.

Yet something has shifted. Perhaps. As with the image of the murdered fourteen-year-old Emmett Till in his casket in 1955, as with the image of police attack dogs being set on Black children in Birmingham, Alabama, in 1963, the image of Floyd agonizing beneath a white cop's knee has triggered a reckoning.

The United States is never still.

The McMichaels did not get away with their murder. It took seventy days and an intense social-media campaign with the hashtag #IRunWithMaud before they were arrested. In January 2022, they were sentenced to life imprisonment without parole. Chauvin is behind bars serving a long sentence.

A Black Lives Matter Plaza stands a few hundred yards from the White House. The Georgia of the vast, diverse, and growing Metro Atlanta sprawl defeated the rural Georgia of Confederate flags and entrenched racism, tipping the 2020 election decisively toward Biden in what had been the Republican stronghold of Georgia.

When I met Wanda Cooper-Jones, Arbery's dignified mother, during the summer of 2020, I asked her what she would say to the McMichaels, who had not yet been tried: "To the father I would say, as mother to father, our job as parents is to train our children in the way to go. I think you failed Travis in that. How can you love and teach them hate? To Travis I would say, 'I don't really know,' but my heart goes out to him because he was deprived of love."

She thought for a moment. "People who are hurt, hurt other people. People who are loved love other people."

As James Baldwin wrote: "It demands great spiritual resilience not to hate the hater whose foot is on your neck, and an even greater miracle of perception and charity not to teach your child to hate."

If ever it was possible to read "whose foot is on your neck" as a metaphor, it no longer is.

Nobody has believed more in the mythology of America, or been more often disappointed by it, than the Black community. The march of progress toward racial justice has resembled a crab walk. The civil-rights legislation of the 1960s, even a Black presidency, have accomplished less than they promised.

Yet there is forward movement, both in the United States and in South Africa, where white rule ended in 1994 with the swearing-in of Mandela as president.

In 1963, *The Selma Times-Journal* in Alabama urged every reader to do everything possible to uphold segregation. It told them to keep repeating the question: "What have I personally done to maintain segregation?" The article requested contributions and asked: "Is it worth four dollars to you to prevent sit-ins, mob marches and wholesale Negro voter registration efforts in Selma?"

Forty-five years later, a Black man, Barack Obama, was elected president. In 2022, the University of Alabama renamed a building that had been known as Bibb Graves Hall, after a Ku Klux Klan leader who was also a two-term governor of Alabama in the 1920s and 1930s. It is now named after Autherine Lucy Foster, who became the university's first Black student in 1956.

Still, the struggle to facilitate voter registration—and restore key provisions of the Voting Rights Act of 1965 that have been struck down or weakened by the Supreme Court—continues, because Republicans perceive expanded voting as more Black votes. It is that simple, and that abhorrent.

In 1966, in Cape Town, Bobby Kennedy addressed apartheid South Africa:

> But the help and the leadership of South Africa and the United States cannot be accepted if we—within our own countries or in our relations with others—deny individual integrity, human dignity, and the common humanity of man. If we would lead outside our borders, if we would help those who need our assistance, if we would meet our responsibilities to

mankind, we must first, all of us, demolish the borders which history has erected between men within our own nations—barriers of race and religion, social class and ignorance.

His words still resonate.

CONFORMITY WINS, DEMOCRACY DIES

A short time after we met, Wanda Cooper-Jones was invited to the White House to see Trump sign an executive order banning police chokeholds "unless an officer's life is at risk," as he put it, and encouraging the adoption of less lethal weapons.

How did she feel, I asked her, about meeting Trump?

"I was criticized, but he gave time to listen to a mother in pain and that is what mattered," she said. "I respect him as the president, as a man and a human being."

America could use more listening across its lines of violent fracture. Confronting racial injustice involves recognition and reconciliation, however painful. That was Mandela's message. It appeared to be Cooper-Jones's message, too. As a Black woman whose son had been murdered because he was Black, she was ready to meet a president bent on preserving the dominance of white America makes her unusual in a polarized country. She is a bridge, not a wall, person.

Moving forward as a society, reinventing an American commons, cannot be achieved on the basis of one tribe's contempt for another. Nobody ever had his or her mind changed by being made to feel stupid. When contemptuous liberal certainties—Hillary Clinton's dismissal of all the nation's "deplorables," for example—confront Red State rage, America loses. Every American wants to be *seen.*

The unfashionable idea that freedom is served by open debate, even with people holding repugnant views, is worth defending to the last. If conformity wins, democracy dies. If there is only one correct way to view a question, every deviant from that "correctness" risks getting canceled. This is the death of thought.

It could also be the death of journalism as an exercise in openness.

A battle has been joined over what constitutes "journalistic integrity." Wesley Lowery, a Black journalist who left *The Washington Post* after he clashed with the paper's white executive editor, Marty Baron, over the *Post*'s social-media policy, tweeted in June 2020: "American view-from-nowhere, 'objectivity'-obsessed, both-sides journalism is a failed experiment. . . . We need to rebuild our industry as one that operates from a place of moral clarity."

A place of moral clarity sounds enticing, but it can easily translate into holding that there is only one truth. A stifling culture insistent on conformity with that "moral clarity" instills more fear than justice. It freights with tendentious conviction sentences that should be allowed to speak for themselves.

Good journalism cannot survive in an atmosphere where everyone is looking over their shoulder worrying about whether they have trespassed against the new moral order. If legitimate subjects are deemed off-limits for fear of giving offense, open inquiry atrophies. Journalism depends on vigorous freedom for ideas, even bad ones, and acceptance of the fact that less of life transpires in the light of absolute truths than in the shadow of troubling complexity.

Minds need to be opened, not closed. America needs the conversations it is not having. Americans need to travel abroad in their own country. To see what's over there, you have to get out of over here. That is the essence of foreign correspondence.

In a fissured nation, where fear stalks the land, there are fewer moments of genuine meeting between rival tribes, each confined in its ideological cage. Jury duty is one small setting in which such encounters happen.

Service as a grand juror in 2010 was instructive. We started with the impression we would never be able to agree on anything, but after a couple of weeks we got to know one another's tics, and, having dealt with killing and rape and assault and insurance fraud, we all embraced at the end. Oh, unthinkable act, we'd done something selfless for the commonweal, learned to listen to one another, accepted differences, and argued our way to compromise and decisions.

It can be done.

ACTIVE FATALISM

Every column, in its way, was a shedding of my skin. No wonder each of them was such a struggle. We all have something that makes us tick. In my case, when an issue or question weighs on me, I have to write it out in order to move forward.

Timing is everything. Ripeness, as Shakespeare wrote, is all. I remove the silvery snake skin from the branch outside my window and lay it on my desk. It is translucent, a palimpsest. Fingering it, as I touched the leaf that summoned the ridged surface of my father's thumbnail, I feel the brittleness of life. I marvel at the elaborate miracle of its patterned surface.

The view of the aspens, so unburdened, is different now. I gaze anew. The trace of the snake is gone. Several deer appear and, immobile, they gaze at me.

What is going on around them? The plague turns and turns in its narrowing gyre. It's over, yet it never will be. It has its political uses, not least in Xi Jinping's China. Groundhog Day. Stuck in a time loop within a small radius.

The seasons increasingly resemble one another. Gone is the bracing cold, best remedy for a hangover, replaced by a mild interlude of shorter days masquerading as winter on a warming planet. The browning mountains, the desiccated streams, the parched earth speak of insidious death, pushing millions of migrants out into a world where they are often unwanted.

Gone is the break between the working week and the weekend, now a blur of undifferentiated activity. Gone is the convivial office moment, the fecundity of an unscheduled exchange. We are as lonely as those little planes over the Atlantic in onboard video navigation maps. Gone, too, is the innocuousness of the word "variants."

Gone, baby, gone.

The feeble Zoom wave of the hand, accompanied by a wan smile, comes more naturally than some in-person greeting—an elbow bump or a "Namaste" or a squirming retreat from an impetuous handshake. The physical embrace loses out to the evasive coronavirus swerve. If you get desperate at your home desk, a short walk from your home bed, there's always Siri or Alexa, who are so obliging and never sleep and remain at an appropriate antisocial distance.

Distractions abound. Cool gear is available to buy for your avatar in the dystopian metaverse; and nonfungible tokens may be acquired for a price. Why own something in the real world when you can have your very own noninterchangeable unit of data stored on a blockchain for your exclusive delectation, priced in crypto-currency?

I would not know. I am drawn to texture, the feel of fabrics, the density of oil paint, the animal, the tactile. I cannot dissociate "meta" from metastasize.

But there is no halting the world as it hurtles toward its alter ego in virtual space. "Remote meeting" is no longer an oxymoron. People actually say, "We met *in person*." Intelligence is replaced by its twenty-first-century successor, an intelligence that is *artificial*.

As the past piles up, all that life already lived, days somehow negotiated, everything and everyone becomes, with growing intensity, "a possibility for resemblance." The ghosts of repetition stir.

In Camus's book *The Plague*, one of the most powerful moments comes in an exchange between the doctor at the center of the novel, Bernard Rieux, and a journalist named Raymond Rambert. Rieux has been battling the pestilence day after day, more often defeated than not. Rambert has been plotting escape from the city to be reunited with his loved one. Rieux speaks his mind:

> "I have to tell you this: this whole thing is not about heroism. It's about decency. It may seem a ridiculous idea, but the only way to fight the plague is with decency."
>
> "What is decency?" Rambert asked, suddenly serious.
>
> "In general, I can't say, but in my case I know that it consists of doing my job."

The next day, Rambert tells the doctor he wants to work with him in the emergency teams battling the plague. Later in the novel, Rieux says, "I feel more solidarity with the defeated than with saints. I don't think I have any taste for heroism and sainthood. What interests me is to be a man."

These are almost forgotten ideas in an age much given to a senti-
mental or gimmicky "heroism." I prefer the approach to life summed
up by Camus as "active fatalism." For Camus, "One must imagine Sisyphus happy."

The gods have punished Sisyphus by condemning him to push a
boulder up a hill, only for it to roll down again and again, obliging him
to renew the effort through all eternity. The labor of Sisyphus is the
embodiment of the absurd. But what else is the human condition? Sisyphus, Camus suggests, is freed by lucid acceptance of his task.

Active fatalism. Or serene stoicism. Not the belief in some utopia or a
paradise of virgins, but the belief that the inner swine can be vanquished
through decency and getting the job done. It does not matter that the
sandcastle gets washed away. The thing that mattered was building it.

Bear witness. Trust the view from the ground. Believe in the flicker-
ing light on the sea. Hold power to account. Meet that deadline. Affirm,
always affirm, even when it is hopeless, the flame of humanity in the
darkness.

Wipe the smirk from the swine's face.

William Ernest Henley's poem "Invictus" was affixed to the wall of
Mandela's cell: "It matters not how strait the gate, / How charged with
punishment the scroll, / I am the master of my fate, / I am the captain of
my soul." Over twenty-seven years in prison, still the captain of his soul.

The hero is unsung, putting in a daily shift, absorbing punishment
yet unbowed, placing food on the table for children, giving them an
education and a roof over their heads. Rieux says, "Salvation is too big
a word for me. I don't go that far. What interests me is man's health, his
health first of all."

The Israeli poet Yehuda Amichai evokes the same idea in his poem
"Tourists." How many times, in the Middle East and the Balkans, have I
listened to sterile arguments about who came first to the land millennia
ago, who built the first synagogue or mosque or church, who slaughtered whom in what distant battle, whose land claims have been blessed
by God and whose cursed, who will never forget, who will one day prevail in an orgy of bloodletting.

Vengeance, like alcoholism, is a relapsing condition that leads
nowhere.

Yet there is another way to look at things. It's not that complicated. The past is gone, the faces of children are innocent, and more blood will not efface injustice. The trusting eyes of the child do not deserve to be dulled by slaughter, emptied by rape, clouded by trauma.

Amichai writes of a scene in Jerusalem:

> Once I was sitting on the steps near the gate at David's Citadel and put down my two heavy baskets beside me. A group of tourists stood there around their guide, and I became their point of reference. "You see that man over there with the baskets? A little to the right of his head there's an arch from the Roman period. A little to the right of his head." "But he's moving, he's moving!" I said to myself: Redemption will come only when they are told, "Do you see that arch over there from the Roman period? It doesn't matter, but near it, a little to the left and then down a bit, there's a man who has just bought fruit and vegetables for his family."

The deed, always the deed, however small, that opens the way to some better future. Forget the Roman arch or the lost olive tree. Neither will put a bowl of rice on the table. Not even God can remake the past.

THE VIOLENCE OF HOPE

The sap is irrepressible. At Verdun, from the blood-filled earth, a forest grows. Animals make their nests in shell craters. Butterflies flutter over the ruins of a fort.

Hope, my mother would say, is the last to die. She would have known. Fall down seven times, stand up eight, the Japanese say.

As a young man in Paris I would stand on the Pont Mirabeau, immortalized in a poem by Guillaume Apollinaire, and murmur my favorite line from it: *"Comme la vie est lente et comme l'Espérance est violente"*—"How slow life is, and how violent hope." Some things just sound better in French.

Hope is an irrational but necessary response to hatred. The

temptation to exclude, subjugate, and exploit "the other" is always there—whether the shtetl Jew, the "kaffir" of South Africa, the Black man in Alabama, the oppressed Palestinians, the Muslims of Europe. But no people has more ethical or empirical reason to resist the inebriation of domination than the Jews, most of whose history has involved exclusion.

Long strangers in strange lands, knowing statelessness in their bones, mindful of Hillel's summation of the Torah—"What is hateful to yourself, do not do to your fellow man"—the Jews at last found a homeland in Israel. They came to the reluctant conclusion that they could not rely on the kindness of strangers.

Zionism was born of the conviction, shaped by experience, forged in suffering, that Jews needed a nation-state because no other place would ever be home.

There was a problem, though: the existence of another people, the Palestinians, in the same narrow stretch of territory between the Mediterranean Sea and the Jordan River, with an attachment to the land, and a claim to it, as fierce as that of the Jews. This is the reality behind the repetitive wars that have marked the Israeli-Palestinian conflict.

I am a Zionist because the story of my wandering forebears convinces me that Jews needed the homeland voted into existence by United Nations Resolution 181 of 1947, calling for the establishment of two states—one Jewish, one Arab—in Mandate Palestine. (The blueprint is still a pretty good one, even if now unattainable.) I am a Zionist who believes in the words of Israel's founding charter of 1948, declaring that the nascent state would be based "on freedom, justice and peace as envisaged by the prophets of Israel."

What I cannot accept, however, is the perversion of Zionism that has seen the inexorable growth of a messianic Israeli nationalism claiming all the land between the Mediterranean and the Jordan River; that has, for a half century now, produced the systematic oppression of another people in the West Bank; that has led to the steady expansion of Israeli settlements on the very West Bank land of any Palestinian state; that isolates moderate Palestinians in the name of divide-and-rule; that pursues policies that will make it impossible to remain a Jewish and democratic state; that seeks tactical advantage rather than the strategic breakthrough of a two-state peace; that blockades Gaza with some 1.8 million people locked in its prison and is then surprised by the periodic eruptions of the inmates; and that responds disproportionately to attack in a way that kills hundreds of children.

This, as a Zionist, I cannot accept. Jews, above all people, know what oppression is. Over millennia, children were the transmission belt of Jewish survival, the object of what Amos Oz and his daughter Fania Oz-Salzberger have called "the intergenerational quizzing that ensures the passing of the torch."

The Talmud portrays humanity as beginning from a single person and declares on this basis: "Whoever destroys one life, it is as if he destroyed an entire world, and whoever sustains one life, it is as if he sustained an entire world." The Talmud also says: "Hold too much, and you will hold nothing."

An ethical covenant held Jews together through the millennia of the diaspora, but ethics of course are not enough to face down enemies bent on their destruction now that they have created the modern state of Israel. Still, to abandon the covenant is to abandon the backbone of Jewishness. Israel, facing movements like Hamas that call for its destruction, in thrall to fears that no amount of power allays, has succumbed to the very temptation of unrestrained rule over others that the Jewish experience most decries. Israel cannot be a Jewish and democratic state and at the same time control the lives of millions of disenfranchised Palestinians who live on land under its dominion.

But that is not the only truth of the Holy Land. It is important, if difficult, to avoid embracing one truth to the exclusion of another.

Recent years have seen the development of an anti-Zionism derangement syndrome that spills over into anti-Semitism. It is ahistorical in nature. It denies the long Jewish presence in, and bond with, the Holy Land. It disregards the fundamental link between murderous European anti-Semitism and the decision of surviving Jews to embrace Zionism in the conviction that only a Jewish homeland could keep them safe. It dismisses the legal basis for the modern Jewish state in United Nations Resolution 181. The Jewish state was not an act of "colonialism" but an expression of the post-Holocaust will of the world. Arab armies went to war against it and lost. Putative Palestine shrank and went on shrinking.

As Alan Johnson, a British political theorist, has put it, "That which the demonological Jew once was, demonological Israel now is." Johnson, writing in *Fathom Journal*, outlined three components to left-wing anti-Semitic anti-Zionism. First, "the abolition of the Jewish homeland; not Palestine alongside Israel, but Palestine instead of Israel." Second, "a demonizing intellectual discourse" that holds that "Zionism is racism" and pursues the "systematic Nazification of Israel." Third, a global social movement to "exclude one state—and only one state—from the economic, cultural and educational life of humanity."

Criticism of Israel is one thing; it is needed in vigorous form. Demonization of Israel is another, a familiar scourge refashioned by the very politics—of identity and "liberation"—that should comprehend the millennial Jewish struggle against persecution. That Zionism should have become a dirty word in Europe—of all places!—is grotesque. As Simon Schama, the British historian, has written, the Israel of 1948 came into being as a result of the "centuries-long dehumanization of the Jews."

Perhaps there is no better definition of active fatalism than working for a two-state outcome in the Holy Land. As a Zionist critical of Israeli overreach, I still see no other way to bring peace.

ACTUAL RESPONSIBILITY

In his "Letter from a Region in My Mind," James Baldwin wrote, "It seems to me that we ought to rejoice in the *fact* of death—ought to decide, indeed, to *earn* one's death by confronting with passion the conundrum of life. One is responsible to life: It is the small beacon in that terrifying darkness from which we come and to which we shall return."

Responsibility to life cannot be resignation. As Shakespeare's Henry V declares: "We would not seek a battle, as we are; / Nor as we are, we say we will not shun it." We are admonished, in the words of Supreme

Court Justice Oliver Wendell Holmes, to wear the "heart out after the unattainable."

Such is our affirming flame.

Journalism can be a "cheap shot" when it's self-congratulatory, or voyeuristic, smug, or shallow. The journalist evokes suffering and moves on; the suffering tends to endure. In some circumstances, professionalism must cede to humanity: drop your notebook, twist the tourniquet tighter, save a life.

But journalism is the most facile of targets. An independent press is essential to any liberal democracy. For the people who do not want such democracies, the cry of "fake news" is therefore part of their authoritarian political program. Max Weber, the German sociologist, came close to the truth in a lecture given in Munich shortly after World War I. He told students:

> Not everyone realizes that to write a really good piece of journalism is at least as demanding intellectually as the achievement of any scholar. This is particularly true when we recollect that it has to be written on the spot, to order, and that it must create an immediate effect, even though it is produced under completely different conditions from that of scholarly research. It is generally overlooked that a journalist's actual responsibility is far greater than the scholar's.

This "actual responsibility" is onerous.

There's a moment in the movie *Gandhi* when the fictional *New York Times* correspondent, Vince Walker, having witnessed the brutal British assault on a nonviolent protest by Gandhi supporters at the Dharasana Salt Works, phones in his dispatch. He's sweating, under pressure, close to tears, as he reads out the last graph: "Whatever moral ascendancy the West held was lost here today. India is free, for she has taken all that steel and cruelty can give, and she has neither cringed nor retreated."

It's all there: the head and the heart fused, lucidity and emotion, a nudge to history from a correspondent bearing witness lest anything be forgotten. To be there at the cusp of change is a rare gift. I started out filing by telex from the Commodore Hotel in Beirut in 1983, lining up to feed encoded paper tape into the machine. Everything in journalism has changed except the essential.

When I was very young, I'd go to the Kruger National Park in South Africa. It seemed that nature was slow, with sudden bursts of acceleration. Nothing moved as the heat of the day rose. Then the air quickened. An eagle soared, elephants charged. Life then was a question of waiting and timing. It might idle for many years before packing several into a single one.

Journalism is like that, lulls and accelerations, adrenaline and troubled questioning. It's not for nothing that journalists drink. They go in the opposite direction from the crowd, toward disaster. In wartime Sarajevo, a man, half Serb, half Muslim, a man therefore with nowhere to go, a man whose legs had just been blown off by Serbian shelling, whose wife had given birth on the floor below his at the hospital, who was drinking heavily as we spoke, emptying a bottle of whiskey, told me that his father had admonished him: "A child needs his father even if he is just sitting in the corner."

Be obstinate, for that which seems lost may not be. As Hannah Arendt observed of acts of courage that may seem futile in the light of early death: "The holes of oblivion do not exist. Nothing human is that perfect, and there are simply too many people in the world to make oblivion possible. Hence, nothing can ever be 'practically useless,' at least, not in the long run."

Far from practically useless, there have been moments when words seemed vital: finding in Paraguay two of those Argentine children stolen by the military; being there at Pinochet's downfall in Chile; chronicling the Bosnian war until at last NATO intervened; giving voice to brave Iranians in Tehran in 2009.

After a botched attempt at an execution in 2018, the State of Alabama and lawyers for Doyle Lee Hamm reached a settlement that spared a life. I'd written a column called "Death Penalty Madness in Alabama." Bernard Harcourt, Hamm's lawyer, told me, "Without your piece, I don't think we'd be where we are today. It made all the difference."

A single life saved, that feels like enough for a lifetime.

This era feels more dangerous than any other moment I have known. Putin's war in Ukraine stemmed from the restoration of dangerous ideas that led to the twentieth century's greatest horrors and had seemed consigned to the past. Fritz Stern, the great historian of postwar Germany, once wrote that he was born, in the Germany of 1926, "into a world on the cusp of avoidable disaster." For Stern, "the fragility of freedom" was "the simplest and deepest lesson of my life and work."

Freedom is hard to recover once lost. The people of Ukraine have fought not only for their own liberty but for that of every human being. If the Russian butchery in Bucha goes unmet, if the quest for justice is abandoned, barbarism extends its tentacles. We stand always at "the cusp of avoidable disaster," separated from it only by vigilance and courage.

As I learned long ago in South Africa, disaster *is* avoidable if the truth is upheld, dignity prized, and the intrinsic value of every being human recognized. The words of W. H. Auden in 1939, on the eve of a world war that would take tens of millions of lives, should be read today in every classroom across our small, vulnerable planet:

> *Defenceless under the night*
> *Our world in stupor lies;*
> *Yet, dotted everywhere,*
> *Ironic points of light*
> *Flash out wherever the Just*
> *Exchange their messages:*
> *May I, composed like them*
> *Of Eros and of dust,*
> *Beleaguered by the same*
> *Negation and despair,*
> *Show an affirming flame.*

PARIS, JUNE 2022

COLUMNS

ONE CLEAR CONSCIENCE, SIXTY YEARS AFTER AUSCHWITZ

Confronted by a regime of terror that may threaten their lives, most people become bystanders, making their small accommodations with evil. A few, however, will not. They resist, at whatever price. Here I considered a then unknown Pole, Mieczysław Kasprzyk, who saved a young Jewish girl in Poland. Later, as a result of the column, he was recognized by Israel as "Righteous Among the Nations," an honorific accorded to non-Jews who risked their lives during the Holocaust to save Jews.

JANUARY 30, 2005

As the sixtieth anniversary of the liberation of Auschwitz is marked with solemn exhortations never to allow the infamy of the Nazi death camps to return, I find myself thinking of a Pole with a bad leg and dirty fingernails who did not need such lessons in the nature of evil.

His name is Mieczysław Kasprzyk. He lives in a shack atop a hill outside the southern Polish town of Wieliczka, near Kraków. Clucking chickens are his principal companions. Now seventy-nine, Mr. Kasprzyk stands ramrod straight. He squints at the world through thick spectacles and he likes his vodka, but he sees clearly enough, always has.

His bad leg dates to 1936, when it was broken in an accident. Then, in 1941, the leg was injured again: he was shot while trying to smuggle a message to his father in the Polish underground. Without that leg, I might not have found him.

I am pleased that I did, pleased that I witnessed his reunion with a Jewish woman, born Amalia Gelband, whose life he saved by hiding her from the Nazis during World War II. Over more than fifty years, a lot is forgotten, but Mr. Kasprzyk's limp stuck in Amalia's mind, an awkward mnemonic.

She was eleven, a child adrift in the Nazi-terrorized Europe of 1942, when Mr. Kasprzyk, risking his life, hid her in his family's farmhouse outside Wieliczka. Her mother, Frimeta, was already dead, killed that year by the Germans. Her father was overseas, unreachable.

Mr. Kasprzyk took her in, along with her older brother, Zygmunt. Encouraged by his mother, he hid them in the attic of their isolated home. The children were known to him through an uncle who knew their uncle Pinkus Sobel, a horse trader. "How can you not help if a child asks?" Mr. Kasprzyk said to me.

How indeed? How can simple humanity be drained from so many people? But it was. Millions of Germans, and those complicit with them in countries the Nazis overran, must have known that what they were doing, or allowing to happen, was vile and unconscionable. It must have occurred to them to try to stop the mass murder.

But almost every one of them, after whatever internal debate occurred, acting out of fear or opportunism or anger or for simple convenience, sided with complicity, active or passive. They knew and nodded, or they knew and looked away, or they told themselves they really did not know.

Not Mr. Kasprzyk. Soon after the German invasion of Poland in 1939, he understood. Polish police officers ordered him to bring a small group of Jews to a local Jewish cemetery in his horse cart. The Jews were stripped and shot dead, their jewelry distributed to local officials.

"It was the first time I had seen a naked woman," said Mr. Kasprzyk, who was fourteen at the time.

The episode stuck in his throat. "Someone who does not know the difference between good and evil is worth nothing," he said. "In fact, such a person belongs in a mental institution."

When the attic hiding-place seemed too vulnerable, Mr. Kasprzyk ushered Amalia to greater safety. Late in 1942, he helped her and her brother find work on two farms near Pleszów, on the outskirts of Kraków.

Amalia assumed the name Helena Kowalska, went to church every Sunday, slept on the kitchen floor, peeled potatoes, and told anyone who asked that she was a Catholic whose father was a prisoner of war and whose stepmother had driven her out. The Gebala family, who put her to work, never knew her true identity. In 1945, when Poland was liberated, Amalia, alias Helena, left the farm and found refuge with her brother in a Jewish orphanage in Kraków.

War's end brought no relief from penury for the modest Pole who protected them. People, he noted, talked for a while about the missing Jews, but soon the blur of discomfiting names was lost in silence.

Hidden in the woods above Wieliczka stands a monument to the town's murdered Jews. No road or path leads there. Weeds and nettles advance. An inscription records the slaughtered "Polish Jews." Somebody has tried to scratch out the word "Polish."

Forgotten Jewish cemeteries, defaced headstones, and crumbling little monuments to dead Jews dot Poland and Hungary. I saw a monument last year in Göncz, Hungary, that listed each of the town's Christian World War II dead by name; at the bottom it mentioned that 168 Jews also died.

Mr. Kasprzyk, a righteous Pole, should have his name widely known. He did not do well after the war: the same nonconformism that led him to defy the Nazis with decency also led him to defy communist authority. "I was never a member of the party, and you had to be to get ahead," he said. "I do not belong to anyone, not even Christ. I do not like anyone to give me orders."

Instead of all the pious speeches surrounding this sixtieth anniversary, I wonder why Europe does not clean up some of those little monuments in towns like Wieliczka and Göncz, and does not honor the likes of Mr. Kasprzyk.

As Fritz Stern, the great historian of Germany, said recently: "Even in the darkest period, there were individuals who showed active decency, who, defying intimidation and repression, opposed evil and tried to ease suffering. I wish these people would be given a proper European memorial not to appease our conscience, but to summon the courage of future generations."

In this particular case, I confess to a personal interest in the memorializing of Mr. Kasprzyk. I see him limping toward Amalia as they met again after almost six decades. I see their embrace serenaded with clucking. I hear his tender words: "Malvinka, Malvinka."

The "Malvinka" he saved, now Amalia Baranek, a Brazilian citizen, is the mother of my wife.

THE POLISH SEMINARY STUDENT AND THE JEWISH GIRL HE SAVED

A little-known story from the youth of Pope John Paul II reveals his humanity as a twenty-four-year-old seminary student. It helps explain his core conviction that "a degradation, indeed a pulveriza-tion, of the fundamental uniqueness of each human being" lay be-hind fascism and communism, the mass movements of the twentieth century that produced killing on an epic scale. Karol Wojtyła saved the life of a thirteen-year-old Jewish girl in Poland, whose other family members had been murdered by the Nazis.

APRIL 6, 2005

Here is a family story of Pope John Paul II, an intimate tale of his humanity.

During the summer of 1942, two women in Kraków, Poland, were denounced as Jews, taken to the city's prison, held there for a few months, and then sent to the Belzec death camp, where in October they were killed in primitive Nazi gas chambers by carbon monoxide from diesel engines.

Their names were Frimeta Gelband and Salomea Zierer; they were sisters. As it happens, Frimeta was my wife's grandmother. Salomea—known as Salla—had two daughters, one of whom survived the war and one of whom did not.

The elder of these daughters was Edith Zierer. In January 1945, at age thirteen, she emerged from a Nazi labor camp in Częstochowa, Poland, a waif on the verge of death. Separated from her family, unaware that her mother had been killed by the Germans, she could scarcely walk.

But walk she did, to a train station, where she climbed onto a coal wagon. The train moved slowly, the wind cut through her. When the cold became too much to bear, she got down at a village called Jędrzejów. In a corner of the station, she sat. Nobody looked at her, a girl in the striped and numbered uniform of a prisoner, late in a terrible war. Unable to move, Edith waited.

Death was approaching, but a young man approached first, "very good-looking," as she recalled, and vigorous. He wore a long robe and appeared to be a priest. "Why are you here?" he asked. "What are you doing?" Edith said she was trying to get to Kraków to find her parents.

The man disappeared. He came back with a cup of tea. Edith drank. He said he could help her get to Kraków. Again the mysterious benefactor went away, and returned with bread and cheese. They talked about the advancing Soviet Army. Edith said she believed that her parents and younger sister, Judith, were alive.

"Try to stand," the man said. Edith tried and failed. He carried her to another village, where he put her in the cattle car of a train bound for Kraków. Another family was there. The man got in beside Edith, covered her with his cloak, and made a small fire.

His name, he told Edith, was Karol Wojtyła. Although she took him for a priest, he was still a seminarian who would not be ordained until the next year. Thirty-three more years would pass before he became Pope John Paul II and embarked on a papacy that would help break the communist hold on Central Europe and so transform the world.

What moved this young seminarian to save the life of a lost Jewish girl cannot be known. But it is clear that his was an act of humanity made as the two great mass movements of the twentieth century, the twin totalitarianisms of fascism and communism, bore down on his nation, Poland.

Here were two people in a ravaged land, a twenty-four-year-old Catholic and a thirteen-year-old Jew. The future pope had already lost his mother, father, and brother. Edith, although she did not know it yet, had already lost her mother at Belzec, her father at Majdanek and her little sister at Auschwitz. They could not have been more alone.

Pope John Paul II is widely viewed as having been a man of unshakable convictions that some found old-fashioned or rigid. But perhaps he offered his truth with the same simplicity and directness he showed in proffering tea and bread and shelter from cold to an abandoned Jewish girl in 1945, when nobody was watching.

It was based in the belief that, as he once put it, "a degradation, indeed a pulverization, of the fundamental uniqueness of each human being" was at the root of the mass movements of the twentieth century, communism and fascism.

Stalin once contemptuously asked, "How many divisions has the pope?" Starting with his 1979 visit to Poland, John Paul gave an answer.

Perhaps the strength that enabled him to play a central role in ending communism and the strength that led him to save Edith Zierer did not differ fundamentally. Like his healing ecumenism, those acts required the courage born of a core certitude.

Edith fled from Karol Wojtyła when they arrived at Kraków in 1945. The family on the train, also Jews, had warned her that he might take her off to "the cloisters." She recalls him calling out, "Edyta, Edyta!"—the Polish form of her name—as she hid behind large containers of milk.

But hiding was not forgetting. She wrote his name in a diary, her savior, and in 1978, when she read in a copy of *Paris Match* that he had become pope, she broke into tears. By then Edith Zierer was in Haifa, Israel, where she now lives.

Letters to him went unanswered. But at last, in 1997, she received a letter from the Vatican in which the pope recalled their meeting. A year later, they met again at the Vatican. Edith thanked the pope for saving her. He put one hand on her head, another hand in hers, and blessed her. As she parted, he said, "Come back, my child."

CHINA VERSUS U.S.: DEMOCRACY CONFRONTS HARMONY. STAY TUNED

This was an early look at the "new bipolar world whose centers are Washington and Beijing." Developing countries know American aid often comes with strings attached: democracy and the rule of law. China cares nothing for values, so long as there is economic benefit. Beijing is ideologically agnostic, with its gaze set on running the world by 2050.

NOVEMBER 22, 2006

HANOI—The American-dominated unipolar world that emerged from the abrupt end of the Cold War is already history. In retrospect, it will be viewed as the seventeen-year interlude that produced the Iraq war and much disquiet before the emergence of a new bipolar world whose centers are Washington and Beijing.

Those centers are unequal for the moment, U.S. power being greater, but the China of President Hu Jintao has now come far enough on the road to superpower status and the articulation of how its muscle will be used to establish a new bipolarity. Countries once again have options: the American road or the Chinese.

At the twenty-one-nation Asia-Pacific Economic Cooperation summit meeting here, this new world was apparent. President George W. Bush was largely hidden from view for security reasons while Hu set out his vision of "peaceful development." His speech dwelt heavily on "harmony," a Chinese buzzword, and called for an increase in "official development assistance with no strings attached."

We all know what the American "strings" are: democracy, freedom, human rights, the rule of law—the whole Iraq-tarnished lexicon of the luminous "city upon a hill." When the West offers money or simply its embrace, it wants these things in return.

China has no such preoccupations or scruples. If the Washington consensus is ideologically interventionist, the emerging Beijing consensus looks ideologically agnostic. It prizes peace, development, and trade. It cares not a hoot what a country's political or economic model is, so long as oil and raw materials are flowing.

In this regard, the APEC speech of Secretary of State Condoleezza Rice was interesting. She inveighed against the governments of Myanmar and North Korea for having "chosen to reject the path of cooperation."

Hu mentioned neither country. China has undercut American sanctions on Myanmar, designed to prod the government to free the opposition democracy leader Aung San Suu Kyi and recognize her victory in 1990 elections, and is investing heavily in oil and gas. Beijing's economic support keeps the brutal and now nuclear-armed North Korean regime of Kim Jong-il afloat.

The ideological differences in the new bipolar world are not as great as those of the Cold War chasm between Washington and Moscow. Foreign investment of $72.4 billion in China last year, much of it American, is one measure of how interlinked a once-fractured world has become. But they are increasingly clear.

The United States has waged war in Afghanistan and Iraq in the past five years. By contrast, "China's primary strategic objective today is not conflict, but the avoidance of conflict," as Cheng Li, a professor at Hamilton College, has put it.

Hu's accent on peace, part clever marketing in a world that disparages America-the-bellicose, is above all a long-term strategic bet on the fruits 10 percent annual growth will bring. It also reflects the scars of conflict in China, scars also evident in Vietnam, another fast-growing Asian country more interested in money than in painful memory.

China is not in the business of exporting war, development models, or political blueprints. It wants to do business, morality be damned. Democracy, in its worldview, comes in a very distant second to growth—if it comes in at all. The kindest view of the Chinese position is this: growth solves most problems, and no problems, be they of poverty or enslavement, are solvable without it.

Nowhere have the Chinese differences with Washington been clearer than in Africa. While the leading industrial nations of the G-8 tie aid for Africa to democracy and "zero tolerance for corruption," China does energy deals of the kind cemented at the recent China-Africa forum in Beijing.

"African countries can now play to multiple audiences," said Jeffrey Herbst, the provost of Miami University and an Africa expert. "The G-8 has been eclipsed and the big losers are Bono and Jeffrey Sachs and the charity crowd. The Chinese are not interested in the internal governance or human-rights affairs of African states."

The Chinese approach has the merit of seeing potential rather than cause for conscience-salving charity in Africa; it has the drawback of helping thugs like Robert Mugabe of Zimbabwe. As in Myanmar, it diminishes American influence by standing in opposition to it.

In general, the Chinese have tried to wield their new power discreetly. But the recent election in Zambia, where China has made major investments in copper, suggested the limits of that policy.

When the opposition candidate, Michael Sata, denounced Chinese labor practices and expressed support for Taiwan, China made clear Zambia would pay a heavy price if Sata won. He lost.

China was a hot Zambian election issue in the same way Bush's America has been in recent European elections. A discreet superpower is an oxymoron. Harmony may be the goal, but disharmony is part of the global burden any superpower must confront. Over time, Beijing will discover that.

Meanwhile, Washington is discovering how many roads lead to Beijing. After Bush met Hu here, Christopher Hill, the chief American negotiator with North Korea, was dispatched to China in search of a deal believed to involve economic incentives to Pyongyang in exchange for a North Korean commitment to dismantle some nuclear facilities and admit inspectors from the International Atomic Energy Agency.

That was a good summation of the new bipolar, American-Chinese world. In the push to the Iraq war in 2003, the Bush administration was dismissive of the IAEA and global opinion generally. IAEA inspectors left Iraq and North Korea the year the war started. Good riddance, was America's response.

But the seventeen-year unipolar age is dead, and the United States now knocks with deference at the Chinese door. "A very important nation" is how Bush describes China. Iraq has shown the limits of America the all-powerful.

The era of struggle between democratic capitalism and one-party capitalism has begun, a fight between Washington's banner of multi-party freedom and Beijing's banner of no-strings-attached growth.

Democracy confronts harmony. Stay tuned.

THE MacARTHUR LUNCH

How, over lunch, the Bush administration took a decisive wrong turn in Iraq.

AUGUST 27, 2007

Zalmay Khalilzad, the American ambassador to the United Nations, is a twinkle-eyed hawk. The defeat of Soviet imperialism in Afghanistan, the unfinished business of the 1990–1991 Persian Gulf war, and his own liberating odyssey from an Afghan childhood to the University of Chicago convinced him the world needs the transformational power of the United States.

Since 9/11, he has fared better than most of the Bush brigade. As a Beirut-educated, Farsi-speaking Sunni Muslim, he actually has a clue about the Islamic world. He was prepared to sip tea rather than set edicts.

In his shepherding of Hamid Karzai to power in Kabul, his forging of Sunni cooperation now bearing fruit in Iraq's Anbar Province, and his recent prodding of the UN to a fuller Iraqi role, "Zal," as he's known, has suggested shrewdness explains the twinkle.

So, as the September storm clouds gather over America-in-Iraq, I was intrigued to find Zal looking back in anguish. President Bush now alludes to "the mistakes that have been made," but is unspecific. There's such an array that everyone has a favorite: a nonexistent casus belli, skimpy troop levels, the end of the Iraqi army, aberrant planning.

Khalilzad's anguish centers on May 6, 2003. That's the day he expected Bush to announce his return to Iraq to convene a grand assembly—something like an Afghan *loya jirga*—that would fast-forward a provisional Iraqi government.

Instead, the appointment of L. Paul Bremer III to head a Coalition Provisional Authority was announced. Khalilzad, incredulous, went elsewhere. In the place of an Afghan-American Muslim on a mission to empower Iraqis, we got the former ambassador to the Netherlands for a one-year proconsul gig.

"We had cleared both announcements, with Bremer to run things and me to convene the *loya jirga*, both as presidential envoys," Khalilzad told me. "We were just playing with a few final words. Then the game plan suddenly changed: we would run the country ourselves."

Alluding to former secretary of state Colin Powell and his successor, Condoleezza Rice, who was then national security adviser, Khalilzad continued: "Powell and Condi were incredulous. Powell called me and asked, 'What happened?' And I said, 'You're secretary of state and you're asking *me* what happened!' "

Powell confirmed his astonishment. "The plan was for Zal to go back," he said. "He was the one guy who knew this place better than anyone. I thought this was part of the deal with Bremer. But with no discussion, no debate, things changed. I was stunned."

The volte-face came at a Bush-Bremer lunch that day, where Bremer made a unity-of-command argument to the Decider. "I put it very directly to the president: you can't have two presidential envoys running around Iraq," Bremer told me.

A MacArthur-Karzai debate had raged within the administration for months: Should the United States run Iraq like General Douglas Mac-

Arthur in postwar Japan or seek a local Karzai-like leader and operate behind the scenes?

Bremer still believes the MacArthur route was imperative. An exile-dominated Iraqi government would have had no legitimacy or competence. Nor would it have changed the legal fact of the U.S. occupation.

"The way we did it gave Iraqis the best chance of a sustainable political process," he argued.

Nonsense, Khalilzad believes. "I feel strongly that the U.S. ruling was wrong. We could have had an interim Iraqi government. I argued, based on Afghanistan, that with forces, diplomacy, and money, nothing can happen anyway without your support."

Powell agrees. "Everything was Bremer, the suit, the boots, the whole nine yards." It was a mistake not to move "more rapidly to putting an Iraqi face on it."

Khalilzad and Powell are right. The insurgency that took hold after Bremer's arrival had a clear target: the guy in Timberlands. Given the extent of its post–Cold War power, the United States must wield it with subtlety. This was the sledgehammer approach.

And chosen over lunch. "Unfortunately, yes, the way that decision was taken was typical," Powell said. "Done! No full deliberations. And you suddenly discover, gee, maybe that wasn't so great, we should have thought about it a little longer."

Do such mistakes redouble American responsibility in Iraq or demonstrate the hopelessness of the task? I say the former. The little miracle of Khalilzad's free-thinking life is just one example of the positive transformations this country can fashion when resolve and coordination shape policy, not precipitous whim.

DOWNTIME FROM MURDER

In Nazi Germany, Santa Claus was really the Gasman, as Günter Grass put it. That did not stop the murderers from enjoying their downtime.

SEPTEMBER 24, 2007

So now we know where Eva from Mannheim and Angela from Dort-mund and Irmgard from Dresden ended up during the war years—jiving in pleated skirts to the strains of an accordion, or gorging themselves on blueberries, or lounging on deck chairs in the shadow of the Auschwitz-Birkenau crematoriums.

How fresh-faced and playful the SS women look in the 116 photo-graphs that, sixty-two years after the liberation of the Nazi camp, have found their way by a circuitous route to the United States Holocaust Memorial Museum. It is not easy to imagine these young ladies moving on from a picnic to administer death wholesale.

In thinking about the Holocaust, we have grown accustomed to images of the Nazis' victims: shadowy naked figures on the edge of ditches about to be dispatched by the SS-Einsatzgruppen; huddled wide-eyed children; skeletal human simulacra; piles of bones. Getting the perpetrators in focus is harder.

But here, revealed by these newly discovered photographs, are the German murderers in all their dumb humanity, flirting and joking and lighting Christmas trees, as if what awaited them after the frolicking were just the bus to some dull job in a dental office rather than the super-vision of Auschwitz's industrialized killing machine.

If they were downwind of the camp, did some trace of the acrid-sweet stench of death ever mess with the merrymaking? Did the image of a Jewish girl from Budapest being herded toward the gas mar a mouth ful? Did conscience stir or doubt impinge? Was it clear that the children had to die in order to eradicate not only a people, but also their memory? Such questions are useless. The facts must speak for themselves.

Goethe's hero Faust declared: "Two souls, alas, are housed within my breast, and each will wrestle for mastery there." The light and dark of Germany, the disturbing proximity of civilization and barbarism, speak of that battle and its universal echoes.

I wish I could say I was surprised by the photos (on display at the museum's Web site—www.ushmm.org). My years in Germany eroded my capacity for shock. The walk from Buchenwald's brick-chimneyed crematorium to the genteel streets of Weimar—home to Schiller and

Goethe, birthplace of the Bauhaus—is illusion-stripping. In 1942, Buchenwald prisoners were ordered to make wooden boxes to protect Schiller's work.

Germans, through distinct postwar stages, have engaged in a painful examination of who the people giving and obeying such orders were and how, in Günter Grass's words, an "entire credulous nation" believed in Santa Claus, but "Santa Claus was really the Gasman."

Just how hard that introspection has been was illustrated when Grass, a moral reference to the Bundesrepublik, broke a sixty-one-year silence and revealed that he served as a seventeen-year-old in the Waffen-SS.

More such revelations are needed; the threads of truth's tapestry are not all tied. Germans will gaze at these photographs and ask: Is that my grandmother or great-aunt? If not, might they have been? Jews and Germans are tied at their hip in their contemplation of the two sides of the crime.

Historians are voyeurs; they like nothing more than reading other people's mail. They need to pry to put names to these faces of "ordinary Germans" doing their jobs at Auschwitz.

The album was kept by Karl Höcker, the adjutant to the camp commandant. Höcker's father was killed in World War I; his mother struggled. And what of the stories of Eva and Angela and Irmgard? Will any Germans step forward to claim these young women and give them real names rather than those invented here?

Hans Magnus Enzensberger wrote in 1960 of a Germany "overcrowded with absentees," full of people "who happen to be in this country / fleeing from this country." With the years, Germany has gained confidence, pried open locked drawers, filled some of the absences. But these photos are an invitation to do more.

Inevitably, they pose the question: What would you have done? Filled your mouth with blueberries or balked and paid the mortal price? Perhaps no single question is more important. The voyeur has the luxury of posing it whereas those living then had to answer it. The overwhelming majority acquiesced to the unspeakable.

It has become banal to quote Hannah Arendt. But she encapsulated these photos' conundrum when she wrote: "Under conditions of terror most people will comply but some people will not," adding, "Humanly speaking, no more is required, and no more can reasonably be asked, for this planet to remain a place fit for human habitation."

Like Germany's unfinished but already remarkable postwar voyage from self-amputation to self-realization, these words bear pondering.

TERROR AND DEMONS

The terrible end, in a holding cell at Phoenix Airport, of a forty-five-year-old woman from South Africa who had suffered from postpartum depression triggers memories of my often-suicidal mother, who was also plucked out of South Africa. A column may be envisaged long in advance or may, like this one, surge abruptly fully formed.

OCTOBER 8, 2007

History happens, but only just. The lives of individuals, as of nations, may hinge on a millimeter's difference in the trajectory of a bullet, a road not taken on a whim, or the random spray of shrapnel. But there is no undoing what is done.

Nothing, for example, can bring back the life of Carol Ann Gotbaum, forty-five, whose terrible end in a holding cell at the Phoenix Airport was chronicled in a *Times* report by Eric Konigsberg. Depressive and fighting alcoholism, Carol missed a connection by minutes. She became hysterical and was subdued, handcuffed, shackled, abandoned, and found dead with the shackle across her neck.

All this happened fast. We can hear her cry: "I'm not a terrorist. I'm a sick mother."

We can see the heavy-handed police officers, their sense of mission redoubled by the alcohol on her breath, muscling Carol to the ground.

In their zeal—for American airports are now temples of zealotry—
they would not have imagined her three young children, her distraught
husband, much less the dislocated life that had put her en route, alone,
to an Arizona addiction-treatment clinic.

As it happened, on another perfect New York morning, redolent
of the endless summer of 2001 (a time when sunlight mocked pain), I
was particularly affected by Carol's story; and here I am writing about
her, rather than brave monks in Burma, because certain signals are too
powerful to ignore.

In many particulars—her South African upbringing, her uprooted
life, her acute postpartum depression after the birth of her last child, her
hardworking and often absent husband, her radiant smile overlying pain,
and her powerlessness before her own self-destructive urges—Carol
resembled my mother.

So, having read about Carol, my head filled with her disoriented
rage before punitive officialdom, I did something I rarely do. I went back
and read my mother's suicide note of July 25, 1978.

The note reads in part: "It's as though I've turned to stone. I can't
relate, I can't communicate and I can no longer bear the pain and gloom
I cause to those I love most. I feel I'll never completely throw off this
mood and hopelessness and depression. I know I have everything to
thank God for and be thankful for, which only makes my ordeal worse
and worse."

In conclusion, my mother asks if "my body—any part of it—can
be used for research." With that, she downed Valium, antidepressant
drugs, and gin.

That was almost the end of the story, or the start of a different story
of anguish, but my father, a doctor, found her just in time. Her life hung
in the balance and was salvaged. Other suicide notes would follow—
one of June 15, 1982, says, "I'm just too tired to fight anymore"—but
never again was the attempt so serious.

Technology leaps forward. Medicine advances. Lives grow longer.
Diseases are vanquished. But the brain, and in particular the vagaries
of mental illness, present mysteries as deep as the elusive enigma of life
itself.

When Carol, raised in Cape Town, had her postpartum depression after the birth of her now three-year-old son, she was a relative newcomer in New York. When my mother, raised in Johannesburg, had hers after the birth of my sister in 1957, she was new to London, with its chill postwar pall.

The things that happened to my mother in the 1950s—insulin shock therapy, electric shock treatment, hospitalization in harrowing wards—things about which she could never speak without a shudder—were of that time. Nobody would have treated Carol's despair, or anybody's, like that today.

But the riddle remains, etched in radiant mothers' faces clutching laughing children, faces that seem to mock the very idea of panic, delusion, and suicidal self-hatred, but contain them nonetheless.

You can look at Carol's end in many ways: as an innocent's devastating encounter with terror-obsessed police, as a ghastly but haphazard event, as a death foretold.

In the days of the Irish Republican Army's terrorism in London, my mother was thrown into what amounted to a holding cell at Fortnum & Mason, the department store, after she left a bag unattended. Under questioning, she became hysterical, confused, unhinged—and was locked up. There was no shackle, however.

The affairs of the world intersect with individuals' pain. The upshot then rests on a razor's edge. Lives veer into a vortex.

Carol Ann Gotbaum and June Bernice Cohen are dead. Cancer took my mother in 1999; she viewed the illness as a trifle beside depression. Her favorite book, unsurprisingly, was *Anna Karenina*. Her favorite line was from *Othello*: "What wound did ever heal but by degrees?"

A ONCE AND FUTURE NATION

Afghanistan inches toward progress, but the West's stomach for the very long haul required may be limited.

OCTOBER 22, 2007

QALAT, Afghanistan—Once upon a time there was a country, more a space than a nation, landlocked, mountainous, impoverished, and windblown.

There resided many peoples, including Pashtuns and Tajiks and Uzbeks and Turkmen, and a new tribe called the Americans.

They had come, the Americans, after thirty years of bloodshed, to bring peace to this land called Afghanistan. But what did they know—what could they know—of life behind burkas, or on the other side of mud walls, or inside minds made mad by war?

Past goatherds and yellowing almond trees, the helmeted Americans drove armored Humvees. Beside lurching stacks of battered tires, children gathered in villages and, unlike those in another broken land called Iraq, they smiled and waved.

The Americans talked about empowering Afghans. Sometimes they took to Blackhawk choppers and swooped along the dun-colored riverbeds and sent goats scurrying for cover.

The twenty-six thousand U.S. troops meant well. They wielded billions of dollars. They calculated "metrics" of progress. They had learned, to their cost, how this faraway place—invaded and used and at last abandoned to pile rubble upon rubble—could nurture danger.

Not only was it once home to the American-financed Islamists who humbled the Soviet empire. It also housed their jihadist offspring, who, like sorcerers' apprentices, turned on a distracted sponsor and brought the dust of two fallen towers to Manhattan.

To help forge a better Afghanistan—or merely an Afghanistan—the Americans involved their NATO friends. An alliance forged to defend the West against the Soviets was transformed into an agent of democratic change in southwest Asia.

How strange! The enemy now was Taliban Islamofascists rather than Kremlin totalitarians. On a hillside in southeastern Afghanistan rose "Camp Dracula," a garrison of seven hundred Romanian soldiers on this NATO mission.

It would take a great fabulist to make up such stories. Yet they wrote themselves after reports that the Cold War's conclusion marked the end of history proved greatly exaggerated.

And so, one recent morning, Lieutenant Colonel James Bramble, a reservist from El Paso, Texas, with a job there as a pharmaceuticals executive, found himself visiting the Romanian forces and then going to the nearby village of Morad Khan Kalay.

Nations are built one village at a time. Or so Colonel Bramble has come to believe. He is a thoughtful man, commanding a NATO provincial reconstruction team, one of twenty-five across the country, at a base in Qalat, between Kandahar and Kabul. His team is supposed to deliver the development and good governance that will marginalize the Taliban.

That's the theory. The practice looks like this. Seven armored U.S. Humvees form a "perimeter" on the edge of the village and newly trained members of the Afghan police—the "Afghan face" on this mission—are dispatched to bring out village elders.

Looking apprehensive, the Afghans appear swathed in robes and headgear whose bold colors mock dreary U.S. Army camouflage. Staff Sergeant Marco Villalta, of San Mateo, California, steps forward. "We would like to ask you some questions about your village," he says.

The following is elicited: There are three hundred families using twenty-five wells. Their irrigation ditches get washed away in winter. A small bridge keeps collapsing. They send their children to a school in nearby Shah Joy, but it's often closed because of Taliban threats to teachers.

Sergeant Villalta takes notes. "We'll share this information with the governor and make sure that something is done."

"No! No!" says Sardar Mohammed. "We don't trust the governor. If he gets food, he gives it to ten families. He puts money in his pocket. We trust you more than him. Bring aid directly to us."

Bramble's view is that the governor is as good as officials get around here. The U.S. officer, like his country and NATO, is caught in the hall of mirrors of contested nation-building. The exchange at the village has traversed cultures, civilizations, and centuries. For Western soldiers trained to kill, and now in the business of hoisting an Islamic country from nothing as fighting continues, that's challenging.

Still, Bramble thinks this first contact will lead to others, and perhaps he can arrange for the bridge to be bolstered soon. Another community will be brought around in "the good war" against death-to-the-West Islamists.

This process will be very slow. The West's stomach for investing blood and treasure here for another decade is unclear. But I see no alternative if Afghanistan is to move from its destructive gyre and the global threat that brings.

The children's smiles suggest hope still flickers. To lose Afghanistan by way of smile-free Iraq—and do so on the border of a turbulent nuclear-armed Pakistan—would be a terrible betrayal and an unacceptable risk.

That, alas, is no fairy tale.

BAMIYAN'S BUDDHAS REVISITED

The fifteen-hundred-year-old Buddhas of Bamiyan, in Afghanistan, are gone, replaced by two gashes in the reddish-brown cliff. They were destroyed in March 2001 by the Taliban in their quest to rid the country of the "gods of the infidels." The fanatical soldiers of Islam blasted the ancient treasures to fragments. Here, I reflected on fanaticism.

OCTOBER 28, 2007

BAMIYAN, Afghanistan—People still speak of the Buddhas as if they were there. The Buddhas are visited and debated. A "Buddha road" just opened. It boasts the first paved surface in Afghanistan's majestic central highlands and stretches all of a half mile.

But the fifteen-hundred-year-old Buddhas of Bamiyan are gone, replaced by two gashes in the reddish-brown cliff. They were destroyed in March 2001, by the Taliban. The fanatical soldiers of Islam blasted the ancient treasures to fragments.

"It is easier to destroy than to build," Mawlawi Qudratullah Jamal, then the Taliban information minister, noted on March 3, 2001. True enough, but few in the United States or elsewhere listened.

Memory, however, is another matter. It is stubborn and volatile and hard to eradicate. The keyhole-like niches in the rock face are charged. Absence is presence. The visitor is drawn into the void as if summoned, not by vacancy, but by the towering Buddhas themselves.

Yet they are in pieces. Nasir Mudabir, twenty-nine, a director of the site, ushered me into a makeshift shelter where boxes filled with sandstone and plaster fragments from the two Buddhas are kept. Metal remnants of the bombs that destroyed them are preserved separately: they are jagged whereas the stones are smooth to the touch.

Why keep evidence of the barbarians' arsenal? "It's part of the story," Mudabir said. "It's history, bad or good. Instead of going forward, we went backward."

In Bamiyan, Hazara refugees, who have returned from Iran after Afghanistan's decades of conflict, eke out an existence in Taliban-despoiled caves once covered with bright murals.

That this is a holy place, sought out by Buddhist pilgrims over the centuries, is written in light, form, and stone.

The smaller, eastern Buddha, known locally as *Shamama*, stood 125 feet tall and has now been dated to the year 507. The larger, called *Salsal*, rose to 180 feet. It was constructed in 554. One theory holds that the builders were dissatisfied with the first and erected its neighbor in the pursuit of perfection.

I climbed the steep staircase in the rocks beside *Shamama*'s absence, reaching a rickety platform at the level of the vanished Buddha's head. "The head was comfortable," said Mohammed Qassim, my guide. "Ten people could sit and sip tea."

They could. I sat on the Buddha's head myself in 1973, gazing in wonder. The Afghan king, Mohammad Zahir Shah, had just been ousted after a forty-year reign. The coup would soon usher in the turmoil that has taken Afghanistan backward.

We knew nothing of that. We were travelers without a map. The "hippie trail" had taken us, at the wheel of a Volkswagen Kombi called "Pigpen" (named for the Grateful Dead keyboardist who died that year), from London across Iran to this noble, generous country

Looking again, after thirty-four years, at this beautiful place, first from the top of the smaller niche and then from the larger ("Twenty people could sit on this head," said Qassim), I wondered: Was it my own innocence that was gone, or the world's?

The Cold War ended, only to be replaced by the explosive conflict of secular and theocratic worlds. What began here in March 2001 has spread. The Taliban are back, sort of, seeping across the Pakistani border in a campaign fed by an Internet-borne jihadist message. The Web is a force multiplier for any guerrilla movement.

This was the Afghan burning of the books. The Nazis burned Brecht. The Taliban, then sheltering Osama bin Laden, blew up the "un-Islamic" Buddhas. The burning presaged war. The destruction presaged 9/11: two Buddhas, two towers.

Heinrich Heine noted, "When they burn books, they will, in the end, burn human beings." When Buddhas buckle, people will be crushed.

There is talk of reassembling the Buddhas, or of using solar power to beam laser holograms of their forms onto the cliff. I say, reassemble one, for hope, but not both. Absence speaks, shames, reminds.

"Peace and love" was our mantra back in 1973. So what I take from Bamiyan revisited are children in the early morning, the girls in white hijabs, walking toward a newly built primary school, dust dancing behind them. I fear for their world, and ours, but fear is not the answer.

OBAMA'S AMERICAN IDEA

An interview with Barack Obama the year before he was elected president.

DECEMBER 10, 2007

I asked Senator Barack Obama if he's tough enough for a dangerous world. Sometimes the Democratic candidate treads so carefully, and looks so vulnerable to a gust of wind, that the question of whether his legal mind can get lethal arises.

"Yes, I'm tough enough," he responded during a half-hour conversation. "What I've always found is people who talk about how tough they are aren't the tough ones. I'm less interested in beating my chest and rattling my saber and more in making decisions that build a safer and more secure world."

Obama, speaking less than a month before the Iowa caucus on January 3, continued: "We can and should lead the world, but we have to apply wisdom and judgment. Part of our capacity to lead is linked to our capacity to show restraint."

That was striking: an enduring belief in U.S. leadership coupled with a commitment to, as he also put it, acting "with a sense of humility." Skepticism about the American idea and American global stewardship has grown fast during the Bush years.

There are many reasons: the failures in Iraq; the abyss between U.S. principle and practice (Abu Ghraib); the rise of other nations (China); startling displays of American incoherence (Iran); economic vulnerability (the dollar as declining store of value); and general resentments stirred by any near hegemonic power.

All this has led some to conclude that the world would be better off if America slunk home. As Joyce Carol Oates wrote in *The Atlantic*: "How heartily sick the world has grown, in the first seven years of the twenty-first century, of the American idea!" It has become a "cruel joke."

If a global survey were taken, that might prove to be a minority opinion, but I doubt it.

Still, Obama stands by the universality of the American proposition: life, liberty, and the pursuit of happiness under a constitutional government of limited powers. "I believe in American exceptionalism," he told me, but not one based on "our military prowess or our economic dominance."

Rather, he insisted, "our exceptionalism must be based on our Constitution, our principles, our values, and our ideals. We are at our best when we are speaking in a voice that captures the aspirations of people across the globe."

It is dangerous, of course, to speak of being exceptional; people tend to resent it. If the United States said its ambition was to be normal, few would object. But Obama is right to retain a belief in America's capacity to inspire; it remains unique. And I still see no credible stabilizing alternative to the far-flung American garrisons that act as the offsetting power to old rivalries in Asia and Europe.

Pax Americana, being neither perfect nor peaceful, is not popular. Only its absence would convince its detractors of its worth.

Obama's main Democratic rivals, Senator Hillary Clinton and former Senator John Edwards, have joined him in calling for a shift from fear, militarism, and unilateralism toward interaction, including with enemies. But Obama's global engagement seems visceral in unusual ways.

"If, as president, I travel to a poor country to talk to leaders there, they will know I have a grandmother in a small village in Africa without running water, devastated by malaria and AIDS," he said. "What that allows me to do is talk honestly not only about our need to help them, but about poor countries' obligation to help themselves. There are cousins of mine in Kenya who can't get a job without paying an exorbitant bribe to some midlevel functionary. I can talk about that."

Referring to the time he spent in Indonesia, Obama said: "I have lived in the most populous Muslim country in the world, had relatives who practiced Islam. I am a Christian, but I can say I understand your worldview, although I may not agree with how Islam has evolved. I can speak forcefully about the need for Muslim countries to reconcile themselves to modernity in ways they have failed to do."

Al Qaeda attacked the West in Kenya, Bali, and New York. Obama's father was Kenyan. The senator was schooled partly in Indonesia. He attended college in New York. The parallels are strange. They can also be a source of the toughness married to intuition for which he still seeks complete expression.

Nowhere in American history has the gulf between ideals and sordid practice been greater than on questions of race. It is precisely the gulf between high principle—not least habeas corpus—and unprincipled actions that has done the most damage to America's image in recent years. Once again, Obama appears to bridge and reconcile.

"We can't entirely remake the world," he told me. "What we can do is lead by example."

BEYOND CONSPIRACY, PROGRESS

Normality is dull for those enjoying its fruits. For the traumatized, as Afghanistan illustrates, it is a distant dream.

DECEMBER 27, 2007

On the outskirts of Kandahar in Southern Afghanistan, there's a junk-yard of the Soviet empire. It's filled with the hulls of T-55 and T-62 tanks and the tubes of multiple rocket launchers. Some of the tanks are intact. I guess high-explosive, antitank missiles penetrated the turrets and coated the interior of the steel shells with blood.

I drove past this modest memorial to imperial hubris a couple of months ago on my way to a base of the nascent U.S.-trained Afghan Army. The army needs money. It might sell those metal carcasses for scrap. Why not? The detritus of human events, and their constant ebb and flow, turn the head.

Military guys deal in worst-case scenarios. But no Soviet-era planner of the 1979 invasion could have imagined being humbled in the Hindu Kush by a bunch of Islamic holy warriors; and no American Cold War strategist could have imagined those CIA-funded Islamists turning on the United States and bringing down the Twin Towers in 2001.

Yet all this happened. Just as it happened that the Soviets were once our allies and communists from Central Asia raised the hammer and sickle on the Reichstag as Hitler's Germany burned in 1945.

And then, the Soviets became our enemies while the Japanese, despite Pearl Harbor, became our friends. And, at last, the Soviets became Russians who were no longer enemies but rivals.

The mantle of enemy passed with the Cold War's end. It went to purveyors of another totalitarianism, haters of modernity, atavistic murderers of unbelievers (and their own), fanatics for whom free will and sexuality are so intolerable that a savage God must be raised up to suppress them in jihad's name.

The relation of these jihadists to Islam is as twisted as Stalin's to Marx, or the Gulag's to the liberation of the masses, but the draw of absolutism has not abated.

The problem with liberal societies is that they are as dull as they are successful. The mortgage, the tax man, the lobbyist, and the vote leave a thirsting. Revolutions are made for freedom, but its exercise is mundane, which can be intolerable. Only the terrorized—from East Berlin or Baghdad—understand that "Give me normality" is a rousing cry. For a Pole, the absence of drama feels like paradise.

But history lurches. Its strangeness prompts some to believe that there must be a hidden hand. Conspiracy theory is the refuge of the feebleminded; that has not stopped it becoming rampant in an age where every voice has a digital loudspeaker.

Americans and Canadians training young Afghan recruits near Soviet junkyards in a faraway land must be the work of someone, a plot of international speculators, or perhaps Mossad agents, who, for the grotesquely conspiracy-minded, planned 9/11.

Most of life, however, is unplanned. It's banal, capricious, a frustration to any puppet master, which does not make it any less precious, of course, or fragile.

At a Kandahar airport, I overheard two U.S. soldiers:

"I don't wanna die," the first said.

"Yeah," the second concurred. "Keep your head down."

They parted. Their fear stayed with me. I've been thinking of them and other U.S. servicemen and servicewomen this holiday season. What we all want is pretty simple. Home about sums it up. The place they have to take you in.

I boarded a U.S. military flight to Kabul and some special-forces guys—no uniforms, sniper scopes on their assault rifles—got on board, too. One sat next to me. I asked: "What's your line of business?"

"Oh, doing some private work for the government, but it would be too long a story to tell you."

I nodded. He was from Perth, Australia: a long story, indeed. Perhaps he'd been out in the badlands on the Afghan-Pakistani border battling the Taliban, or down in the southwest, where the Iranian border area is said to be full of guys without uniforms.

Afghanistan, like Poland, is a small country flanked by larger ones. Unlike Poland, it has not found the means to contain those larger countries' interests. The "Great Game" goes on.

Its continuation may suggest that nothing changes, or changes only to stay the same. But that would be a pessimistic view. On a train the other day, gliding through the mists of Belgium along pale lines of poplar trees, I thought of the slaughter at Passchendaele ninety years ago. European peace is a miracle; we forget too many miracles.

More recently, there was the Passchendaele-like slaughter of the Iran-Iraq War, with its one million dead for nothing, its Cold War fog and its Cold War intrigues. Openness is advancing, even in the Middle East. This is the age of empowerment. The back-to-the-Caliphate boys cannot resist it. Their own junkyard awaits them.

HERE COMES KOSOVO

A reflection on the birth of the independent state of Kosovo, the last piece of a dismembered state, Yugoslavia, to go its own way. Russia will be angered, I wrote. Vladimir Putin added Kosovo's independence from Serbia, a fellow Slav nation, to his long list of grievances against the West.

FEBRUARY 14, 2008

Europe will get a new state, Kosovo, on Sunday, and the long, bloody unraveling of Yugoslavia will be concluded seventeen years after the first war of its dissolution broke out in Slovenia. That is cause for celebration.

I say celebration although Serbia will rail against what its prime minister calls "this fictitious state on Serbian territory," and the Russian bear will growl, and Balkan tensions will flare for a while, and lawyers will fret over precedent.

The fact is, the independence of Kosovo is justified, unique, and unavoidable. There is no other way. Serbia lost a nationalist gamble on Kosovo a long time ago; the differences stemming from it are unbridgeable. Further delay of the inescapable can only damage the region.

So, come Sunday, I am reliably told, Kosovo will proclaim independence, and early next week major powers—including the United States, France, Britain, and Germany—will recognize the new state.

European Union foreign ministers meet Monday and may agree on a "platform" statement saying conditions for recognition have been met. A clear majority of the twenty-seven European Union members—certainly no fewer than twenty—are expected to recognize Kosovo rapidly.

Cyprus, with its Turkish-occupied northern third, will lead the holdouts. Other European Union states that are recognition-reluctant, some out of concern over separatist minorities, include Spain, Romania, Slovakia, Greece, and Bulgaria.

Unanimity would be nice, but broad consensus is sufficient. Thanks largely to the work of Wolfgang Ischinger, the German ambassador to Britain, the European Union will be united enough. More important, the United States and Europe will march in step, not a frequent occurrence of late.

"This has been a common endeavor illustrating the way we and Europe ought to work together," said Frank Wisner, the former U.S. ambassador to India, who labored fruitlessly with Ischinger last year to bring Kosovo and Serbia closer. Wisner's view: "There was never an attempt by anyone in Belgrade to reach out to a Kosovar Albanian."

Reaching out to Kosovo had scarcely been the Serbian thing in recent decades. Slobodan Milošević, the late dictator, set Serbia's murderous nationalist tide in motion on April 24, 1987, when he went to Kosovo to declare that Serbian "ancestors would be defiled" if ethnic Albanians had their way.

Milošević's quashing of Kosovo's autonomy was central to his conversion of Yugoslavia into "Serboslavia." The revolt against his bullying brought independence to former Yugoslav republics from Croatia to

Macedonia. Serbs will kick and scream, but Kosovo is just the last piece of a dead state to go its inevitable way.

Albanians, accounting for about 95 percent of a Kosovo population of 2.1 million, cannot be reconciled with a Serbia that suppressed, beat up, evicted, and killed them until NATO's 1999 intervention. Belgrade is not Bern: a Pristina inside Serbia would always be Pariahville.

But, Serbs protest in their blind pursuit of an untenable moral equivalency, the Kosovo Liberation Army were no kittens. Nor, once the Serbian genocide against Bosnian Muslims of April to September 1992 was completed, was the emergent Bosnian Army. That's right: persecute a people with enough savagery and they will in the end unite, rise up, fight, and go their own way.

What will Serbia do now? Vojislav Koštunica, the nationalist prime minister, says he won't allow "such a creation to exist for a minute."

That's been the nihilistic Serbian drumbeat ever since United Nations Resolution 1244 of 1999 made clear that a UN-overseen and NATO-protected autonomy in Kosovo would extend only until "a final settlement." Belgrade never wanted to settle.

I expect Serbia to make modest trouble but stop short of violence and cutting off Kosovo's electricity. Some of the 120,000 Serbs in Kosovo may hit the road. Serbs in the pocket north of Mitrovica may be encouraged to go for partition.

But the recent election of a pro-Western Serbian president, Boris Tadić, will be a force for restraint. So will U.S. and European pressure on Albanians. Kosovo's prime minister, Hashim Thaçi, has been making gestures to Serbs: that's positive.

Russia will call an emergency United Nations Security Council meeting. It will scream. But it's backed the wrong horse. Europe is right to demonstrate that it will not cave to Moscow's pressure. Ultimately, Serbia will want to move toward European Union membership.

Kosovo is not Transnistria or Abkhazia or South Ossetia. It is an anachronistic remnant of a now defunct country, Yugoslavia, a province that has been under UN administration for eight years pending a final settlement impossible within Serbia. Milošević rolled the dice of genocidal nationalism and lost.

In the long run, I believe this outcome will be positive for Serbia.

Instead of dwelling on medieval battles, victory-in-defeat symbolism, shrinking borders, and a poisonous culture of victimization, Serbia will begin to see what it wrought and look forward—to the West rather than the East.

KARADŽIĆ AND WAR'S LESSONS

As Radovan Karadžić, the Bosnian Serb leader, was at last arrested to be tried for war crimes at the International Criminal Tribunal for the former Yugoslavia in The Hague, I reflected on an interview I had had with him during the Bosnian war and on my memories of several of his victims.

JULY 23, 2008

CHÉRENCE, France—After covering a war, a friend said, buy yourself a house. I did. I came to this French village where church bells chime the rhythm of the days, married here, raised children, and parked Bosnia somewhere in a corner of my mind.

I had to forget. I had to write a book, so the horror would never be forgotten, in order to forget just enough to go on. There is always a measure of guilt in survival when so many have died. There are faces, in death and bereavement, that can never be eclipsed.

It's peaceful here. I'd been out watching crows in the stubble when I returned to discover Radovan Karadžić had been arrested in Belgrade, thirteen years after the end of the war, to face charges of genocide and crimes against humanity.

The years fell away, fear resurfaced, and I've been unable to sleep. I find myself back in Pale with you, Dr. Karadžić, back in that two-bit ski resort you parlayed into the Bosnian Serb capital and bestrode with your killer hairdo, back asking you questions you never could answer.

Objectivity and neutrality are not synonymous. The head is useless without the heart. War teaches that better than journalism school. The unseeing eyes of young Sarajevan women penetrated by shrapnel had taught me the rights and wrongs of the war long before I met you. Still, I wanted to look you in the eye.

"Unhinged" would be a kind description. You talked of your "love" for Sarajevo, the ethnically mixed city your boozy forces kept shelling. You told me, thirty-two months into the fighting, that you were ready "to declare a state of war." I stared in disbelief and asked about Ruždija Šestović.

Names dispel a numbing when the death toll rises toward a hundred thousand. Šestović had been seized from his home in eastern Bosnia on June 20, 1992, by masked Serbian forces, and had disappeared.

He was one of thousands of Bosnian Muslims to meet this fate in the sharp burst of Serbian violence that opened the war and "cleansed" wide swaths of the country of non-Serbs, many processed through murderous concentration camps. Pits of bones form the bitter harvest of this genocidal Serbian season.

"Ethnic cleansing was not our policy," Karadžić responded with nonchalance. "It happened because of fear. Fear and chaos. I was not informed on a daily basis of what was happening in the first months of the war, although we got some information from our troops and police. But the fate of men like Šestović was beyond our control."

An international court in The Hague will now examine that contention. I don't doubt the outcome. Justice is important—for Bosnia and for amnesia-afflicted Serbia with its everyone-was-guilty evasiveness. But justice won't change the faces brought back to me now across the years.

Amra Džaferović, beautiful Amra, telling me in the desperate Sarajevo summer of 1995: "Here things are black and white, they are, there is evil and there is good, and the evil is up in the hills, so when you say you are just a journalist, an observer, I understand you but I still hate you. Yes, I hate you."

I took that away from the war: the fierceness of moral clarity.

Pale Faruk Šabanović watching a video of the moment he was shot in Sarajevo and saying: "If I remain a paraplegic, I will be better, anyhow, than the Serb who shot me. I will be clean in my mind, clean with respect to others, and clean with respect to this dirty world."

I took that away from the war: the quietness of courage.

Ron Neitzke, noblest of American diplomats, handing me his excoriation of the U.S. government and State Department for "repeatedly and gratuitously dishonoring the Bosnians in the very hour of their genocide" and urging future Foreign Service officers to be "guided by the belief that a policy fundamentally at odds with our national conscience cannot endure indefinitely—if that conscience is well and truthfully informed."

I took that away from the war: the indivisibility of integrity and the importance of a single dissenting voice.

Nobody labored with fiercer lucidity to inform America's conscience about Karadžić's crimes than Kurt Schork, the Reuters correspondent killed in Sierra Leone in 2000. I wish he were here.

Schork would be smiling—and chiding me for being careless with my Bosnian lessons in the onward rush of life. The precious is no less important for being unbearable.

IN THE SEVENTH YEAR

A biblical rendering of the post-9/11 sundering of the United States, whose extent became clear as the 2008 financial crisis hit. The line "In the seventh year the land is to have a sabbath of rest" (Leviticus 25:4) had stuck in my mind. It gave me the lilt for this column. Writing is cadence.

SEPTEMBER 10, 2008

NEW YORK—And in the seventh year after the fall, the dust and debris of the towers cleared. And it became plain at last what had been wrought.

For the wreckage begat greed; and it came to pass that while America's young men and women fought, other Americans enriched themselves. Beguiling the innocent, they did backdate options and they did package toxic mortgage securities and they did reprice risk on the basis that it no more existed than famine in a fertile land.

Thereby did the masters of the universe prosper, with gold, with silver shekels, with land rich in cattle and fowl, with illegal manservants and maids, with jewels and silk, with Gulfstream V business jets; yet the whole land did not prosper with them. And it came to pass, when the housing bubble burst, that Main Street had to pay for the Wall Street party.

For Bush ruled over the whole nation and so sure was he of his righteousness that he did neglect husbandry.

And he took his nation into desert wars and mountain wars but, lo, he thought not to impose taxation, not one heifer nor sheep nor ox did Bush demand of the rich. And it came to pass that the nation fell into debt as boundless as the wickedness of Sodom. For everyone was maxed out.

So heavy was the burden of war and of bailing out Fannie Mae and financing debt with China that not one silver shekel remained to build bridges, nor airports, nor high-speed trains, nor roads, nor even to take care of wounded vets; and the warriors returning unto their homes from distant combat thought blight had fallen on the land.

So it was in the seventh year after the fall of the towers. And still Bush did raise his hands to the Lord and proclaim: "I will be proved right in the end!"

And around the whole earth, which had stood with America, there arose a great trouble, for it seemed to peoples abroad that a great nation, rich in flocks and herds and land and water, had been cast among thorns and Philistines; its promise betrayed, its light dimmed, its armies stretched, its budget broken, its principles compromised, its dollar diminished.

And it came to pass that this profligate nation, drinking oil with an insatiable thirst, could not cure itself of this addiction, and so its wealth was transferred to other nations that did not always wish it well. Wherefore the balance of power in the world was altered in grievous ways; and new centers of authority arose, and they were no more persuaded by democracy than was the Pharaoh.

For Bush ruled over the whole nation and so sure was he of his righteousness that he did neglect the costs of wanton consumption. And he believed that if the Lord created fossil fuel, fossil fuel must flow without end, as surely as the grape will yield wine.

Therefore, in the seventh year after the fall, with 1,126 of the slain still unidentified, their very beings rendered unto dust, their souls inhabiting the air of New York, it seemed that one nation had become two; and loss, far from unifying the people, had sundered the nation.

For the rich, granted tax breaks more generous than any blessing, grew richer, and incomes in the middle ceased to rise, and workers saw jobs leaving the land for that region called Asia. And some fought wars while others shopped; and some got foreclosed while others got clothes; and still Bush spake but few listened.

Behold, so it was in the seventh year, and it seemed that America was doubly smitten, from without and within. And, lo, a strange thing did come to pass. For as surely as the seasons do alternate, so the ruler and party that have brought woe to a nation must give way to others who can lead their people to plenty. How can the weary, flogged ass bear honey and balm and almonds and myrrh?

Yet many Americans believed the weary beast could still give them bounty. They did hold that a people called the French was really to blame. They did accuse a thing called the United Nations. They did curse the ungodly folk of Gotham and Hollywood and the sinful city of Chicago; and, lo, they proclaimed God was Republican, and carried a gun, and almost certainly hailed from Alaska.

For Bush ruled over the whole nation and so sure was he of his righteousness that he did foster division until it raged like a plague.

And in the seventh year after the fall, the dust and debris of the towers cleared. And it became plain at last what had been wrought—but not how the damage would be undone.

THE KING IS DEAD

With the American economy in meltdown, I wrote a lament for the fact that the finest young minds in the country are drawn no longer to public service but to the big money on Wall Street. I appealed for a change in mentality as Lehman Brothers, after 158 years, went under.

SEPTEMBER 17, 2008

They're listening to Coldplay down on Wall Street:

> *I used to rule the world*
> *Seas would rise when I gave the word*
> *Now in the morning I sleep alone*
> *Sweep the streets I used to own*

The leverage party's over for the masters of the universe. Shed a tear. When you trade pieces of paper for other pieces of paper instead of trading them for real things, one day someone wakes up and realizes the paper's worth nothing. And Lehman Brothers, after 158 years, has gone poof in the night.

We're witnessing the passing of more than a venerable firm. We're seeing the death of a culture.

For years, accountants, rating agencies, and Wall Street executives decided to shoot craps and collect fees. Regulators, taking their cue from a distracted President Bush, took a nap. The two "M"s—Money and Me—became the lodestones of the zeitgeist, and damn those distant wars.

The biggest single-day market drop since 9/11 reminded me that when trading reopened on September 17, 2001, and the Dow plunged 684.81 points, some executives backdated their options to reprice them at this post-attack low to increase their potential gains.

So that's what "financial killing" really means. No better illustration exists of a culture where private gain has eclipsed the public good, public service, even public decency, and where the cult of the individual has caused the commonwealth to wither.

That's the culture we've lived with. It's over now. Some new American beginning is needed.

When I taught a journalism course at Princeton a couple of years ago, I was captivated by the bright, curious minds in my class. But when I asked students what they wanted to do, the overwhelming answer was: "Oh, I guess I'll end up in i-banking."

It was not that they loved investment banking, or thought their purring brains would be best deployed on Wall Street poring over a balance sheet, it was the money and the fact everyone else was doing it.

I called one of my former students, Bianca Bosker, who graduated this summer and has taken a job with the Monitor Group, a management consultancy firm (she's also writing a book). I asked her about the mood among her peers.

"Well, I have several friends who took summer internships at Lehman that they expected to lead to full-time jobs, so this is a huge issue," she said. "You can't believe how intensely companies like Merrill would recruit at Ivy League schools. I mean, when I was a sophomore, if you could spell your name, you were guaranteed a job."

But why do freshmen bursting to change the world morph into investment bankers?

"I guess the bottom line is the money. You could be going to grad school and paying for it, or earning six figures. And, knowing nothing about money, you get to move hundreds of millions around! No wonder we're in this mess: turns out the best and the brightest make the biggest and the worst."

According to *The Harvard Crimson*, 39 percent of workforce-bound Harvard seniors this year are heading for consulting firms and financial-sector companies (or were in June). That's down from 47 percent—almost half the job-bound class—in 2007.

These numbers mirror a skewed culture. The best and the brightest should think again. Barack Obama put the issue this way at Wesleyan

University in May: Beware of the "poverty of ambition" in a culture of "the big house and the nice suits."

College seniors might start by reading "A New Bank to Save Our Infrastructure" in the current edition of *The New York Review of Books*, an impassioned plea from Felix Rohatyn (who knows something of financial rescues) and Everett Ehrlich for the creation of a National Infrastructure Bank, or NIB.

Its aim, at a time when the Chinese are investing two hundred billion dollars in railways and building ninety-seven new airports, would be to use public and private capital to give coherence to a vast program of public works. "This can improve productivity, fight unemployment, and raise our standard of living," Rohatyn told me.

It's absurd that earmarks—the self-interested budgetary foibles of senators and representatives—should dictate the progressive dilapidation of America. How can the commonwealth thrive when its bridges sag, its levees cede, its public transport creaks?

So, young minds, sign up for the NIB! Before doing so, read Nick Taylor's stirring *American-Made: The Enduring Legacy of the WPA: When FDR Put the Nation to Work*. It shows how the Works Progress Administration, a linchpin of Roosevelt's New Deal, put millions of unemployed to work on dams, airports, and the like. It's a book about how imaginative political leadership can rally a nation in crisis.

They're listening to Coldplay down on Wall Street:

> *Now the old king is dead! Long live the king!*

Yes, the death of the old is also the birth of the new. In my end is my beginning. It's time for the best and the brightest to step forth and rediscover the public sphere.

IRAN'S DAY OF ANGUISH

Every now and again a journalist gets to witness the hinge of history, epochal events that could go either way. For a couple of weeks after the June 2009 election, Iran's Islamic Republic stood on a knife-edge. Huge crowds in the streets of Tehran protested the evident fraud that delivered "victory" to President Mahmoud Ahmadinejad. The Islamic regime might have fallen if the millions in the street had marched on the seats of power.

JUNE 14, 2009

TEHRAN—She was in tears, like many women on the streets of Iran's battered capital. "Throw away your pen and paper and come to our aid," she said, pointing to my notebook. "There is no freedom here."

And she was gone, away through the milling crowds near the locked-down Interior Ministry spewing its pickups full of black-clad riot police. The "green wave" of Iran's pre-election euphoria had turned black.

Down the street, outside the ghostly campaign headquarters of the defeated reformist candidate, Mir Hussein Moussavi, the baton-wielding police came in whining phalanxes, two to a motorbike, scattering people, beating them.

"Disperse or we'll do other things and then you'll really know." The voice, from a police megaphone, was steady in its menace. "You, over there, in a white hat, I'm talking to you."

Anger hung in the air, a sullen pall enveloping the city, denser than its smog, bitter as smashed hope.

I say "defeated." But everything I have seen suggests that Moussavi, now rumored to be under house arrest, was cheated, the Iranian people defrauded, in what Moussavi called an act of official "wizardry."

Within two hours of the closing of the polls, contrary to prior practice and electoral rules, the Interior Ministry, through the state news agency, announced a landslide victory for President Mahmoud Ahmadinejad, whose fantastical take on the world and world history appears to have added another fantastical episode.

Throughout the country, across regions of vast social and ethnic disparity, including Azeri areas that had indicated strong support for Moussavi (himself an Azeri), Ahmadinejad's margin scarcely wavered, ending at an official 62.63 percent. That's 24.5 million votes, a breathtaking eight million more than he got four years ago.

No tally I've encountered of Ahmadinejad's bedrock support among the rural and urban poor, religious conservatives, and revolutionary ideologues gets within six million votes of that number.

Ahmadinejad won in other candidates' hometowns, including Moussavi's. He won in every major city except Tehran. He won very big, against the backdrop of an economic slump.

He won as the Interior Ministry was sealed, opposition Web sites were shut down, text messages were cut off, cell phones were interrupted, Internet access was impeded, dozens of opposition figures were arrested, universities were closed, and a massive show of force was orchestrated to ram home the result to an incredulous public.

Overnight, a whole movement and mood were vaporized, to the point that they appeared a hallucination.

The crowds called it a "coup d'état." They shouted *"Marg bar dictator"*—"Death to the dictator." Eyes smoldered.

I've argued for engagement with Iran and I still believe in it, although, in the name of the millions defrauded, President Obama's outreach must now await a decent interval.

I've also argued that, although repressive, the Islamic Republic offers significant margins of freedom by regional standards. I erred in underestimating the brutality and cynicism of a regime that understands the uses of ruthlessness.

"Here is my country," a young woman said to me, voice breaking. "This is a coup. I could have worked in Europe but I came back for my people." And she, too, sobbed.

"Don't cry, be brave," a man admonished her.

He was from the Interior Ministry. He showed his ID card. He said he'd worked there thirty years. He said he hadn't been allowed in; nor had most other employees. He said the votes never got counted. He said numbers just got affixed to each candidate.

He said he'd demanded of the police why "victory" required such oppression. He said he'd fought in the 1980-88 Iraq war, his brother was a martyr, and now his youth seemed wasted and the nation's sacrifice in vain.

Quoting Ferdowsi, the epic poet, he said, "If there is no Iran, let me be not." Poets are the refuge of every wounded nation—just ask the Poles—and nowhere more so than here in this hour.

Iran exists still, of course, but today it is a dislocated place. Angry divisions have been exposed, between founding fathers of the revolution—Ayatollah Ali Khamenei, the supreme leader, and Ali Akbar Hashemi Rafsanjani, the former president—and between the regime and the people.

Khamenei, under pressure from Rafsanjani, appeared ready to let the election unfold, but he reversed course, under pressure, or perhaps even diktat, from the Revolutionary Guards and other powerful constituencies.

A harsh clampdown is under way. It's unclear how far, and for how long, Iranians can resist.

On Vali Asr, the handsome avenue that was festive until the vote, crowds swarmed as night fell, confronting riot police and tear gas. "Moussavi, Moussavi. Give us back our votes," they chanted.

Majir Mirpour grabbed me. A purple bruise disfigured his arm. He raised his shirt to show a red wound across his back. "They beat me like a pig," he said, breathless. "They beat me as I tried to help a woman in tears. I don't care about the physical pain. It's the pain in my heart that hurts."

He looked at me, and the rage in his eyes made me want to toss away my notebook.

A SUPREME LEADER LOSES HIS AURA AS IRANIANS FLOCK TO THE STREETS

In the streets of Tehran, protesters were hurling themselves against serried ranks of police. The battle, it seemed for a moment, could go either way.

JUNE 20, 2009

TEHRAN—The Iranian police commander, in green uniform, walked up Komak Hospital Alley with arms raised and his small unit at his side. "I swear to God," he shouted at the protesters facing him, "I have children, I have a wife, I don't want to beat people. Please go home."

A man at my side threw a rock at him. The commander, unflinching, continued to plead. There were chants of "Join us! Join us!" The unit retreated toward Revolution Street, where vast crowds eddied back and forth, confronted by baton-wielding Basij militia and black-clad riot-police officers on motorbikes.

Dark smoke billowed over this vast city in the late afternoon. Motorbikes were set on fire, sending bursts of bright flame skyward. Ayatollah Ali Khamenei, the supreme leader, had used his Friday sermon to declare high noon in Tehran, warning of "bloodshed and chaos" if protests over a disputed election persisted.

He got both on Saturday—and saw the hitherto sacrosanct authority of his office challenged as never before since the 1979 revolution birthed the Islamic Republic and conceived for it a leadership post standing at the very flank of the Prophet. A multitude of Iranians took their fight through a holy breach on Saturday from which there appears to be scant turning back.

Khamenei has taken a radical risk. He has factionalized himself, so losing the arbiter's lofty garb, by aligning himself with President Mahmoud Ahmadinejad against both Mir Hussein Moussavi, the opposition leader, and Ali Akbar Hashemi Rafsanjani, a founding father of the revolution.

He has taunted millions of Iranians by praising their unprecedented participation in an election many now view as a ballot-box putsch. He has ridiculed the notion that an official inquiry into the vote might yield a different result. He has tried pathos and he has tried pounding his lectern. In short, he has lost his aura.

The taboo-breaking response was unequivocal. It's funny how people's obsessions come back to bite them. I've been hearing about Khamenei's fear of "velvet revolutions" for months now. There was nothing velvet about Saturday's clashes. In fact, the initial quest to have Moussavi's votes properly counted and Ahmadinejad unseated has shifted to a broader confrontation with the regime itself.

Garbage burned. Crowds bayed. Smoke from tear gas swirled. Hurled bricks sent phalanxes of police, some with automatic rifles, into retreat to the accompaniment of cheers. Early-afternoon rumors that the rally for Moussavi had been canceled yielded to the reality of violent confrontation.

I don't know where this uprising is leading. I do know some police units are wavering. That commander talking about his family was not alone. There were other policemen complaining about the unruly Basijis. Some security forces just stood and watched. "All together, all together, don't be scared," the crowd shouted.

I also know that Iran's women stand in the vanguard. For days now, I've seen them urging less courageous men on. I've seen them get beaten and return to the fray. "Why are you sitting there?" one shouted at a couple of men perched on the sidewalk on Saturday. "Get up! Get up!"

Another green-eyed woman, Mahin, aged fifty-two, staggered into an alley clutching her face and in tears. Then, against the urging of those around her, she limped back into the crowd moving west toward Freedom Square. Cries of "Death to the dictator!" and "We want liberty!" accompanied her.

There were people of all ages. I saw an old man on crutches, middle-aged office workers, and bands of teenagers. Unlike the student revolts of 2003 and 1999, this movement is broad.

"Can't the United Nations help us?" one woman asked me. I said I doubted that very much. "So," she said, "we are on our own."

The world is watching, and technology is connecting, and the West is sending what signals it can, but in the end that is true. Iranians have fought this lonely fight for a long time: to be free, to have a measure of democracy.

Ayatollah Ruhollah Khomeini, the leader of the Islamic Revolution, understood that, weaving a little plurality into an authoritarian system. That pluralism has ebbed and flowed since 1979—mainly the former—but last week it was crushed with blunt brutality. That is why a whole new generation of Iranians, their intelligence insulted, has risen.

I'd say the momentum is with them for now. At moments on Saturday, Khamenei's authority, which is that of the Islamic Republic itself, seemed fragile. The revolutionary authorities have always mocked the cancer-ridden Shah's ceding before an uprising, and vowed never to bend in the same way. Their firepower remains formidable, but they are facing a swelling test.

Just off Revolution Street, I walked into a pall of tear gas. I'd lit a cigarette minutes before—not a habit but a need—and a young man collapsed into me shouting, "Blow smoke in my face." Smoke dispels the effects of the gas to some degree.

I did what I could and he said, "We are with you," in English, and with my colleague we tumbled into a dead end—Tehran is full of them—running from the searing gas and police. I gasped and fell through a door into an apartment building where somebody had lit a small fire in a dish to relieve the stinging.

There were about twenty of us gathered there, eyes running, hearts racing. A nineteen-year-old student was nursing his left leg, struck by a militiaman with an electric-shock-delivering baton. "No way we are turning back," said a friend of his as he massaged that wounded leg.

Later, we moved north, tentatively, watching the police lash out from time to time, reaching Victory Square, where a pitched battle was in progress. Young men were breaking bricks and stones to a size for hurling. Crowds gathered on overpasses, filming and cheering the protesters. A car burst into flames. Back and forth the crowd surged, confronted by less-than-convincing police units.

I looked up through the smoke and saw a poster of the stern visage of Khomeini above the words "Islam is the religion of freedom."

Later, as night fell over the tumultuous capital, gunfire could be heard in the distance. And from rooftops across the city, the defiant sound of *"Allah-u-Akbar"*—"God is great"—went up yet again, as it has every night since the fraudulent election. But on Saturday it seemed stronger. The same cry was heard in 1979, only for one form of absolutism to yield to another. Iran has waited long enough to be free.

A JOURNALIST'S "ACTUAL RESPONSIBILITY"

Once I was back in New York from Tehran, the distance felt like betrayal of a journalist's "actual responsibility," which is to bear witness. There is no substitute for what Martha Gellhorn, one of America's great war correspondents, called "the view from the ground." Journalists are supposed to move on. Most of the time, like insatiable voyeurs, we do. But once a decade or so, we get undone.

JULY 5, 2009

NEW YORK—Journalism is a matter of gravity. It's more fashionable to denigrate than to praise the media these days. In the twenty-four/seven howl of partisan pontification, and the scarcely less constant death knell din surrounding the press, a basic truth gets lost: that to be a journalist is to bear witness.

The rest is no more than ornamentation.

I confess that, out of Iran, I am bereft. I have been thinking about the responsibility of bearing witness. It can be singular, still. Interconnection is not presence.

A chunk of me is back in Tehran, between Enquelab (Revolution) and Azadi (Freedom), where I saw the Iranian people rise in the millions to reclaim their votes and protest the violation of their Constitution.

We journalists are supposed to move on. Most of the time, like insatiable voyeurs, we do. But once a decade or so, we get undone, as if in love, and our subject has its revenge, turning the tables and refusing to let us be.

The Iranian Constitution says that the president is to be elected "by the direct vote of the people," not selected through the bogus invocation of God's will. Ayatollah Ruhollah Khomeini, the leader of the 1979 revolution, said in 1978: "Our future society will be a free society and all the elements of oppression, cruelty, and force will be destroyed."

The regime has been weakened by the flagrance of its lie, now only sustainable through force. No show trials can make truth of falseness. You cannot carve in rotten wood.

I was one of the last Western journalists to leave the city. Ignoring the revocation of my press pass, I went on as long as I could. Everything in my being rebelled against acquiescence to the coterie around President Mahmoud Ahmadinejad, whose power grab has shattered the balances of the revolution's institutions and whose goal is plain: no eyewitnesses to the crime.

Of course, Iranians have borne witness—with cell-phone video images, with photographs, through Twitter and other forms of social networking—and have thereby amassed an ineffaceable global indictment of the usurpers of June 12.

Never again will Ahmadinejad speak of justice without being undone by the Neda Effect —the image of eyes blanking, life abating, and blood blotching across the face of Neda Agha-Soltan.

Iran crushes people with its tragedy. It was unbearable to go. It remains so. Images multiply across the Web, but the work of foreign correspondents is to distill truth—and they are gone now.

Still, the world is watching. As we Americans celebrate the Declaration of Independence, let's stand with Iran by recalling the first democratic revolution in Asia. It began in 1905 in Iran, driven by the quest to secure parliamentary government and a Constitution from the Qajar dynasty.

Now, 104 years on, Iranians demand that the Constitution they have be respected through Islamic democracy and a government accountable to the people. They will not be silenced. The regime's base has narrowed dramatically. Its internal splits are growing with the defection of much of the clerical establishment.

One distinguished Iran scholar, Farideh Farhi, wrote this to me: "So I cry and ask why we have to do this to ourselves over and over again. Yet I do have hope, perhaps for purely selfish reasons—because I don't want to cry all the time, but also because of the energy you keep describing. We have a saying in Persian, I assume out of historical experience, to the effect that Iran ultimately tames the invaders."

That transported me to Ferdowsi Square, on June 18, and a woman who, with palpable passion, told me: "This land is my land."

She called Ahmadinejad "the halo without light"—a line from the anthem of the Iran demanding its country back, the Iran still saying "No" by lifting its unbending chorus into the night.

From far away, I hear it, and this distance feels like betrayal—of those brave rooftop voices and of what Max Weber, the German sociologist, called a journalist's "actual responsibility."

THE MEANING OF LIFE

Two monkeys, two diets, two stories. Is it preferable to live well at the risk of dying young, or live a life of strict dietary discipline in the hope of living longer?

JULY 15, 2009

NEW YORK—What's life for? That question stirred as I contemplated two rhesus monkeys, Canto, aged twenty-seven, and Owen, aged twenty-nine, whose photographs appeared last week in *The New York Times*.

The monkeys are part of a protracted experiment in aging being conducted by a University of Wisconsin team. Canto gets a restricted diet with 30 percent fewer calories than usual, while Owen gets to eat whatever the heck he pleases.

Preliminary conclusions, published in *Science* two decades after the experiment began, "demonstrate that caloric restriction slows aging in a primate species," the scientists leading the experiment wrote. Whereas just 13 percent of the dieting group has died in ways judged due to old age, 37 percent of the feasting monkeys are already dead.

These conclusions have been contested by other scientists for various reasons I won't bore you with—boredom definitely shortens life spans.

Meanwhile, before everyone holds the French fries, the issue arises of how these primates—whose average life span in the wild is twenty-seven (with a maximum of forty)—are feeling and whether these feelings impact their desire to live.

Monkeys' emotions were part of my childhood. My father, a doctor, worked with them all his life. His thesis at the University of Witwatersrand in Johannesburg, South Africa, was on the menstrual cycle of baboons. When he settled in Britain in the 1950s, he had some of his baboons (average life span thirty) shipped over, and ultimately donated a couple to the London Zoo.

Upon visiting the zoo much later, he got a full-throated greeting from the baboons, who rushed to the front of their cage to tell him they'd missed him. Moral of story: Don't underestimate monkeys' feelings.

Which brings me to low-cal Canto and high-cal Owen: Canto looks drawn, weary, ashen, and miserable in his thinness, mouth slightly agape, features pinched, eyes blank, his expression screaming, "Please, no, not another plateful of seeds!"

Well-fed Owen, by contrast, is a happy camper with a wry smile, every inch the laid-back simian, plump, eyes twinkling, full mouth relaxed, skin glowing, exuding wisdom as if he's just read Kierkegaard and concluded that "Life must be lived forward, but can only be understood backward."

It's the difference between the guy who got the marbleized rib-eye and the guy who got the oh-so-lean filet. Or between the guy who got a Château Grand Pontet Saint-Émilion with his Brie and the guy who got water. As Edgar notes in *King Lear*, "Ripeness is all." You don't get to ripeness by eating apple peel for breakfast.

Speaking of Saint-Émilion, scientists, aware that most human beings don't have the discipline to slash their calorie intake by almost a third, have been looking for substances that might mimic the effects of caloric restriction. They have found one candidate, resveratrol, in red wine.

The thing is, there's not enough resveratrol in wine to do the trick, so scientists are trying to concentrate it, or produce a chemical like it in order to offer people the gain (in life expectancy) without the pain (of dieting).

I don't buy this gain-without-pain notion. Duality resides, indissoluble, at life's core—Faust's two souls within his breast, Anna Karenina's shifting essence. Life without death would be miserable. Its beauty is bound to its fragility. Dawn is unimaginable without the dusk.

When life extension supplants life quality as a goal, you get the desolation of Canto the monkey. Living to 120 holds zero appeal for me. Canto looks like he's itching to be put out of his misery.

There's an alternative to resveratrol. Something is secreted in the lovesick that causes rapid loss of appetite—caloric restriction—yet scientists have been unable to reproduce this miracle substance, for if they did they would be decoding love. Because love is too close to the divine, it seems to defy such breakdown.

My mother died of cancer at sixty-nine. Her father lived to ninety-eight, her mother to 104. I said my mother died of cancer. But that's not true. She was bipolar, and depression devastated her. What took her life was misery.

We don't understand what the mind secretes. The process of aging remains full of enigma. But I'd bet on jovial Owen's outliving wretched Canto. I suspect those dissenting scientists I didn't bore you with are right.

My ninety-eight-year-old grandfather had a party trick, making crisscross incisions into a watermelon, before allowing it to fall open in a giant red blossom. It was as beautiful as a lily opening.

When my father went to pick up his baboons at Heathrow Airport, he stopped at a grocery store to buy them a treat. "Two pounds of bananas, please," he said. But there were none. "Okay," he said, "then I'll take two pounds of carrots." The shopkeeper gave him a very strange look before hurriedly handing over the carrots.

I can hear my eighty-eight-year-old father's laughter as he tells this story. Laughter extends life. There's little of it in the low-cal world, and little doubt pudgy Owen will have the last laugh.

ADVANTAGE FRANCE

The American and French relationships to food diverge radically. The French don't believe what they're eating is genuine unless they've seen gritty proof of provenance. In the United States, best remove all trace—blood and blemishes—from the produce on offer.

AUGUST 30, 2009

CHÉRENCE, France—Arrival is usually defined as reaching a destination, but of course it's more than that, it's the moment when you have shed enough of where you came from to be present at the place you've reached. This off-loading of layers takes time, like peeling an onion.

My French arrival this year was time-consuming. Iran, which is another story, had me. But the moment came, and when it came, it was not the dawn swooping of starlings, the softness of the dusk light through the sycamores, or the chiming of a village bell that delivered me to "la douce France," but the sight of glistening guts.

The guts in question were being coaxed by a hand—ungloved—from the belly of a four-pound sea bass—unfarmed—at the market in the Norman town of Vernon, which has one stand devoted solely to watercress. The fish, iridescent, its gills bright scarlet, was fresh from the waters off Dieppe.

My friend Marcel Bossy, who had made the predawn drive from the coast with his glossy load, had his hand deep in the fish. He was laughing about something as the guts slithered onto a scale-coated chopping board.

My eleven-year-old daughter, Adele, covered her eyes, but I was riveted. Marcel's wife, Sandrine, also laughing—something ribald between them—was gutting firm mackerel with swift incisions and finger movements, when one dropped to the ground. She scooped the fish up and resumed work on it, putting me in mind of Julia Child's famous statement about a miss-flipped potato pancake: "You can always pick it up."

Since Child, in *Mastering the Art of French Cooking,* and in her groundbreaking 1960s television show *The French Chef,* brought Gallic secrets to riveted Americans, the shameless gutting and picking-up of real food in ungloved hands has given way to the hurried-hermetic-hygienic U.S. fever of plastic gloves, processed foods, and precooked meals.

Those fish guts delivered me to France because, although this country has its share of fast-food outlets, it has preserved a relationship to food distinguished from the American in three essential respects: fear, time, and *terroir.*

If Americans want their fish pre-filleted, their chicken breasts excised from surrounding bone and conveniently packed, their offal kept from view and the table, and any hand that touches a slice of ham or lox sealed inside a glove, it is because fear of the innards that will not speak their name, the guts that reek of life, and the germs we all carry has become rampant.

By contrast, the French don't believe what they're eating is genuine unless they've seen gritty proof of provenance. They like the alchemy of the peasant hand that does the pâté grip.

American anxiety is related to the American perception of time, which is always short in a land that prizes efficiency above all. Precooked meals—food divorced from its origins, food without guts—is faster to prepare and therefore attractive.

I bought a couple of the female ducklings the French call *canettes* the other day. It took fifteen minutes for the cutting-off of head, feet, and wing tips; for the innards to be removed; for the placing in the cleansed insides of the liver, kidneys, and neck; for singeing over a gas burner; and

for discussion as to whether I wanted the plump ducks trussed for rotis-
serie cooking (I did not).

Most stores in New York don't bother selling ducklings—they're
inefficient birds in that the meat-to-size ratio is low—and if they did,
such protracted preparation would be unthinkable. Time bows at the
altar of gastronomy in France. In the United States time is the altar.

The third fundamental difference relates to *terroir*, the untranslat-
able combination of soil, hearth, and tradition that links most French
people to a particular place. France sees American mobility with a
sacred immobility; attachments trump restlessness.

These are attachments of the gut, which brings us back to why the
French take such pleasure in those hands at work cleansing a sea bass or
a duckling, and why a stand selling watercress (with the unique taste of a
particular patch of soil) is viable.

The French Paradox, so-called, is really the French self-evidence.
Change your relationship to fear, time, and place, and you change your
metabolism. This has less to do with the specific foods eaten, or the specific wine drunk (although of course they count), than it has to do with
how food is approached.

According to the 2009 *CIA World Factbook*, the estimated average life expectancy in France is 80.98 (84.33 for women and 77.79
for men), against 78.11 for the United States (80.69 for women and
75.65 for men). France ranks ninth in the world; America ranks fiftieth.
There's something to be said for ungloved hands picking mackerel from
the ground.

The American health-care debate is skewed. It should be devoting
more time to changing U.S. culinary and eating habits in ways that cut
the need for expensive care by reducing rampant obesity, to which anxiety, haste, and disconnectedness contribute. France has much to teach,
guts and all.

THE MAGIC MOUNTAIN

The Iranian-American conflict, unresolved in the almost half century since the Iranian revolution of 1979, had led to sterile paralysis. "Death to America," went the chant heard every Friday in Iran. Americans tend to equate all Iranians with bearded religious fanatics intent on destroying Israel. Here, reflecting on a hike in the Alborz Mountains north of Tehran, I gave voice to young Iranians who, up above the city, allow fingertips to touch.

NOVEMBER 5, 2009

TEHRAN—The Alborz Mountains soar above the north side of the megalopolis that is the Iranian capital, their snowy peaks arousing dreams of evasion in people caught by the city's bottlenecks. One day I could resist them no longer.

Near Evin Prison, where thousands languish and executions are frequent, a trail begins. Following a rushing stream, it winds up past teahouses full of the fragrant smoke of hookahs and stalls offering fresh pomegranate juice, into the bracing wild.

Iran's pursuit of liberty, unbowed since the Constitutional Revolution of 1906, remains unfulfilled. The Islamic Revolution has not birthed a totalitarian state; all sorts of opinions are heard. But it has created a society whose ultimate bond is fear. Disappearance into some unmarked room is always possible. So the freedom of the mountains is double in nature.

For young Iranians, the Alborz trails are a physical escape from the city, where jobs are elusive, but also a mental one—from self-censorship, from monochrome dress, and from the morality police ever alert for a female neck revealed, hands fleetingly held, or hair cascading from a headscarf.

Their youthful voices open up. They sing to the haunting sound of the kamancheh, a bowed fiddle. They bellow into the gullies. They recite the poetry of the great Hafez. They allow fingertips, and more, to touch. Their camaraderie is strong: bowling alone is not what repressive societies do. Iran's force—a population younger than its thirty-year-old revolution—is palpable.

At a teahouse around the nineteen-hundred-meter mark, I fell into conversation with a couple, Narges Azizi, twenty-three, and her twenty-six-year-old boyfriend, Behnam Moradi. Students of graphics and design, they hike once a week. She was wearing a loose-fitting blue sweat suit, a sufficient affront to Islamic dress code to have caused her detention back in the city.

"They took my photo, face to the camera, both profiles," Azizi said. "My parents had to get me." I'd heard a similar story from a divorced woman in her mid-thirties stopped for wearing a skirt that reached to her ankles. She was still seething from the humiliation of the experience, parental rescue and all.

"Our relationship is like stealing," Moradi said.

"It's worse than stealing," Azizi said.

Highly educated, lacking the means to marry or acquire their own apartment, dodging parental reproach and dour governmental strictures, dissatisfied but not to the point of rebellion, this young couple is typical enough of a nation in a halfway house of Islam and modernity.

Iran's emblem should be a turbaned mullah on a motor scooter talking on a cell phone; or a young woman who has fashioned a hijab into an article of Parisian elegance.

"Should we leave?" Moradi asked me.

"Not if you're prepared to be patient."

"Change could take two generations," he said.

One is more likely if the United States shows restraint. I thought back to a senior cleric, Mohsen Gharavian, whom I'd met in the holy city of Qom. He'd seemed at ease expounding on the union of Islam, politics, and freedom until the subject of women's attire came up.

"Prostitution is a career for some people in some countries, but here we cannot bear that," Gharavian said. "So the reason this looseness in dressing is not admitted is that this concept may lead gradually to a negation of our values and bring the preconditions for the spread of prostitution."

Right.

Yet the revolution of which this cleric is a bastion has empowered women. In the end, it was only Ayatollah Khomeini who could tell traditional families they had to educate their daughters.

Today, as my colleague Nazila Fathi recently noted, more than 60 percent of university students are women. Laws cannot forever lag the reality of an emancipated mindset.

The irony of the Islamic Revolution is that it has created a very secular society within the framework of clerical rule. The Shah enacted progressive laws for women unready for them. Now the opposite is true: progressive women face confining jurisprudence. At some point something must give.

That is why I suggested Azizi and Moradi be patient. That is also why it is essential that the West engage with Iran and avoid the one thing that could set back the country's inexorable evolution: an act of war that would increase repression and embolden religious nationalism.

It's not easy to be patient. Service in the Basiji, the pro-government volunteer militia, is often a surer path to a good job than a college degree.

Still, up in the Alborz, Iranians' long-held dream of freedom seems within reach. At twenty-one hundred meters, I saw two young women with their hair down. Afraid? They laughed.

Higher still, I met Marjan Safiyar, twenty, an electrical-engineering student. She looked chic in a tight-fitting silvery jacket. Up here, she said, "I breathe." I asked her if she thought Iran would change.

"No," she said, laughing. "Our men don't have the courage."

But its women are another story. They are reason to see Iran as one of the most hopeful societies in the Middle East rather than one of the most threatening.

A MIDEAST TRUCE

I have been and remain a believer that a two-state outcome—with Israel and a Palestinian state existing beside each other in peace and security—is the only way to end the conflict between two peoples claiming the same sliver of land between the Mediterranean Sea and the Jordan River. But even in 2009, I had grown pessimistic. The then 250-mile-long Israeli wall, or separation barrier, had cemented division.

NOVEMBER 16, 2009

I've grown so pessimistic about Israel-Palestine that I find myself agreeing with Israel's hard-line foreign minister, Avigdor Lieberman: "Anyone who says that within the next few years an agreement can be reached ending the conflict simply doesn't understand the situation and spreads delusions."

That's the lesson of early Obama. The president tried to rekindle peace talks by confronting Israel on settlements, coaxing Palestinians to resume negotiations, and reaching out to the Muslim world. The effort has failed.

It has alienated Israel, where Obama is unpopular, and brought the president of the Palestinian Authority, Mahmoud Abbas, close to resignation. It's time to think again.

What's gone wrong? There have been tactical mistakes, including a clumsy U.S. wobble toward accepting Israeli "restraint" on settlements rather than cessation. But the deeper error was strategic: Obama's assumption that he could resume where Clinton left off in 2000 and pursue the land-for-peace idea at the heart of the two-state solution.

This approach ignored the deep scars inflicted in the past decade: the killing of 992 Israelis and 3,399 Palestinians between the outbreak of the Second Intifada in 2000 and 2006; the Israeli Army's harsh reoccupation of most of the West Bank; Hamas's violent rise to power in

Gaza and the accompanying resurgence of annihilationist ideology; the spectacular spread of Jewish settlements in the West Bank; and the Israeli construction of over 250 miles of a separation barrier that has protected Israel from suicide bombers even as it has shattered Palestinian lives, grabbed land, and become, in the words of Michael Sfard, an Israeli lawyer, "an integral part of the West Bank settlement plan."

These are not small developments. They have changed the physical appearance of the Middle East. More important, they have transformed the psychologies of the protagonists. Israelis have walled themselves off from Palestinians. They are less interested than ever in a deal with people they hardly see.

As Ron Nachman, the founder of the sprawling Ariel settlement, comments in René Backmann's superb new book, A *Wall in Palestine*, the wave of Palestinian suicide attacks before work on the barrier began in mid-2002 meant: "Israelis wanted separation. They did not want to be mixed with the Arabs. They didn't even want to see them. This may be seen as racist, but that's how it is."

And that's about where we are.

With Palestinians saying, "Not one inch further will we cede." The myriad humiliations of the looping barrier, which divides Palestinians from one another as well as from Israel, have cemented this *"Nyet."*

On the surface, Obama's decision to tackle settlements first was logical enough. Nothing has riled Palestinians as much as the continued flow of Israeli settlers into East Jerusalem and the West Bank. Both Oslo (1993) and the Road Map (2003) called for settlements to stop, but the number of settlers has risen steadily to over 450,000.

The president was categorical in his Cairo speech: "The United States does not accept the legitimacy of continued Israeli settlements."

Nor do I. But facts are hard—and Obama has tried to ignore them. The history briefly outlined above makes clear that the right-wing government of Prime Minister Benjamin Netanyahu won't deviate from the pattern of settlement growth established since 1967.

Indeed, Backmann's book (from which the Sfard quote is also taken) demonstrates a relentless continuity of Israeli purpose, now cemented by a fence whose aim was in fact double: to stop terrorists but also "to protect the settlements, to give them room to develop."

That is why, even at 250 miles, the barrier (projected to stretch over four hundred miles) is already much longer than the pre-1967 border or Green Line: it burrows into the West Bank to place major settlements on the Israeli side, effectively annexing over 12 percent of the land.

The United States condoned the construction of this settlement-reinforcing barrier. It cannot be unmade—not for the foreseeable future. Peace and walls do not go together. But a truce and walls just may. And that, I must reluctantly conclude, is the best that can be hoped for.

Obama, who has his Nobel already, should ratchet expectations downward. Stop talking about peace. Banish the word. Start talking about détente. That's what Lieberman wants; that's what Hamas says it wants; that's the end point of Netanyahu's evasions.

It's not what Abbas wants, but he's powerless. Shlomo Avineri, a political scientist, told me, "A nonviolent status quo is far from satisfactory, but it's not bad. Cyprus is not bad."

I recall my friend Shlomo dreaming of peace. That's over. The last decade destroyed the last illusions: hence the fence. The courageous have departed the Middle East. A peace of the brave must yield to a truce of the mediocre—at best.

At least until Intifada-traumatized Israeli psychology shifts. I agree with the Israeli author David Grossman when he writes: "We have dozens of atomic bombs, tanks and planes. We confront people possessing none of these arms. And yet, in our minds, we remain victims. This inability to perceive ourselves in relation to others is our principal weakness."

A JEW IN ENGLAND

Being taunted as a "Yid" in high school, and encountering the faint
not-quite-one-of-us bigotry of late-1960s Britain, forged my Jewish
identity, despite an upbringing whose priority was assimilation.

NOVEMBER 30, 2009

NEW YORK—When my father was about to emigrate from South
Africa to England in the 1950s, a friend of the family suggested that a
change of name was in order because it would be unwise to pursue his
career in Britain while called "Cohen."

My dad, a young doctor, said he would think it over. A few days later,
he announced to the friend that he had decided to make the change.

"To what?" she asked with satisfaction. "Einstein," he deadpanned.

And so Sydney Cohen came to London and in time had the title
of Commander of the Order of the British Empire (CBE) bestowed
upon him by the queen, and was named a fellow of the Royal Society
(founded 1660), and, most important to him, became a member of the
Royal and Ancient Golf Club of St. Andrews.

In all, it can hardly be said that he encountered barriers in the land
of Benjamin Disraeli. He embraced his adopted country, my family was
assimilated, and Jewishness became the minor key of our identity.

That was most of the story but not quite all. A couple of things have
recently stirred deep memories of being a Jew in England.

The first was Nick Hornby's screenplay for the movie *An Education*, set in 1960s London and rendering with acuity a subtle current of
prejudice.

It is captured when Emma Thompson, playing the proper headmis-
tress of a girls' school where a precocious sixteen-year-old student has
taken up with an older man, exclaims, "A Jew!" upon discovering the
identity of the rake. Her voice quivers with distaste.

The second was reading my colleague Sarah Lyall's account of the controversy stemming from the Court of Appeal's decision about the Jewishness (or not) of a boy trying to get into the JFS, or Jews' Free School, in London. I won't go into the case here but will say that I found the court's ruling that the criterion for Jewishness must be "faith, how-ever defined"—rather than family ties—quaint. Nobody I know ever defined a Jew, or persecuted one, on the grounds of whether or not he went to synagogue regularly.

An Education put me back in my London complete with Dad's old Rover model. But it wasn't just the cars. It was that faint prejudice floating around with its power to generate I'm-not-quite-one-of-them feelings.

In the late 1960s, I went to Westminster, one of Britain's top private schools, an inspiring place hard by Westminster Abbey, and was occasionally taunted as a "Yid"—not a bad way to forge a proud Jewish identity in a nonreligious Jew.

The teasing soon ended. But something else happened that was related to the institution rather than to adolescent minds. I won a scholarship to Westminster and would have entered College, the scholars' house, but was told that a Jew could not attend College nor hold a Queen's Scholarship. I got an Honorary Scholarship instead.

This seemed normal then but appears abnormal in retrospect. So I wrote to the current headmaster, Stephen Spurr, asking what the grounds were back then on which Jews were not admitted to College; whether the same regulation still exists; when the practice was changed (if it was); and how Westminster defines, or defined, Jewishness.

Spurr e-mailed answers. "I am afraid I do not know" was his response to my query on why Jews were barred from College; "Absolutely not" on whether the regulation still exists; no idea on when it was changed (if it ever existed); and, on the definition question, "We do not try to determine Jewishness."

That piqued rather than satisfied my curiosity, so I wrote to my old English teacher John Field, who inspired my lifelong love of literature, and he was more forthcoming:

"The demography of London began to change markedly in the 1930s with refugees from mainland Europe, and when the school returned to London after five years' evacuation, the number of Jewish

applicants slowly began to increase. The bursar and registrar was an
ex-Indian Army colonel with the kind of views you would expect such a
background to provide. I recall archiving his notes on Nigel Lawson"—
later Britain's chancellor of the exchequer—"when his parents brought
him for interview in 1945 or 46. On the lines of 'Undoubtedly a bright
and clever child. Very Jewish of course.'"

Field continued: "Colonel Carruthers (his real name!) almost certainly operated with a Jewish quota in his mind when admitting people
to the school, and at some point in the early 1960s got the Governing
Body to agree to a new condition of entry to College: the candidate
should 'profess the Christian faith.'"

He added: "So in the 1960's Westminster acquired a reputation for
being unwelcoming to Jewish families. Maybe the examples of yourself
and John Marenbon"—a brilliant Jewish classmate of mine, now a fellow of Trinity College, Cambridge—"prompted John Rae to persuade
the governors to scrap the condition of entry to College." Rae was headmaster from 1970 to 1986.

Westminster, like Britain, has changed. Openness has grown. Bigotry's faint refrain has grown fainter still. But I think my old school
should throw more light on this episode. And I still believe that the
greatest strength of America, its core advantage over the Old World,
is its lack of interest in where you're from and consuming interest in
what you can do.

CHINESE OPENINGS

History enlightens; it can also blind. Ever since covering the Bosnian war in the 1990s, I have been interested in the way history manipulated or repressed can be used to ignite revanchist frenzy. Here I mused on China's manipulation of its history, its airbrushing of events (including the crushing of the Tiananmen uprising in 1989), taking a small cemetery in Chongqing commemorating victims of the 1966–76 Cultural Revolution as my starting point.

JANUARY 18, 2010

CHONGQING, China—The tombstones loomed in the dusk, some of them rising more than twenty-five feet, each telling a forgotten story of China's troubled history. I had come to find them because, for the first time, China has sanctioned the preservation here of a site commemorating the numberless victims of the 1966–76 Cultural Revolution.

That's a hopeful sign. I spent too long covering the bloody wars in the Balkans not to believe that history denied can devour you.

But until now, the communist rulers of China have been relentless in suppressing the history of their worst errors, not least the frenzied attempt of Mao Zedong in the decade before his death to revitalize his rule by spreading terror.

So the decision, made last month by authorities in this gritty central Chinese city, to designate a cemetery containing the remains of 573 people slaughtered during the Cultural Revolution as an official relic worthy of maintenance is a significant opening.

That, it seems to me, is modern China: two steps forward, one back. For every new repression there is some relaxation; for every new abuse, some advance.

Few things have made the capitalist-communist overseers of China's frenzied thrust for modernity as nervous as history. On the one hand, it's a source of pride. On the other, it's a fount of fear.

When an American working in China met a Communist Party cadre recently, he was greeted by a backhanded compliment: "With our five thousand years of history, we in China think you Americans are doing pretty well for your brief history of about 230 years."

To which the American, alluding to the six decades of the People's Republic, responded: "Well, we in the United States think China's not doing badly for its mere sixty years of history!"

The remark did not do a lot for Chinese-American relations, but it has to be said that history is a malleable thing here. China finds comfort in a past whose immensity contains many dynasties that lasted longer than all U.S. history. Posters exalting the Communist Party show the Great Wall, the better to link its rule with immovable authority and nationalist grandeur.

At the same time, China's modern rulers like nothing so much as reducing history to a blank sheet. Everywhere the past—temples, ancient walls, sinuous alleys—is being swept away. Disastrous periods of Mao's rule, including the famine of 1959–61 and the Cultural Revolution, have been airbrushed from history. Like "June 4"—shorthand for the crushing of the Tiananmen uprising in 1989—they are taboo.

Here in Chongqing, the Cultural Revolution took particularly devastating form as rival factions bent on demonstrating their devotion to Mao's wild anti-capitalist, anti-rightist, anti-cadre purge battled one another. The local arms industry fed the frenzy: mass murder in the name of a personality cult.

Outside the walled cemetery in Shaping Park, as I waited for hours to be admitted into the overgrown sanctuary with its whispering of these terrible deeds, a man approached me: "Everyone was shooting in 1967 to protect Mao! I don't know why. Even now I don't know why. I just followed my school with a gun."

He shook his head. "We're not interested in any of that now. All we do is talk of development."

But a few people, like a scholar named Chen Xiaowen, were interested. Now fifty-four, Chen became concerned over the fate of the cemetery in the 1980s and has since campaigned to block the ever-ready bulldozers of real-estate developers.

He was part of a group of scholars who submitted a petition to the

Chongqing authorities requesting the safeguarding of the cemetery as a "cultural preservation site." On December 25, 2009, the request was approved, allowing the eventual devotion of city funds to restoration. "It's progress!" Chen said.

The cemetery, with its 131 graves containing multiple victims, many of them young Red Guards, is a place of hushed mystery. A faded photograph of a young man, his features blurred, is propped against one tombstone. Ferns grow from the stones, weeds advance. Chinese characters peel away. "We can be beaten, struggled against, but we will never bow our revolutionary heads," says one inscription. None of the dead is over fifty-one.

I asked Chen why this past still haunts a party that has hoisted China from destructive folly. "It's a form of rule based on results, efficacy, not on democratic legitimacy," he said. "So, if you dig too deeply into the mistakes of the past, you make yourself vulnerable."

Still, here in Chongqing, China has taken a small step toward a genuine history, an honest accounting, and away from history as merely a vehicle for the consolidation of power. I applaud that. The Chinese people, their wounds assuaged by time, are ready for more openness.

In the fading light, old men come out with their birds, hang the cages on trees, and let the birds sing to one another as they gossip. Some say history is for the birds. I say it needs to be aired or it will turn on you.

A WOMAN BURNS

Nothing is to stand between China and its development, certainly not a single woman resisting the demolition of her house in Chengdu. She had been ordered to move to make way for a new highway. After I reported this column on the self-immolation of Tang Fuzhen, I was detained by police waiting outside her house, which had been reduced to rubble.

JANUARY 25, 2010

CHENGDU, China—Tang Huiqin got between China and its ferocious development push and still bears the scars. I found her, traumatized and trembling, in the northern outskirts of this vast city, where it's common to see old houses with a single Chinese character scrawled in red on the façade: "Demolish."

The thugs from the city demolition squad rolled into her neighborhood, a village called Jinhua now engulfed by urban sprawl, early on November 13. A road was to be built, and nothing—not women, or children, or years of painstaking homebuilding—was to stand in its way.

"They were beating me, beating me, and I could hear my younger sister, on the highest part of the roof, screaming, 'Older sister, older brother, have you been beaten to death?'" Tang, fifty-three, told me. "I could hear her voice but I had blacked out from the beating and could not speak."

We were seated in the courtyard of Tang's simple home, adjacent to her sister's house, now reduced to rubble. Chickens strutted about. Tang had just emerged from the hospital. A large reddish scar cut across her forehead. She was nervous. It can be dangerous in China to speak out, to speak truth to power. Tang stood up and raised her shirt to reveal severe bruising all down her left flank.

Tears filled her eyes. She averted them. Her younger sister was called Tang Fuzhen. She's dead now.

On that day, November 13, as Tang Fuzhen yelled at the demolition brutes to stop the violence against her siblings, as she pleaded with them to leave her house intact, she doused herself three times in gasoline, saying she would set herself on fire, right there on the roof, if the beating of her family continued.

The blows continued to rain down and the self-immolation of Tang Fuzhen, forty-seven, was added to the long list of victims of explosive Chinese development.

The nexus of that growth often comes down to real estate: who owns it, who gets the sweet deals on it, who gets ousted, and who among Communist Party officials and their developer cronies pockets the big bucks from the infrastructure, business, and residential projects that have turned China into a monumental construction site.

The equation of the Chinese growth story that is changing the world (and keeping U.S. Wal-Mart customers happy) is unforgiving: 10 percent annual expansion is the guarantor of the Communist Party's hold on power, and so everything will be done to sustain it. Agonized debate (think U.S. health-care reform or Afghan deployment) is not for China. Bulldozers are more its thing.

The thrill of living in China is this very short distance between words and action. Few Western executives are immune to the frisson. Forget Indian democratic dithering! Nowhere else are projects so intimate with their execution.

That's fundamental to the forced quick-march of 1.3 billion people to modernity. It can be very seductive, this fast train to the future, because you live on the cusp of a great and stirring transformation. You are part of history, an actor in an essential drama, not sitting on the weary European sidelines! But its underside is often trampled lives.

Tang Huiqin's life is in shreds after her sister's death. Her daughter, Wei Jiao, twenty-five, paced about. How long until the police would come and interrupt our conversation? Wei recalled what happened that day, two months ago, when her aunt became a ball of flames.

"I was holding my daughter, who's less than one year old, and they were beating us with lead pipes," she told me. "My daughter fell on me, and they were spraying this stinging substance in our eyes. Then they grabbed my child and they were kicking me in the legs and back. I wanted to cry out, but I couldn't, I was lying on the ground shaking, and I heard them say, 'Take their cell phones!'"

Wei began to cry. "My aunt was a really good person. Everyone got help from her. She liked to make herself pretty and she was very industrious. I never thought she would go to such lengths, that she would want to die. I can hear her still saying, 'I'll come down if everyone leaves. I just want everyone to leave!' They pushed her to this."

Tang Fuzhen was a successful woman. She and her husband had been in Jinhua for more than a decade, building a wholesale clothing business called Aoshiwei. They had been courted by local party officials to install their company in the area and, according to local press reports, had invested close to $450,000 in a three-story building with a factory on the first two floors and their home on the third. They had a son studying in Britain and a teenage adopted daughter.

Although once touted as model entrepreneurs—profiled in newspapers and on local TV—they had, since 2007, run into a familiar conflict in China stemming from the confluence of murky property rights, soaring real-estate prices, land-hungry businessmen, and rampant corruption linking party officials with developers.

"Land use is a huge issue because, in the absence of property taxes, local city authorities have to keep selling land and developing land to stay afloat financially," one Western official told me. "Chengdu gets about thirty percent of its city budget from sales of land owned by the state or the military. The government has to keep monetizing the land through long-term leases, and of course corrupt officials want to make money by getting bribes and other gifts from the buyers."

Arthur Kroeber, an economist, told me that as much as 50 percent of local government revenues came from land sales throughout China in 2009. "The financial interests of a lot of powerful people hinge on the real-estate boom. That's where the big capital gains are." The real-estate bicycle is the get-rich-quick bicycle: everyone in the game has to keep pedaling!

For Tang Fuzhen, who was estranged from her husband, the building local authorities coveted was at once her home and her factory. She derided the offers of compensation, a mere fraction of the market value. Official and market prices often bear no relation to each other in China.

But the city, determined to build a road to a new water-treatment plant, would hear none of her protests.

The conflict came to a head on that roof. Tang Fuzhen burned for a long time. Wei Jiao, her niece, was in the ambulance with her.

"There was no skin on her arms and face, just exposed flesh," she told me. "Her teeth were completely black. She had no eyelashes or hair. And she said, 'Jiao, Jiao, I just want to die, I just want to die.' And I knew it was not the physical pain. It was the feeling in her heart of watching her family being beaten and the house she built with her labor destroyed. And I told her to try to hold on until we got to the hospital."

Tang Fuzhen did hold on for a while. But on November 29, sixteen days after her self-immolation, she succumbed to the burns.

Her suicide was caught on video by a neighbor and spread across the Internet. An outcry ensued. A local inquiry found the demolition process legal, but deemed the eviction "mismanaged," and a city official was fired. Professors at Beijing University Law School wrote to the People's Congress, in theory the highest legislative body, suggesting changes to the law to ensure that compensation is adequate, that it's paid before demolition, that violence is never used, and that owners can sue to contest eviction rulings.

These reforms are urgently needed. They would bring development and individual rights into some balance and slow the fast-money corruption machine. But the entrenched interests behind brutal expropriation are enormous.

Across China, I sensed great anger at the raging real-estate game in which the party plays such a central role. On a vast half-built development in Chongqing, a dozen banners had been draped from windows: "Try to support our peasant brothers in getting the blood, sweat, and tears money owed to them by the developers."

Here in Chengdu, on entire city blocks marked for demolition, there were banners urging China's leaders to "reflect the wishes of the people" by reforming the way land is acquired.

Meanwhile, property seizures continue apace. The road between Jinhua and downtown Chengdu is buried in dust and rubble. Posters and banners beside the road show images of verdant fields, flowering shrubs, trees, superhighways, high-speed trains, gleaming office blocks, elegant executives—an almost comical imagined paradise of affluent twenty-first-century development in the midst of construction mayhem. I saw a man, seated beside a dead bush, overwhelmed by the dust, cleaving a just-killed chicken beneath a photograph of white doves and a white horse bearing a beautiful woman off to her dream home.

"Today's irritation is for tomorrow's convenience," said one sign. Another said, "Create a green culture!" A third tried this: "Be cultural citizens. Construct a cultural city!" And everywhere I looked there was demolition, disarray, destitution.

I asked Tang how she felt now. "Helpless," she said. And when at last I stepped outside, the police were of course waiting. "Your papers," they demanded. A few yards away, workers labored on a road where a home once stood and a woman burned.

THE GLORY OF POLAND

An air crash at Katyn, where thousands of Polish officers were murdered by the Soviet Union at the start of World War II, killed Poland's president Lech Kaczyński. But Poland's democracy, two decades after the country's deliverance from the Soviet imperium, is stable. Vladimir Putin, during his interlude as Russian prime minister, attended the anniversary of the Katyn massacre and denounced the way the truth of Katyn had been hidden. His words would be unthinkable today. A Polish-Russian rapprochement was stillborn.

APRIL 12, 2010

NEW YORK—My first thought, hearing of the Polish tragedy, was that history's gyre can be of an unbearable cruelty, decapitating Poland's elite twice in the same cursed place, Katyn.

My second was to call my old friend Adam Michnik in Warsaw.

Michnik, an intellectual imprisoned six times by the former puppet-Soviet communist rulers, once told me:

> Anyone who has suffered that humiliation, at some level, wants revenge. I know all the lies. I saw people being killed. But I also know that revanchism is never-ending. And my obsession has been that we should have a revolution that does not resemble the French or Russian, but, rather, the American, in the sense that it be for something, not against something. A revolution for a constitution, not a paradise. An anti-utopian revolution. Because utopias lead to the guillotine and the Gulag.

Michnik's obsession has yielded fruit. President Lech Kaczyński is dead. Sławomir Skrzypek, the president of the National Bank, is dead. An explosion in the fog of the forest took them and ninety-four others on the way to Katyn. But Poland's democracy has scarcely skipped a beat. The leader of the lower house of Parliament has become acting president, pending an election. The first deputy president of the National Bank has assumed the duties of the late president. Poland, oft dismembered, even wiped from the map, is calm and at peace.

"Katyn is the place of death of the Polish intelligentsia," Michnik, now the soul of Poland's successful *Gazeta Wyborcza* newspaper, said when I reached him by phone. "This is a terrible national tragedy. But in my sadness I am optimistic, because Putin's strong and wise declaration has opened a new phase in Polish-Russian relations, and because we Poles are showing we can be responsible and stable."

Michnik was referring to Prime Minister Vladimir Putin's words after he decided last week to join, for the first time, Polish officials commemorating the anniversary of the murder at Katyn of thousands of Polish officers by the Soviet Union at the start of World War II. Putin, though defending the Russian people, denounced the "cynical lies" that had hidden the truth of Katyn, said "there is no justification for these crimes" of a "totalitarian regime" and declared, "We should meet each other halfway, realizing that it is impossible to live only in the past."

The declaration, dismissed by the paleolithic Russian Communist Party, mattered less than Putin's presence, head bowed in that forest of shame. Watching him beside Poland's prime minister, Donald Tusk, I thought of François Mitterrand and Helmut Kohl hand-in-hand at Verdun in 1984: of such solemn moments of reconciliation has the miracle of a Europe whole and free been built. Now that Europe extends eastward toward the Urals.

I thought even of Willy Brandt on his knees in the Warsaw Ghetto in 1970, a turning point on the road to a German-Polish reconciliation more miraculous in its way even than the dawning of the postwar German-French alliance. And now perhaps comes the most wondrous rapprochement, the Polish-Russian.

It is too early to say where Warsaw-Moscow relations are headed but not too early to say that ninety-six lost souls will be dishonored if Polish and Russian leaders do not make of this tragedy a solemn bond. As Tusk told Putin, "A word of truth can mobilize two peoples looking for the road to reconciliation. Are we capable of transforming a lie into reconciliation? We must believe we can."

Poland should shame every nation that believes peace and reconciliation are impossible, every state that believes the sacrifice of new generations is needed to avenge the grievances of history. The thing about competitive victimhood, a favorite Middle Eastern pastime, is that it condemns the children of today to join the long list of the dead.

For scarcely any nation has suffered since 1939 as Poland, carved up by the Hitler-Stalin Nonaggression Pact, transformed by the Nazis into the epicenter of their program to annihilate European Jewry, land of Auschwitz and Majdanek, killing field for millions of Polish Jews and Christian Poles, brave home to the Warsaw Uprising, Soviet pawn, lonely Solidarity-led leader of post-Yalta Europe's fight for freedom, a place where, as one of its great poets, Wisława Szymborska, wrote, "History counts its skeletons in round numbers"—20,000 of them at Katyn.

It is this Poland that is now at peace with its neighbors and stable. It is this Poland that has joined Germany in the European Union. It is this Poland that has just seen the very symbols of its tumultuous history (including the Gdańsk dockworker Anna Walentynowicz and the former president-in-exile Ryszard Kaczorowski) go down in a Soviet-made jet and responded with dignity, according to the rule of law.

So do not tell me that cruel history cannot be overcome. Do not tell me that Israelis and Palestinians can never make peace. Do not tell me that the people in the streets of Bangkok and Bishkek and Tehran dream in vain of freedom and democracy. Do not tell me that lies can stand forever.

Ask the Poles. They know.

MODERN ODYSSEYS

A new country offers new hope. But the country, the home, left behind does not release its grip on the mind and soul. In every one of the past three generations, my family moved—from Lithuania to South Africa, from South Africa to Britain, from Britain to the United States. About to move back to London from New York for a few years, I reflected here on the effects of repetitive displacement.

JULY 29, 2010

NEW YORK—Now about to circle back to London after thirty years, I've been thinking about my family's odyssey. We lose sight of the long arc of things in the rapid ricocheting of modern life.

This is just one story among many, with its measure of joy and tragedy, and I recount these events not because I find anything exceptional in them but, rather, because I believe the pain of displacement amounts to a modern pathology.

I'll begin in South Africa, where I recently went to the Jewish Cemetery on the outskirts of Johannesburg. It was a perfect winter's morning on the high plateau, still and luminous. On a wall, beneath pines, there is a plaque inscribed to the memory of my mother, who was born there in 1929 and died in London in 1999.

In Africa, it is your forefathers' graves that identify your land. On that principle, it seems right that my mother be remembered in Johannesburg. Her parents are buried in that cemetery, as is her grandfather, Isaac

Michel, who was a co-founder in 1927 of the OK Bazaars, a pioneering department store. I have a photo of Isaac, chin jutting, suit impeccably pressed, in full tycoon pose—a South African Henry Ford.

Fortunes come and go. His went, which is another story. Well before that happened, my mother enjoyed the fruits of Isaac's entrepreneurship—his Johannesburg mansion was known as Château Michel. Then love of a young doctor, my father, lifted her from that comfortable cocoon into the cold and the rationing of postwar London.

She made the best of it. Uprooting is hard. The surface current of her English life appeared smooth at times, but in the depths the tug of African sun and light never abated. She abhorred the damp.

Hers was the land of avocado trees and dry heat. In her latter years she spent more time in South Africa. It was her soul's home, another reason for putting the plaque there rather than in London.

Where is home? For Robert Frost, "Home is the place where, when you have to go there, / They have to take you in." It's "Something you somehow haven't to deserve."

My mother knew South Africa would always take her in.

You can live somewhere for decades and still in your heart it's no more than an encampment, a place for the night, detached from collective destiny. Across the world today, millions are bivouacked, dreaming of return. The inverse is also true: home can sink its roots in little time, as if in a revelation. But that is rarer than lingering exile.

While in South Africa, I finished reading Christopher de Bellaigue's fine book, *Rebel Land,* which is about a troubled provincial town in Turkey and—because of those troubles—also about the pain of "various diasporas" from it. The author, a wanderer, knows something of such alienation. His mother, who moved to England from Canada, never "quite knew where she belonged."

He writes: "After her death by her own hand, when I was thirteen, as I memorialized, even martyred her, I resented her origins. I felt obscurely that they had contributed to her death."

That jolted me. My displaced mother survived, just. But the bipolar state that led her to try to take her life in 1978 never entirely relaxed its grip. Her will to live was intermittent. Cigarette ends stained with lipstick accumulated in ashtrays around her, red-smudged little death piles.

I myself have wandered and found at last a home in New York. It's the place that will take me in.

Standing in the cool air of that Johannesburg cemetery beside the grave of my great-grandfather Isaac, who left Lithuania as a boy for South Africa, I wondered at our restlessness and at the depressive family gene transposed across continents. I wondered at the bonds of the heart, the bones of forefathers, and the beauty of the world.

And now I move on again to Europe to continue this column from there. For me, it is also a return to something deep and unresolved.

CHANGE OR PERISH

As we hurtle forward, what is gained and what is lost?

OCTOBER 4, 2010

LONDON—Before leggings, when there were letters, before texts and tweets, when there was time, before speed cameras, when you could speed, before graffiti management companies, when cities had souls, we managed just the same.

Before homogenization, when there was mystery, before aggregation, when the original had value, before digital, when there was vinyl, before Made in China, when there was Mao, before stress management, when there was romance, we had the impression we were doing all right.

Before apps, when there were attention spans, before "I've got five bars," when bars were for boozing, before ringtone selection, when the phone rang, before high-net-worth individuals, when love was all you needed, before hype, when there was Hendrix, we got by just the same.

Before social media, when we were social, before thumb-typing, when a thumb hitched a ride, before defriending, when a friend was for life, before online conduct, when you conducted yourself, before "content," when we told stories, we did get by all the same.

Before non-state actors, when states commanded, before the Bangalore back office, when jobs stayed put, before globalization, when wars were cold, we did manage okay, it seemed.

Before celebrities, when there were stars, before Google Maps, when compasses were internal, before umbilical online-ism, when we off-lined our lives, before virtual flirtation, when legs touched, we felt we managed all the same.

Before identity theft, when nobody could steal you, before global positioning systems, when we were lost, before twenty-four/seven monitoring and alerts by text and e-mail, when there was idleness, before spin doctors, when there was character, before e-readers, when pages were turned, we did get by just the same.

Before organic, when carrots weren't categorized, before derivatives, when your mortgage was local, before global warming, when we feared nuclear winters, before "save the planet," when we lived in our corners, before the Greens, when we faced the Reds, it seemed we did somehow manage just the same.

Or did we? Before iPads and "Search," in the era of print, before portable devices, when there were diaries, before the Weather Channel, when forecasts were farcical, before movies-on-demand, when movies were demanding, before chains and brands, in the time of the samizdat, before curved shower-curtain rods, when they were straight, before productivity gains, when Britain produced things, and so did Ohio, did we really and honestly get by just the same?

Before January cherries, when fruit had seasons, before global sushi, when you ate what you got, before deep-fried Mars bars, when fish were what fried, before New World wine, when wine was tannic, before fast food and slow food, when food just was, before plate-size cookies, when greed was contained, before fusion, in scattered division, before the obesity onslaught, in our ordinariness, could we—could we—have gotten by all the same?

Before dystopia, when utopia beckoned, before rap, in Zappa's time, before attention deficit disorders, when people turned on, before the new Prohibition, when lunches were liquid, before Lady Gaga, when we dug the Dead, before "join the conversation," when things were disjointed, before Facebook, when there was Camelot, before reality shows, when things were real, yes, I believe we got by just the same.

Before "I'll call you back," when people made dates, before algorithms, when there was aimlessness, before attitude, when there was apathy, before YouTube, when there was you and me, before Gore-Tex, in the damp, before sweat-resistant fabric, when sweat was sexy, before high-tech sneakers, as we walked the walk, before remotes, in the era of distance, I'm sure we managed just the same.

Before "carbon neutral," when carbon copied, before synching, when we lived unprompted, before multiplatform, when pen met paper, before profiling, when there was privacy, before cloud computing, when life was earthy, before a billion bits of distraction, when there were lulls, before "silent cars," when there was silence, before virtual community, in a world with borders, before cut-and-paste, to the tap of the Selectra, before the megabyte, in disorder, before information overload, when streets were for wandering, before "sustainable," in the heretofore, before CCTV, in invisibility, before networks, in the galaxy of strangeness, my impression, unless I'm wrong, is that we got by quite okay.

Before I forget, while there is time, for the years pass and we don't get younger, before the wiring accelerates, while I can pause, let me summon it back, that fragment from somewhere, that phrase that goes: "The bourgeoisie cannot exist without constantly revolutionizing the instruments of production . . . and with them the whole relations of society."

Yes, that was Marx, when he was right, before he went wrong, when he observed, before he imagined, with terrible consequences for the twentieth century.

And if back in that century—back when exactly?—in the time before the tremendous technological leap, in the time of mists and drabness and dreams, if back then, without passwords, we managed just the same, even in black and white, and certainly not in hi-def, or even 3D, how strange to think we had to change everything or we would not be managing at all.

A REPUBLIC CALLED TAHRIR

Egypt's moment of democratic hope was hard to resist, yet it too would evaporate and, in 2014, President Abdel Fattah el-Sisi, a retired military officer, would be installed as the country's authoritarian president. In Tahrir Square in 2011, as young secular Egyptians and members of the Muslim Brotherhood embraced in shared euphoria, anything seemed possible.

FEBRUARY 6, 2011

CAIRO—Beyond politics there is culture. You don't live on the same patch of land for millennia without acquiring a deep form of it. Egyptian culture is also the product of this nation's scars. Its wisdom, issued from suffering, is rooted in humanity.

Tahrir Square—the locus of a great national awakening from almost six decades of dictatorship, overlooked appropriately enough by a museum that houses the Egyptian heritage and by the headquarters of the long-slumbering Arab League—has become a reflection of that culture. Its spontaneous development into a tolerant mini-republic is a riposte to President Hosni Mubarak's warnings of chaos.

Far from chaos, there is serendipitous order. "We've been organizing as we go; if there's a problem, solve it," Omar el-Shamy, a twenty-one-year-old student who hasn't left the square for a week, told me. Through necessity talent is allotted: the doctor here, the engineer there, the security guy in that corner, and the IT expert in this one.

An infirmary is born. Garbage is collected, defense marshaled. Food is ferried, prayer respected. The Brotherhood coexists with a dynamic sisterhood. As my colleague David Kirkpatrick remarked of a flag-waving youth atop a lamppost: "Where is Delacroix when you need him?"

I spoke to an investment banker. He'd been talking to a guy cleaning the square. In Cairo, where dust is the city's very element! Why, the banker asked, this Sisyphean sweeping? The reply: Just decided to do it. "Never in a million years would that have happened before," the banker tells me.

It's startling what pride reborn will do, what a gleaming eye will see that a sullen eye was blind to.

A square, of course, is not a nation of eighty-three million people. Egypt has its lethargy and its pharaoh's tradition. Mubarak, this boss whose only real idea in three decades has been security and whose sole currency has been fear, now says he will go in September. That's enough for some Egyptians—and now, it seems, for Barack Obama's America.

It's a preposterous idea, really, to imagine that this anti-democrat Mubarak, aided by his longtime henchman Omar Suleiman, can now, at eighty-two, reverse his every instinct and deliver, within seven months, a free and fair election; to believe that this man whose security forces have killed or disappeared dozens (including a Google executive Wael Ghonim) can become a disciple of the rule of law; to ask this Honecker to become Havel.

I don't buy it and I don't think the "Yes-we-can" American president should have adopted the tiptoeing "No-we-can't" that leaves Mubarak as a dead man walking.

Just three months ago, in the farcical November parliamentary elections, my colleague Robert Worth watched regime gunmen burst into a Cairo polling station firing shots into the air. Several hundred people waiting to vote were ordered to disperse: Sorry, too dangerous!

"Why would we trust them now to play it right?" Mounir Fakhry Abdel-Nour, the secretary general of the secular Wafd opposition party, asked me. That's a question the West hasn't answered.

The deeper problem is more cultural than political. To accept the Mubarak-or-chaos argument is a form of disrespect to the civility and capacity of Tahrir Square. It is an expression of Western failure before the exploding Arab thirst for dignity and representative government. It reflects the old conditioning which sees in an Egyptian culture that was, after all, deep enough and realistic enough to accept peace with Israel, no more than a disaster waiting to happen if the iron fist is removed.

Western leaders say events in the Arab world should spur Israelis and Palestinians to peace because they show how unstable the region is. Wrong: these events are themselves the spur to the only sustainable peace, one based on Arab self-respect and self-expression.

"There is one united front calling for one single demand: Mubarak needs to go," Mohamed ElBaradei, the Nobel Prize–winning opposition figure, told me. "People need a new beginning, and psychologically that new beginning is when Mubarak leaves—with all dignity." And, I asked, immunity? Yes, ElBaradei said, in principle—Egyptians are not seeking retribution.

The Western fiction, he said, is "that somehow Arabs are not really ready for democracy, that maybe they have horns." It is time to overcome that fiction and look at what Tahrir says about culture emerging, technology-sped, from a deep sleep.

There is a better way forward. It begins with Mubarak's departure. It involves the installation of a three-member presidential council, including a representative of the army, and a caretaker government of respected figures to oversee constitutional and other reforms needed for free elections a year from now. How can credible political parties emerge by September in Mubarak's wilderness?

That investment banker talked to me about how, early in the uprising, people formed a human chain around the Egyptian Museum to protect the nation's culture. It was one in the stream of acts that have dignified Egypt.

"Look," he said. "If we're capable of doing that, surely you can give me the benefit of the doubt."

MY LIBYA, YOUR LIBYA, OUR LIBYA

Inside Qaddafi's bunker in Libya. He had plotted how to survive in elaborate detail but was dead before he reached his elaborate lair.

APRIL 30, 2011

BAYDA, Libya—I descended fifty-five steps into the labyrinth of Muammar el-Qaddafi's mind. The glow of cell phones and a feeble flashlight lit a passage into the darkness. A netherworld unfolded—bedrooms, bathrooms, kitchens, even saunas—linked by tunnels with six-inch-thick metal doors agape at their mouths. No expense had been spared on this lair.

"You see what the rat planned," said Farage Mohamed, a manager in an oil-pipe company, as he led the way to the base of an escape hatch that emerged deep in the gardens of this sprawling former Qaddafi villa in liberated eastern Libya. "It's like Hitler's Berlin bunker."

So Qaddafi always thought this could happen, even forty-two years into his rule. He feared someone might slice away the myths—Arab nationalist, African unifier, all-powerful nonpresident—and leave him, disrobed, a little man in a vast vault with nowhere left to go. In the twisted mind of the despot now derided here as "the man with the big hair," his own demise was the specter that would not go away.

Strange, then, that the United States and Europe never thought this could happen—not to Qaddafi, or Mubarak, or Ben Ali, or any of the other plunderers, some now gone, others slaughtering their own people, here in Libya, or in Syria, or Yemen. Policy was based on the mistaken belief that these leaders would last forever.

They were paranoid about their fates. We were convinced of their permanence.

Of course, it was not just a conviction about their inevitability that drove U.S. policy toward these dictators. It was a cynical decision to place counterterrorism and security at the top of the agenda, and human rights—in this case Arab rights—at the bottom. It was about Big Oil interests. And, to some degree, it was about the perception of what served the security of America's closest regional ally, Israel.

Oh, sure, an Egyptian human-rights activist might get American support, or a worthy nongovernmental organization, but when they were suppressed, a resounding silence emanated from Washington.

Arab reform was an oxymoron, as was Arab democratization. They were dwarfed by the supposed counterterrorist credentials of these despots, their professed loathing for Al Qaeda or Hamas or any brand of radical Islamism, and their readiness to kill or torture and pass on intelligence. Qaddafi never stopped haranguing U.S. diplomats about his hatred for Al Qaeda and about American support for Al Qaeda's first home, Saudi Arabia.

Yet he, like the other dictators, was also busy creating the problem in order to portray himself as the solution to it.

Passports got into the hands of the Libyans who made their way from the eastern town of Darnah to swell the ranks of Qaeda offshoots in Iraq. Repression fed extremism. Plundering fed desperation.

Hosni Mubarak used the Israeli-Palestinian conflict as a manipulative tool in his repressive arsenal. He was the worst "friend" the Palestinians ever had, sowing division as he preached unity. Like Qaddafi and Ben Ali, he called himself a bulwark against extremism even as his strangled society fostered it.

So, having been in Tunisia and Egypt and now Libya during this Arab Spring, I say: Shine a light—into Qaddafi's bunkers and everywhere. Let people out of their dark houses. Allow them to participate in the making of their societies.

Take the disgruntled and give them opportunities. That's a different counterterrorism policy that may actually work over time. The evolving Middle East, where despotic Islamism is well past its ideological zenith, demands it.

Before visiting Qaddafi's villa, where kids play soccer on the former tennis court, I went to the Bayda home of Mustafa Abdel-Jalil, the mild leader of the Transitional National Council in eastern Libya. "The West's mistake was to support Qaddafi, the first terrorist," he said, citing the downed Pan Am 103 and UTA 772 flights, with a combined total of 440 people killed.

He called for weapons, especially in the embattled west of the country, the intensification of NATO airstrikes, and the ousting of a man "who is challenging the whole world."

There's a debt to repay to the Libyan people; a strong strategic interest in a Tunis-Tripoli-Cairo democratic example; and, with civilians dying daily in Misurata, a powerful UN-backed legal case for bombing that forces the issue: Qaddafi's departure. The attack on Tripoli in which one of Qaddafi's sons appears to have been killed falls into that category. Behind the swagger lurks the coward who built that bunker.

It's a few miles from the Qaddafi villa to the breathtaking ruins at Cyrene, founded in the seventh century b.c. and once known as the "Athens of Africa." I wandered, almost alone, among the Greek and Roman temples and gazed out to the Mediterranean. Libya, brutalized, is reclaiming something deep, its history and culture.

Under the pines I found a few youths with a guitar, two of whom had lost brothers in this war. With a haunting intensity they sang: "We're gonna chase him out of here because we have no fears. My Libya, your Libya, it's our Libya. . . ."

THE FORCE OF THE DEED

Reflections on the killing by U.S. commandos of Osama bin Laden.

MAY 9, 2011

NEW YORK—Watching the talk shows, thinking about the tumultuous last American decade, reflecting on the death of Osama bin Laden, I feel grateful for many things but not least this: the invisibility of the heroes.

For once it is the deed itself that speaks. The deed, so often lost in this age of celebrities and reality shows and Donald Trump's monumental ego, stands unadorned. In its daring, its professionalism, and its effectiveness, the deed is there, making words look cheap.

The deed was that of the seventy-nine U.S. commandos who have met with their commander-in-chief, President Obama, and who are known to one another, but are unknown to us. Secrecy is their covenant.

Dispatched from Jalalabad, Afghanistan, at night, into a triangular compound in the Pakistani military town of Abbottabad, they contrived, in thirty-eight minutes, and despite the loss of one helicopter, to kill the charismatic leader of Al Qaeda and gather the largest intelligence cache on this murderous organization ever found. It was an extraordinary achievement that put to rest a gnawing American self-doubt.

I am grateful that the achievement is not being dissected and adorned in a feeding frenzy of interviews with the Navy Seal forces; that the deed stands whole, not broken down into its component human parts—the work of a team, indivisible and invisible.

So many times these past days, finding myself back in New York beneath skies of a 9/11 blue, I have heard an internal voice saying, "Oh, please." It was responding to complaints that this was "murder," that there was no "justice," that Bin Laden's burial in the North Arabian Sea was "disrespectful." As if turning four planes into missiles and killing almost three thousand people were not an act of war.

If there is greater fatuity than second-guessing the split-second decisions of commandos confronted by gunfire, knowing the compound may be wired to explode, and hunting a serial mass murderer unwilling to surrender, then I am unaware of it.

More than a thousand bodies were so pulverized on 9/11 that no trace of them was found, leaving the downtown air filled with their souls. And we are supposed to worry that this killer—of many Muslims, too—may not have gotten appropriate Muslim rites before sliding to his watery grave.

I am grateful for something else: that Bin Laden has been human-ized. He thought he carried the Prophet's message and was able, through a charisma pornographic in its worship of death, to channel an immense Muslim frustration. In taking on America, and staging his own mega-production one September day, he turned himself into myth.

Yet here he is, hunched, gray-bearded, channel-surfing with his remote in search of images of himself. And here he is, with his beard dyed black, betraying the very vanity of the black-haired Arab gerontocracy he professed to loathe. Bin Laden is very human here—in his boredom, his ego, his foibles, and his weariness.

That is an important reminder. Bin Laden was not the devil. He was a human being. What happened to him, this gentle-eyed killer, can happen: his transformation into a demon is banal. That is why all of our collective vigilance is needed.

Speaking of vigilance, I have to say one word on Pakistan's blindness. If the country were not nuclear-armed, America would not give it another dime. But it is and America must. Before then, however, Congress is right to demand an answer to this question: Why, of all the places on earth, would Bin Laden choose to live in the very town that houses the elite military academy that is Pakistan's West Point?

His advisers must have told him that was not a problem. They must have had a reason for saying it was not a problem. Their reason is America's and the world's problem. Until it is resolved it will do harm.

I must end with the deed. It was also Obama's. He's the guy who said: "It's a go." In the duel of Obama with Osama, there was something of fate. The president kept coming back to him. There is strength in humility. Sometimes you have to keep coming back.

Rilke, in a far different context, had this to say of Cézanne's abiding obsession with apples and wine bottles: "And (like Van Gogh) he makes his 'saints' out of such things: and forces them—forces them—to be beautiful, to stand for the whole world and all joy and all glory, and he doesn't know whether he has succeeded in making them do it for him. And sits in the garden like an old dog, the dog of his work that is calling him again and that beats him and lets him starve."

For America, long starved of the satisfactions sustained purpose brings, the decade-old work is done.

THE BEAUTY OF INSTITUTIONS

The European Union was the greatest political creation of the second half of the twentieth century, a peace magnet and a generator of prosperity.

OCTOBER 24, 2011

LONDON—Loving an entity is hard, given the intangibility of the thing, but I love the bland Brussels institutions that gave my generation a peace denied its forebears. It's a measure of the success of the European Union that peace is now taken for granted by its half-billion inhabitants. Nobody pauses at the memorials to the dead scattered across Europe. These days I find myself wanting to shout: "Remember!"

That's a tall order when people glide from France to Germany and on to Poland, across the killing fields of old, without pause for a border, and the Basque separatists of ETA have just laid down their weapons in Europe's last armed confrontation. Yet I detect a dawning sense of the gravity of Europe's crisis—its political rather than financial peril—in the parallels being drawn between dying for Danzig in 1939 and paying for Athens in 2011.

These are dangerous times. Helmut Schmidt, who as a German is hardwired to the nature of cataclysm and at ninety-two knows what sacrifice brought about a borderless Europe, declared as much the other day, lambasting "anyone who considers his own nation more important than common Europe." There are plenty of such people these days, driven by frustration or boredom or pettiness to the refuge of the tribe.

The euro's creation was an irrevocable political decision. The currency, however, had the misfortune to be birthed just as the idealism that fired Europe's integration sagged. The federalist implications of a common currency met the fissuring rancor of complacent Europeans. They had been lulled by the end of the Cold War, irked by European bureaucracy, and wearied by the EU expansion to postcommunist states. The bad history uppermost in the minds of François Mitterrand and Helmut Kohl had faded. If ever a crisis was foretold, it's the euro crisis.

But the danger is broader. European frustration with remote, seemingly unaccountable institutions has spread into a wider anger against the impunity of the powerful and the richness of the ever richer. Growing numbers of people feel that the levers of globalization's compounding advantages are manipulated by the privileged few. From Manhattan to Milan, the Occupy movement is saying, "Enough already!"

No, European leaders retort, we need more—more budget-cutting, more sacrifice to set our houses in order after the debt-driven binge of this century's first decade. Just as the euro had to row against an unraveling tide, so the austerity prescribed to save the currency now has to row against a tide of skepticism.

Jean Arthuis, a French senator, gave this recent assessment of the state of the West: "Globalization led us, through outsourcing, to give up our productive substance and opt for the comfort of consumption, while other states became the producers of what we consumed on credit: on our side sovereign debts, on the other sovereign wealth funds."

Many Europeans and Americans experience that shift day to day in the form of lost jobs, the disappearance of the credit that cushioned relative decline, growing disparities between rich and poor, a feeling of powerlessness, too many bills to pay, a gathering sense of injustice, and growing anger toward hapless politicians outstripped by markets they cannot control.

"Capitalism is crisis," says a big banner of the Occupy movement at St. Paul's in London. Indeed it is. As Joseph Schumpeter noted, "Economic progress, in capitalist society, means turmoil." The trick is to convince people that crisis is creative more than it is destructive—and that's not happening right now.

The European Union was created for such a moment. It was meant to guarantee the impossibility of the worst—not to deliver Europeans to postmodern bliss but to save them from the hell that began almost a century ago, in 1914, and did not really stop until the Continent lay in ruins in 1945.

Now, fortunately, the big bazookas are financial. Roll them out, whatever the subsequent cost in inflation. "Irrevocable" means just that:

The euro cannot be turned back. There is no soft euro exit imaginable, only mayhem and danger.

Recapitalize the banks. Bulk up on the rescue fund. Turn bankers' Greek haircuts into buzz cuts. Do whatever it takes. Germany, ushered from ruin by the European Union, must lead the safeguarding of the euro or risk the loss of the stability that it prizes above anything.

The best institutions are also self-correcting mechanisms. They work like the checks and balances of the U.S. Constitution. They turn crisis into opportunity. In time, the euro's defense will demand a federative leap forward. That will be good for Europeans even though they cannot see it now.

FRANCE'S GLORIOUS MALAISE

Malaise is not a French word for nothing. Nor is it quite what it seems.

JULY 11, 2013

RAPHÈLE-LES-ARLES, France—It seems this is a time of French malaise, moroseness, and melancholy. I have been reading a lot about the existential anguish of France, a directionless nation under a featureless president. There are even fears for the Fifth Republic.

Here is something I read: "France today is racked by doubt and introspection. There is a pervasive sense that not only jobs—but also power, wealth, ideas and national identity itself—are migrating, permanently and at disarming speed, to leave a vapid grandeur on the banks of the Seine." The article continued: "The country's manicured capital, impeccable roads, high-speed trains, glorious food, seductive scents and deep-rooted savoir-vivre provide a compelling image of wealth and tradition. But just as the golden statuary on the bridges of Paris distracts the eye from the homeless sleeping beneath the arches, so the moving beauty of France tends to mask what amounts to a kernel of despair."

Disturbing stuff all right—and the article noted how the anti-immigrant, rightist National Front was well placed to benefit from the ambient angst.

Well, that was an article I wrote sixteen years ago, in 1997, when I was a Paris-based correspondent. So deep was the *morosité* that a two-part series was planned before my colleague, Bill Keller, then the *New York Times* foreign editor, decided even a malaise so massive could be evoked in a single piece. That was a good call.

For if moroseness is a perennial state, rather than a reaction to particular circumstance, does it really matter? The French are living off their malaise much as the British live off the Royal Family. It's a marketing ploy with its degree of affectation—an object of fascination to foreigners rather than a worrying condition.

Tell a Frenchman what a glorious day it is and he will respond that it won't last. Tell him how good the heat feels and he will say it portends a storm. I recently asked in a French hotel how long it would take for a coffee to reach my room. The brusque retort: "The time it takes to make it."

This surliness is more a fierce form of realism than a sign of malaise. It is a bitter wisdom. It is a nod to Hobbes's view that the life of man is, on the whole, "solitary, poor, nasty, brutish, and short."

Nothing surprises, nothing shocks (especially in the realm of marriage and sex), and nothing, really, disappoints. Far from morose, the French attitude has a bracing frankness. No nation has a more emphatic shrug. No nation is the object of so much romanticism yet so unromantic itself. No nation internalizes as completely the notion that in the end we are all dead.

Now, it is true that France lives with high unemployment in a depressed euro zone; that it is more vassal than partner to Germany these days; that it is chronically divided between a world-class private sector and a vast state sector of grumpy functionaries; that its universalist illusions have faded as its power diminishes; and that its welfare state is unaffordable.

Still, moroseness is a foible in a country with superb medicine, good education, immense beauty, the only wine worth drinking, strong families, and the earthy wisdom of *"la France profonde."*

Malaise and ennui are to France what can-do is to America: a badge of honor.

My daughter Jessica married into a French family, many of whom live in that region of strange, blustery beauty, the Camargue. Émile Trazic, my son-in-law's uncle, has a farm here where he raises bulls and horses. Having lived near Nîmes, in an area "where even snakes die of thirst," he was drawn to the watery flatlands of the Camargue.

I went to see Trazic recently for a long lunch. He lives alone, his wife fifty miles away: simpler like that. He has little time for ecologists—"All these people who love nature and know nothing about nature." He says, "I love the land, I hate folklore." His advice: "If you want to ruin somebody's life, give him a bull." Further counsel: "A leant horse is a sold horse." His deepest conviction, *"Dans la vie il ne faut pas s'emmerder"*—roughly (and slightly less crudely) "In life, don't take any crap." His father always told him, "The make of the bicycle does not matter, just pedal." And he has.

Trazic served a vile fermented cheese called "Cachat." To make it, take all your leftover cheese, crush it, add olive oil, cognac, bay leaves, and thyme, and seal it in a jar for about a year. The stench is staggering, the secret of eating it to take very little. "It's stronger than any antibiotic, cures anything," he said.

Even malaise? No, that is incurable, too dear to the French to be given up. Voltaire, on his deathbed, was asked to renounce Satan and embrace God. He declined, saying this was "no time to be making new enemies."

Better to be miserable than a hypocrite, nauseated than naïve—and far better to be morose than a fool.

CRY FOR ME, ARGENTINA

Argentina is a mystery, a unique case of a vast, wealthy country that somehow, for decades, squandered its bounty.

FEBRUARY 27, 2014

USHUAIA, Argentina—A bon mot doing the rounds in post-commodities-boom South America is that Brazil is in the process of becoming Argentina, and Argentina is in the process of becoming Venezuela, and Venezuela is in the process of becoming Zimbabwe. That is a little harsh on Brazil and Venezuela.

Argentina, however, is a perverse case of its own. It is a nation still drugged by that quixotic political concoction called Peronism; engaged in all-out war on reliable economic data; tinkering with its multilevel exchange rate; shut out from global capital markets; trampling on property rights when it wishes; obsessed with a lost little war in the Falklands (Malvinas) more than three decades ago; and persuaded that the cause of all this failure lies with speculative powers seeking to force a proud nation—in the words of its leader—"to eat soup again, but this time with a fork."

A century ago, Argentina was richer than Sweden, France, Austria, and Italy. It was far richer than Japan. It held poor Brazil in contempt. Vast and empty, with the world's richest topsoil in the Pampas, it seemed to the European immigrants who flooded here to have all the potential of the United States (per capita income is now a third or less of the United States level). They did not know that a colonel called Juan Domingo Perón and his wife, Eva ("Evita"), would shape an ethos of singular delusional power.

"Argentina is a unique case of a country that has completed the transition to underdevelopment," said Javier Corrales, a political scientist at Amherst College.

In psychological terms—and Buenos Aires is packed with folks on couches pouring out their anguish to psychotherapists—Argentina is the child among nations that never grew up. Responsibility was not its thing. Why should it be? There was so much to be plundered, such riches in grain and livestock, that solid institutions and the rule of law—let alone a functioning tax system—seemed a waste of time.

Immigrants camped here with foreign passports rather than go through the nation-forming absorption that characterize Brazil or the United States. Argentina was far away at the bottom of the world, a beckoning, fertile land mass distant enough from power centers to live its own peripheral fantasies or drown its sorrow in what is probably the world's saddest (and most haunting) dance.

Then, to give expression to its uniqueness, Argentina invented its own political philosophy: a strange mishmash of nationalism, romanticism, fascism, socialism, backwardness, progressiveness, militarism, eroticism, fantasy, mournfulness, irresponsibility, and repression. The name it gave all this was Peronism. It has proved impossible to shake.

Perón, who discovered the political uplift a military officer could derive from forging links with the have-nots of Latin America and distributing cash (a lesson absorbed by Hugo Chávez), was deposed in the first of four postwar coups. The Argentina I covered in the 1980s was just emerging from the trauma of military rule. If I have a single emblematic image of the continent, then it is of the uncontrollable sobbing of Argentine women clutching the photographs of beloved children who had been taken from them by the military junta for "brief questioning" only to vanish.

Since 1983, Argentina has ceased its military-civilian whiplash, tried some of the perpetrators of human-rights crimes, and been governed democratically. But for most of that time it has been run by Peronists, most recently Néstor Kirchner and his widow, Cristina Fernández de Kirchner (shades of Perón's widow, Isabel), who have rediscovered redistribution after a Peronist flurry in the 1990s with neoliberalism. Economic whiplash is alive and well. So are reckless spending in good times and lawless measures in bad. So, too, are mawkish evocations of Perón and Evita and Isabel: on earth as it is in the heavens.

Cry for me, my name is Argentina and I am too rich for my own good.

Twenty-five years ago, I left a country of hyperinflation (5,000 percent in 1989), capital flight, currency instability, heavy-handed state interventionism, dwindling reserves, uncompetitive industry, heavy reliance on commodity exports, reawakening Peronist fantasies, and bottom-of-the-world complexes. Today inflation is high rather than hyper. Otherwise, not a whole lot has changed.

As I came ashore at Ushuaia, on Argentina's southern tip, what I saw was a sign saying that the "Malvinas" islands had been under illegal occupation by the United Kingdom since 1833. The second was a signpost saying Ireland was 13,199 kilometers away (no mention of Britain). The third was a packet of cookies "made in Ushuaia, the end of the world."

Hope is hard to banish from the human heart, but it has to be said that Argentina does its best to do so.

THE UNLIKELY ROAD TO WAR

I imagine the way the acts of a Ukrainian patriot, enraged by Russia's annexation of Crimea and the slaying of a fellow student in Kyiv, lead to World War III, starting with the assassination of the Russian defense minister in Sevastopol. Two NATO F-16s are shot down during a reconnaissance flight close to the Lithuanian-Russian border. Russia declares war on Estonia, Latvia, and Lithuania.

MARCH 17, 2014

A nineteen-year-old Ukrainian nationalist from a remote farming village, raised on stories of his family's suffering during Stalin's great engineered famine, embittered by Moscow's long imperialist dominion, enraged by the slaying of a fellow student in Kyiv during the uprising of 2014, convinced any price is worth paying to stop the Russian annexation of Crimea, takes the long road to Sevastopol.

He is a simple angular man, a dreamer, who as a young boy had engraved his initials on a retaining wall of rocks at the back of his family's plot. When asked why, he replied, "Because one day people will know my name."

On the farm, he works hard by day and reads voraciously by night. He is consumed with the long suffering of the Ukrainian peasant laboring in near-feudal conditions.

Neighboring countries have gained their independence and dignity after Soviet occupation. Why, he asks, should Ukraine not do the same?

To this teenager, the issue is simple. The imperial ruler in the Kremlin knows nothing of Ukraine. The twenty-first-century world is changing, but this high officer of the imperium is determined to wind back the clock to the twentieth. A good student, the man travels to Kyiv, where an older brother works. He falls into the "Young Ukraine" movement, a radical student circle in which feelings run high over the shotgun referendum that saw the people of Crimea vote with Orwellian unanimity for union with Russia. At night, he fingers the hand-engraved Browning pistol that was once his father's.

A plot is hatched. The Russian defense minister is to visit Sevastopol with his wife to celebrate the wise choice of the Crimean people and speak of Russia's civilizing influence over this beautiful but backward region. Fanfare follows. "Wide Is My Motherland" booms from loudspeakers as the minister's procession of black limousines snakes along the waterfront. The assassin is waiting at a point where the minister and his wife are to greet local dignitaries.

Two shots ring out. One cuts through the minister's jugular vein. The other penetrates his wife's abdomen. The minister's last words are spoken to her: "Don't die, don't die, live for our children."

Events now move quickly. Russia annexes Crimea. It declares war on Ukraine, takes Donetsk in short order, and annexes the eastern half of the country. The United States warns Russia not to advance on Kyiv.

It reminds the Kremlin of America's binding alliance with Baltic states that are NATO members. European nations mobilize.

Desperate diplomacy unravels. A Ukrainian counterattack flounders but inflicts heavy casualties, prompting a Russian advance on the capital. Two NATO F-16s are shot down during a reconnaissance flight close to the Lithuanian-Russian border. Russia declares war on Estonia, Latvia, and Lithuania. Invoking Article 5 of the North Atlantic Treaty—an attack against one member shall be considered an attack against all—the United States and its European allies come to their defense. China, in what it calls a pre-emptive strike, invades Taiwan, "a potential Crimea." Japan and India declare war on China. World War III has begun.

It could not happen. Of course, it could not happen. The institutions and alliances of a connected world ensure that the worst cannot happen again. The price would be too high, no less than nuclear annihilation. Civilization is strong, humanity wise; safeguards are secure.

Anyone who believes that should read Tim Butcher's riveting *The Trigger*, a soon-to-be-published account of the long road traveled from a remote Bosnian farm to Sarajevo by Gavrilo Princip, the nineteen-year-old Bosnian Serb nationalist whose assassination of Archduke Franz Ferdinand in Sarajevo on June 28, 1914, ignited what Churchill called "the hardest, the cruelest and the least-rewarded" of all wars.

Yes, the Great War, the end of empires and the old order, was triggered by a teenager. And, as Butcher writes, "It was out of this turbulent collapse that Bolshevism, socialism, fascism and other radical political currents took root." They would lead to World War II.

Princip acted with a small group of accomplices bent on securing the freedom of the south Slavs from the Austro-Hungarian Empire. Luck helped him, diplomatic ineptitude force-multiplied his deed, and by the age of twenty-three this farm boy whose name would be remembered was dead of tuberculosis in a Habsburg military prison.

Then, too, exactly a century ago, it could not happen. The world had finessed other moments of tension. Yet very quickly Austria-Hungary had declared war on Serbia, prompting Russia to mobilize in defense of Belgrade, prompting the Kaiser's Germany to attack France pre-emptively and Britain to declare war on Germany. The war haunts us still.

The unthinkable is thinkable. Indeed, it must be thought. Otherwise, it may occur—soldiers reduced, in Butcher's words, to "fodder locked in the same murderous morass, sharing the same attrition of bullet and barrage, disease and deprivation, torment and terror."

IN SEARCH OF HOME

Where would you go if you had only a few weeks to live? Where lies the landscape of childhood, the scents that soothe, the feel of consolation?

APRIL 3, 2014

LONDON—In a fascinating recent essay in the *London Review of Books*, called "On Not Going Home," James Wood relates how he "asked Christopher Hitchens, long before he was terminally ill, where he would go if he had only a few weeks to live. Would he stay in America? 'No, I'd go to Dartmoor, without a doubt,' he told me. It was the landscape of his childhood."

It was the landscape, in other words, of unfiltered experience, of things felt rather than thought through, of the world in its beauty absorbed before it is understood, of patterns and sounds that lodge themselves in some indelible place in the psyche and call out across the years.

That question is worth repeating: If I had only a few weeks to live, where would I go? It is a good way of getting rid of the clutter that distracts or blinds. I will get to that in a moment.

In the essay, Wood, who grew up in England but has lived in the United States for eighteen years, explores a certain form of contemporary homelessness—lives lived without the finality of exile, but also without the familiarity of home.

He speaks of existences "marked by a certain provisionality, a structure of departure and return that may not end."

This is a widespread modern condition; perhaps it is *the* modern condition. Out of it, often, comes anxiety. Wood does not focus on the psychological effects of what he calls "a certain outsider-dom," but if you dig into people who are depressed you often find that their distress at some level is linked to a sense of not fitting in, an anxiety about belonging: displacement anguish.

Wood describes looking at the familiar life of his Boston street, "the heavy maple trees, the unkempt willow down at the end, an old white Cadillac with the bumper sticker 'Ted Kennedy has killed more people than my gun,' and I feel . . . nothing: some recognition, but no comprehension, no real connection, no past, despite all the years I have lived there—just a tugging distance from it all. A panic suddenly overtakes me, and I wonder: How did I get here?"

Having spent my infancy in South Africa, grown up and been educated in England, and then, after a peripatetic life as a foreign correspondent, found my home in New York, I understand that how-did-I-get-here panic. But Wood and I differ. He has no desire to become an American citizen.

He quotes an immigration officer telling him, "'A Green Card is usually considered a path to citizenship,'" and continues: "He was generously saying, 'Would you like to be an American citizen?' along with the less generous: 'Why don't you want to be an American citizen?' Can we imagine either sentiment being expressed at Heathrow airport?"

No, we can't. And it's that essential openness of America, as well as the (linked) greater ease of living as a Jew in the United States compared with life in the land of Lewis Namier's "trembling Israelites," that made me become an American citizen and elect New York as my home. It's the place that takes me in.

But it is not the place of my deepest connections. So—what if I had a few weeks to live? I would go to Cape Town, to my grandfather's house, Duxbury, looking out over the railway line near Kalk Bay Station to the ocean and the Cape of Good Hope. During my childhood, there was the scent of salt and pine and, in certain winds, a pungent waft from the fish-processing plant in Fish Hoek. I would dangle a little net in rock pools and find myself hypnotized by the silky water and quivering life in it. The heat, not the dry high-veld heat of Johannesburg but something denser, pounded by the time we came back from the beach at lunchtime. It reverberated off the stone, angled into every recess. The lunch table was set and soon enough fried fish, usually firm-fleshed kingklip, would be served, so fresh it seemed to burst from its batter. At night the lights of Simon's Town glittered, a lovely necklace strung along a promontory.

This was a happiness whose other name was "home."

Wood writes: "Freud has a wonderful word, 'afterwardness,' which I need to borrow, even at the cost of kidnapping it from its very different context. To think about home and the departure from home, about not going home and no longer feeling able to go home, is to be filled with a remarkable sense of 'afterwardness': It is too late to do anything about it now, and too late to know what should have been done. And that may be all right."

Yes, if we are not quite home, acceptance, which may be bountiful, is what is left to us.

FROM DEATH INTO LIFE

On the death, at the age of ninety-five, of my beloved uncle Bert, I mused on the mystery of the small bird that settled on his shoulder when he was in Florence in October 1944. It remained there for five days. Florentines thought Bert Cohen of the Sixth South African Armored Division, Nineteenth Field Ambulance, was a saint. He was not that, but he was an immense presence in my life.

APRIL 7, 2014

On July 21, 1944, my uncle Bert Cohen of the Sixth South African Armored Division, Nineteenth Field Ambulance, reached Italy's Monte Cassino, abandoned by German forces a few weeks earlier after repeated Allied assaults. Appalled by the destruction, he thought photographs of it should be circulated in every schoolroom.

This was the memento mori proposed by my uncle, then aged twenty-five and recently arrived in a bloody continent called Europe.

Those pictures were not circulated; and the miracle and fragility of European peace is too often forgotten.

In April of that year, Captain Cohen, born in the last year of World War I and now thrust into World War II, had crossed from Egypt to Italy, sailing beneath searchlights that "deftly flick their fingers across the face of the sky."

War is a gale. It scoops up routine lives and (when it does not end them) scatters them here and there, never again to be reconstituted in the same form. Whether my uncle would in any event have emigrated from South Africa is impossible to know.

He left first for Chicago, where he gained a master's degree in dental science from Northwestern University in 1948, and ultimately went to London, where, in 1960, he became the first Nuffield Research Professor of Dental Science at the Royal College of Surgeons of England. An oral pathologist of great distinction, he was above all a scientist of wide-ranging interests, a man passionate about literature and art, a stranger to the narrow specialization in vogue today. In 1982, he was appointed CBE (Commander of the Order of the British Empire), an honor he accepted but never talked about. He wore his many accomplishments lightly.

I relate all this because my uncle died last month at the age of ninety-five and I have since found my life consumed by his. Each of us is allotted one life. Bert needed two. As the fragments from his diary suggest, he wanted to be a writer.

Early short stories showed promise. He talked his way, as a teenager, into becoming South African correspondent of the boxing magazine *The Ring*, and filed many a fine dispatch. His diary places him, more than once, on the brink of giving up dentistry for a life of writing. It was not to be. Reading of the road not taken, I understood better Bert's passionate interest in my work. Childless, he was living through me what he had wanted to do.

Now he lives in me. The living are the custodians of the souls of the dead, those stealthy migrants. Love bequeaths this responsibility.

I might never have known him. On April 24, 1945, he was ordered into a bend in the Penaro River where a Nazi column was trapped. The fighting was brutal. An artillery battery pulverized the enclave.

Wounded horses, nostrils flared in gasping horror, bayed—a terrible sound. In the carnage, ammunition exploded and tires burst. One dead German in particular caught Bert's eye: a blond, square-jawed young man, hair flecked with blood and smoke, legs twisted grotesquely, abdomen ripped open, coils of gut spilling through a ragged gash into the dust, sightless blue eyes gazing at infinity.

Beside the corpse lay letters from the soldier's mother in Hamburg. She talked about *der Angriff*, the Allied bombardment of the city. Uncertain what to do, Bert returned the letters to the dead man's pocket. That single German corpse haunted my uncle. Bert dwelt on him as if this death was his responsibility, or as if he, a Jew from South Africa, might somehow have brought this handsome young man, Hitler's model Aryan, back to the life denied him. Bert thought that he should have kept the letters, perhaps to return them to a bereaved mother in Hamburg.

This tantalizing image stayed with me. So did another. On October 14, 1944, near Florence, a small bird settled on Bert's shoulder. It remained there for five days. This extraordinary encounter, caught in a photograph on the banks of the Arno, caused Florentines to prostrate themselves, name Bert "Captain Uccellino" (or "Little Bird") and proclaim him a saint. He was far from that, but he had about him something magical.

Of that the days since his death have left no doubt. He is now that bird on my shoulder, reminding me to take care with my spelling and be aware that love alone redeems human affairs.

CHINA'S MONROE DOCTRINE

History is not rich in peaceful transitions of power from one hegemon to another. Will China want to put an end to the United States as
an Asian power, enforcing its own Monroe Doctrine? The theory put
forward by John Mearsheimer of the University of Chicago is plausible. But the United States is needed in Asia to offset China's rise.

MAY 8, 2014

HO CHI MINH CITY, Vietnam—In the new edition of his classic *The
Tragedy of Great Power Politics,* John Mearsheimer of the University
of Chicago makes a powerful case for the inevitability of war in Asia as
China rises:

> My argument in a nutshell is that if China continues to grow economi-
> cally, it will attempt to dominate Asia the way the United States dominates
> the Western Hemisphere. The United States, however, will go to enor-
> mous lengths to prevent China from achieving regional hegemony. Most
> of Beijing's neighbors, including India, Japan, Singapore, South Korea,
> Russia and Vietnam, will join with the United States to contain Chinese
> power. The result will be an intense security competition with consider-
> able potential for war.

This is the core strategic question of the twenty-first century. History is not rich in peaceful transitions of power from one hegemon to
another. China needs resources. It will seek them near and far—and find
America in its path. As with the Soviet Union, but without the ideological conflict, the issue will be whether the evident potential for a conflagration can be finessed through alliances or forestalled through the
specter of mutually assured destruction.

The seeds of conflict are evident. On his recent visit to Asia, President Obama made clear how the tensions between Japan and China

over the Senkaku Islands (Diaoyu Islands to Beijing) could draw in the United States. His declaration that the Japan-administered rocks in the East China Sea "fall within the scope of Article 5 of the U.S.-Japan Treaty of Mutual Cooperation and Security" incensed China, which claims the islands.

Mind your own business and get over the Cold War, was the essence of the Chinese message to Washington.

Vietnam and China also have maritime conflicts that have flared in recent days as a result of a Chinese decision to place an oil rig in the South China Sea. Chinese ships escorting the rig rammed and fired water cannons at Vietnamese vessels attempting to stop the move in potentially oil-and-gas-rich waters claimed by Hanoi.

The U.S. response in support of Vietnam, its erstwhile enemy turned pivot-to-Asia partner, was firm: "China's decision to introduce an oil rig accompanied by numerous government vessels for the first time in waters disputed with Vietnam is provocative and raises tensions," Jen Psaki, a State Department spokeswoman, said in a statement. "This unilateral action appears to be part of a broader pattern of Chinese behavior to advance its claims over disputed territory in a manner that undermines peace and stability in the region."

China is asserting sovereignty in the South China Sea, angering the Philippines and Vietnam. Its actions appear to vindicate Mearsheimer, who writes that a more powerful China can "be expected to try to push the United States out of the Asia-Pacific region, much as the United States pushed the European great powers out of the Western Hemisphere in the nineteenth century. We should expect China to devise its own version of the Monroe Doctrine"—the nineteenth-century keep-out-of-this-hemisphere message of the United States to Europe.

The push here in Vietnam to hedge against China by strengthening ties with the United States is evident. The "comprehensive partnership" announced last year indicates how far the wounds of war have healed. Cooperation extends across trade, investment, education (Vietnam is the eighth-largest provider of foreign students to the United States), and defense areas. The proposed trade agreement known as the Trans-Pacific Partnership, in which Vietnam would be a participant (but not China), is luring manufacturing investment from China. So are lower wages. A joint U.S. exercise with the Vietnamese Navy was recently conducted.

Vietnam looks at virtually everything through the lens of relations with China. The fraternity of one-party communist systems is seen as insufficient insurance against vassal-state status. France and the United States were latecomers to this corner of Southeast Asia. The Vietnamese creation story is one of a thousand-year struggle to free itself from Chinese rule. So Vietnam looks to the United States as its offshore balancer.

Other smaller Asian nations will do the same as China rises. These American alliances, if firm, could be powerful deterrents to war. Economic interdependence, which did not exist during the Cold War standoff, could also prevent conflict. Competitive cooperation is a possible scenario. The Chinese seem bent on peaceful development, at least for now; harmony is at the core of the national vocabulary.

The Vietnamese pivot to the United States demonstrates how real its fears of China are. The little naval battle being fought around a Chinese rig suggests they have cause. The Mearsheimer prediction is not inevitable, as he acknowledges, but it is plausible.

American retrenchment would make it more so. Rising hegemons seize on weakness when they see it. Deterrence is far preferable to war.

GETTYSBURG ON THE MAIDAN

I visited the Maidan, or Independence Square, where Ukrainians have paid in blood to resist Russian aggression. A landscape of makeshift barricades and shrines unfolded before me. Eight years before Russia's full-scale war in Ukraine, it was clear that the country had become the nexus of a renewed fight between freedom and imprisoning imperium.

MAY 19, 2014

KYIV, Ukraine—Ukrainians are reluctant to dismantle the symbols of their revolution on streets that have become the hallowed ground of democracy and a nation-constituting struggle. On Independence Square, known as the Maidan, and in the surrounding area, makeshift barricades of tires and timber, impromptu shrines to the more than one hundred dead, and Ukrainian flags flanked by that of the European Union constitute a stage set of defiance against Russian aggression.

This unusual urban landscape, at once stirring and vulnerable, surrounds the office of Arseniy P. Yatsenyuk, the acting prime minister and a man now forged, like many young Ukrainians, in the bloodshed of defiance.

"Putin is caught in the cell of his own propaganda," Yatsenyuk said of the Russian president. "We can offer him an off-ramp. It is called 'Get out of Crimea.' I spoke to his envoy and I told him that even the Roman emperors disappeared, and one day we will have Crimea back."

His words may appear quixotic, given Russian might and Ukrainian weakness, but Yatsenyuk's determination reflects a clear choice that has emerged from the success of the Maidan uprising and the ousting of the former president and corrupt Putin toady, Viktor F. Yanukovych: in favor of European pluralism and against a Eurasian imperium.

Ukraine is today the pivot of a struggle between individual freedom and imprisoning empire. There is no halfway house in this confrontation and no escaping the imperative of moral clarity in picking sides. Vladimir V. Putin's unleashed nationalism and Crimean land grab represent a return to Europe's darkest days. Americans and Europeans need to stand together to resist this threat.

"I don't know what's in Putin's head or what his final destination is," Yatsenyuk said. "Luhansk? Lviv? Lisbon? Ask our Polish friends. They are afraid of Russian troops. A permanent member of the United Nations Security Council has decided to grab the land of an independent country."

The prime minister was speaking to a small group of American, Canadian, and European visitors, including the Polish author and former dissident Adam Michnik; the former French foreign minister Bernard Kouchner; the literary editor of *The New Republic*, Leon Wieseltier; and the Yale historian Timothy Snyder.

Snyder has recently written in *The New Republic:* "We easily forget how fascism works: as a bright and shining alternative to the mundane duties of everyday life, as a celebration of the obviously and totally irrational against good sense and experience."

The fact that Putin has chosen the label "fascists" for the likes of Yatsenyuk in Kyiv (even as the Kremlin maintains excellent relations with extreme-right parties in Western Europe) only underscores the Orwellian mind games of his resurgent nationalism. It is typical of fascism to twist history into a narrative of national humiliation justifying the apotheosis of an avenging leader bent on righting these supposed wrongs—be they in the Sudetenland or Ukraine.

During an hour-long conversation, Yatsenyuk said Russia would do its best to "disrupt and undermine" Ukraine's May 25 election, suggesting there were now up to twenty thousand armed people in the eastern part of the country orchestrated by several hundred well-trained Russian agents. Nevertheless, he said, a credible election across most of Ukrainian territory is possible. "We need a legitimate president," he said.

He rejected the federalization of Ukraine—"Buy every governor; that is the Russian planning behind so-called federalization"—but spoke strongly in favor of the devolution of power and the rights of Russian speakers. "My wife speaks Russian and she does not need any protection from President Putin," he declared.

Putin must recognize that Ukraine is a "European state" that will go ahead with its contested association agreement with the European Union and recognize the results of the election, Yatsenyuk said. He said Ukraine is ready to pay its debts to Gazprom, the Russian energy company, on condition that Russia adopts "a market-based, not a politically based approach"—cutting off trade when it suits Putin to punish Kyiv.

Asked about American policy toward Ukraine, the prime minister sighed deeply. He said he recognizes that every nation has its limits and constraints. But he continued: "The United States is the leader of the free world. You have to lead. If someone crosses a red line, he is to be prosecuted for this in all ways." As for American military support, he said, "I never ask in case I don't get it," adding that he would of course be "happy to have Patriot missiles on Ukrainian soil."

There is no question that Putin has exploited a perception of American weakness that began in Syria with President Obama's retreat there from his "red line" against the use of chemical weapons—a retreat that at once underwrote President Bashar al-Assad, strengthened Putin, and undermined American credibility. Ukrainians have now died fighting for American and European values of liberty and pluralism. After its Gettysburg on the Maidan, a free and independent Ukraine is a critical U.S. interest and test.

POOR ANGRY, MAGNETIC EUROPE

I am struck by the dissonance between irritation and anger within the European Union and the union's magnetic pull beyond its borders. On the Maidan, where Ukrainians died in numbers to escape the rule of an incompetent kleptomaniac backed by Putin, the European Union flag was draped down the façade of the Foreign Ministry.

MAY 22, 2014

BERLIN—Europe at the centenary of the war that devoured it is voting in elections for the European Parliament that will no doubt reflect the anger, disillusionment, and boredom of people inclined to cast their ballots for an array of protest parties, many from the xenophobic right, some from the pander-to-Putin left.

Political sentiment across the Continent has converged at a grumpy and small-minded nadir. There is anger about high unemployment. There is pessimism over the future.

There is irritation at immigration. There is alienation from the European Union. What, the chorus goes, has Brussels ever done for me? The answer, of course, is that it has brought peace, removed borders, and spread once-unimaginable prosperity. But this achievement is no longer enough, or no longer deemed relevant.

In some ways Europe's mood resembles America's. Focus has narrowed and solidarity atrophied. Europe, like America, does not want to die for anyone else. It has turned inward, wanting its own problems solved, and damn the Libyans and Syrians and Ukrainians and whoever else may be making demands through their plight.

Anyone who believes the spread of freedom, democracy, and the rule of law matters is a "warmonger." The sharing economy is in vogue because it affords a better deal on a car ride or a room. Sharing politics is not, because it may involve sacrifice for faraway people with strange names.

So the National Front in France, and the U.K. Independence Party in Britain, and Jobbik in Hungary, and Die Linke (the Left) in Germany—parties from right and left that have expressed varying degrees of admiration for President Vladimir Putin and his homophobic irredentism (Russian-speaking gays need not apply for admission to the imperium)—are all likely to benefit from a diffuse anger, in which anti-Americanism mingles with general spleen.

Never have the idea and the ideal of the twenty-eight-member European Union been so weakened, at least within its borders, to the point where several fringe parties take Putin's Eurasian Union, with its promise of good times in Belarus, seriously. Just outside the union, it is a different story. Europe is magnetic still. The dissonance between the union as perceived by many of its more than five hundred million citizens, and the union as it is idealized and ached for by millions on its fringes or in faraway lands, is complete.

The European Parliament election coincides with a critical election Sunday in Ukraine, where Putin has created havoc by annexing Crimea, dispatching thugs to stir unrest in the eastern part of the country, and inventing a "fascist" threat in Kyiv to conceal his own growing affinities with such politics (his beloved, much-lamented Soviet Union of course allied with Nazi Germany in 1939 before Hitler tore up the pact in 1941; attraction to fascism is nothing new in Moscow).

On Kyiv's Independence Square, known as the Maidan, where Ukrainians died in numbers to escape the rule of an incompetent kleptomaniac backed by Putin, the European Union flag flies in several places. It is equally visible on surrounding streets. It is draped down the façade of the Ukrainian Foreign Ministry. It stands for something important in Kyiv, something that seems almost unimaginable to Europeans in the confusion of their bile: the glowing possibility of freedom and dignity and pluralism, the possibility of a normal life.

"Europe is a promise of liberty," said Nataliya Popovych, an activist in the Maidan movement. "As for Putin's Eurasian Union, we have been in that cage before. Why would we go back? Through Maidan, Ukrainians killed *Homo Sovieticus* in themselves. In Russia and some parts of the east of Ukraine, *Homo Sovieticus* is still alive."

It is not dead in Western Europe, either. As my colleague Andrew

Higgins noted, Aymeric Chauprade, the National Front's top European Parliament candidate for the Paris region, trooped off to Moscow last year to declare, "Russia has become the hope of the world against new totalitarianism." We live in a time when sentences need to be turned on their heads. The "new totalitarianism" is of course emanating from Moscow.

But Europe is suddenly full of what Germans now call the *Putinversteher*—literally, someone who understands Putin; more loosely, a Putin apologist. Europeans of different stripes see him standing up to America, incarnating "family values," countering a loathed European Union, and just being tough. Germans in surprising numbers are discovering their inner sympathy for Russia, a complex emotion in which anti-Americanism, romanticism, guilt, and gratitude for Moscow's acceptance of unification all play a part.

The old temptation in Germany to look eastward is not entirely overcome after all.

Europeans would do well to lift their gaze from the small world of their current anger toward those blue-and-gold flags fluttering on the Maidan, the better to recall what freedom means and with what sacrifice it has been attained.

ZIONISM AND ITS DISCONTENTS

It has always been interesting to me how many Americans focus on my *criticism* of Israel whereas many Europeans focus on the fact I am a *Zionist,* something close to a dirty word in Europe. It can never be a self-interested act to criticize Israel in the United States, or to declare oneself a Zionist in Europe.

JULY 29, 2014

My great-grandfather's brother, Michael Adler, was a distinguished rabbi who in 1916 compiled the *Prayer Book for Jewish Sailors and Soldiers* at the front during World War I. As "chaplain," he toured battlefields administering last rites. At the end of the war, he asked if British Jews had done their duty.

"Did those British citizens of the House of Israel to whom equality of rights and equality of opportunity were granted by the State some sixty years ago, did these men and women do their duty in the ordeal of battle?" he wrote. "Our answer is a clear and unmistakable YES! English Jews have every reason to be satisfied with the degree of their participation both at home and on the battlefronts in the struggle for victory. Let the memory of our sacred dead—who number over 2,300—testify to this."

The question for European Jewry was always the same: belonging. Be they French or German, they worried, even in their emancipation, that the Christian societies that had half-accepted them would turn on them. Theodor Herzl, witnessing French anti-Semitism during the Dreyfus case, wrote *The Jewish State* in 1896 out of the conviction that full acceptance for the Jews would never come.

Herzl was prescient. Zionism was born of a reluctant conclusion: that Jews needed a homeland because no other place would ever be home. Scrawny scholars would become vigorous tillers of the soil in the Holy Land. Jews would never again go meekly to the slaughter.

The ravages of European nonacceptance endure. I see within my own family how the disappearance of a Jewish woman grabbed by Nazis on the streets of Kraków in 1941 can devour her descendants. I understand the rage of an Israeli, Naomi Ragen, whose words were forwarded by a cousin: "And I think of the rest of Europe, who rounded up our grandparents and great-grandparents, and relatives—men, women and children—and sent them off to be gassed, no questions asked. And I think: They are now the moral arbiters of the free world? They are telling the descendants of the people they murdered how to behave when other anti-Semites want to kill them?"

Those anti-Semites would be Hamas, raining terror on Israel, whose annihilation they seek. No state, goes the Israeli case, would not respond with force to such provocation. If there are more than a thousand Palestinian deaths (including two hundred children), and more than fifty Israeli deaths, Israel argues, it is the fault of Hamas, for whom Palestinian victims are the most powerful anti-Israeli argument in the court of world opinion.

The Israeli case for the bombardment of Gaza could be foolproof. If Benjamin Netanyahu had made a good-faith effort to find common cause with Palestinian moderates for peace and been rebuffed, it would be. He has not. Hamas is vile. I would happily see it destroyed. But Hamas is also the product of a situation that Israel has reinforced rather than sought to resolve.

This corrosive Israeli exercise in the control of another people, breeding the contempt of the powerful for the oppressed, is a betrayal of the Zionism in which I still believe.

TRUTHS OF A FRENCH VILLAGE

When I decided to sell my village house, the realtor pleaded with me not to do it. The house, she said, is the repository of irreplace-able good things and family memories. She felt this in her bones.

SEPTEMBER 22, 2014

A few weeks ago I was in France, where I've owned a village house for almost twenty years that I am now planning to sell. A real-estate agent had taken a look at the property and we had made an appointment to discuss how to proceed. She swept into the kitchen, a bundle of energy and conviction, with an impassioned appeal:

"Monsieur Cohen, whatever you do, you must on no account sell this house!"

I gazed at her, a little incredulous.

"You cannot sell it. This is a family home. You know it the moment you step in. You sense it in the walls. You breathe it in every room. You feel it in your bones. This is a house you must keep for your children. I will help you sell it if you insist, but my advice is not to sell. You would be making a mistake."

This was, shall we say, a cultural moment, when a door opens and you gaze, if not into the soul of a country, at least into territory that is distinct and deep and almost certainly has greater meaning than the headlines and statistics that are supposed to capture the state of a nation, in this case one called France, whose malaise has become an object of fascination. I tried to imagine an American or British real-estate agent, presented with a potentially lucrative opportunity, deciding to begin the pitch with a heartfelt call not to sell the property because it was the repository of something important or irreplaceable. I came up blank.

There were no circumstances in which self-interest, or at least professional obligation, would not prevail. Price would be pre-eminent, along with market conditions and terms. Yet in this French village, across a wooden kitchen table set on a stone floor, the setting of economic interest below emotional intuition seemed a natural outcrop of soil and place.

I thought of this exchange the other day as Prime Minister Manuel Valls, a modernizing socialist, faced a confidence vote in the National Assembly over yet another plan to cut public spending, make the job market more flexible, and break the French logjam of high unemployment, a bloated state sector, and handouts that can have the perverse effect of making work in the official economy an unattractive proposition. "What matters today is effectiveness and not ideology," Valls said.

He prevailed even though thirty-two members of his own party abstained in protest at a perceived attack on socialist principles. More than any other party of the center-left in Europe, the French socialists have had trouble jettisoning ideological baggage ill-adapted to twenty-first-century global competition. More than any other Western country, France has resisted modernity, at least in the way it thinks of itself. So my feeling listening to Valls talk about "effectiveness" could be summed up in two words: Good luck!

The prime minister is up against something deeper than the resistance of labor unions or his own party: a culture that views the prizing of efficiency as almost vulgar.

Effectiveness had no place in my chat with the real-estate agent.

Effectiveness does not seem to enter into it as I contemplate French butchers bard a chicken or prepare a cut of beef with deft incisions. Effectiveness is not the rule in French shopping habits. It lies at a far remove from the long conversations between shopkeepers and clients. Efficiency for the French is a poor measure of the good life, just as making a buck from the sale of a house pales before the expression of feeling about what a house may represent. Whether this is good or bad hardly matters. It is often bad for the French economy but good for a balanced life.

These distinctive cultural components of nations are probably underestimated as globalization and homogenization create the impression that the same standards or systems can be pursued everywhere. I used to be impatient with such thinking. The Russians need a czar! The Egyptians need a pharaoh! The French need to strike! No, I would think, the Russians and the Egyptians and the French are like everyone else, they want to be free, they want governance with the consent of the governed, they do not want their lives subjected to arbitrary rules, or to live less well than they could without czars and pharaohs and strikes.

Now I feel I was wrong about that. Globalization equals adaptation to insurmountable differences as much as it equals change. Some things do not change, being the work of centuries.

A couple of days after my meeting, I was having a beer with my sons in a French café. The bill was fourteen euros. The waitress was going to take a credit card, then saw I had a ten-euro note. "Just give me that," she said. "Don't worry about the rest."

THE COMMUNITY OF EXPULSION

Reflections on the community of explusion, known over millennia by Jews, known today by Palestinians.

OCTOBER 6, 2014

LONDON—Attending services at a Reform synagogue during the High Holy Days in London, I heard sermons of great worthiness from British rabbis. One was about Alzheimer's and dementia among the elderly and the need to honor the "fragment of the divine in everyone." Another was about changes to the prayer book, including the dropping of the term "Lord," with its male overtones.

I listened with interest but without feeling challenged. The one subject not addressed was the one most on the minds of congregants: Israel and its recent war in Gaza, with the deaths of more than seventy Israelis and more than twenty-one hundred Palestinians, including about five hundred children. Surely I was not alone in hearing words like "fragment" and finding my mind turn to the moral dilemmas of the modern Israeli condition with its power and precariousness, its prosperity and violence, its uncertainty and contaminating dominion. The divine was in those dead Palestinian children, too. They just happened to have lived their brief lives in the hell of encircled Gaza with its tunnels and terrorists and Hamas operatives bent on the destruction of Israel.

Every human instinct recoils from the killing of children. It recoils even as Israel's right to defend itself from rockets is clear; and the excruciating difficulty of waging war against an enemy deployed among civilians is acknowledged; and the readiness of Israel's foes to kill any Jew is confronted. However framed, the death of a single child to an Israeli bullet seems to betoken some failure in the longed-for Jewish state, to say nothing of several hundred. The slaughter elsewhere in the Middle East cannot be an alibi for Jews to avoid this self-scrutiny.

Throughout the diaspora, the millennia of being strangers in strange lands, Jews' restless search in the scriptures for the ethics contained in sacred words formed a transmission belt of Judaism. For as long as the shared humanity of the other is perceived and felt, such questioning is unavoidable. The terrible thing about the Holy Land today is the denial of this humanity to the stranger. When that goes, so does essential self-interrogation. As mingling has died, separation has bred denial and contempt.

Perhaps I should not have been surprised by the anodyne sermons in London. I had read my colleague Laurie Goodstein's recent account of the incendiary sensitivity of Israel as subject matter, of the reticence of rabbis, of some feeling "muzzled," and of the difficulties faced by one New York rabbi, Sharon Kleinbaum, when she read the names of Israeli soldiers and Palestinian children, alike, killed in Gaza. She was accused of spreading Hamas propaganda. No, she was trying, in a small, brave way, to keep hearts and minds open.

That is the only way out of the impasse; neither people is going away. It is sixty-seven years since the United Nations called for the establishment of two states, one Jewish, one Arab, in Mandate Palestine; forty-seven years since the Israeli occupation of the West Bank began; forty-two days since the Gaza war ended. Palestinians have made a profession of failure. But to deny Israel's share of that failure is to opt for delusion.

Of course, sermons are only part of the story. The High Holy Days are days to look inward, to be still. I found my eyes straying to a passage from Stefan Zweig's *The World of Yesterday* reprinted in the prayer book. It read:

> Only now, since they were swept up like dirt in the streets and heaped together, the bankers from their Berlin palaces and sextons from the synagogues of Orthodox congregations, the philosophy professors from Paris, and Romanian cabbies, the undertaker's helpers and Nobel prize winners, the concert singers, and hired mourners, the authors and distillers, the haves and the have-nots, the great and the small, the devout and the liberals, the usurers and the sages, the Zionists and the assimilated, the Ashkenazim and the Sephardim, the just and the unjust, besides which the confused horde who thought that they had long since eluded the curse,

the baptized and the semi-Jews—only now, for the first time in hundreds of years, the Jews were forced into a community of interest to which they had long ceased to be sensitive, the ever-recurring—since Egypt—community of expulsion. But why this fate for them and always for them alone? What was the reason, the sense, the aim of this senseless persecution? They were driven out of lands but without a land to go to.

Two phrases leapt out: "community of expulsion," and "driven out of lands but without a land to go to." The second embodied the necessity of the Jewish state of Israel. But it was inconceivable, at least to me, without awareness of the first. Palestinians have joined the ever-recurring "community of expulsion."

The words of Leviticus are worth repeating for any Jew in or concerned by Israel today: Treat the stranger as yourself, for "you were strangers in the land of Egypt."

THE CONSOLATIONS OF ITALY

Italy defies the rules of modern life, inviting important questions as to where wisdom lies.

DECEMBER 4, 2014

ROME—It is always a pleasure to return to Rome and find that some things never change. I dissipated part of my youth here in a trance of happiness and, even at this distance, I find that happiness accessible. As we grow older, memory gains in importance, a labyrinth of infinite possibility.

So much of life today is jolting that a measure of dilatory inefficiency becomes comforting. The transactional relationships of London or New York or Singapore give way to the human relationship of Rome.

People actually take a few seconds to look at one another. They chat without purpose.

The heavy hotel-room key (rather than anonymous key card); the perfect *carciofi alla romana* (little artichokes Roman-style) dissolving in the mouth; the unchanging answer to any man-in-the-street question about the state of the Italian Republic ("*fa schifo*"—it stinks); the *manifestazione*, or demonstration, that closes a wide area of central Rome; the style of the *barista* making three espressos, two lattes, and two cappuccinos at once (eat your heart out, plodding Starbucks); the focus of the maître grating truffles with the clinical majesty of a matador; the grumbling and the small courtesies; the sound of voices rather than engines; the high-ceilinged apartments in their cool half-light; the whining scooters on the banks of the muddy Tiber; the shutters clattering down on stores at lunchtime, only to reopen in the late afternoon. All of this consoles in its familiarity.

Rush on, world, the voice of Rome seems to murmur: ambition will founder, conquest will unravel, riches will be lost, power will be dissipated, palaces will crumble, great loves will end, borders will be redrawn; and you, shed at last of your illusions, will be left to find comfort in beauty, family, your corner of the city, and a steaming plate of *bucatini all'amatriciana*.

It was Giuseppe Tomasi di Lampedusa who observed that everything must change so that everything stays the same. Here it sometimes seems that everything must stay the same so that one or two things may change (the city clocks, unlike when I used to live here thirty years ago, now tend to function).

Then, of course, there is politics. Prime Minister Matteo Renzi, aged thirty-nine, is a revolutionary politician in that his youth, direct language, dynamism, and relative transparency have shaken up old habits. There is something of the young Tony Blair about him. He is a showman pushing change through force of character. His ambition for Italy, he has said, "is not to do better than Greece but to do better than Germany."

Fighting words: After the Berlusconi years, Italy needed this shake-up desperately. Renzi's "Jobs Act," the cause of the current demonstrations, is an attempt to make it a little easier for corporations to fire employees.

That, by Italian standards, would be big. Renzi's slogan, in effect, is: Change or die. Unemployment is over 13 percent, public debt continues to climb, and Italy has known three recessions in six years. The country is problematic. Still, caution with official numbers is advisable. Family solidarity, private wealth, and the black economy cushion the crisis the statistics declare. Italy is poor; Italians are richer than it.

Like almost all Europeans, they are being outpaced by the hunger for wealth, long working days, and unregulated economies of the emergent world, where most people scarcely know what social security means. Still, Italians contrive to live better than seems possible in a declining economy.

There is nothing that unusual for a Roman about going home for lunch (or even having *la Mamma* prepare it). Resistance to change can also be healthy. It is a buffer against dislocation and loneliness, preserving the ties of family and sociability. Cultural skepticism about change runs deep. Unlike Americans, Italians have no desire to reinvent themselves. Rome restrains the itch to believe all can be changed utterly. Style is its refuge.

Italy needs change; Renzi is right to push for it. New investment will only come when the bureaucratic rigidities that curtail the economy are overcome. But change will always have its limits here. Behind Italian frivolity lies a deep-seated prudence.

The past year has been sobering. A quarter century on from the fall of the Berlin Wall, we see how deluded we were to imagine, even for a moment, that the old battles of nation-states and rival ideologies would give way to a world driven by enlightened self-interest and the shared embrace of Western liberal democracy and the rule of law.

Al Qaeda, Vladimir Putin, and the Chinese Communist Party thought otherwise. Powers still do what they do: seek to further their interests, accumulate resources, and advance their ideologies, at the expense of others if necessary. Beheadings and plague have not been banished from the world.

Italians tend to shrug. They knew this all along. There are compelling reasons to prefer beauty to the squalid affairs of the world.

WESTERN ILLUSIONS
OVER UKRAINE

Here, in this call to arm Ukraine, are unheeded words about the threat to Europe from Vladimir Putin. Nobody was much interested seven years ago. A few sanctions were imposed on Moscow. But Europe's dependence on Russia's oil and gas increased all the way to February 24, 2022.

FEBRUARY 9, 2015

MUNICH—The most difficult thing for a communist, it has been observed, is to predict the past. I was reminded of this as I listened to Russian Foreign Minister Sergei Lavrov, in full Soviet mode at the Munich Security Conference, suggesting that after World War II it was "the Soviet Union that was against splitting Germany."

People laughed; they guffawed. Germans recall the Soviet clamp on the east of the country and the Berlin Wall. But in a way Lavrov was right: the Soviet Union would have been quite happy to swallow all of Germany, given the chance.

Today, in similar fashion, President Vladimir Putin's Russia would be quite happy to absorb all of Ukraine, which it views as an extension of the motherland, an upstart deluded by the West into imagining independent statehood.

Lavrov's performance here reflected the alternate universe in which the Russian spaceship has docked almost a quarter century after the collapse of the Soviet Union. George Orwell's doublethink scarcely begins to describe his assertions.

Russia's annexation of Crimea was, he insisted, a popular uprising, the people "invoking the right of self-determination" as per the United Nations Charter. Ukrainians were engaged in an orgy of "nationalistic violence" characterized by ethnic purges directed against Jews and Russians. The United States was driven by an insatiable desire for global dominance and, in Ukraine, had orchestrated the "coup d'état" last year that led to the ousting of President Viktor Yanukovych. Europe post-1989 had turned its back on building "the common European house," declining the prospect of a "free economic zone" from Lisbon to Vladivostok in favor of the expansion of NATO eastward to the doorstep of Mother Russia.

Dream on, Sergei.

In fact, the Russian annexation of Crimea tore up by forceful means "the territorial integrity" and "political independence" of Ukraine, in direct violation of Article 2 of the United Nations Charter. It also shredded Russia's formal commitment under the Budapest Memorandum of 1994 to respect Ukraine's international borders. The "nationalistic violence" that has again raised issues of war and peace in Europe stems not from Kyiv but from Moscow, where Putin has cultivated a preposterous fable of encirclement, humiliation, and Western depredation to generate hysteria and buttress Russian aggression in eastern Ukraine.

Similarly, the fascism Lavrov purports to locate in Ukraine through allusions to attacks against Jews and other ethnic groups can in fact be far more persuasively identified back home. Putin has reminded humankind that the idiom fascism knows best is untruth so grotesque it begets unreason. The Russian leader has invoked history the better to turn it into farce. He has persevered in the nonsense that all the Russian forces and matériel in eastern Ukraine are figments of the world's imagination.

Lavrov's "coup" in Ukraine was nothing of the sort: it was a popular uprising against a corrupt Russian puppet strong-armed into turning his country away from closer association with the West. Ukrainians find the allure of Warsaw or Berlin greater than that of sunny Minsk. When they hear "common European house" they translate it as "Soviet imperium."

Two plus two equals five, was a Soviet slogan. It was deployed in 1931 in support of the notion that Stalin's five-year plan could be completed in four. Two plus two equals five is still the "truth" emanating from Moscow. This is worth recalling in all negotiations over Ukraine.

There was much talk here of a possible Franco-German-engineered cease-fire; of there being "no military solution" to the Ukrainian conflict (except, of course, the one Putin has in mind); of the advisability or not for the West of sending weapons to support the Ukrainian government

(Chancellor Angela Merkel is opposed); and of the need to be resolute, at least in word.

It's time to get real over Putin. He has not poured tanks and multiple-launch rocket systems over the Ukrainian border because he is about to settle for anything less than a weak Ukraine, sapped by low-level conflict in the Donetsk region, a country with its very own pro-Russian enclave à la Abkhazia or Transnistria, firmly within the Russian sphere of influence: the symbol of his definitive strategic turn away from closer cooperation with the West toward the confrontation that shores him up as oil prices and the currency plunge. He will not let Ukraine go.

There is a language Moscow understands: antitank missiles, battle-field radars, reconnaissance drones. Bolster the Ukrainian Army with them and other arms. Change Putin's cost-benefit analysis. There are risks, but no policy is risk-free. Recall that Ukraine gave up more than eighteen hundred nuclear warheads in exchange for that bogus commitment from Russia back in 1994 to respect its sovereignty and borders. Surely it has thereby earned the right to something more than night-vision goggles. The West's current Ukraine diplomacy is long on illusion and short on realism. Two plus two equals four, in war and peace.

THE VAST REALM OF "IF"

What if? The idea of the road not taken is tenacious.

MARCH 3, 2015

LONDON—What happens only just happens; then inevitability is conferred upon it. Between the lived and the not-quite-lived lies the little word "if." It's a two-letter invitation to the vast realm of the hypothetical, the counterfactual, and all the various paths not taken over the course of a life.

When I lived in Brazil in the 1980s, I would run along the beach from Leblon to Ipanema and back. After the workout, I'd always pay a couple of cents for coconut water. I liked to watch the way the beach-shack dude cupped the coconut in one hand and then, with three or four languorous but unerring swipes of his machete, opened up the top. He'd insert a straw. The iced water was always perfect.

I'd count his fingers. The blade never slipped. There were always ten.

Of course, if I'd thought of putting the coconut water in a bottle thirty years ago, marketing its health benefits, and selling it worldwide, I would not be writing this column today. It was too simple to think of that.

When I lived in Rome, before Brazil, I liked to watch the barmen ratcheting ground coffee into a receptacle, tapping the grains down, twisting the container into a socket, placing cups on a metal ledge-cum-filter beneath the coffee-yielding spouts, pouring milk with the requested dose of foam, and placing the various coffees on the counter. The quicksilver movements seemed all part of a single pirouette.

My then wife and I would travel from Rome to the Midwest, where she is from, and remark on the fact that it was near impossible to get a good coffee. She liked the idea of opening a coffee shop in the Twin Cities that would serve coffee as good as we'd become accustomed to drinking in Italy. Perhaps we could even grow the business across the United States!

Of course, if we'd done that in 1983, coffee aficionados might be speaking of St. Paul today the way they speak of Seattle. We'd be visiting our coffee shops in Chengdu and Glasgow. But it was too simple to do that.

Before Rome, when I lived in Brussels, I'd watch the chocolatiers down near the Grand Place apply their tongs (most useful and under-rated of culinary implements!) to the cocoa-dusted truffles and place them, one by one, in small white boxes until the chocolates were arrayed in many-layered order, one temptation nestling against another.

It would have been easy enough, in 1980, to make those chocolates more widely available, and it did occur to me that they should be, but of course I did nothing about the thought. If I had, who knows?

When I was in Afghanistan in 1973, before all the trouble started, or, rather, at the moment the trouble started with the overthrow of the king, I should have brought back all those Afghan rugs, and perhaps picked up a few in Iran (in that one could drive across the country then without any problem or mention of nukes); and certainly I should have hung on to our VW Kombi called Pigpen, after the keyboardist of the Grateful Dead who died that year, but I did not imagine then what a vehicle like that, adorned with Afghan paintings, might go for on eBay today, or how the VW bus would one day be prized from Hay-on-Wye to Haight-Ashbury. I don't even recall where in England I left Pigpen to die.

Hypothetically speaking, we need countless lives. There is not enough time. Or so it may seem. In the next one I will be a baker or a jeweler or a winemaker. I will make things. I will stay in one place.

Absent what might have been, I went on writing. In *The Debt to Pleasure*, the English novelist John Lanchester has this to say about my profession:

> "Your precipitate social decline cannot fail to alarm your well-wishers," I told my brother. "You started as a painter, then you became a sculptor, now you're basically a sort of gardener. What next, Barry?
>
> "Street-cleaner? Lavatory attendant? Journalism?"

That is a little harsh on what happened in the absence of what might have.

There is beauty in our dreams of change, our constant what-ifs.

Days begin in the realm of solemn undertakings—to eat less, to exercise more, to work harder, or to go gentler. They end with wobbles into compromise, or collapses into indulgence, with the perennial solace of the prospect of another day. The good-intentions dinner, a salad with a couple of slivers of chicken, turns into a burrito with cheese and avocado and salsa and chicken.

It's an illusion to think it would have been simple to change. We live lives that reflect our natures. Memory grows, a refuge, a solace, a repository so vast that what happened and what almost did begin to blur.

OF CATFISH WARS
AND SHOOTING WARS

History devours some societies, but not others. Just as the capacity
for civilized disagreement is one indication of a healthy society, so
is the capacity to get over the wounds of the past.

MARCH 26, 2015

THANH BINH, Vietnam—I drove out through a watery landscape, the
rice paddies shimmering, watermelon being planted in muddy fields.
There were ducks on the canals, graves and shrines in the light-green
rice fields, the dead among the living, not hidden but recalled daily.
Women in conical hats pushed bicycles over rickety wooden bridges.
The breeze was warm, the viscous coffee sweet. Cafés set with ham-
mocks, some advertising Wi-Fi, offered sugarcane juice pressed through
small hand-cranked mills. Everything felt liquid, soft, fluid here in the
Mekong Delta, an aqueous microclimate.

Yes, the dead among the living: four decades gone by since the war,
the bombs and the napalm—twitchy young Americans at the other side
of the world wondering what menace lurked in this lush vegetation.
America mired in the mud of an unwinnable war.

Now, if anything, the Vietnamese wonder whether the United
States military would protect them against the Chinese, if it ever came
to that. The temporary enemy has become a partner of sorts against the
eternal enemy. Annual trade between Vietnam and the United States
has soared from a mere $220 million in 1994 to $29.6 billion in 2013.

The wars over, the Vietnamese did not want to dwell on them. They
wanted to sow seeds of commerce rather than grievance. Asia could
offer this lesson to other parts of the world where I have spent too much
time. Vengeance and victimhood wither the soul. The life-giving rice
growing around the dead is an image fecund with acceptance. Even the
mud yields.

At its banks the lazy Mekong seems boundless. Business along the river has boomed. I watched with Huynh Khanh Chau, the vice-general director of Asia Commerce Fisheries, as large blue plastic containers of live fish were unloaded from boats into a pipe system that swept them in a watery gush into a nearby factory. The fish are raised on nearby farms; aquaculture has become a big industry in the Mekong.

The name of the small-headed, fat-bodied fish is a matter of some dispute. It is catfish-like. So it has been called Vietnamese catfish. In the United States it is sometimes called *swai*. It has also been dubbed *basa* and in Europe is often referred to as *pangasius*.

This has not been a mere lexicographical game. The "catfish wars" between the United States and Vietnam have been bitter.

The U.S. catfish industry initially pressed Congress to prohibit label-ing *basa* as catfish. The first anti-dumping duties against "certain frozen fish fillets from Vietnam" went into effect in 2003. They have not been lifted. More recently, Vietnam has been angered by an attempt to reclas-sify *basa* as catfish, which could lead to stricter United States Depart-ment of Agriculture inspection standards. Where are Joseph Heller and *Catch-22* when you need them?

Huynh has no doubt this is a simple case of American protectionism. When it comes to catfish, Vietnam, with its ideal climate and cheap labor, is more competitive. Its fish tastes good—or at least just as good. Still, better catfish war than hot war.

His company has had to adjust. It's exporting more to China, but the Chinese taste is only for large fillets. Europe likes medium-sized fil-lets. By contrast, the United States, ever the omnivore, "is a great market because it likes large, medium-sized, and small fillets!"

Inside, the fish are killed by workers with a single throat-cutting thrust of the knife through the gill. Blood drips down a stainless-steel chute into a pool. The fish are cleaned. Another team of men in brown, numbered uniforms does the initial filleting, knives sweeping in prac-ticed incisions through the pale-pink flesh to leave, in seconds, a carcass of head and bone. The men pile the fillets in blue trays and add a disc with their number; pay depends on productivity.

Now it is the turn of blue-uniformed women, whose work is more skilled. It is easy to tear the fillet. With precision and speed, they nip, they scrape, they flip, they excise—until every blemish is gone. The factory floor is a sea of young women and quicksilver knife movements. Fillets are then sorted by size and color, before freezing. From live fish to the frozen fillet ready to be boxed and exported to Western or Chinese supermarkets, no more than an hour elapses.

Outside, in a café, I met a worker, Nguyen Van Tu, from the adjacent Hung Ca fish factory and exporter. He said he works a twelve-hour shift, six days a week, with a one-hour lunch break and two twenty-minute pauses. He earns about $220 a month. Next time I eat a frozen fish fillet in New York or blackened catfish in Louisiana I'll think of his smiling face, his low pay, flashing knives in female hands, fish wars versus shooting wars, the peace of the watery Delta, and those graves in the glistening rice paddies.

COUNTERREVOLUTIONARY RUSSIA

Here are more wasted words on the threat from Putin's Russia. All American eyes were on the so-called war on terror. To suggest Russia was a major threat was to be ridiculed.

JUNE 25, 2015

TALLOIRES, France—For much of the twentieth century Russia was a revolutionary state whose objective was the global spread of communist ideology. In the twenty-first century it has become the pre-eminent counterrevolutionary power.

The escalating conflict between the West and Moscow has been portrayed as political, military, and economic. It is in fact deeper than that. It is cultural. President Vladimir Putin has set himself up as the guardian of an absolutist culture against what Russia sees as the predatory and relativist culture of the West.

To listen to pro-Putin Russian intellectuals these days is to be subjected to a litany of complaints about the "revolutionary" West, with its irreligious embrace of same-sex marriage, radical feminism, euthanasia, homosexuality, and other manifestations of "decadence." It is to be told that the West loses no opportunity to globalize these "subversive" values, often under cover of democracy promotion and human rights.

Putin's Russia, by contrast, is portrayed in these accounts as a proud bulwark against the West's abandonment of religious values, a nation increasingly devout in its observance of Orthodox Christianity, a country convinced that no civilization ever survived by "relativizing" sacred truths.

Beyond Putin's annexation of Crimea and stirring-up of a small war in eastern Ukraine (although large enough to leave more than six thousand dead), it is his decision to adopt cultural defiance of the West that suggests the confrontation with Russia will last decades.

Communism was a global ideology; Putinism is less than that. But a war of ideas has begun in which counterrevolution against the godless and insinuating West is a cornerstone of Russian ideology. To some degree, President Recep Tayyip Erdogan of Turkey shares Putin's view of the West. China, meanwhile, finds uses in it.

Gone is the post–Cold War illusion of benign convergence through interdependence. Something fundamental has shifted that goes far beyond a quarrel over territory. Putin has decided to define his power in conflict with the West. The only question is whether he has limited or all out conflict in mind.

This Russian decision has strategic implications the West is only beginning to digest. It involves an eastward pivot more substantial than President Obama's to Asia. Putin is now more interested in the Shanghai Cooperation Organization, whose core is China and Russia, than he is in cooperation with the G-8 (from which Russia has been suspended) or the European Union.

China reciprocates this interest to some degree, because a Moscow hostile to the West is useful for the defense of its own authoritarian political model and because it sees economic opportunity in Russia and former Soviet Central Asian countries. But China's fierce modernizing drive cannot be accomplished through backward looking Russia.

There are clear limits to the current Chinese-Russian rapprochement.

As a senior European official attending a conference organized by Harvard University's Weatherhead Center for International Affairs put it, Russia's is a "loser's challenge" to the West, because it has given up on modernization and globalization, whereas China's is potentially a "winner's challenge," because it is betting everything on a high-tech, modern economy.

Of course, being irrational and quixotic, losers' challenges are particularly dangerous. Putin has gobbled a chunk of Ukraine after it pursued a trade pact with the European Union. He has said he's adding forty intercontinental ballistic missiles to Russia's stockpile. He has increased flights of nuclear-capable bombers. The message is clear: We're leaning in on nukes.

How should the West respond? It cannot alter the appeal of its values to the world—witness the hordes of people dying in the attempt to get into the European Union. (Rich Russians have also been pouring into the West in search of the rule of law.) So what Russia sees as Western "subversion" (like the tilt of sane Ukrainians toward Europe) will continue—and it should.

The West must protect the right of peoples in the East-West in-between lands. The citizens of Ukraine, Moldova, Armenia, Georgia, and other states have the right to attain Western prosperity through Western institutions if they so choose. Poland and the Baltic States, now protected by membership in NATO, are inevitably magnets to them.

This new protection should borrow from the policies behind Cold War protection of Germany: firmness allied to dialogue. The West, in the words of Tomasz Siemoniak, Poland's defense minister, has been "excessive" in its caution. Holding NATO exercises in Latvia, creating a new five-thousand-strong rapid-reaction NATO "spearhead force," and moving 250 tanks and other equipment into temporary bases in six East European nations is something. But the permanent and significant deployment of heavy weapons in the region is needed to send a message to Putin, as is greater European defense spending, and a clear commitment to maintain sanctions as long as Ukraine is not made whole with full control of its borders.

In the end, the very Western ideas and institutions Putin demeans will be the West's greatest strength in the long looming struggle against Russian counterrevolution.

BATTERED GREECE AND ITS REFUGEE LESSON

Greece, despite great economic hardship, takes care of more than two hundred thousand refugees, mainly from Syria. It gives a lesson to countries like Hungary in the thrall of anti-immigrant nationalism.

SEPTEMBER 21, 2015

MOLYVOS, Greece—Here's a rough guide to the modern world: More efficiency, less humanity. Technology is principally at the service of productivity. Acts of irrational grace are not its thing. They have no algorithm.

Greece has made me think about everything statistics don't tell you. No European country has been as battered in recent years. No European country has responded with as much consistent humanity to the refugee crisis.

Greater prosperity equals diminishing generosity. Device distraction equals inability to give of your time. Modernity fosters the transactional relationship over the human relationship. The rules are not absolute, but they are useful indicators.

More than two hundred thousand refugees, mainly from Syria, have arrived in a Greece on the brink this year, almost half of them coming ashore on the island of Lesbos, which lies just six miles from Turkey. They have entered a country with a quarter of its population unemployed.

They have found themselves in a state whose per capita income has fallen by nearly 23 percent since the crisis began, with a tenuous banking system and unstable politics.

Greece could serve as a textbook example of a nation with potential for violence against a massive influx of outsiders.

In general, the refugees have been well received. There have been clashes, including on Lesbos, but almost none of the miserable bigotry, petty calculation, schoolyard petulance, and amnesiac small-mindedness emanating from European Union countries farther north, particularly Hungary.

For several hours, I crisscrossed Lesbos with a driver, Michalis Papagrigoriou, who had volunteered to help transport refugees from Molyvos, in the north of the island, to the port in Mytilene, about forty-five miles away. His bus, normally used to ferry pale North European tourists in search of Mediterranean sun, had been leased by the International Rescue Committee (IRC) to help the more than two thousand refugees arriving in inflatable rafts every day.

Papagrigoriou, besieged by calls to take his bus here and there, was in an irrepressible mood. Around each switchback on the hills between Kalloni, in the middle of the island, and Molyvos, in the north, refugees came into view: children, old men, pregnant women trudging through pine woods.

They raised their arms. They pleaded. They lay slumped against backpacks. Discarded water bottles traced their path. Papagrigoriou, with an appointment to pick up a busload in Molyvos, could not help immediately, but each group prompted an impassioned soliloquy about injustice and shared humanity. On the way back, although his bus was full, he would bend the rules to squeeze in an extra woman and child. He would also accept a plea from his village, Mantamados, to pick up refugees there, although it meant working deep into the night.

In Molyvos, refugees lined up by the side of the road. Papagrigoriou's was the second-last bus of the evening. The great golden orb of the sun was already halfway through its riveting plunge below the horizon. IRC officials explained how they try to stop refugees setting off on foot to Mytilene, but some are too impatient to wait.

I got talking on the bus to Taleb Hosein, an Afghan refugee. He'd been on the road for a long time, how long he could not say. The worst was a walk of several days without food from Iran into Turkey. He looked very young. I asked how old he was. He did not know. In Afghanistan, he said, there are often no birth records. "I think I am about seventeen or eighteen," he said. Where was he headed? "I want a safe place, I don't care where, but Britain would be my favorite, because I study English."

A twenty-six-year-old Syrian dentist from Damascus who had been listening to us told me he had gotten married two weeks ago. His wife was sleeping, her head on his shoulder. "This is our honeymoon," he said.

Night had fallen. The groups of walking refugees held feeble flashlights. Many had stopped, having decided to sleep by the side of the road. One young man stood in the path of the bus until the last moment. Papagrigoriou, slowly negotiating the switchbacks, talked about how certain situations demand that human beings help one another, other considerations be damned.

Exhausted silence enveloped the bus. Hosein and the other Afghans disembarked into a camp surrounded by barbed wire. The Syrian transit camp is less forbidding; Greek authorities quickly hand out a permit to stay for six months. Most refugees want to move north to Germany, where they believe they will find jobs.

They will be lucky if they find Papagrigoriou's humanity. The world hardens in technology's vise. The productivity of generosity cannot be measured.

I asked Alexis Papahelas, the executive editor of the Greek daily *Kathimerini*, what Greece could teach the world: "That dignity and decency can be preserved, even through the hardest times."

It's a powerful, important lesson that Alexis Tsipras, re-elected as Greece's left-wing prime minister, should carry forward.

OBAMA'S DOCTRINE
OF RESTRAINT

I examined, in two columns, the cost of Barack Obama's foreign policy.

OCTOBER 12, 2015

One way to define Barack Obama's foreign policy is as a Doctrine of Restraint. It is clear, not least to the Kremlin, that this president is skeptical of the efficacy of military force, wary of foreign interventions that may become long-term commitments, convinced the era of American-imposed solutions is over, and inclined to see the United States as less an indispensable power than an indispensable partner. He has, in effect, been talking down American power.

President Vladimir Putin has seized on this profound foreign-policy shift in the White House. He has probed where he could, most conspicuously in Ukraine, and now in Syria. Obama may call this a form of Russian weakness. He may mock Putin's forays as distractions from a plummeting Russian economy. But the fact remains that Putin has reasserted Russian power in the vacuum created by American retrenchment and appears determined to shape the outcome in Syria using means that Obama has chosen never to deploy. For Putin, it's clear where the weakness lies: in the White House.

Russia's Syrian foray may be overreach. It may fall into the category of the "stupid stuff" (read: reckless intervention) Obama shuns. Quagmires can be Russian, too. But for now the initiative appears to lie in the Kremlin, with the White House as reactive power. Not since the end of the Cold War a quarter century ago has Russia been as assertive or Washington as acquiescent.

Obama's Doctrine of Restraint reflects circumstance and temperament. He was elected to lead a nation exhausted by the two longest and most expensive wars in its history. Iraq and Afghanistan consumed trillions without yielding victory. His priority was domestic: first recovery from the 2008 meltdown and then a more equitable and inclusive society. The real pivot was not to Asia but to home.

Besides, American power in the twenty-first century could not be what it was in the twentieth, not with the Chinese economy quintupling in size since 1990. The president was intellectually persuaded of the need to redefine America's foreign-policy heft in an interconnected world of more equal powers, and temperamentally inclined to prudence and diplomacy over force. Republican obstructionism and the politicization of foreign policy in a polarized Washington did not help him. American power, in his view, might still be dominant but could no longer be determinant.

As Obama put it to *The New Republic* in 2013, "I am more mindful probably than most of not only our incredible strengths and capabilities, but also our limitations." After Iraq and Afghanistan, giant repositories of American frustration, who could blame him?

But when the most powerful nation on earth and chief underwriter of global security focuses on its limitations, others take note, perceiving new opportunity and new risk. Instability can become contagious. Unraveling can set in, as it has in the Middle East. The center cannot hold, because there is none.

"I think Obama exaggerates the limits and underestimates the upside of American power, even if the trend is toward a more difficult environment for translating power and influence," Richard Haass, the president of the Council on Foreign Relations, told me. "By doing so, he runs the risk of actually reinforcing the very trends that give him pause. Too often during his presidency the gap between ends and means has been our undoing."

In Afghanistan, in Libya, and most devastatingly in Syria, Obama has seemed beset by ambivalence: a surge undermined by a date certain for Afghan withdrawal; a lead-from-behind military campaign to oust Libya's dictator with no follow-up plan; a statement more than four years ago that "the time has come" for President Bashar al-Assad to "step aside" without any strategy to make that happen; and a "red line" on chemical weapons that was not upheld. All this has said to Putin and China's President Xi Jinping that this is a time of wound-licking American incoherence.

Yet Obama does not lack courage. Nor is he unprepared to take risks. It required courage to conclude the Iran nuclear deal—a signal achievement arrived at in the face of a vitriolic cacophony from Israel and the Republican-controlled Congress. It took courage to achieve a diplomatic breakthrough with Cuba. The successful operation to kill Osama bin Laden was fraught with risk. His foreign policy has delivered in significant areas.

America has wound down its wars. The home pivot has yielded a revived economy (at least for some) and given nearly all Americans access to health insurance.

Yet the cost of the Doctrine of Restraint has been very high. How high we do not yet know, but the world is more dangerous than in recent memory. Obama's skepticism about American power, his readiness to disengage from Europe, and his catastrophic tiptoeing on Syria have left the Middle East in generational conflict and fracture, Europe unstable, and Putin strutting the stage. Where this rudderless reality is likely to lead I will examine in my next column.

OBAMA'S WHAT NEXT?

More on President Obama's weak foreign policy.

OCTOBER 15, 2015

Throughout the Obama years, when international crises and possible American intervention were discussed in the Situation Room, one question from the president was likely to recur: "Okay, but what happens after that?"

It could be the establishment of a no-fly zone in Syria, or setting up a safe area for Syrians fleeing, or putting troops back in Iraq after Islamic State militants overran Mosul—always there was concern over a slippery slope. President Obama, under his Doctrine of Restraint described in my last column, has been the king of the slippery-slope school of foreign policy. His decision to keep thousands of troops in Afghanistan, rather than withdraw them as previously planned, appears to reflect an acknowledgment that American retrenchment can be perilous.

The thing about the president's what-next refrain was that it inevitably led to a range of dire scenarios. Suppose an American forward air controller in Iraq gets captured by Islamic State and burned alive? Suppose you've cratered the airfields in Syria, and President Bashar al-Assad, rather than suing for peace, steps up his brutal ground campaign and resists? Well, take out his air-defense sites and fast-forward arming the opposition. But then you get Russians and Iranians and Hezbollah pouring in to help Assad, and before you know it you've got 150,000 American troops on the ground invested in another intractable war.

Okay, but what happens after that?

Obama came to office at a time when sins of commission (read: Iraq and Afghanistan) outweighed sins of omission. Inclined to lawyerly prudence, yet not without Wilsonian idealism, he was determined to reverse that.

He has sought, with some conspicuous exceptions, including the important Iran nuclear deal, what Robert Blackwill, a senior fellow at the Council on Foreign Relations, described to me as "a risk-free foreign policy." For example, drone attacks on nations without air defenses are near risk-free.

But because there are always reasons not to act, the pursuit of the risk-free tends to pass the initiative to adversaries who believe they can escalate with no fear of American reprisal—see Russia and China. That is the freelance world we now live in. Syria is the American sin of omission par excellence, a diabolical complement to the American sin of commission in Iraq—two nations now on the brink of becoming ex-nations.

A pivotal moment came in 2013, when Obama was on the verge of a military response to Assad for crossing the American "red line" on chemical weapons. The British Parliament had voted against participation. Obama spoke to David Cameron, the British prime minister, who explained the situation. He spoke to François Hollande, the French president, who said France stood shoulder-to-shoulder with America. Targets had been identified. A long meeting of Obama's top advisers was held on Friday, August 30. The consensus was that the British vote did not change the calculus for action. The president asked if he had the constitutional authority to go ahead. He was told he did. When the meeting broke up, military action was imminent.

Then the president went for a now famous walk and in effect changed his mind. As a result, America's word is worth less in the world. Syria could not be worse off than it is. "When your strongest asset, your military, is not ready to engage, people will factor you out," Vali Nasr, the dean of the John Hopkins University Paul H. Nitze School of Advanced International Studies, told me.

But could it have been otherwise? American power in 2015 is not American power in 1990. Hyper-connectivity and the rise of the rest will constrain any president even if the United States, as Hillary Clinton put it, is not Denmark.

Suppose—that word—Obama had been frank and said: "My job is to reduce the footprint of America in a changed world and empower other countries to do more." That's a sinker in American politics.

It's unthinkable because most Americans are still hardwired to American exceptionalism, the notion that America is not America if it gives up on spreading liberty. So it becomes hard to find a foreign-policy language that's aligned to reality but does not smack of "declinism"— fatal for any politician. Republican bloviating about "weakling" Obama notwithstanding, any future president will face this foreign-policy dilemma: the distance between America's idea of itself and what it can plausibly achieve is widening.

That said, I believe Obama has sold America short. The foreign-policy pendulum that swings between assertiveness and retrenchment has swung too far. His shift from indispensable power to indispensable partner has backfired when partner after partner—the Afghan Army, the Iraqi Army—has proved ineffective. The United States is not even at the Minsk table on the Ukraine crisis. Germany is.

"Just do it" might have served Obama better at times than "What next?" Between paralysis and 350,000 troops on the ground there are options. Not every intervention is a slippery slope. The question, post-Syria, is whether the next president can make American power credible enough to stop this crisis or another in the Middle East, the Baltics, or the South China Sea, from spiraling out of control.

THE DANGER OF PLACING
YOUR CHIPS ON BEAUTY

I wrote about France just after the Jihadi terrorist attacks there that killed 130 people and wounded almost 500. Paris felt vulnerable. A shadow was cast over France that in the years to come would feed the rise of a hard-right anti-immigrant nationalist movement.

NOVEMBER 21, 2015

PARIS—Memories, the French poet Guillaume Apollinaire wrote, are like the sound of hunters' horns fading in the wind. I have loved in Paris, had children, dreamed, wandered, gotten lost, found myself again. At every intersection there is an invitation, on every bridge a memory.

The wound from the attack suppurates in the damp air. Anybody attuned to Paris feels it. The French have seen a lot, acquired a fierce realism that refuses to prettify life, and mastered the indifferent shrug. They will endure. Still, they are shaken. There is a void in streets too empty, a new suspicion in appraising glances, a wary numbness.

The Paris Métro reports a 10 percent decline in passengers since the Islamic State slaughtered 130 people at random just over a week ago. Jumpy people run from phantom sounds. A friend, Anne Salazar Orvig, a professor of linguistics at the Sorbonne, tells me she tried to teach a freshman class but had to abandon it because "the students were simply not there."

Paris is afflicted with absences—the dead, of course; visitors frightened away; minds frozen by fear; and tranquility lost. The city feels vulnerable. Its luminous tolerance is intolerable to the jihadi fanatics. In this sense it is a symbol of a Western civilization and an openness that now seem fragile. Terrorists are interested in potent symbolism.

Perhaps no metropolis carries as much symbolism as the French capital, home to the Enlightenment and the Declaration of the Rights of Man.

"Do they attack us for what we do or do they attack us for what we are?" Dominique Moïsi, a political scientist, asked me, wondering if France was a target because of its far-flung military campaigns against armed Islamist zealots or because it is a free and democratic country that has banished God from the political sphere. I think France is attacked above all for what it is. That in turn is terrifying.

Any member of French society, or, by extension, of our civilization, becomes a target. Of course, the threat is not new, but, like a cancer metastasizing, it suddenly feels ubiquitous. I don't think Paris has ever felt so precious or precarious to me as it did over the past week.

Insouciance is a Parisian pleasure. This is the city of aimless wandering and casual delight. But today, insouciance feels freighted with danger. There is too much of it in the West. The enemy has been underestimated. His maxim is maximum damage. He defies classification. He may be the middle-class, private-school-educated son of Moroccan immigrants in Belgium. Saving Paris from the Islamic State will take ruthlessness—but save it we must.

I went back this week to the area at the bottom of the Rue Mouffetard where I first lived in 1975. Aside from a Starbucks in place of the fruit-and-vegetable store where I once shopped, it looked familiar.

Paris has changed just enough to stay the same. Gone is the Gitane-Gauloise pall of the cafés, gone the mouth-puckering midmorning sauvignons blancs downed by red-eyed men, gone the horse butchers and the garlic whiff of the early-morning Métro. Where artisans hammered and workers toiled in the ateliers of the Tenth and Eleventh Arrondissements, restaurants now attract a young crowd—of the kind cut down last week by the jihadi fanatics.

Yet, despite its gentrification, Paris has resisted the brand-obsessed homogenization of our age. If capitalism works less well here, it also works less cruelly. The city is still itself—with its parks of satisfying geometry, its strong Haussmannian arteries, its gilt and gravel, its islands pointing their prows toward the solemn bridges. It is a refuge of our hopes, a repository of our fantasies, a redoubt of a quaint old word—solidarity.

Paris has placed its chips on beauty, a gamble of course, because beauty invites destruction from those who would subjugate rather than uplift the human spirit. The barbarians multiply. Look at Palmyra in Syria, or what is left of it.

Halfway up the Rue Mouffetard I met Nicos Moraitis, a Greek immigrant who came to live in Paris thirty years ago. He owns a crêpe restaurant called, predictably enough, Chez Nicos, and his crêpe maker, less predictably, is an Indian called Nishan Singh. An Indian who makes French crêpes for a Greek—that, too, I thought, is Paris. Moraitis told me business had been down about 40 percent since the attack. People are staying home. "I'm fifty-seven, I've lived my life, I don't worry about myself; if I die, well, goodbye; I don't believe in God. But I do worry about the next generation and my grandchildren."

What, Moraitis asked, do they want, these slaughterers? He came to France, adopted it, took a loan, started a business, and eventually bought a small apartment. His family benefited from free health care and education. France's model worked for him, as it has for generations of immigrants.

Then, abruptly, the model buckled with the arrival of millions of North African immigrants, many hostile to their former colonial overlords, some living in Saint-Denis, just north of the city, where the police fought a pitched battle with a jihadi cell this week. Europe's border-banishing integration is more threatened than at any time since 1945. "We need tranquility," Moraitis told me. "This is a city where, if you feel sad, going for a stroll can lift your mood. But one more attack and all bets are off."

Only a fool would say another attack is impossible. I asked an old friend, Goran Tocilovac, a Serbian writer who long ago adopted Paris, what he thought of Moïsi's question about the motives for the attack. "I think it's above all what we do in Mali or Syria," he said. "But that is the result of what we are. We are accustomed to loving certain liberties and we will defend them."

That answer consoled me somewhat. Democracies are slow to anger but formidable when aroused. I'm not sure if—after Afghanistan, after Iraq—the greatest democracy of all, the United States, has the capacity to rouse itself to a convincing military response against the Islamic State. For Paris, as well as New York, it must.

"We'll always have Paris"—Humphrey Bogart's comment to Ingrid Bergman in *Casablanca*—is one of the most famous movie lines. Yet her desperate question that precedes it is sometimes forgotten: "But what about us?" Bogart is telling Bergman to leave him and be with her husband so that the Paris of their brief but eternal affair can be preserved. He is telling her that Paris—their Paris, the Paris of so many dreams—is a delicate and infinitely precious thing whose survival requires painful, courageous decisions such as his.

TRUMP'S WEIMAR AMERICA

My first column on Trump, in which I predicted the seriousness of his threat. Trump is a clown. No, he is not. He's in earnest and he's onto something.

DECEMBER 14, 2015

NEW YORK—Welcome to Weimar America: It's getting restive in the beer halls. People are sick of politics as usual. They want blunt talk. They want answers.

Welcome to an angry nation, stung by two lost wars, its politics veering to the extremes, its mood vengeful, beset by decades of stagnant real wages for most people, tempted by a strongman who would keep all Muslims out and vows to restore American greatness.

"We're going to be so tough and so mean and so nasty," Donald Trump says in response to the San Bernardino massacre. People roar. He calls for a "total and complete shutdown of Muslims entering the

United States." People roar. "People want strength," he says. People roar. His poll numbers go up. Pundits, even the longtime guru of Republican political branding, Karl Rove, shake their heads.

Trump is a clown. No, he is not. He is in earnest. And he's onto something. It is foolish not to take him seriously.

A near-perfect storm for his rabble-rousing is upon the United States. China is rising. American power is ebbing. The tectonic plates of global security are shifting. Afghanistan and Iraq have been the graveyards of glory. There is fear, after the killing in California inspired by the Islamic State, of an enemy within.

Over more than a decade, American blood and treasure have been expended, to little avail. President Obama claims his strategy against Islamist jihadist terrorism, which he often sugarcoats as "violent extremism," is working. There is little or no evidence of that.

A lot of Americans struggle to get by, their pay no match for prices.

Along comes Trump, the high-energy guy. He promises an American revival, a reinvention, even a renaissance. He insults Muslims, Mexicans, the disabled, women. His words are hateful and scurrilous. They play on fears. They are subjected to horrified analysis. Yet they do not hurt him. He gets people's blood up. He says what others whisper. He cuts through touchy-feely all-enveloping political correctness. This guy will give Putin a run for his money! His poll numbers rise.

It would be foolish and dangerous not to take him seriously. His bombast is attuned to Weimar America. The United States is not paying reparations, as Weimar Germany was after World War I. Hyperinflation does not loom. But the Europeanization of American politics is unmistakable.

America, like Europe, is rattled by Islamic State terrorism and unsure how to respond to the black-flagged death merchants. Its polarized politics seem broken. The right of Donald Trump and the right of France's Marine Le Pen overlap on terrorism and immigration. On the American left, Bernie Sanders sounds like nothing so much as a European social democrat. But that's another story.

Le Pen is now a serious candidate for the French presidency in 2017. Her strong first-round performance in regional elections was not matched in the second round. She faded. But, like Trump, she answers the popular call for an end to business as usual after two Paris massacres this year in which the Islamic State had a role. The three jihadists who killed ninety Friday-night revelers in the Bataclan club were French citizens believed to have been trained in Syria.

"Islamist fundamentalism must be annihilated," Le Pen says. People roar. "France must ban Islamist organizations," she says. People roar. It must "expel foreigners who preach hatred in our country as well as illegal migrants who have nothing to do here." People roar.

There is no question that Le Pen is being taken seriously in France. Europe's watchword is vigilance. Its entire postwar reconstruction has been premised on the conviction that peace, integration, economic union, and the welfare state were the best insurance against the return to power of the fascist right.

That conviction is shaken. The rise of the Islamic State, and the Western inability to contain it, leads straight to the Islamophobia in which Trump and Le Pen traffic with success. It would be hard to imagine an atmosphere better suited to the politics of fear. Americans say they are more fearful of terrorism than at any time since 9/11.

"Every time things get worse, I do better," Trump says. He does. They may get still worse.

The Europeanization of American politics is also the Europeanization of American political risk. The unthinkable has happened in Europe. It is not impossible in America.

It would be wrong not to take Trump very seriously. It would be irresponsible. It would be to forget European history, from whose fascist example he borrows. In Weimar America, politics are not what they were. The establishment looks tired. The establishment has not understood the fact-lite theater of the contemporary world.

The Weimar Republic ended with a clown's ascent to power, a high-energy buffoon who shouted loudest, a bully from the beer halls, a racist, and a bigot. He was an outsider given to theatrics and pageantry. He seduced the nation of Beethoven. He took the world down with him.

THE ASSASSINATION IN ISRAEL THAT WORKED

My reflections on the assassination of Yitzhak Rabin, the warrior turned peacemaking prime minister, two decades after his death. The assassination by a fanatical Jew proved effective. Reason ebbed. Rage flowed. Messianic Zionism supplanted secular Zionism of the kind that believes in a state of laws.

DECEMBER 17, 2015

The assassination two decades ago of Yitzhak Rabin, the warrior who became Israel's peacemaking prime minister, has proved one of the most successful in history.

Like Mahatma Gandhi, assassinated by a Hindu fanatic, Rabin was killed by one of his own, a fanatical Jew who could not abide territorial compromise for peace. Yigal Amir, the assassin, was a religious-nationalist follower of Baruch Goldstein, the American-born killer of twenty-nine Palestinian worshipers in Hebron in 1994.

Reason ebbed. Rage flowed. The center eroded. Messianic Zionism, of the kind that claims all the land between the Mediterranean Sea and the Jordan River as God-given real estate, supplanted secular Zionism of the kind that believes in a state of laws.

An opportunistic right-wing politician named Benjamin Netanyahu, who had compared Rabin to Chamberlain, rose to power. He may supplant David Ben-Gurion as Israel's longest-serving prime minister, but his legacy looks paltry beside the founding father of Israel.

A warrior-peacemaker was lost to an assassin's bullet in 1995. A marketer-fearmonger eventually replaced him. Leadership, in its serious sense, disappeared. Without leadership, every problem is insurmountable. With it, no problem is unsolvable.

It will soon be a half century since Israel took control of the West Bank and backed the settlement movement that now sees several hundred thousand Jews living east of the Green Line, enjoying Israeli citizenship and various state handouts. Why, then, has Israel not asserted its sovereignty over all territory and granted the vote and other democratic rights to all inhabitants?

The answer is simple: too many Palestinians. Asserting sovereignty would have meant the end of the Jewish state. Israel chose instead the undermining of its own democracy. As Gershom Gorenberg has put it, Israel has "behaved as if the territories were part of Israel for the purpose of settlement, and under military occupation for the purpose of ruling the Palestinians."

This policy is corrosive. No democracy is immune to running an undemocratic system on part of the land it controls. Across the Green Line, millions of inhabitants are noncitizens. This is the combustible "one-state reality" of which Secretary of State John Kerry spoke this month.

The noncitizens are Israel's colonized Palestinians. Oppression and humiliation are hewn into the topography of the West Bank. Israel, through the settlement movement, has undermined its Zionist founders' commitment to a democratic state of laws.

Vikram Seth, the novelist, has observed: "The great advantage of being a chosen people is that one can choose to decide who is unchosen."

The great disadvantage of messianic Zionism is that it makes it impossible for Israel to be a Jewish and democratic state. It makes violence inevitable.

Since October, more than twenty Israelis and more than a hundred Palestinians have been killed in what some are calling a third intifada. This is the status quo. Three Gaza wars since 2008 are the status quo. Israel today is a miracle of rapid development perched on the brittle foundation of occupation. Stabbings are the status quo.

The Palestinian leadership has been hopeless. It is divided. It is corrupt. It lacks democratic legitimacy. It has wallowed in the comforting embrace of injustice rather than making the tough decisions to end it. It has opted for theater over substance. It incites against Jews. Time, as the last sixty-seven years demonstrate, is not on the Palestinian side.

None of this annuls Palestinians' right to a state called Palestine in the West Bank and Gaza, or the long-term interest of both sides in working to that end. Rabin hated what Palestinians had done. Still, for Israel's security, he chose peace.

The cornerstone of Israel's United Nations–backed legality was territorial compromise, as envisaged in Resolution 181 of 1947, calling for two states, one Jewish, one Arab, in the Holy Land. This was humankind's decision, not God's.

The covenant Jews bore around the world was a covenant of ethics, not a covenant granting Jews the hills of Judea and Samaria forever. Its core is the idea that what is hateful to yourself should not be inflicted on your fellow human being. It must apply to the strong Jew of Israel as much as to the cowed Jew of the pre-Israel diaspora.

As the liberal Israeli daily *Haaretz* has recently chronicled, various U.S. entities and nonprofit organizations, for which donations are tax-deductible, provide funding for the settler movement opposed by the United States government.

Daniel Kurtzer, a former American ambassador to Israel, summed up why this is unacceptable: "The government—and we, the public—are subsidizing an activity which undermines government policy."

The Obama administration has understandably tired of providing the fig leaf of a "peace process" to Israeli and Palestinian leaders. But it can set down a marker by making public its view of a territorial compromise at or close to the 1967 lines, with agreed swaps. It can seek leverage in its opposition to settlement growth. It can close American tax loopholes that benefit Israeli settlers. It can try to make Rabin's assassination a little less successful.

WAYS TO BE FREE

A diary sent to me, like a message in a bottle, takes me back to my youth. How much freer, in many ways, we were then.

JANUARY 21, 2016

When you grew up in an unmapped, unwired world and find yourself in this one—observing the panic when GPS fails or the extent of online-status anxiety—you can't help wondering if somewhere along the way freedom got lost.

Freedom is still out there. We all have our idea of it, the deferred dream. Your psyche builds layers of protection around your most vulnerable traits, which may be closely linked to that precious essence in which freedom resides. Freedom is inseparable from risk.

Three things recently caused me to ponder these matters. The first was the appearance, like a letter in a bottle, of a diary from 1973, recording a time when I was in Afghanistan as a seventeen-year-old hippie. The second was reading *Barbarian Days*, William Finnegan's wonderful surfing memoir. The third was a question from my son. I'll take them in order.

The diary, written by Leslie Starr, covers three weeks that, as a young woman, she spent with me in Kabul, Bamiyan (its Buddhas still intact), Band-e-Amir, and Mazar-i-Sharif.

Starr, from Annapolis, traveled in a VW Kombi, named Pigpen after the keyboardist of the Grateful Dead, that I had driven with two friends to Afghanistan. It took her only forty-three years to transcribe her jottings and so reverse time's arrow.

There I am, on August 2, 1973, my eighteenth birthday, in a cave beside the beautiful lakes of Band-e-Amir, "propped against bundles, surrounded by chickens, beautiful children, a kitten, a goat, women in the corners" eating. There, the next day, on the "terrible road" from Bamiyan to Mazar, "zooming, crashing along into the night."

There again, on August 10, at the Salang Pass (12,723 feet), camped out and cold with the engine bust. The next day, "we coasted 40 kilometers, stopped in desperation." Back in Kabul, I try a cake inspired, let us say, by the writings of Thomas De Quincey. It leads me to swoon. Starr writes, "During the night I heard Roger talking to Marcus about dying." Oh, man. She observes these three young men "about to enter Oxford" who "sit around and write in notebooks or read Turgenev."

I'm struck by the haphazardness of that journey; the fact that we drove across Iran; the way names likes Mazar and the Salang Pass have become synonymous with war; the idea of us teenagers thousands of miles from our parents, out of contact.

How much freer, in many ways, we were. I don't think it's that the world's more dangerous. I think it's that people are more frightened. Fear is a much-trafficked commodity.

Which brings me to Finnegan's wonderful book, a kind of hymn to freedom and passion. Freedom is inside you. It's the thing that cannot be denied. For Finnegan, that's surfing and writing. "How could you know your limits unless you tested them?" he asks—a question as true before the ferocious energy of the wave as before the infinite possibilities of the written form.

He's a near contemporary, embracing Kerouac and the Dead, contemptuous of what a friend calls "Suckcess," hitting the road without a map to find the perfect wave somewhere between Guam and Cape Town, a child of a zeitgeist he describes as "hippie culture, acid rock, hallucinogens, neo-Eastern mysticism, the psychedelic aesthetic." Like me he laments the loss of the lost places, the beaches he was first to tread.

A patch of coast may demand a lifetime of study. Wave love, he observes, "is a one way street." The wave, implacable, will turn on you. "Scenes feel mythic even as they unfold. I always feel a ferocious ambivalence: I want to be nowhere else; I want to be anywhere else." One near escape produces this catharsis: "On my knees in the sand, in the twilight, absolutely spent, I was surprised to find myself sobbing."

My son Blaise, who is twenty-one, asked was whether it's still possible to have such adventures. He thought not—too much control, too much Google Earth. I suggested that he might be wrong and that, on graduation, he might drive from New York to Patagonia. It's important to experience that "ferocious ambivalence," the threshold of freedom.

SYRIA'S WHITE ROSE

As people slumber, the horror unfolds. Some things never change.

FEBRUARY 18, 2016

BERLIN—At the end of Bertolt Brecht's *Life of Galileo*, there is a sharp exchange. Andrea Sarti, a student of the astronomer, says, "Unhappy is the land that breeds no hero." To which Galileo shoots back: "No, Andrea. Unhappy is the land that needs a hero."

Michael Wolffsohn, a German historian, mentioned Galileo's line the other evening with reference to Syria, an unhappy land of the dead and dying in need of heroes to redeem humanity. The hopelessness of resistance does not diminish its redemptive power in terrorized societies; in fact, hopelessness may even be one of the defining characteristics of heroic resistance.

Abdalaziz Alhamza, the young man sitting beside Wolffsohn at the German Council on Foreign Relations in Berlin, prompted the historian's reflections. "We don't have the necessity today to resist in Germany, because this is a free country," Wolffsohn said. "Resistance is the readiness to incur lethal personal risk."

That is what Alhamza has done. He is from Raqqa, the stronghold of the Islamic State, a town now synonymous with beheadings, immolation, enslavement of women, and every form of barbarism. Alhamza, who is twenty-four, left Syria two years ago and in April 2014 founded a resistance organization called Raqqa Is Being Slaughtered Silently (RBSS). ISIS has killed four of its members.

I was in the southern Turkish town of Sanliurfa in November to write about one of those murders. On October 30, ISIS beheaded Ibrahim Abdel Qader, age twenty-two. Qader had been working to publicize and document ISIS atrocities in Raqqa through online video and other reportage.

"We won't stop," Alhamza said. "We have too many friends and family dead. The only way we will stop is if ISIS kills us all or we go back home."

RBSS will not stop its efforts to spread word of the crimes of ISIS. To record is to resist evil; to forget is to permit its spread. As Czesław Miłosz wrote: "The poet remembers. / You may kill him—another will be born."

Wolffsohn drew a parallel between Alhamza's resistance to ISIS and that of the White Rose group to the Third Reich. Formed in 1942 by Munich University students and their professor, the White Rose, in the face of certain death, distributed leaflets denouncing Nazism. The first read: "Who among us has any conception of the dimensions of shame that will befall us and our children when one day the veil has fallen from our eyes and the most horrible of crimes—crimes that infinitely outdistance every human measure—reach the light of day?"

The "dimensions of shame" awaiting the perpetrators of and the bystanders to the crimes of the Syrian war are as yet unknown, but they will be ample. German has a better word than "bystander" for those—always the majority—who make their accommodations with evil. That word is *Mitläufer*—roughly, "fellow traveler."

There has been a lot of discussion of the origins of ISIS, of the complexity of defeating it, of its digital slickness, but little of its pure evil—its desecration of human life and its exaltation of death (even delivered by children).

To dwell on the group's iniquity—its contempt for humanity—would be to suggest the necessity of its immediate extirpation; and no Western government wants to deploy soldiers to do that. That is a moral capitulation, whatever else it may be.

Of course, ISIS is far from the Third Reich, as Wolffsohn conceded, even if its "absence of consideration for human life" is identical. But the parallels between the White Rose and RBSS are strong. As the historian told me: "The White Rose knew from the very beginning that they would lose but that their loss was necessary to show that humanity and human dignity cannot be wiped out completely. It's the same with the Raqqa group."

The White Rose distributed leaflets, six before its members were executed. The work of RBSS, some of whose members are still in Raqqa, is the digital leaflet. On the existence of that work our humanity hinges.

Alhamza, like most RBSS members in exile, now lives in Germany, having moved on from Turkey, where the ISIS threat was too great. His younger brother drowned trying to escape Syria. Countless family members and friends are dead. One friend, a doctor, joined ISIS; he needed money. Terror bends most people's will. But not all.

"It's been more than two years," Alhamza told me. "Western powers have held a lot of meetings, made speeches, and done nothing, although the Syrian regime crossed every red line. The regime created ISIS. We do not believe the West will help."

The second White Rose leaflet spoke of how hundreds of thousands of Jews had been killed by the Nazis in Poland while "the German people slumber on in dull, stupid sleep and encourage the Fascist criminals."

The United States and its allies slumber on. The loss and the risk are all of humanity's.

AN ANTI-SEMITISM OF THE LEFT

A look at growing British anti-Semitism. The rise of the leftist Jeremy Corbyn to the leadership of Britain's opposition Labour Party appeared to have empowered a far left for whom support of the Palestinians is uncritical and demonizaton of Israel necessary.

MARCH 7, 2016

LONDON—Last month, a co-chairman of the Oxford University Labour Club, Alex Chalmers, quit in protest at what he described as rampant anti-Semitism among members. A "large proportion" of the club "and the student left in Oxford more generally have some kind of problem with Jews," he said in a statement.

Chalmers referred to members of the executive committee "throwing around the term 'Zio,'" an insult used by the Ku Klux Klan; high-level expressions of "solidarity with Hamas" and explicit defense of "their tactics of indiscriminately murdering civilians"; and the dismissal of any concern about anti-Semitism as "just the Zionists crying wolf."

The zeitgeist on campuses these days, on both sides of the Atlantic, is one of identity and liberation politics. Jews, of course, are a minority, but through a fashionable cultural prism they are seen as the minority that isn't—that is to say, white, privileged, and identified with an "imperialist-colonialist" state, Israel. They are the anti-victims in a prevalent culture of victimhood; Jews, it seems, are the sole historical victim whose claim is dubious.

A recent Oberlin alumna, Isabel Storch Sherrell, wrote in a Facebook post of the students she'd heard dismissing the Holocaust as mere "white on white crime." As reported by David Bernstein in *The Washington Post*, she wrote of Jewish students, "Our struggle does not intersect with other forms of racism."

Noa Lessof-Gendler, a student at Cambridge University, complained last month in *Varsity*, a campus newspaper, that anti-Semitism was felt "in the word 'Zio' flung around in left-wing groups." She wrote, "I'm Jewish, but that doesn't mean I have Palestinian blood on my hands," or should feel nervous "about conversations in Hall when an Israeli speaker visits."

The rise of the leftist Jeremy Corbyn to the leadership of Britain's opposition Labour Party appears to have empowered a far left for whom support of the Palestinians is uncritical and for whom, in the words of Alan Johnson, a British political theorist, "that which the demonological Jew once was, demonological Israel now is."

Corbyn is perhaps no anti-Semite. But he has called Hamas and Hezbollah agents of "long-term peace and social justice and political justice in the whole region," and once invited to Parliament a Palestinian Islamist, Raed Salah, who has suggested Jews were absent from the World Trade Center on 9/11. Corbyn called him an "honored citizen." The "Corbynistas" on British campuses extol their fight against the "racist colonization of Palestine," as one Oxford student, James Elliott, put it. Elliott was narrowly defeated last month in a bid to become youth representative on Labour's national executive committee.

What is striking about the anti-Zionism derangement syndrome that spills over into anti-Semitism is its ahistorical nature. It denies the long Jewish presence in, and bond with, the Holy Land. It disregards the fundamental link between murderous European anti-Semitism and the decision of surviving Jews to embrace Zionism in the conviction that only a Jewish homeland could keep them safe. It dismisses the legal basis for the modern Jewish state in United Nations Resolution 181 of 1947. This was not "colonialism" but the post-Holocaust will of the world: Arab armies went to war against it and lost.

The Jewish state was needed. History had demonstrated that. That is why I am a Zionist—now a dirty word in Europe.

Today, it is Palestinians in the West Bank who are dehumanized through Israeli dominion, settlement expansion, and violence. The West Bank is the tomb of Israel as a Jewish and democratic state. Palestinians, in turn, incite against Jews and resort to violence, including random stabbings.

The oppression of Palestinians should trouble every Jewish conscience. But nothing can justify the odious "anti-Semitic anti-Zionism" (Johnson's term) that caused Chalmers to quit and is seeping into British and American campuses.

I talked to Aaron Simons, an Oxford student who was president of the university's Jewish Society. "There's an odd mental noise," he said. "In tone and attitude, the way you are talked to as a Jew in these left political circles reeks of hostility. These people have an astonishingly high bar for what constitutes anti-Semitism."

Criticism of Israel is one thing; it's needed in vigorous form. Demonization of Israel is another, a familiar scourge refashioned by the very politics—of identity and liberation—that should comprehend the millennial Jewish struggle against persecution.

THE MAP OF MY LIFE

A hymn to the hundreds of maps I could not quite throw away because they mapped my life.

MARCH 10, 2016

Life, among other things, is accumulation—of objects, papers, photographs, paintings, tax returns, love letters, and assorted things in the backs of drawers, the bottoms of closets, and the recesses of cellars. Stuff gathers. It piles up through the acquisitive instinct, nostalgia, and inertia. Some of it may be useful, a lot of it not.

Possessions can be uplifting if they are beautiful or merely comforting, signposts to a life, recalling the places they were acquired and with whom. On the other hand, they can feel imprisoning. Who has not had the urge just to be rid of everything and roam free? Humanity may broadly be divided into hoarders and disposers. They tend to have disagreements, especially when bound in a couple.

These thoughts crossed my mind as I picked my way through a bedroom I have used for several months for storage, mostly of books without shelves to place them on, but also of boxes I felt disinclined to open. Making a home is not a steady process but comes about in bursts, interspersed with inactivity.

In the midst of my clutter-clearing push, I stumbled on my maps—hundreds of maps, produced by companies like Michelin or Rand McNally or the British Ordnance Survey, charting the roads, tracks, and railroads of the Marseille region through Jerusalem to Paraguay by way of the Cheddar Gorge. Bearing witness—what journalists must do—involves moving around; for a long time there was only one way to get oriented. A good map in a bad place was a lifesaver.

The maps looked otherworldly, like old sewing machines or transistor radios from another era. I fingered them, unsure what to do. Google

Maps and GPS have taken over. A disembodied voice guides you to a destination whose geographic context is irrelevant. Technology siphons people into furrows. When the GPS breaks down, there is panic.

I thought of throwing all the maps away. Why keep them if I would no longer need them? Because I love maps—the way they render contour and scale, invite exploration. But that hardly seemed reason to hoard.

Then my eye fell on two maps of a country that no longer exists—Yugoslavia—and another map of the countries born from its death—Slovenia, Croatia, Bosnia, Serbia, etc.—and I was back in the wars of Yugoslavia's destruction in the 1990s. The smash of a shell in Sarajevo, the contraction in my stomach, the tapering valley and the death-spewing mountains, sweet coffee in the old city, a sign on the road south of Split pointing left to Sarajevo and straight to Dubrovnik. I always turned left, away from the sea, toward the besieged Bosnian capital. That was the road where, in 1994, I flipped over, crashed into a field, ended upside-down with Bosnian peasants trying to extricate me from the wreck.

I was alive, somehow. My son was born a few days later in Paris.

Life pivots on very little. It has its roads and byways. Italy was well represented—maps of Lake Como, Campania, Sicily. Covering Italy in the 1980s was a joy. Now I was back in Italy: that interview with then Prime Minister Bettino Craxi, who exuded an animal force and ended badly in Tunisia. The call, its menace unmistakable, in the midst of a Palermo night when I was investigating a four-part series on the Mafia for *The Wall Street Journal*. The umbrella pines in the Villa Borghese, the clay tennis courts playable through winter, the talkative Umbrian agro-scientist convinced he could cultivate truffles, the beans at Nino on the Via Borgognona, that shattering Velázquez portrait in Rome of Pope Innocent X.

These maps, it occurred to me, mapped my life more or less. I was transported. The Old City in Jerusalem near the Damascus Gate, market stalls piled with dates and pomegranates, Palestinians emerging from the Al-Aqsa Mosque on the El-Wad Road, Orthodox Jews bumping into them as they head toward the Western Wall, a crowd of Philippine Christians emerging from the Via Dolorosa carrying a crucifix they try to maneuver through these Arabs and Jews.

I was back there, too. Life is mingling and coupling despite the effort of every Middle Eastern fanatic to draw division. Yugoslavia died bloodily because it took such force to unmingle it.

I could not dispose of my redundant maps. My own borders were written into them. I do not want to live without them.

A confession, then: I tend toward hoarding, perhaps through trauma. A vivid memory is of my father standing in the garden in the London house where I spent most of my childhood, piling objects onto a fire. Into the flames went old toys, files, papers, and the "Don Bradman" cricket bat I had used as a child and he had used before me. That was after my mother's first suicide attempt, in preparation for a disastrous move.

After which the family was lost in unmapped territory.

BRITAIN'S BREXIT LEAP
IN THE DARK

Anger at growing inequality, the impunity of elites, and immigration erupted as Britain turned its back on the European Union. Trump's election, a shock of equal dimensions, was just months off.

JUNE 24, 2016

LONDON—The British have given the world's political, financial, and business establishment a massive kick in the teeth by voting to leave the European Union, a historic decision that will plunge Britain into uncertainty for years to come and reverses the integration on which the Continent's stability has been based.

Warnings about the dire consequences of a British exit from President Barack Obama, Britain's political leaders, major corporations based in Britain, and the International Monetary Fund proved useless. If anything, they goaded a mood of defiant anger against those very elites.

This resentment has its roots in many things but may be summed up as a revolt against global capitalism. To heck with the experts and political correctness was the predominant mood in the end. A majority of Britons had no time for the politicians that brought the world a disastrous war in Iraq, the 2008 financial meltdown, European austerity, stagnant working-class wages, high immigration, and tax havens for the superrich.

That some of these issues have no direct link to the European Union or its much-maligned Brussels bureaucrats did not matter. It was a convenient target in this restive moment that has also made Donald Trump the presumptive Republican nominee—and may now take him further still on a similar wave of nativism and antiestablishment rage.

David Cameron, the British prime minister prodded into holding the referendum by the right of his Conservative Party, said he would resign, staying on in a caretaker capacity for a few months. This was the right call, and an inevitable one. He has led the country into a debacle.

The pound duly plunged some 10 percent to its lowest level since 1985. Global markets were rattled. Mainstream European politicians lamented a sad day for Europe and Britain; rightists like Marine Le Pen in France exulted. The world has entered a period of grave volatility.

Ever-greater unity was a foundation stone since the 1950s not only of peace in Europe, putting an end to the repetitive wars that had ravaged generations of Europeans, but also of the global political order. Now all bets are off. A process of European unraveling may have begun. A core assumption of American foreign policy—that a united Europe had overcome its divisions—has been undermined.

Geert Wilders, the right-wing anti-immigrant Dutch politician, tweeted: "Hurrah for the British! Now it is our turn. Time for a Dutch referendum!" The European Union is more vulnerable than at any point since its inception. The sacred images of old—like French President François Mitterrand and German Chancellor Helmut Kohl hand-in-hand at Verdun—have lost their resonance. The travails of the euro, the tide of immigration (both within the European Union, from poorer to richer members, and from outside), and high unemployment have led to an eerie collective loss of patience, prudence, and memory. "Anything but this" has become a widespread sentiment; irrationality is in the air.

The colossal leap in the dark that a traditionally cautious people—the British—were prepared to take has to be taken seriously. It suggests that other such leaps could occur elsewhere, perhaps in Trump's America. A Trump victory in November is more plausible now, because it has an immediate precedent in a developed democracy ready to trash the status quo for the high-risk unknown.

Fifty-two percent of the British population was ready to face higher unemployment, a weaker currency, possible recession, political turbulence, the loss of access to a market of a half-billion people, a messy divorce that may take as long as two years to complete, a very long subsequent negotiation of Britain's relationship with Europe, and the tortuous redrafting of laws and trade treaties and environmental regulations—all for what the right-wing leader Nigel Farage daftly called "Independence Day." Britain was a sovereign nation before this vote in every significant sense. It remains so. Estrangement Day would be more apt.

The English were also prepared to risk something else: the breakup of the United Kingdom. Scotland voted to remain in the European Union by a margin of 62 percent to 38 percent. Northern Ireland voted to remain by 56 percent to 44 percent. The Scots will now likely seek a second referendum on independence.

Divisions were not only national. London voted overwhelmingly to remain. But the countryside, small towns, and hard-hit provincial industrial centers voted overwhelmingly to leave and carried the day. A Britain fissured between a liberal, metropolitan class centered in London and the rest was revealed.

Europe's failings—and they have been conspicuous over the past decade—are simply not sufficient to explain what Britain has done to itself. This was a vote against the global economic and social order that the first sixteen years of the twenty-first century have produced. Where it leads is unclear. The worst is not inevitable, but it is plausible. Britain will remain an important power. But it will punch beneath its weight. It faces serious, long-term political and economic risk.

Anger was most focused on the hundreds of thousands of immigrants coming into Britain each year, most from other European Union nations, like Poland. Farage's U.K. Independence Party, abetted by much of the press, was able to whip up a storm that conflated EU immigration with the trickle from the Middle East. Wild myths, like imminent Turkish membership in the European Union, were cultivated. Violence entered the campaign on a wave of xenophobia and take-our-country-back rhetoric.

In this light, it is not surprising that Trump supporters were delighted. Sarah Palin welcomed the "good news." One tweet from a supporter read: "I'm thrilled with U.K. 1st step—time 4 all the dominoes 2 fall, every country to leave & end the E.U."

Trump arrived in Britain on Friday, a timely visit. He said the vote to quit the EU was "a great thing" and the British "took back their country." He did not say from whom.

It is quite likely that Cameron's successor will be Boris Johnson, the bombastic, mercurial, and sometimes fact-lite former London mayor with his trademark mop of blond hair. Johnson was a leader of the campaign for "Brexit"; he may now reap his political reward. The Era of the Hair looms.

Timothy Garton Ash, the historian, paraphrasing Churchill on democracy, wrote before the referendum: "The Europe we have today is the worst possible Europe, apart from all the other Europes that have been tried from time to time."

It was a wise call to prudence in the imperfect real world. Now, driven by myths about sovereignty and invading hordes, Britain has ushered in another time of treacherous trial for the European Continent and for itself.

My nephew wrote on Facebook that he had never been less proud of his country. I feel the same way about the country I grew up in and left.

MY DAUGHTER THE POLE

My daughter decided to become a Pole in order to remain a European Union citizen after Brexit. She opted to be a citizen of the country where her great-grandmother Frimeta Gelband was gassed by the Nazis as a Jew.

AUGUST 22, 2016

The British vote to leave the European Union has had many consequences, among them a plunge in sterling, sagging business confidence, an identity crisis in Britain's two main political parties, confusion, and uncertainty. One of its less known results is that my daughter Adele is now contemplating becoming a Pole.

"Dad," she said to me the other night over dinner in Brooklyn, "if Britain starts up this Article 50 thing, I'm going to get Polish citizenship." Article 50 of the Lisbon Treaty lays out how a country quits the European Union. Because it is in a muddle over what to do, the British government has not yet triggered this procedure. But it almost certainly will.

On the face of it, Adele's choice is a curious one. The Nazis gassed her maternal great-grandmother Frimeta Gelband in Poland. Adele's grandmother Amalia Gelband, aged eleven in 1942, found herself alone in Nazi-occupied Poland, a Jewish girl hounded. She changed her name to Helena Kowalska, passed herself off as a Catholic, found work on a farm, and survived Germany's attempted annihilation of European Jewry.

After the war, Polish authorities stuck Amalia in a Jewish orphanage in Kraków, where she remained for three years. All she wanted of Poland was to get out of it. Her mother, her cousins, aunts, and uncles had all been slaughtered.

Amalia Baranek, her married name, is now a Brazilian citizen living in Rio. She has been celebrating the wondrous Olympics that have just ended. She has little time for denigrators of Brazil, the country that took her in. She has been living in Rio since 1948, the year she was at last reunited with her father, who had left Poland shortly before the war. There is no prouder Brazilian than Amalia. She knows a country whose spirit is generous.

Adele, who is eighteen and a sophomore at the University of Southern California, adores her Brazilian grandmother. Still, she's ready to become a Pole.

I am not sure whom to blame for this, or whether "blame" is the right word (see below). The world was full of fear and anger in the 1930s, enough to propel a deranged hatemonger and anti-Semite to power in Germany. It is full of fear and anger again today, enough to propel Britain out of the European Union and a man as flawed as Donald Trump to the brink of the American presidency.

The troubled psyche requires a scapegoat. For Hitler, it was the Jews, among others. Today scapegoats are sought everywhere for the widespread feeling that something is amiss: that jobs are being lost; that precariousness has replaced security; that incomes are stagnant or falling; that politicians have been bought; that the bankers behind the 2008 meltdown got off unscathed; that immigrants are free riders; that inequality is out of control; that tax systems are skewed; that terrorists are everywhere.

These scapegoats, on either side of the Atlantic, include Syrian refugees, African migrants, Polish workers in Britain, Mexicans, Muslims, and, now that it's open season for hatred, just about anyone deemed "foreign."

After the madness against otherness comes remorse. The descendants of families murdered in or driven out of Poland during the Holocaust are now eligible to apply for ancestral citizenship. Some of Adele's close relatives have already become Poles.

Of course, a Polish passport today is also a passport to work anywhere in the European Union, the greatest political creation of the second half of the twentieth century, a borderless union of half a billion people (at least until Britain leaves). Young people—including all the young Britons who voted overwhelmingly to remain—want to live, love, and work anywhere in Europe they choose.

Adele is one of them. She loves London, where she completed high school. She loves its openness. She cannot believe her British passport may soon—unless sanity is somehow restored—no longer be a European Union passport. And so Poland beckons, just as Germany, with a similar law, has beckoned since Brexit for some British Jews of German origin. History comes full-circle.

In a way, this doubling back is right. Adele owes her existence to a brave Pole named Mieczysław Kasprzyk, who in 1942 risked his life to hide Amalia in the attic of his family's farmhouse near Kraków. He knew the Gelband family, had been outraged by the killing of Jews, and wondered in disbelief, as he once said to me, "How can you not help if a child asks?"

Plenty of Poles collaborated, but some did not. May Kasprzyk's moral clarity inspire Adele, as a Pole or not, and may the world never again descend into the darkness he felt bound to resist.

WE NEED
"SOMEBODY SPECTACULAR":
VIEWS FROM TRUMP COUNTRY

I visited Kentucky and concluded, two and a half months before the election, that Trump could well win. In Trump country, people were clear-eyed and lucid and ready to take a wild risk for change in full knowledge of Trump's flaws.

Appalachian voters know perfectly well the candidate is dangerous.
But they're desperate for change.

SEPTEMBER 9, 2016

PARIS, Kentucky—After Bill Bissett, the president of the Kentucky Coal Association, told me, "President Obama cares more about Paris,

France, than he does about Paris, Kentucky"—a sentiment that seems broadly shared around here—I decided to check out this little town with a big name set amid the verdant undulations of picket-fenced Kentucky horse country. Soon enough I ran into Cindy Hedges, whose boot store stands on Main Street and whose hours, as described by a sign on the door, are: "If I'm here, I'm here. If I ain't, I ain't."

Straight talk, the way the people of this particular Paris like it, is the kind of talk they recognize in Donald J. Trump. Hedges is a garrulous woman who says she's "never met a stranger." But recent times have tried her affability. Her business has been slow. Her husband, Mitch, lost his job as the coal business collapsed, she has been withdrawing money from savings, and the couple are struggling to afford health insurance. All of which has led her to the conviction that the country is off-track and needs "somebody spectacular to get us halfway straight."

For her, that somebody is Trump. She voted for Barack Obama in 2008, and says her political choices are gut-driven rather than party-driven. "I have never been this political," she tells me. "This is the most fired up I've ever been for a candidate." She believes Trump will get business going, revoke trade deals she sees as draining domestic jobs, and "clean up the mess Obama has left us." But what, I ask, of Trump's evident character flaws? "Sure, he's kind of a loose cannon, but he tells it the way it is and, if elected, people will be there to calm him down a bit, tweak a word or two in his speeches. And I just don't trust Hillary Clinton."

Kentucky voted twice for Bill Clinton before going solidly Republican in presidential elections. Now Kentuckians are clambering aboard the Trump train—and to heck with its destination. Obama is blamed for the collapse of coal, particularly in eastern Kentucky, and the ever-more-stringent standards of the Environmental Protection Agency. Beyond that, the blame is aimed at airy-fairy liberals more concerned about climate change—often contested or derided—than about Americans trying to make their house payments.

The number of Kentucky coal jobs has plunged to fewer than sixty-five hundred from about eighteen thousand when Obama took office; the number fell 6.9 percent between this April and June alone. Hillary Clinton's words in Ohio—"We're going to put a lot of coal miners and coal companies out of business"—echo on Republican radio ads, plucked out of context from her pledge to replace those jobs with opportunities in clean, renewable energy. By contrast, Trump declared in West Virginia in May that miners should "get ready, because you are going to be working your asses off!"

"I don't believe Obama has a whiteboard on how he's going to torture us, but he has," Bissett told me at his office in Lexington. "I cannot tell you how rabid the support for Trump is."

That support is proving resilient. The postconvention Trump free fall has run into the obstinacy of his appeal—an appeal that seems to defy every gaffe, untruth, and insult. The race is tightening once again because Trump's perceived character—a strong leader with a simple message, never flinching from a fight, cutting through political correctness with a bracing bluntness—resonates in places like Appalachia, where courage, country, and cussedness are core values.

"Trump's appeal is nationalistic, the authoritarian shepherd of the flock," Al Cross, an associate professor at the University of Kentucky, told me. "That's why evangelical Christians are willing to vote for this twice-divorced man who brags about the size of his penis. There's a strong belief here still in America as special and exceptional, and Obama is seen as having played that down."

But the Trump magnetism goes deeper than resentment at Obama's regretful tone from Havana to Hiroshima. It seems to go beyond the predictable Republican domination in this part of the country. There's a sense, crystallized in coal's steady demise, that, as the political scientist Norman Ornstein put it to me, "Somebody is taking everything you are used to and you had"—your steady middle-class existence, your values, your security. It's not that the economy is bad in all of Kentucky; the arrival of the auto industry has been a boon, and the unemployment rate is just 4.9 percent. It's that all the old certainties have vanished.

Far from the metropolitan hubs inhabited by the main beneficiaries of globalization's churn, many people feel disenfranchised from both main political parties, angry at stagnant wages and growing inequality, and estranged from a prevailing liberal urban ethos. I heard a lot about how Obama has not been supportive enough of the police, about how white lives matter, too, and about how illegal—as in illegal immigrant—means illegal, just as robbing a bank is. For anyone used to New York chatter, or for that matter London or Paris chatter, Kentucky is a through-the-looking-glass experience. There are just as many certainties; they are simply the opposite ones, whether on immigration, police violence toward African Americans, or guns. America is now tribal, with each tribe imbibing its own social-media-fed ranting.

The Clintons were feted here in the 1990s, but two decades on, Hillary Clinton is viewed with cool suspicion. That's because both the economy and values have moved on, too. Jobs went south to Mexico or east to Asia. Somewhere on the winding road from whites-only bathrooms to choose-your-gender bathrooms, many white blue-collar Kentucky workers—and the state is 85.1 percent white—feel their country got lost. The FDR Democrats who became Reagan Democrats and then Clinton Democrats could well be November's Trump Democrats.

America is no longer white enough for that to be decisive, but it is significant. To these people, Trump's "Make America Great Again" is not the empty rhetoric of a media-savvy con artist from Queens but a last-ditch rallying cry for the soul of a changing land where minorities will be the majority by the middle of the century.

Hazard, set in the mountains of eastern Kentucky, is a once-bustling town with its guts wrenched out. On Main Street, the skeleton of a mall that burned down last year presents its charred remains for dismal contemplation. Young people with drugged eyes lean against boarded-up walls on desolate streets. The whistle of trains hauling coal, once as regular as the chiming of the hours, has all but vanished. So have the coal trucks spewing splinters of rock that shattered windshields. In the age of cheap natural gas and mountaintop removal mining, a coal town is not where you want to be.

Hazard is in Perry County, where unemployment is above 10 percent. On a bench opposite the county courthouse, on the Starbucks-free Main Street, I found Steve Smith and Paul Bush. Smith used to work underground at the Starfire mine. He earned as much as fifteen hundred dollars a week, but was laid off a while ago. His unemployment has dried up and he has four children to feed. His family scrapes by on his wife's income as a nurse. He'd been in court over a traffic offense; now an idle afternoon stretched away.

"Trump's going to get us killed, probably!" he told me. "But I'll vote for him anyway over Hillary. If you vote for Hillary you vote for Obama, and he's made it impossible to ship coal. This place is about dried up. A job at Wendy's is the only thing left. We may have to move."

"Yeah, another year without change and they'll be shutting Hazard down," Bush suggested.

He was awaiting his son, in court on a drug charge for the painkiller Percocet. A retired operator of heavy equipment for the Road Department, Bush said his son did nothing, "just a few odd jobs." He continued: "Obama's probably never known hardship. He and Hillary don't get it. At least Trump don't hold nothing back: if he don't like something, he tells you about it."

His son's girlfriend emerged from the courthouse. "They locked him up," she said.

"Why?"

"He failed one of the drug tests."

"Well, ain't nothin' we can do about it," Bush said.

There are people here who are not resigned, people thinking about what can be done about a post-coal Hazard. Self-reliance remains an important Appalachian value even if many people are "on the draw." An initiative backed by Congressman Hal Rogers, a Republican, to bring broadband access to rural areas in Kentucky has been announced.

Jenny Williams, an English teacher at Hazard Community and Technical College, told me it's past time to get over divisions between "Friends of Coal"—a popular movement and bumper sticker—and anti-coal environmentalists to forge a creative economy around agriculture, ecotourism, education, and small-scale manufacture. Coal, she observed, was never going to last forever. "How could any idiot support Trump?" she said. "But when you've been on seventy thousand dollars a year in coal mines, and your life's pulled out from under you, who else can you be mad at but the government?"

That anger simmers. It's directed at Obama, and by extension Clinton, and by further extension a Democratic Party that, as the former Democratic senator Jim Webb from Virginia told me, "has now built its constituency based on ethnic groups other than white working people." The frustration of these people, whether they are in Kentucky, or Texas, or throughout the Midwest, is acute. They are looking for "someone who will articulate the truth of their disenfranchisement," as Webb put it. Trump, for all his bullying petulance, has come closest to being that politician, which is why millions of Americans support him.

Bissett, the Coal Association president, made clear to me that he did not dismiss the emissions concerns about coal; what bothers him is what he sees as Obama's and the EPA's refusal to seek a reasonable balance between the economy and the environment. The administration, he argues, has moved the goalposts to kill coal. It is this that feels punitive. For example, the EPA's Clean Power Plan, first presented in 2014 with no backing from Congress, requires every state to submit proposals for reducing carbon-dioxide emissions by 2018. The Supreme Court, in a five-to-four decision, blocked the initiative early this year. But that was just before Justice Antonin Scalia died. "We need Trump for a reasonable Supreme Court and an EPA no longer skewed against fossil fuels," Bissett argued. "A lot of jobs here still depend on coal and cheap electricity. That's why Clinton is toxic right now."

At Jabo's Coal River Grille, a popular restaurant in Hazard, I met Phillip Clemons, known as "Jabo" ("perhaps because I used to box"). He owns the Locust Grove Mining Company, with fifteen employees, down from 150. As a hedge, he opened the restaurant, where he was working a shift to keep payroll down. He called the election a "terrible choice," but he's with Trump, because he believes that, as a businessman, Trump will respect the need to "balance the books," past bankruptcies notwithstanding. "Obama just hates coal," he said. "I don't dislike people because of their color. I liked Herman Cain a lot. I can tell you the only Black person who's ever been mean to me is Barack Obama."

What's happened to eastern Kentucky is devastating, but far from unique. At France's Diner, another popular Hazard hangout, Daniel Walker, who works from home for a medical-software company, told me: "Look, I lived for a while in Mansfield, Ohio, and General Motors moved its stamping plant there to Mexico, with the loss of thousands of factory jobs. The decent middle-class life is gone." There are many places, here and abroad, where people feel shoved aside by technology and cheap global labor, leading them to seek radical political answers. Trump is one of those answers; Brexit, the surprise British vote to leave the European Union, was another; the fall of Chancellor Angela Merkel of Germany next year could be a third, after she trailed an anti-immigrant party in a local election this month.

Trump can't reverse globalization. Nor is he likely to save coal in an era of cheap natural gas. His gratuitous insults, evident racism, hair-trigger temper, and lack of preparation suggest he would be a reckless, even perilous, choice for the Oval Office. I don't think he is a danger to the Republic, because American institutions are stronger than Trump's ego, but that the question even arises is troubling.

Still, in a climate where disruption is sought at any cost (whether political in Hazard or economic in Silicon Valley), it would be foolhardy to suggest that Trump cannot win. He can; and he can in part because of the liberal intellectual arrogance that dismisses the economic, social, and cultural problems his rise has underscored. Whatever happens in November, these problems will persist, and it will take major public and private investment and an unlikely rebirth of bipartisanship in Washington to make any dent in them.

Back in Paris—the Kentucky one—I sit down in a coffee shop with Cindy Hedges and her husband, Mitch. He worked for more than thirty years as a welder and then a supervisor in a factory that refurbished mining equipment. It was dirty work—coal is black, grease is black, hydraulic oil is black—but it was a good living. He lost his job in February, before returning on a temporary contract a couple of weeks ago, and when I ask him why his full-time employment disappeared, the answer is by now familiar: the EPA and Obama, for whom, like his wife, he voted in 2008. But when I turn to this political season, he springs a surprise.

"Look, there's nobody to vote for," he says. "Trump is an idiot, he pisses everyone off, he's scary, he'll pump his mouth off to some foreign country and we'll be at war. He's a billionaire on a power trip with as much reason to be president as I have. If Trump had shut up, he'd win the election. So do you vote for the one who's going to lie, or the one who takes you to war? I'm leaning Hillary."

"Oh, come on, Mitch!" says Cindy.

"What? With Bill Clinton the economy was rolling. I was working a fifty-hour week and my 401(k) outperformed my salary. He's going to be advising Hillary, suggesting she needs to do this or this."

"They don't get along, Mitch."

"Well, I'm scared of Trump."

"I guess we'll cancel each other out, then," says Cindy.

At the boot store, Carrie McCall, a FedEx driver, appears with a package.

"I love Trump," she declares. "He shoots from the hip."

But, I ask, isn't that dangerous?

"I don't care. After all we've been through, I just don't care."

HOW DICTATORSHIPS ARE BORN

An early warning of Trump's threat to American democracy.

OCTOBER 14, 2016

PALO ALTO, California—"Something is happening here but you don't know what it is / Do you, Mister Jones?"

Of course Bob Dylan deserved the Nobel Prize for Literature. We're all Mister Jones now. It's the wildest political season in the history of the United States.

Just to make his pedigree clear, Donald Trump is now suggesting that Hillary Clinton "meets in secret with international banks to plot the destruction of U.S. sovereignty, in order to enrich these global financial powers, her special interest friends, and her donors."

What was it the Nazis called the Jews? Oh, yes, "rootless parasites," that's it. For Stalin they were rootless cosmopolitans. Just saying.

Societies slide into dictatorship more often than they lurch, one barrier falling at a time. "Just a buffoon," people say, "and vulgar." And then it's too late.

Today, millions of Americans who plan to vote for Trump are apparently countenancing violence against their neighbors, people who might be different from them, perhaps Muslim or Latino. It's easy to inject the virus of hatred: just point a gun.

That Trump traffics in violence is irrefutable. His movement wants action—deportations, arrests, assassination, and torture have been mooted. The most worrying thing is not that Trump likes Vladimir Putin, the butcher of Aleppo, but that he apes Vladimir Putin.

Speaking of Latinos, here's what happened the other day to Veronica Zuleta, who was born in El Salvador and became an American citizen more than a decade ago. She was in the upscale Draeger's Market in Menlo Park when the man next to her said: "You should go to Safeway. This store is for white people."

Zuleta was shocked. Never had she encountered a comment like that about her brown skin. But even the Democratic bastion of Silicon Valley is not immune to the Trump effect: once-unsayable things can now be said the world over. "Go back to where you came from" is the phrase du jour.

In the three months after the Brexit vote in Britain, homophobic attacks rose 147 percent compared with the same period a year earlier. It's open season for bigots.

Financial and emotional pressures have been mounting on Zuleta. She lives in what the visionaries of Google, Facebook, and the like consider the center of the universe. Where else, after all, are people thinking seriously about attaining immortality; or life on Mars; or new floating cities atop the oceans; or a universal basic income for everyone once the inevitable happens and artificial intelligence renders much of humanity redundant?

Y Combinator, a big start-up incubator, has announced it will conduct a basic-income experiment with a hundred families in Oakland, giving them between one and two thousand dollars a month for up to a year. Just to see what people do when they have nothing more to do. Oh, brave new world.

Back in the present, prices for real estate have soared. Zuleta lives in a modest rented place on what used to be the wrong side of the tracks, in East Menlo Park, east of Route 101, which runs down the Valley. As it happens, her home is now a couple of blocks from Facebook's sprawling headquarters, designed by Frank Gehry, which opened last year. She asked about a job in the kitchen, to no avail. She struggles to make ends meet.

Facebook, she told me, "is intimidating for people like me. It's, like, get out of here if you don't know anything about technology."

For its part, Facebook says it cares about and invests in the local community—$350,000 in grants donated to local nonprofits this year and last, new thermal-imaging cameras for the local fire district, and so on. Its revenue in 2015 was $17.9 billion.

Zuleta works from six-thirty in the morning until midnight, cleaning homes, driving children to school and activities, running errands for wealthy families (like shopping for them at Draeger's), and cleaning offices at night. In between she tries to care for her two young children. The other day, she was in the kitchen, collapsed, and found herself in the hospital.

"The doctor said I need to sleep and relax," she told me. "But I can't!"

Life is like that these days for many Americans: implacable and disorienting. As a Latina, Zuleta said she would never vote for Trump, but she feels overwhelmed.

Something is happening here but you don't know what it is, do you, Mister Jones?

BROKEN MEN IN PARADISE

Refugees do not flee out of choice but because they have run out of choices. I traveled to Manus, Papua New Guinea, to document the way Australia had consigned more than nine hundred asylum seekers from some of the most terrifying places on earth to a long season of hell.

DECEMBER 9, 2016

MANUS, Papua New Guinea—The plane banks over the dense tropical forest of Manus Island, little touched, it seems, by human hand.

South Pacific waters lap onto deserted beaches. The jungle glistens, impenetrable. At the unfenced airport, built by occupying Japanese forces during World War II, a sign welcomes you to "our very beautiful island paradise in the sun."

It could be that, a sixty-mile-long slice of heaven. But for more than nine hundred asylum seekers from across the world banished by Australia to this remote corner of the Papua New Guinea archipelago, Manus has been hell: a three-and-a-half-year exercise in mental and physical cruelty conducted in near secrecy beneath the green canopy of the tropics.

A road, newly paved by Australia as part payment to its former colony for hosting this punitive experiment in refugee management, leads to Lorengau, a capital of romantic name and unromantic misery. Here I find Benham Satah, a Kurd who fled persecution in the western Iranian city of Kermanshah. Detained on Australia's Christmas Island after crossing in a smuggler's boat from Indonesia and later forced onto a Manus-bound plane, he has languished here since August 27, 2013.

Endless limbo undoes the mind. But going home could mean facing death: refugees do not flee out of choice but because they have no choice. Satah's light-brown eyes are glassy. His legs tremble. A young man with a college degree in English, he is now nameless, a mere registration number—FRT009—to Australian officials.

"Sometimes I cut myself," he says, "so that I can see my blood and remember, 'Oh, yes! I am alive.'"

Reza Barati, his former roommate at what the men's ID badges call the Offshore Processing Center (Orwell would be proud), is dead. A fellow Iranian Kurd, he was killed, aged twenty-three, on February 17, 2014. Satah witnessed the tall, quiet volleyball player being beaten to death after a local mob scaled the wall of the facility. Protests by asylum seekers had led to rising tensions with the Australian authorities and their Manus enforcers.

The murder obsesses Satah but constitutes a mere fraction of the human cost of a policy that, since July 19, 2013, has sent more than two thousand asylum seekers and refugees to Manus and the tiny Pacific island nation of Nauru, far from inquiring eyes. (Unable to obtain a press visa to visit Manus, I went nonetheless.)

The toll among Burmese, Sudanese, Somali, Lebanese, Pakistani, Iraqi, Afghan, Syrian, Iranian, and other migrants is devastating: self-immolation, overdoses, death from septicemia as a result of medical negligence, sexual abuse, and rampant despair. A recent United Nations High Commissioner for Refugees report by three medical experts found that 88 percent of the 181 asylum seekers and refugees examined on Manus were suffering from depressive disorders, including, in some cases, psychosis.

The world's refugee crisis, with its sixty-five million people on the move, more than at any time since 1945, knows no more sustained, sinister, or surreal exercise in cruelty than the South Pacific quasi-prisons Australia has established for its trickle of the migrant flood.

Australia, like Europe but on a much smaller scale, faces a genuine dilemma: What to do about desperate migrants trying by any means to gain asylum? Their journeys across the world have fueled rightist movements in many developed societies. Anxiety, whether related to jobs or to terrorism, is high and, as Donald Trump demonstrated, scapegoating is effective. Approaches to the crisis have varied. Angela Merkel, the German chancellor, has taken in more than a million. But the Australian government argues that toughness is the only way to prevent the country from being overwhelmed.

It has "stopped the boats" and the Indonesian smugglers behind them: this is the essence of Australia's case. The government says it has prevented deaths like those in the Mediterranean, where more than four thousand migrants have drowned this year. By turning back the "queue jumpers," a phrase that resonates in a nation devoted to a "fair go" for all, it has safeguarded Australia's right to select who gets to people a vast and empty country. The official vow that those marooned on Manus and Nauru will never live in Australia has assumed doctrinal vehemence.

In Peter Dutton, the immigration minister, the country has its own little Trump. Last May he portrayed the asylum seekers as illiterates bent on stealing Australian jobs, and he has suggested "mistakes" were made in letting in too many Lebanese Muslim immigrants. His soft bigotry resonates with enough voters to sway elections.

At the same time, Manus and Nauru are a growing embarrassment to Australia, a party to all major human-rights treaties. "There is an increasing realization that this is unsustainable," Madeline Gleeson, an Australian human-rights lawyer, told me.

Prime Minister Malcolm Turnbull knows this and needs a way out. After Omid Masoumali, a young Iranian, burned himself to death on Nauru this year, a cartoon by Cathy Wilcox captured Australia's shame. Above a man in flames was the caption "Not drowning."

The result is a one-time agreement with the United States, announced last month. America will, over an unspecified period, take in an unspecified number of the refugees, with priority going to the women, children, and families who are on Nauru. The single men on Manus would presumably bring up the rear, if accepted at all with Trump in office.

Turnbull has said he's confident Trump will not torpedo the deal. But when I asked Benham Satah if he thought he would soon be in the United States, he drew on a cigarette and gazed out to sea. "After three years suffering here, I know only this: unless you see it, don't believe it."

In the early morning at the Lorengau covered market, another Australian-funded project, women lay out produce and wares. Pickings are slim: pineapples, papaya, and small bunches of peanuts. Giant turtles with prices scrawled on their bellies flap in expiration as the sun rises and flies hover.

Betel nut has pride of place on many tables. Chewing the nut is a Manus habit often manifested in scarlet lips and rotting teeth. Betel, a mild stimulant, prompts what June Polomon, who works in the market, called "our tendency to be nonstop chatterers, just like our noisy friarbirds."

Visiting Manus in 1928, Margaret Mead, the American anthropologist, described a scene little changed nine decades later: "He puts a betel nut in his mouth, leisurely rolls a pepper leaf into a long funnel, bites off the end, and dipping the spatula into the powdered lime, adds a bit of lime to the mixture he is already chewing vigorously."

As they chew, the people of Manus discuss property (familial attachment to land is fierce), daughters' dowries, and the many hundreds of asylum seekers who—unexpected and unexplained—were deposited in 2013 at the island's Lombrum Naval Base, originally established by United States forces in 1944 under General Douglas MacArthur.

"If Australia had cared, it would have told us something, talked to our village leaders, who are important," Polomon told me. "We've been used in a neocolonial way."

That is also the view of Charlie Benjamin, the Manus governor, whom I found in an indignant mood. "It's just morally wrong to dump these people here and then say, 'Never Australia,'" he said. "Our understanding was, we'd help a process, and genuine refugees would move on, but no process exists." He described endless wrangling with the Australian authorities over roads he believes they should pay for—the western half of the island is still so inaccessible the governor said it took him six hours to drive the fifty miles to his village.

Under the money-for-migrants deal between Canberra and the Papua New Guinea government in Port Moresby, Australia promised its former colony hundreds of millions of dollars, but chiefly for projects outside Manus. The sixty thousand inhabitants of Manus were never consulted. Nor, of course, were the asylum seekers and refugees. When they arrived, they had no idea where they were. Seeing Black Papuans, many thought they were in Africa. For almost three years, they were held in the detention camp, humiliated, and intermittently terrorized.

Last April, the Papua New Guinea Supreme Court ordered an end to "the unconstitutional and illegal detention of the asylum seekers or transferees at the relocation center on Manus"; it was an offense "against their rights and freedoms." To which Dutton, the immigration minister, promptly responded that nobody in Manus "will settle in Australia."

The only change resulting from the ruling is that refugees can now leave the camp during the day and take buses into Lorengau.

"We're just in a bigger prison," Abdirahman Ahmed, a Somali refugee, told me. The Shabab jihadi militia killed his father and brother in Mogadishu. "Sometimes I think maybe if I die it's better. If you die there's no question in front of you, no interpreter between you and God, no immigration, no Australia. We are not human, just a signpost: If you want to come to Australia you will end up in Manus with three years of trauma and torture."

They are the walking dead, suspended in a dreamland, staring out at shimmering islets. Abdul Aziz Muhamat's lips are trembling. He is from Darfur and recalls how Sudanese government forces bound a villager's

limbs to four horses "and they tore him up." The soldiers put children
in a fuel-doused hut and torched it. "I can see it like yesterday," he says.

With an uncle's help, Aziz—the name he now uses—fled: Khartoum
Airport, Yemenia Airways Flight 632 ("I still remember the number") to
Sana, on to Dubai, and from there to Jakarta. He is met by a Sudanese
man who whisks him south to Bogor, where he hides in a house with
Iranians, Pakistanis, Burmese, and others. It is mid-August 2013.

They move on by truck at night, then paddle in canoes to an island,
and board a rickety boat crammed with fifty people. "I asked where we
were going," Aziz tells me, "and this guy said Australia." But after twelve
hours at sea, with the boat foundering, they turn back. Five people
drown.

When Aziz tries again, in October, his boat is intercepted by the
Australian Navy and he is thrown into a detention center on Christmas
Island with more than forty others. Finally, an Australian immigration
officer tells them they will be flown to Manus, "a very dangerous place
full of contagious diseases—if you touch a local, sanitize yourself."

"I have a question," Aziz says.

"That's it. I cannot answer questions," says the immigration officer.

"If you know these things exist on Manus Island, why do you want
to send us there?"

Aziz says he's in a cage. The whole island is a cage. Then he says he's
in a hole. He has no feelings, no desire. There's no point asking why. It's
been too long. At first conditions in the detention center are primitive,
hundreds of men crammed into makeshift compounds or tents, scant
food, bullying expat staff contracted by Australia, constant threats from
a special Papuan police riot squad flown in at Australian expense—and
no information, no "process." Nothing.

Frustration boils up in early 2014. For weeks, there are peaceful
protests every evening, chants of "Freedom." But they have no effect,
and the asylum seekers are told that "processing" could take a decade:
Kafka in the tropics. Anger turns to rage. Two Iranians try to escape and
are beaten up. Local thugs with machetes and bush knives, drunk on
moonshine, goaded and abetted by some international security staff,
pile into the camp. Shots are fired. Reza Barati is killed. Aziz, his toe broken, finds himself in the clinic among "a hundred and seventy guys lying

on concrete, some conscious, some unconscious, bodies full of blood. I thought I was back in Darfur."

Dump men in the middle of nowhere, confine them, abuse them, suspend them in limbo, and this is what you get.

The riot changes nothing.

A year later, in January 2015, hundreds of men begin a hunger strike. Several sew their mouths shut. The strike persists for two weeks. The authorities break it by throwing Aziz, Benham Satah, and others into solitary confinement in windowless containers known as the *chauka* (named after a bird unique to Manus).

The hunger strike changes nothing.

Australia has relied on the remoteness and secrecy of its program: out of sight, out of mind. Keep the press out. Impose draconian nondisclosure clauses in contracts for everyone who works there. Even pass a federal law that can send whistle-blowers to prison. On the whole, it has worked.

Still, the ugliness is beginning to seep out. In forty-one months, these stranded men have had only two pieces of good news: the Papua New Guinea Supreme Court ruling, and now the Australian deal with the United States.

"The deal represents a long-overdue concession from the government that it cannot leave people on Manus and Nauru forever," Daniel Webb, a lawyer at the Melbourne Human Rights Law Centre, told me. "That concession is way overdue, but it does not end their suffering."

Aziz, a smart young man who now has dreams of becoming a human-rights lawyer, said the policy is "not about stopping boats. I think it's about using innocent people as political tools to win elections."

Moving the asylum seekers elsewhere to be processed was not in itself unlawful, so long as the process was fair and efficient and met basic human-rights standards. There should have been explanatory sessions with the local authorities, clarity over who was running facilities, zero detention, and an Australian-led regional effort to secure a decent life for the refugees. None of this occurred.

Instead, Australia, briefly under a Labour Party government and then under the Conservatives, has effectively argued that the end (discouraging human smuggling) justifies the means (cruelty). As Hugh

Mackay, a social researcher, observed, this is "the very same principle used to justify torture." And even so, boats are still being turned around by a huge naval deployment.

A strange hysteria about the "boat people" seems to have blinded Australia to what is being perpetrated in its name. The country was founded on a similar principle to "offshore processing": Britain's dispatch in the late eighteenth century of convicts to a faraway land in Oceania, where they, too, would be invisible.

Its subsequent history has included the slaughter and incarceration of the native Aboriginal people; the White Australia policy, under which a vast land mass was seen as threatened by Black people and other nonwhites emanating from places like Papua New Guinea; the "stolen generation" policy, under which tens of thousands of Aboriginal children were taken from their families and placed in white homes; and now this disgraceful consignment of asylum seekers, many of them dark-skinned and Muslim, to faraway islands where they are left to fester with the "natives."

"Australians have a tendency to feel vulnerable," Amelia Lester, the editor of the magazine *Good Weekend*, told me. "We're so far from anywhere, it breeds a kind of paranoia."

Just twenty-four million people live in Australia, a country twice the size of India, where 1.25 billion live. Might there be room to squeeze in two thousand more? Australia has not known a recession in a quarter century. Perhaps it is hard to imagine what humiliation and despair are. But it is time to imagine; they are right here, across the water.

"Whatever the policy challenge, deliberate cruelty to thousands of innocent people is never the solution," Webb told me.

One measure of the government's obsession is that it has introduced legislation to impose a lifetime ban from Australia for anyone held at one of the camps. So, in theory, a man from Manus could go to the United States under the recently announced deal, become a Harvard professor, and never be able to visit Sydney.

Another is that it insists that the roughly 370 people who were moved from Manus or Nauru to Australia as "transitory persons" because they were injured in riots, or sexually assaulted, or were dying, or pregnant, or had broken down (like the wife of the Iranian who self-immolated) cannot stay in Australia. If they want to be considered for the American deal, they would have to return to one of the islands to be "processed." The "transitory persons" include about forty children. This is madness.

Lynne Elworthy, a mental-health nurse, is one Australian who knows the agony of Manus and Nauru. She's worked on both islands, and spoke to me in brave defiance of the nondisclosure rules meant to gag her. "Some cope better, focus on gym, and seem to do okay," she said. "But many men in Manus are withdrawn, skinny, depressed, and worn out, hopeless, with plummeting lows. It's quite obvious to see this. They exist in a lifeless pit."

She continued: "Apart from the way the whites treated the Aborigines when they first arrived—that was worse—this will come in second by the time Manus and Nauru are considered for their absolute cruelty. I imagine one day a royal commission will look into the illegal imprisonment, the damage caused, the agony, and the injury."

On my last day in Manus I managed to get through the navy checkpoint at the entrance to the camp. Rain was falling heavily. I drove past General MacArthur's old house, and an American-built church, and down to the high metal fences and barbed wire. Dozens of Australian border guards were exercising in a field. Jeeps and white SUVs splashed by. I saw the barracks—Oscar and Delta and Mike and Foxtrot—and by now it was easy to imagine the suffering endured within.

Behrouz Boochani, another Iranian refugee, had broken down in front of me a couple of days earlier, crying uncontrollably. "I can't sleep," he said. "I want justice," he said. "I have one million pages of incriminating documents," he said. Emaciated, with pale-green eyes, a ponytail, and a beard, he was a broken but still-determined man: "We are here because of all Australia, all the people who are silent, who have done nothing."

Among the refugees is Nayser Ahmed, a Rohingya who fled persecution in Myanmar on July 2, 2013. Now sixty-three, he made his way to Indonesia with his wife and six children. But when they boarded the bus to go to the boat, he was unable to squeeze in alongside. His family reached Australia before the imposition of the Manus and Nauru policy, and now live in Sydney. He did not. Every effort to be reunited with his family since he arrived in Manus on November 15, 2013, has failed.

Ahmed's nose and ribs were broken in the 2014 riot. A daughter got married in Sydney two years ago; he told her to stay well and not think too much. He blames himself for missing the bus.

"I think all the time about what happened," he told me. "When I close my eyes, I can see that bus leaving." He said he was "shouting and screaming, 'My family is gone, someone help me!'"

What is incumbent on Australia now is clear enough. Prevail on Trump to take as many of the refugees as possible. Reunite Nayser Ahmed with his family. Recognize that the country has incurred a moral debt to the myriad people it has mistreated on the islands and allow those who do not go to the United States to build a decent life in Australia. Make the "transitory persons" already in Australia permanent residents. Close this foul chapter that stains Australia and echoes the darkest moments in its history.

Aziz had been reading Mandela's biography. One of these men, allowed a chance, might yet make Australia proud.

TRUMP'S MANY SHADES OF CONTEMPT

I examined Trump's contempt for the State Department, for the American patriots across the globe dedicated to the American idea as a force for good in the world.

MARCH 3, 2017

This is a column about contempt. Let's start with the utter contempt that President Trump has shown for the State Department since taking office six weeks ago. Some seventy thousand American patriots across the globe, dedicated to the American idea as a force for good in the world, have been cast adrift.

Rex Tillerson, the secretary of state, is a near phantom. He has no deputy, having seen his first choice nixed by Trump. No State Department press briefing, once a daily occurrence, has been held since Trump took office. The president has proposed a 37 percent cut in the State Department budget. An exodus of senior staff members continues. The State Department has taken on a ghostly air.

The message is clear. America has no foreign policy, so nobody is needed to articulate it. All we have are the feverish zigzags of the president, a man who thinks NATO is obsolete one day and glorious the next. There is no governing idea, only transactional hollowness. One midlevel officer told Julia Ioffe of *The Atlantic*: "It's reminiscent of the developing countries where I've served. The family rules everything, and the Ministry of Foreign Affairs knows nothing."

Jared Kushner, Trump's son-in-law, has become the foreign service of the United States of America.

Trump does not buy into the American idea. He buys, if anything, into Vladimir Putin's macho authoritarianism and spheres of influence for the great powers. This amounts to a dramatic break with American policy as superbly articulated last month by one of the departing diplomats, Daniel Fried, who joined the Foreign Service in 1977 and served with great distinction, particularly in Central and Eastern Europe.

Fried had this to say in his parting remarks: "Few believed that Poland's Solidarity movement could win, that the Iron Curtain would come down, that the Baltic States could be free, that the second of the twentieth century's great evils—communism—could be vanquished without war. But it happened, and the West's great institutions—NATO and the EU—grew to embrace one hundred million liberated Europeans. It was my honor to have done what I could to help. I learned never to underestimate the possibility of change, that values have power, and that time and patience can pay off, especially if you're serious about your objectives. Nothing can be taken for granted, and this great achievement is now under assault by Russia, but what we did in my time is no less honorable. It is for the present generation to defend and, when the time comes again, extend freedom in Europe."

Donald Trump, our ahistorical Russophile president, should frame these words and hang them in the Oval Office as his first history lesson.

Fried noted America's long-held opposition to spheres of influence, a recipe for war, and made this critical point: "We are not an ethno-state, with identity rooted in shared blood. The option of a White Man's Republic ended at Appomattox. On the contrary, we are 'a new nation, conceived in liberty and dedicated to the proposition that all men are created equal.'" And so, "That rough sense of equality and opportunity, embedded in us, informed the way that we brought our American power to the world, America's Grand Strategy. We have, imperfectly, and despite detours and retreat along the way, sought to realize a better world for ourselves and for others, for we understood that our prosperity and our values at home depend on that prosperity and those values being secure as far as possible in a sometimes dark world."

There could be no finer rebuke to Trump's dangerous contempt.

But there is a deeper contempt, even more treacherous. It is for the Constitution. Trump has attacked the freedom of the press enshrined in the First Amendment, and the independence of the judiciary. His reckless travel ban raised issues of due process and religious discrimination. Serious questions exist as to whether "aid or comfort" was given by the Trump entourage to an American enemy—in this case Russia—during the presidential campaign and after his victory on November 8.

This contempt was signaled in his inaugural speech when Trump said, "The oath of office I take today is an oath of allegiance to all Americans." No, the president's oath is to "preserve, protect and defend the Constitution of the United States." It is to the law, not the *volk*.

Barnett Rubin, a political scientist and an Afghanistan expert who served at the State Department, recalled to me in an e-mail how he never thought of the oath he took to defend the Constitution "against all enemies, foreign and domestic," even when confronting the Taliban, but that these days the words have acquired meaning.

I know what Rubin means. I am a naturalized American, and so I took the oath to "support and defend the Constitution and laws of the United States of America against all enemies, foreign and domestic."

This column about contempt amounts, in a way, to fulfillment of that oath.

SONS WITHOUT FATHERS

My father, Sydney, died at ninety-five, leaving me more bereft than I had imagined.

JUNE 14, 2017

In her novel *The Bird's Nest*, Shirley Jackson writes:

> I was thinking what it must feel like to be a prisoner going to die; you stand there looking at the sun and the sky and the grass and the trees, and because it's the last time you're going to see them they're wonderful, full of colors you never noticed before, and bright and beautiful and terribly hard to leave behind. And then, suppose you're reprieved, and you get up the next morning and you're not dead; could you look again at the sun and the trees and the sky and think they're the same old sun and sky and trees, nothing special at all, just the same old things you've seen every day?

I've been looking at the world as a condemned man these past few weeks. Or, rather, I've been contemplating it with the eyes of my dying, now dead, father. This sunset, this light glinting on the water, this birdsong at dawn, this sweet breeze, this soft rain from the heavens—all seen and felt as if for the last time. Now Sydney Cohen, at the age of ninety-five, has merged with the nature he loved, as sea and sky merge beyond the Eden Estuary he would gaze at from his window in St. Andrews, Scotland.

There is no preparation for the loneliness of a world from which the two people who put you in it have gone. The death of parents removes the last cushion against contemplating your own mortality. The cycle of life and death becomes internal, bone-deep knowledge, a source now of despair, now of inspiration. The earth acquires a new quality of silence.

A physician, my father had the hands of the healer. He knew, and was at one with, the natural world. No terrain was so forbidding that he could not conjure a garden from it. His elements were water, trees, grass, flowers, wind, and sky. From them he conjured patterns and in them he found peace.

Readers of my writings may be passingly familiar with Sydney. How he was born in 1921 in Johannesburg, then, as he wrote, "a burgeoning town, younger than most of its inhabitants, arisen from a hectic mining camp." How chickens pecking around the yard of his modest home squawked in terror if picked for a Sunday lunch. How he studied medicine at the University of the Witwatersrand and, in 1945, reached England ten days after the end of the war in Europe. How he treated war-injured at the Royal Berkshire Hospital in Reading, where he encountered an astounding sight for a South African: a white woman on her hands and knees cleaning the floor.

How, above all, he strove over forty-nine years of marriage to cope with the mental illness of my mother, June. This constituted, as he once wrote to me, "the deepest and most sacred element of my life."

We are left with a human being: an exterior grown forbidding, dissolved by a luminous smile; a life sometimes double; and a soul whose innocence was preserved over almost a century. As Whitman noted, to be human is to "contain multitudes."

Sydney contained them. Displacement from South Africa to England overcame my mother, who first broke down with postpartum depression in 1958, the year after their emigration, and underwent electric-shock treatment.

Still, Britain brought some relief. His last post in South Africa was as dean of the one remaining residence for Black students at Wits. He would tell me of the infuriating ordeal of extricating his talented Black students from arbitrary arrest by some dumb Afrikaner cop. When Douglas Smit House was shut down in 1963 under the tightening grip of apartheid, Sydney was disgusted.

By then he was gone. Before he emigrated in 1957, a relative suggested he should change his name. "Cohen" was too conspicuously Jewish for professional success in Britain. He said that was a wonderful idea—only to add he would call himself "Einstein" instead. That was Sydney: a cool eye for human foibles and a pitch perfect sense of humor.

Mr. Cohen did all right in Britain. He became a professor at Guy's

Hospital, was elected a fellow of the Royal Society and was appointed CBE by the queen in 1978. These honors, worn lightly, reflected his pioneering work on the pursuit of a vaccine for malaria, a scourge of his beloved Africa. A landmark paper in *Nature*, co-written in 1961 with Ian McGregor, chronicled how immunoglobulin from immune Gambian adults had an antiparasitic effect when administered to infected children; it is still cited today.

On all this he turned his back thirty years ago, dedicating himself to gardening and carpentry, painting and golf. He knew what the affairs of the world were worth beside the majesty of the mountaintop.

After Mom died in 1999, and another relationship came to the surface, Dad wrote that he had tried in every way to cherish and sustain her.

My last moments with Sydney, in which the obdurate reserve of fathers and sons dissolved, will always be a reference in this quest:

"You have a lovely family," I said.

"I sure do."

"All very intelligent, just like you."

"Darling, you are very kind to say that."

"And funny, like you."

"Darling" (with a faint smile).

"We had a lot of fun together."

"Oh, yes."

"You'll always be with me."

"That's for sure."

The other evening, everything was aglow. They are not "the same old sun and sky and trees." That must be because my father is in them. To what degree the glow endures will be the measure of how far I can honor that deepest, vulnerable part of Sydney whose beauty I was lucky enough to know.

DAYDREAMING IN GERMANY

Yom Kippur in Berlin. My mind turned to the complications of having a mother tongue that was also the murder tongue.

OCTOBER 17, 2017

On Yom Kippur, last month, I was in Berlin. I am not a religious Jew, but on the High Holy Days I like to be in a synagogue, listen to the ancient lilt of Hebrew prayer and allow my mind to drift from daily cares. It is a form of respite. We all need that these days. Worry has become an early riser.

I closed my eyes. The sounds of Jewish worship in the Pestalozzi-strasse Synagogue were followed from time to time by instructions or explanations in German. This linguistic alternation, in Berlin, was more freighted than it might be elsewhere. It was an affirmation of healing, but not without a shadowy undertow.

My mind turned to the complications for a postwar German Jew, or indeed any German, of having a mother tongue that was also the murder tongue. Nothing after the Holocaust is ever straightforward in Germany, not even the jovial smile of the rabbi who conducted the service that day.

Berlin is a city of absences. The *Stolpersteine*, or stumbling stones, are now everywhere: the small brass bricks inlaid in sidewalks that recall a single Jewish life curtailed. What a beautiful name they have! You do stumble. You catch your breath. You are reminded of the everyday reach of the Nazi dragnet, of what diligence it took to decompose the German Jewish world.

This is a time of growing fears, in Europe and the United States. Ghosts have stirred. Humanity never quite grows out of the buffoon's attractions: the scapegoats he offers; the fast money; the rush of violence; the throb of nation and flag; the adrenaline of the mob; the glorious future that will, he insists, avenge past humiliations.

The Enlightenment was not the end of the story. Nor was 1989, that giddy moment for the liberal-democratic idea, deemed self-evidently all-conquering. An autocratic, nativist, xenophobic, nationalist reaction is now in full swing on both sides of the Atlantic—as the election in Austria demonstrates again. It demands resolute vigilance. It also demands that we listen, try to understand, and resist fracture.

On the wall of the synagogue, opening my eyes, I noticed these words: "*Zerstört*, Nov. 9, 1938, *Wieder eingeweiht*, September 1947"—destroyed in 1938, rededicated in 1947, eight months before the founding of the modern state of Israel. In those nine years—one more than a two-term American presidency—the German Jewish tapestry of Berlin, of Germany, was shredded. A whole universe disappeared. Hitler was a buffoon of ruthless intuitions who contrived to take the world down with him. That's worth recalling today.

Millions of European Jews, none more patriotic than the German, went to the gas.

All that, of course, was in the twentieth century, now disappearing from view at alarming speed. Few things are more dangerous than amnesia. But of course the things you remember best are things lived. What's the Cold War or the Berlin Wall to a thirty-year-old today?

The reconciliation of German and Jew after the Holocaust was unimaginable. Death was Paul Celan's "master from Germany"; how could such a master proffer a hand across the ashes to those who slipped through the net? And yet, just as there could be poetry after Auschwitz, there could, over generations, be a new understanding between perpetrator and victim, even German-Jewish friendship.

I moved very reluctantly from Paris to Berlin in 1998. By the time I left, in 2001 (a couple of weeks before the world changed), I was a convert to the *Bundesrepublik*. No nation guilty of a great crime has pursued an honest reckoning and atonement with greater rigor than Germany. It did not come immediately or easily. The country zigzagged its way to a full accounting. There were long silences and significant evasions. But Germany got there.

To me it has yielded a mystery or two, kept others back. You watch, in October, a naked woman emerging from Berlin's Krumme Lanke lake to the hissing of a swan, watch swans' wings thwacking the water in the struggle to get airborne, listen to the rhythmic clack-clack of hikers' poles on the paths in the dark woods—and it is as if you are being allowed to glimpse some secret. Still, you wonder.

The *Bundesrepublik* is America's child. It was forged under American tutelage and inspired by high American ideals of liberty. President Trump therefore poses a particular problem for Germany, more acute than for any other European nation. If the United States has forsaken these ideals, if the nation of "We the people" is no longer a universal idea but projects only a pay-up-now mercantilism, Germany will one day have to think again.

So will all allies of the United States. America's word is a devaluing currency. Across Europe, people roll their eyes at the mere mention of the American president.

Just last week Trump tweeted: "With all of the Fake News coming out of NBC and the Networks, at what point is it appropriate to challenge their License? Bad for country!"

This is Putin-Erdogan territory (and they don't use insane capitalization). Worse, this is the territory where books get burned.

We don't know yet how far the president is prepared to go in silencing critics who do not meet his test of patriotism, perhaps further than Russia and Turkey. We do know already that he has little idea of what his oath to the Constitution meant.

I am a Lithuanian-South-African-British-American Jew who, strangely, does not like walls, fences, hard borders, messianic nationalism, or race-baiting bigotry. Tell me, how did we get to the point where spewing hatred is the best way to prove contempt for the politically correct?

When I was on the way back from Brandenburg an der Havel to Berlin this month, after interviewing a member of Germany's ascendant rightist party, Alternative for Germany, a violent storm erupted. Loads were blown off trucks. Trees came down. One of them killed Sylke Tempel, a prominent foreign-policy expert and passionate Atlanticist, in Berlin.

The storm—so strange, almost otherworldly—felt like a warning. The waters of the Wannsee lake, generally so placid, churned like the North Atlantic; the Wannsee, where the "evacuation" of European Jewry to a "final solution" was decided in early 1942—and words had already lost their meaning.

MYANMAR IS NOT A SIMPLE MORALITY TALE

In Burma, I considered the evaporation of the halo of Daw Aung San Suu Kyi, long the world's persecuted champion of democracy, who fell silent as the Rohingya genocide unfolded. After such investment in her goodness, the world was livid at being duped. But perhaps the world was always deluded about her election victory in 2015. She was never the real leader of the country. Five years after this was written, she has again been imprisoned by the Burmese military.

NOVEMBER 25, 2017

NAYPYIDAW, Myanmar—As world capitals go, this is one of the weirdest. Six-lane highways with scarcely a car on them could serve as runways. The roads connect concealed ministries and vast convention centers. A white heat glares over the emptiness. There is no hub, gathering place, or public square—and that is the point.

Military leaders in Myanmar wanted a capital secure in its remoteness, and they unveiled this city in 2005. Yangon, the bustling former capital, was treacherous; over the decades of suffocating rule by generals, protests would erupt. So it is in this undemocratic fortress, of all places, that Daw Aung San Suu Kyi, long the world's champion of democracy, spends her days, contemplating a spectacular fall from grace: the dishonored icon in her ghostly labyrinth.

Seldom has a reputation collapsed so fast. Aung San Suu Kyi, daughter of the assassinated Burmese independence hero, Aung San, endured fifteen years of house arrest in confronting military rule. She won the Nobel Peace Prize. Serene in her bravery and defiance, she came to occupy a particular place in the world's imagination and, in 2015, swept to victory in elections that appeared to close the decades-long military chapter in Myanmar history. But her muted evasiveness before the flight across the Bangladeshi border of some 620,000 Rohingya, a Muslim minority in western Myanmar, has prompted international outrage. Her halo has evaporated.

After such investment in her goodness, the world is livid at being duped. The city of Oxford stripped her of an honor. It's open season against "The Lady," as she is known. Why can she not see the "widespread atrocities committed by Myanmar's security forces" to which Secretary of State Rex Tillerson alluded during a brief visit this month, actions the State Department defined last week as "ethnic cleansing"?

Perhaps because she sees something else above all: that Myanmar is not a democracy. It's a quasi-democracy at best, in delicate transition from military rule, a nation at war with itself and yet to be forged. If she cannot walk the fine line set by the army, all could be lost, her life's work for freedom squandered. This is no small thing. Not to recognize her dilemma—as the West has largely failed to do so since August—amounts to irresponsible grandstanding.

The problem is with what the West wants her to be. Kofi Annan, the former United Nations secretary general, who delivered a report on the situation in Rakhine State, in western Myanmar, just as the violence erupted there, told me that people in the West were incensed about Aung San Suu Kyi because "We created a saint and the saint has become a politician, and we don't like that."

Certainly Aung San Suu Kyi has appeared unmoved. She has avoided condemning the military for what the United Nations has called a "human-rights nightmare." She shuns the word "Rohingya," a term reviled by many in Myanmar's Buddhist majority as an invented identity. Her communications team has proved hapless, and opacity has become a hallmark of her administration as she has shunned interviews. At a rare appearance with Tillerson at the Foreign Ministry here, she said, "I don't know why people say that I've been silent." It's untrue, she insisted. "I think what people mean is that what I say is not interesting enough. But what I say is not meant to be exciting, it's meant to be accurate. And it's aimed at creating more harmony."

"Harmony" is a favorite expression of hers, as is "rule of law." Both lie at a fantastic distance from the reality in Myanmar. It is a fragmented country still confronting multiple ethnic insurgencies and "always held together by force," as Derek Mitchell, a former American ambassador, told me. Since independence from British imperial rule in 1948, the army, known as the Tatmadaw, has ruled most of the time, with ruinous consequences.

In many respects, the military continues to rule. When her National League for Democracy won the 2015 election, Aung San Suu Kyi did not become president. The world rejoiced—and glossed over this detail. The 2008 Constitution, crafted by the military, bars her from the presidency because she has children who are British citizens. So she labors under the contrived honorific of "state counselor." The Ministries of Defense, Home Affairs, and Border Affairs—all the guns—remain under military control, as do the National Defense and Security Council and 25 percent of all seats in Parliament.

This was not a handover of power. It was a highly controlled, and easily reversible, cession of partial authority.

Aung San Suu Kyi's decisions must be seen in this context. She is playing a long game for real democratic change. "She is walking one step by one step in a very careful way, standing delicately between the military and the people," said U Chit Khaing, a prominent businessman in Yangon. Perhaps she is playing the game too cautiously, but there is nothing in her history to suggest she's anything but resolute.

The problem is, she's a novice in her current role. As a politician, not a saint, it must be said, Aung San Suu Kyi has proved inept. This is scarcely surprising. She lived most of her life abroad, was confined on her return, and has no prior experience of governing or administering.

You don't endure a decade and a half of house arrest, opt not to see your dying husband in England, and endure separation from your children without a steely patriotic conviction. This is her force, a magnetic field. It can also be blinding. "Mother Suu knows best," said David Scott

Mathieson, an analyst based in Yangon. "Except that she's in denial of the dimensions of what happened."

The hard grind of politics is foreign to her. Empathy is not her thing. Take her to a refugee camp; she won't throw her arms around children. She sees herself as incarnating the inner spirit of her country, a straight-backed Buddhist woman with a mission to complete what her father, whom she lost when she was two, set out to do: unify the nation. Yet the road to that end remains vague. Even Myanmar's ultimate identity—a Buddhist state dominated by her own ethnic Bamar majority or a genuinely federalist, multireligious union—remains unclear. Her voice is absent.

Could she, short of the military red lines that surround her, have expressed her indignation at the immense suffering of Rohingya civilians, and condemned the arson and killing that sent hundreds of thousands of terrified human beings on their way? Perhaps. But that would demand that she believes this is the essence of the story. It's unclear that she does; she's suspicious of the Rohingya claims and what she sees as manipulation of the media. It would also demand that she deem the political risk tolerable in a country that overwhelmingly supports her in her stance. Certainly she did not order the slaughter. Nor did she have the constitutional powers to stop it.

What is clear is that Aung San Suu Kyi's reticence has favored obfuscation. It has left the field open for a ferocious Facebook war over recent events. The Rohingya and Buddhists inhabit separate realities. There are no agreed facts, even basic ones. This is the contemporary post-truth condition. As the Annan report notes, "Narratives are often exclusive and irreconcilable."

In Rakhine State, where all hell broke loose last August, the poverty is etched in drawn faces with staring eyes. The streets of its capital, Sittwe, a little over an hour's flight from Yangon, are dusty and depleted. Its beach is overrun with stray dogs and crows feeding on garbage. As the town goes, so goes all of Rakhine, now one of the poorest parts of Myanmar, itself a very poor country. The violence that ripped through the northern part of the state was a disaster foretold.

There was an earlier eruption, in 2012, when intercommunal violence between Rakhine Buddhists and Muslims left close to two hundred people dead and about 120,000 people marooned in camps. There they have rotted for five years. Government promises have yielded nothing. The camps are closed off. Former Rohingya districts in town have been emptied, a shocking exercise in ghettoization.

I spoke by phone with Saed Mohamed, a thirty-one-year-old teacher confined since 2012 in a camp. "The government has cheated us so many times," he told me. "I have lost my trust in Aung San Suu Kyi. She is still lying. She never talks about our Rohingya suffering. She talks of peace and community, but her government has done nothing for reconciliation."

Rakhine, also called Arakan, was an independent kingdom before falling under Burmese control in the late eighteenth century. Long neglect from the central government, the fruit of mutual suspicion, has spawned a Rakhine Buddhist independence movement, whose military wing is the Arakan Army. "We are suffering from seventy years of oppression from the government," Htun Aung Kyaw, the general secretary of the Arakan National Party, whose objective is self-determination for the region, told me.

The steady influx over a long period of Bengali Muslims, encouraged by the British Empire to provide cheap labor, exacerbated Rakhine Buddhist resentments. The Muslim community has grown to about one-third of Rakhine's population of more than 3.1 million and, over time, its self-identification as "Rohingya" has become steadily more universal.

Within Myanmar, this single word, "Rohingya," resembles a fuse to a bomb. It sets people off. I could find hardly anybody, outside the community itself, even prepared to use it; if they did they generally accompanied it with a racist slur. The general view is that there are no Rohingya. They are all "Bengalis."

U Nyar Na, a Buddhist monk, seemed a picture of serenity, seated at the window of a Sittwe monastery beside magenta robes hanging on a line. But when our conversation turned to the Rohingya, he bristled.

"The whole problem lies in that word; there are no Rohingya among the one hundred and thirty-five ethnic groups in Myanmar," he told me, alluding to the indigenous peoples listed in connection with the country's 1982 citizenship law. "This is not an existing ethnic group—they just created it. So, if they believe it, the belief is false."

He reached down for his smartphone, and found an Internet image supposedly representing the secessionist plans of the "Bengali Muslims." It showed Rakhine, shaded green, under the words "Sovereign State of Rahamaland, an independent state of Rohingya people." He looked at me as if to say: There, you see, empirical proof of their diabolical intent.

Such fears run deep. Aung San Suu Kyi is inevitably sensitive to them. A combination of more than a century of British colonial subjugation, the looming presence of China to the east and India to the west, with their 2.7 billion people (Myanmar has fifty-four million), and its own unresolved internal ethnic conflicts have marked the national psyche with a deep angst over sovereignty. U Ko Ko Gyi, a politician long imprisoned by the military but now in full support of the army's actions in Rakhine, told me, "Our in-bone conviction from our ancestors is to resist outside pressure and fight until the last breath to survive."

Myanmar, with its bell-shaped golden pagodas dotting the landscape, shimmering in the liquid light, often seems gripped these days by a fevered view of itself as the last bastion of Buddhism, facing down the global advance of Islam in Afghanistan, Bangladesh, Pakistan, and elsewhere. The Rohingya have come to personify these fears.

Many conversations here reminded me of my time covering the Balkan wars of the 1990s, when Serbs, in the grip of a nationalist paroxysm, often dismissed the enemy—Bosnian Muslims, Kosovo Albanians—as nonexistent peoples. But as Benedict Anderson observed, all nations are "imagined communities." The Rohingya exist because they believe they exist.

It does not matter when exactly the name was coined—dispute rages on this question—or when exactly the Muslims of Rakhine embraced it in their overwhelming majority. Nothing is more certain to forge ethno-national identity than oppression. By making Rakhine Muslims stateless—by granting them identity cards of various hues that at various times seemed to confer citizenship or its promise, only to withdraw them—and by subjecting them to intermittent violence, the military of Myanmar and its Rakhine Buddhist militia sidekicks have done more than anyone to forge a distinct Rohingya identity.

Out of such desperation emerged the Arakan Rohingya Salvation Army, or ARSA, the Rohingya insurgent group whose attacks on several police outposts close to the Bangladeshi border on August 25 ignited a devastating military response. A persecuted people will take up arms. When you attempt to destroy a people you don't believe exists, fury may get the upper hand.

In September, with hundreds of thousands of Rohingya already displaced in camps in Bangladesh, Aung San Suu Kyi told the *Nikkei Asian Review* she was puzzled as to why the exodus had continued after military operations slowed. She speculated: "It could be they were afraid there might be reprisals. It could be for other reasons. I am genuinely interested because if we want to remedy the situation, we've got to find out why—why all the problems started in the first place."

Her tone, weirdly academic, seemed almost plaintive. The problems started because of an abject failure over decades. Military governments failed Rakhine Buddists; they failed Rakhine Rohingya even more, their policy laced through with racism. Aung San Suu Kyi's own government has prolonged that failure. The arson, killing, and rape followed. This should be clear.

It's less clear what should be done now. More than half a million terrorized people find themselves homeless. Bangladesh and Myanmar announced an agreement last week to begin returning displaced people within two months, but details were murky. Repatriation is urgent, but contentious, and will be meaningless unless Myanmar lays out an unambiguous and consistent path to citizenship, or at least legal residency, for the Rohingya, who today constitute some 10 percent of all the world's stateless people. Denying the possibility of citizenship to people resident in Myanmar for a long time is unworthy of the democracy Aung San Suu Kyi wants to forge as her last legacy.

This Burmese transition to democracy stands on a knife-edge. Its ultimate success is of critical importance, with forms of authoritarianism ascendant the world over. Criminal actions should be punished under the "rule of law" Aung San Suu Kyi cites so often. But the sanctions being called for by more than twenty senators and by groups including Human Rights Watch, and even the targeted individual sanctions envisaged by the State Department, would undermine a parlous economy, entrench the Burmese in their sense of being alone against the world, and render any passage to full democracy even harder.

The country is now in the sights of jihadist groups enraged by the treatment of the Rohingya. Already there is an ugly and significant movement of extremist Buddhist monks. Pope Francis, who plans to visit Myanmar this week, faces a delicate task in trying to advance conciliation. His first quandary will be whether to use the word "Rohingya," which the Annan report avoided, in line with the request of Aung San Suu Kyi. (She believes that both "Rohingya" and "Bengali" are needlessly provocative.) He should. The Rohingya exist, have suffered, and through suffering have arrived at an identity that is unshakable.

Now in her seventies, Aung San Suu Kyi has to find her voice. Harmony is all very well, but meaningless without creative, energetic politicking. She knows she can't throw the military under the bus if she wants to complete what she began through her brave defiance of the army in 1988. The world should understand this, too. It might be better to focus on Min Aung Hlaing, the commander-in-chief who presided over a ludicrous military report on the atrocities that exonerated the army. Tillerson rightly demanded an independent inquiry. Taking down Aung San Suu Kyi's portrait is easy for people in comfortable places who have never faced challenges resembling hers.

In her book *Letters from Burma*, Aung San Suu Kyi wrote of the suffering of Burmese children: "They know that there will be no security for their families as long as freedom of thought and freedom of political action are not guaranteed by the law of the land."

The work of removing, once and for all, that anxiety from all the inhabitants of Myanmar and establishing the rule of law is far from done, as the devastating violence in Rakhine has amply illustrated. But Aung San Suu Kyi, a woman who faced down guns, remains the best hope of completing the task. Turning saints into ogres is easy. Completing an unfinished nation, clawing it from the military that has devastated it, is far more arduous—the longest of long games.

THE YEAR NOT TO
DEFER DREAMS

Because I travel a lot, I am forever asked how long I will be in town. Forever, I feel like saying, not leaving New York City ever again. Here, on the Staten Island Ferry, I journeyed into all that was most familiar.

DECEMBER 26, 2017

From my window in Brooklyn Heights, I've watched the Staten Island Ferry come and go for more than two years now, a big orange boat criss-crossing the water. That's when I'm home, which is not much.

At night, I hear the foghorn, a reassuring sound, fading slowly, like memories. On the road, in yet another hotel room where my hand can't locate by instinct the light switch, I imagine that sound sometimes. It makes me smile. Home is little things, the clunk of the door closing on your world.

There's a lot going on out my window: joggers on the promenade, barges plowing the East River, choppers landing on the prow of Manhattan, planes nosing down into Newark Airport, cars on the first traffic-free stretch of FDR Drive, where hope surges, only to collide with reality at a bottleneck. The view always reminds me of a children's picture book. Yes, my love, that's a helicopter.

I don't look out on all that enough. Water is life, a mirror one day, a maelstrom the next. Do I live in New York or camp in it? Sometimes I wonder. I resent the inevitable question: How long are you in town for? Forever, I feel like saying. That's right, the farthest I'm going for the next six months is the convenience store on Montague.

Home's important. Belonging is important, right there behind love in terms of human needs. Watching an old movie on your couch is important. That's what holidays are for. I watched *Shampoo,* a minor Hal Ashby masterpiece. "You never stop moving," Jill (Goldie Hawn) tells her feckless hairdresser boyfriend, George (Warren Beatty). "You never go anywhere."

The movie's set on the eve of Nixon's 1968 election. A TV blares in the background. There's Nixon. He says the American flag won't be "a doormat." He says "the great objective" of his administration will be to "bring the American people together."

That which is new under the sun is meager. Funny, Nixon's not looking so bad these days, compared with the orange apparition in the White House.

Speaking of orange, I figured, what the heck, I'm paying, like every New Yorker, for the free Staten Island Ferry service. I gaze at the boat, imagine it, and it goes to a mysterious place where the Great Leader triumphed in the presidential election. A cleansing end-of-year wind was gusting. I boarded the ferry, not to go anywhere, just to be transported.

Some cities waste the water on which they are set. London used to. Rome still does. Paris is the aqueous gold standard. I've watched New York embrace its waterfront over the years. Right beneath my window a lawn has been taking shape this year on Pier 3, Brooklyn Bridge Park's last pier to be converted, and set to open in 2018. It will include a labyrinth.

The ferry's a commuter service, of course. But at this time of year, it's full of tourists gasping at the sunlight falling on the serried towers of Lower Manhattan, on the Statue of Liberty, on the derricks, like gangling metal dinosaurs, of New Jersey. New towers go up, yet to acquire, or having half-acquired, their gleaming outer coats of armor. How handsome the Verrazzano-Narrows Bridge is!

The boat crosses to Trump country, but its brief passage evokes the centuries of American hope invested in this city, seen by so many immigrants for the first time from this expanse of water. Here, suffering, famine, and the endless gyre of Old World conflict were set aside, or at least cushioned by New World possibility.

At this low point for the United States, when truth itself is mocked from on high, that liberating message is worth recalling. Certainly, no naturalized American, as I am, who has witnessed the rites of passage of people drawn by hope from every corner of the earth to the rights and responsibilities of citizenship, can be indifferent to it.

I made the journey to Staten Island—beyond Montague, I know. We can't always live up to our word. But we must keep trying. Avoid a high moral tone. Pay attention to detail. Wander aimlessly. Know, with Cavafy, "what these Ithacas mean." Believe in, and provide for, the children who will inherit this earth. Yes, darling, that's a boat. And that's a labyrinth.

The night I took the Staten Island Ferry, I went to a party. Each of us, after eating well, was asked to read or recount something close to the heart. One guest read Langston Hughes's "Harlem":

> *What happens to a dream deferred?*
>
> Does it dry up
> like a raisin in the sun?
> Or fester like a sore—
> And then run?
> Does it stink like rotten meat?
> Or crust and sugar over—
> like a syrupy sweet?
>
> Maybe it just sags
> like a heavy load.
>
> *Or does it explode?*

In 2018, take the time, dear reader, to gaze at the familiar, board the ferry to nowhere—and do not, at risk of an explosion, defer your dreams.

HOLY CITY
OF STERILE STREETS

I journey to Hebron, nexus of the Israeli-Palestinian conflict.

JANUARY 20, 2018

HEBRON, West Bank—The Israeli soldier stands at the entrance to Shuhada Street. The street is deserted; its stores are shuttered, doors welded shut. The old center of Hebron has been a ghost town for many years. The Israel Defense Forces refer to *tzir sterili*, or sterile roads, because no Palestinian is allowed on them, whether in a car or on foot.

The occupation of the West Bank is a half century old. That's a long time. Jews did not go to the Holy Land to deploy for another people the biological metaphors of classic racism that accompanied their persecution over centuries. But the exercise of overwhelming power is corrupting, to the point where "sterile" streets, presumably freed of disease-ridden natives, enter the lexicon.

The soldier at the checkpoint is a young man with a ready smile. He tells me he's visited New York. He asks where I bought my watch. I ask him what he's done to merit the punishment of Hebron. He laughs, a little uneasily. He's clearly uncomfortable with his mission, enforcing segregation, and wants to connect. No doubt he'd rather be on the beach in Tel Aviv, enjoying a beer.

If there's an end point to the terrible logic of an occupation driven in part by a fanatical settler movement abetted by the state of Israel, that place is the historic center of Hebron. Once home to the souk and the jewelry market, a bustling maze of commerce, it is now a stretch of apocalyptic real estate. Wires trail down crumbling walls. Garbage accumulates. Mingling is obliterated.

Security demands separation.

The soldier, armed with an M-16 rifle, talks to a Hebrew-speaking friend of mine. He says it's good that we are seeing soldiers for who they really are. Who they really are, often, translates as young Israelis in impossible situations doing their patriotic duty but troubled by what they see. I recall my cousin, who served in Hebron in the early 1990s, telling me: "You are treating families in a way you would not want your own family to be treated. It's as simple as that."

I was last here in 2004. It's gotten worse. I wrote then: "Every loss is nursed, proof of the irremediable barbarism of the enemy. The past is pored over, an immense repository of spilt blood that justifies more bloodshed." Hebron, home to about 215,000 Palestinians, and about eight thousand settlers between adjacent Kiryat Arba and the city itself, festers. The status quo is not static. Everybody knows there will be another explosion. Nobody knows when.

There's the boom of stun grenades in the distance. Palestinian kids have been throwing stones; the Israel Defense Forces respond. The soldier is waiting for a call from his commander. Until he gets it, we cannot pass.

I stand at the checkpoint with Yehuda Shaul, who served in the infantry in Hebron and later became a founder of Breaking the Silence, an advocacy group that collects testimonies from former Israeli soldiers troubled by their service. Shaul's a well-known figure in Hebron. He calls a lawyer for his organization. A half-hour later, we are allowed to proceed.

Abraham is buried in Hebron. He is the first patriarch to the Jews. For Muslims, he's a prophet called Ibrahim and a model for humankind. To settlers, this is the first Jewish city in the biblical hills of Judea. To the Palestinian majority, this is their centuries-old home, under Israeli military occupation.

Like every Israeli-Palestinian argument, this one has no resolution. Other than to say the past is gone and what matters is the future.

Ever backward the violence spirals: the execution-style killing of an incapacitated Palestinian attacker by an IDF soldier in 2016; the stabbing to death that year of a thirteen-year-old Jewish girl in Kiryat Arba by a Palestinian attacker; the killing of twelve Israelis by Palestinian snipers in 2002; the 1994 murder of twenty-nine Muslims at prayer by

Baruch Goldstein. A sign on Shuhada Street says: "This land was stolen by Arabs following the murder of 67 Hebron Jews in 1929."

There is no end to this without leadership.

Shaul came to Hebron as an IDF soldier during the Second Intifada. He remembers a mission statement on a wall: "To protect and defend the inhabitants of the Jewish community of Hebron." He was ordered to fire a grenade machine gun into a heavily populated Palestinian residential area. He saw a Palestinian medical clinic destroyed. Doubts grew.

"It's not defense, or prevention. It's offense against Palestinian independence. That is the mission," Shaul says. "The view is that between the river and the sea there is room for one state only, so it better be us." Inevitably, the settlers, however extreme, become a vehicle of this strategic aim.

"People have no clue," Shaul continues. "We are sent to do the job. But nobody knows what the job is. The job stays here." Tel Aviv is a ninety-minute drive away. Soon enough I am back on the beach, wondering if I imagined all this.

ONE HONORABLE AMERICAN'S LOVE OF TRUMP

You can't dismiss tens of millions of Americans. You have to get out there to understand what produced the Trump phenomenon. Shannon Kennedy, retired military officer, ex-stockbroker, Obama voter (twice), explained why he jumped on the Trump train.

FEBRUARY 9, 2018

SYRACUSE—Shannon Kennedy, son of Jack, retired military officer, ex-stockbroker, voted twice for Barack Obama ("so poised, a really got-it-together guy") before his conversion to Donald Trump. Now he's a true believer, even if he thinks "Donald definitely needs to button it sometimes."

His dad, named John but universally known as Jack, "was such a charmer, he could charm hungry pups from a meat wagon." Married three times with eight kids, Jack was a Democrat and "a very capable political operative who ran a couple of campaigns here in Syracuse." For a while he sold used cars at Shamrock Motors, then opened a bar, Kennedy's Club K, which, his son observes, "was not a great occupation for an alcoholic."

Jack was dry at the time. He said he'd put tea in the whiskey bottles, nobody would know, and he'd drink from those. That worked, until it didn't. He was dead at forty-nine.

We are driving around Syracuse, population 143,000. It's pretty bleak. Most industry and manufacturers are long gone. Poverty and drugs are scourges, as in countless towns across America. Service industries and Syracuse University are significant providers of jobs now. Kennedy recalls a different town in his youth, a thriving magnet to immigrants. After his parents divorced, and his mother died young in 1961, he was raised by his grandmother.

"She was so tight, she wouldn't spend a nickel to watch the Statue of Liberty swim back to France!" Kennedy says. "She kept me busy. I mowed lawns in summer, raked leaves in the fall, and shoveled snow in winter to make a buck. Her message was: Never spend a dime when you can spend a nickel."

So there's that in Kennedy's makeup: the scrappy, can-do fighter who's known hard times and believes there's no substitute for a day's work. Then came the military. He served in Japan, in a naval hospital, from 1970 to 1971, treating war-wounded from Vietnam. "We'd get the injured twelve to twenty-four hours out of Vietnam, generally with at least one limb missing. We'd sew, or suture, or ligate stumps. They were my age. My thought was, 'I could be them!'"

Later, he trained at Fort Bragg; was commissioned as an officer; and served in Saudi Arabia, Somalia, and Egypt, among other countries, retiring with the rank of major in 1997. He recalls, "When I was in Sinai, I would be asked by my commanding officer, 'What did you do for the taxpayer today?'"

If there's a main source of Kennedy's anger, it's that this has become such a quaint, outmoded question in today's America of lobbyists and line-my-pockets politics. "Trust the Clintons? Not with the Lord's breakfast," he says.

He tells me he leans right, but he believes that every American should have a functioning public-transit system ("as in Germany and Japan") and a good national health service. He thought Obama could be "a breath of fresh air," and was initially in favor of "Obamacare," until it "went off the rails because the exchanges were not competitive."

Then along came Trump. "The thing about him," Kennedy tells me, "is that there's forward energy. He's like a horse with blinders at the Kentucky Derby. If there's another horse in the way, knock it out and ride the rail. I listened to him, on immigration, on draining the swamp, on lobbyists, and I liked that. As I recall, it was 'We the people,' not 'We the empowered.'"

Immigration was an important factor in Kennedy's lurch from Obama to Trump. Though he favors the Dreamers program, which shielded some young immigrants from deportation, he says, "There are too many people running around who have no business being here." America First was important: too many working Americans have lost jobs to unbalanced trade deals.

A little over a year in, Kennedy remains a fervent Trump supporter. He insists that he has no illusions. Trump is "brash," a "rogue." He's also "a fighter, a scrapper, the kind of guy who says, 'Damn the torpedoes, full speed ahead.'" He's proving his stamina against the naysayers "who hate the man with a vileness that is very un-American." He's draining Washington "of people with contempt for the people they represent." The tax cut will be "beneficial."

And what of the president's racism, lies, warmongering outbursts, vulgarity, and attacks on a free press and the judiciary? "Go beyond the noise," Kennedy tells me. "Don't take him at face value. If I thought he was a racist, I'd be off the train so fast you'd have to mail me my shadow. Respect the office of the presidency."

I disagree. Respect for the office must begin with Trump, who's sullied it with mendacity, bigotry, and autocratic contempt for the Constitution. Still, I respect Kennedy. He's served his country. He's a patriot.

He's no "deplorable." He's smart. The Democratic Party should listen to him, or risk losing in 2020.

The message is clear. The same old, same old (for example, Joe Biden) won't work. A whiff of got-the-system-rigged elitism from the Democrats will be fatal. A strong economic program for working Americans is essential. Look to purple-state America, not blue-state coastal America, for a candidate who is grappling with the country's toughest issues and is strong on can-do, down-to-earth values.

DEATH PENALTY MADNESS
IN ALABAMA

After I was told the details of a botched attempt to execute Doyle Lee Hamm, aged sixty-one, I argued that Governor Kay Ivey of Alabama should grant him clemency and allow him to serve the rest of his life in prison. She did.

FEBRUARY 27, 2018

A man suffering from cancer strapped to a gurney after spending thirty years on death row in Alabama. An intravenous team probing him, jabbing him, for hours in an attempt to find a usable vein to administer the lethal, secret drug cocktail. Going into his groin a half-dozen times, puncturing his bladder, penetrating his femoral artery. Until, a little before the midnight deadline, they abandon the botched execution with its puncture-mark traces tattooed across the man's legs and groin.

Doyle Lee Hamm, age sixty-one, becomes one of the rare prisoners to walk out of an execution chamber. "This was a bit of butchery that can only be described as torture," his attorney, Bernard Harcourt, tells me.

Not all is rosy in Alabama, a state long prominent in the United States death belt, where these events unfolded last Thursday. The state was the darling of the world in December when *Le Monde*, among other leading global newspapers, gave Alabama a front-page headline for defeating the ultraconservative Republican bigot and accused sexual predator Roy Moore, and electing a Democrat to the United States Senate. But Alabama is a place where old habits die hard.

Corrections Commissioner Jeff Dunn was unmoved by the grotesque unexecution. "I wouldn't necessarily characterize what we had tonight as a problem," he said. That might just qualify, against stiff competition from the highest office in the land, as the dumbest statement of 2018.

This was an abomination foretold. Harcourt, who has been representing Hamm since 1990, had been arguing for months that Hamm's case presented an unconstitutional risk of a "cruel and unnecessarily painful execution." Hamm, convicted of the 1987 murder of a motel clerk, Patrick Cunningham, has advanced lymphatic cancer and carcinoma. He's dying. An examination in September by a doctor from the Columbia University Medical Center found that Hamm had no usable veins and that "the state is not equipped to achieve venous access in Mr. Hamm's case."

So began a macabre dance characterized by an unseemly determination to execute Hamm. The Alabama Supreme Court set an execution date late last year. U.S. Chief District Judge Karon Bowdre of the Northern District of Alabama granted a stay on January 31. After an emergency appeal to the Eleventh Circuit Court of Appeals, that stay was vacated on February 13 and a medical examination ordered.

The examination found that Hamm's arms and hands were unusable but his legs and feet, or "lower extremities," were workable. On February 20, Bowdre ordered that the execution could proceed on February 22. Then the Eleventh Circuit required that a doctor be present with ultrasound equipment. A final appeal to the Supreme Court was denied last Thursday evening, setting in motion the ghoulish proceedings.

To state the obvious, this is obscene. I won't get into the merits of Hamm's conviction here; suffice it to say there were oversights and misrepresentations. Nor will I dwell on the fact that, under international law, thirty years on death row constitutes torture.

I oppose the death penalty on the ground that it's barbaric and increasingly unworkable. It's also irreversible in a world where human error is so inescapable as to disqualify such absolute judgment. Even if you are not an abolitionist, however, the Hamm case must give pause.

"This experience teaches us a deep fallacy in our justice system," Harcourt says. "When federal courts so eagerly get into the business of trying to find novel ways to execute a man, when the most august judges get their fingers bloody in this way, I think it does an injustice to justice."

Alabama has executed sixty-one people since the Supreme Court allowed executions to resume in 1976. United States Attorney General Jeff Sessions was long the grim reaper of Alabama, eagerly seeking executions when he was the state's attorney general. In President Trump, Sessions has a strong capital-punishment ally. Trump tweeted "SHOULD GET DEATH PENALTY" for a New York terrorist suspect in November, one of more than a dozen tweets calling for the death penalty since 2012. He has hinted strongly that he thinks the death penalty is the way to solve America's drug crisis. The president lusts for blood.

The country, however, is moving in another direction. The number of executions has fallen to twenty-three in 2017, from ninety-eight in 1999. Illinois, Connecticut, New Mexico, and Maryland abolished the death penalty in recent years. Over twenty companies, including Pfizer, have prohibited their products from being used for lethal injections.

Harcourt was moved to help Hamm after learning of the abject quality of legal protection afforded indigent defendants in capital cases. After the Supreme Court denied his appeal on Thursday, and the execution looked inevitable, Harcourt told me he had said to Hamm, "I did everything I possibly could have done but had let him down, and I apologized."

Hamm, he said, tried to console his longtime attorney: "We did everything possible."

It is now time, after Thursday's lesson in the consequences of inhumanity, for Governor Kay Ivey of Alabama to grant Hamm clemency and allow him to serve the rest of his life in prison.

TRUMP'S WORLD AND THE
RETREAT OF SHAME

Around the world, autocrats felt strengthened by Trump. With respect to Putin, Trump was incapable of uttering a critical word. His
conduct was so strange that it suggested the Russian president
had a mysterious hold over him.

MARCH 9, 2018

After Aleppo, now comes the agony of Eastern Ghouta. This suburb
of Damascus, the last rebel-held enclave close to the Syrian capital, is
bombarded by Bashar al-Assad's forces for weeks on end, with Russian
air support. More than nine hundred people, including many children,
are killed. Hospitals are targeted in what François Delattre, the French
ambassador to the United Nations, has called "a siege worthy of the
Middle Ages." Pregnant women bleed to death. Some four hundred
thousand people are trapped.

France and Britain convene an emergency meeting of the Security
Council and press for enforcement of last month's Resolution 2401,
calling for an immediate cessation of hostilities. In this effort, the United
States is nowhere, silent, AWOL, as President Vladimir Putin and his
Syrian sidekick do their worst. The message to Moscow is clear: Donald
Trump's America does not care about Syria, or war crimes, or human
rights. Russian cynicism and American absence produce disaster.

Yes, it has come to this.

Emmanuel Macron, the French president, calls Putin. He dis-
patches his foreign minister to Moscow and Tehran in an attempt to
stop the slaughter. Trump, to whom moral indignation—indeed, morality itself—is a stranger, does not care. His Middle East foreign policy has
two components: back Israel, bash Iran. With respect to Putin, he is
compromised, or enamored, to the point of incapacity. Let Syria burn.

Yes, it has come to this.

In Hungary, a European Union country, committed by treaty to the union's founding principles of "the rule of law and respect for human rights," Viktor Orbán, the prime minister, declares, "We do not want to be diverse and do not want to be mixed; we do not want our own color, traditions, and national culture to be mixed with those of others." Now, what color, precisely, are Hungarians, and what color were the nearly 440,000 Jews deported by the Nazis, mostly to Auschwitz, in 1944 with the cooperation of Hungarian authorities?

Mateusz Morawiecki, the prime minister of Poland, another European Union member state, defends a new law that makes it a crime to accuse "the Polish nation" of complicity in any "Nazi crimes committed by the Third Reich." He says there were also "Jewish perpetrators" of the Holocaust.

These illiberal European leaders are empowered by Trump's dalliance with despotism and by his indifference to the distinction between truth and lies. They have the wind at their backs. They can lie lightly. The values-based American pushback against bigotry, in the name of liberty, human rights, and the rule of law, has vanished. If the American idea is indivisible from America, Trump is an impostor.

Yes, it has come to this.

Zeid Ra'ad al-Hussein, the outgoing United Nations high commissioner for human rights, tells it like it is: "Today oppression is fashionable again; the security state is back, and fundamental freedoms are in retreat in every region of the world. Shame is also in retreat. Xenophobes and racists in Europe are casting off any sense of embarrassment." He continues with a question: "Have we all gone completely mad?"

Yes, shame is in retreat; decency too. Freedom is in retreat. The American president expresses semi-joking approval for Xi Jinping, the Chinese president, extending his rule indefinitely.

It has come to this.

A counterrevolution against liberal democracy is in full swing. The preceding revolution, as the author Paul Berman put it to me, was "large-scale." It may be traced from 1968, a half century ago, through the revolutions of 1989, and on to the Arab Spring that began in late 2010. It involved women's rights; the civil-rights movement; anti-authoritarianism in all forms; the spread of liberal-democratic practices into formerly communist European states; and the Arab uprising—now largely dashed—against despotism and for the personal agency that only freedom offers.

Why the illiberal counterrevolution? "First," Berman tells me, "because there's always a counterrevolution! Second, fear. You can only understand the macho cartoons that are Putin and Trump through the fear aroused by the revolution in women's rights. Fear of globalization, too, and then we have this cultural collapse that leads so many Americans to be incapable of seeing at a glance that Trump should not be president."

Yes, it has come to this. It's dangerous and it's frightening.

Seventy years ago this year, the Universal Declaration of Human Rights was adopted, founded on Franklin Roosevelt's four pillars of "freedom of speech and belief and freedom from fear and want." It reflected a core premise of the postwar, American-led order: that "human rights should be protected by the rule of law" if cycles of violence were to be avoided. At its fiftieth anniversary, in 1998, it seemed the world had united around these principles.

Trump knows nothing, and cares even less, about these now threatened values. It has come to this.

Yet the fight for Eastern Ghouta is no less than the fight for this planet's decency. It must and will continue. As Bernard-Henri Lévy notes in *The Empire and the Five Kings*, his forthcoming book, "the last word is never said."

HOW DEMOCRACY
BECAME THE ENEMY

I traveled to Hungary and Poland to look at how the illiberal coun-
terrevolutions there have turned the West into a threat, and how a
new nationalism has emerged to confront Western "decadence."

APRIL 6, 2018

Hungary had a horrendous twentieth century of lost territory and freedom, but Budapest, a handsome city set on a broad sweep of the Dan-
ube, suggests its wounds have healed. Trams hum along boulevards
lined with elegant cafés and clogged with the cars German companies
manufacture here. The country has escaped from what Milan Kundera, the Czech writer, called the "kidnapped West," the great swath
of Europe yielded to the Soviet empire after World War II, and has
returned to the Western family.

Or so it seems, until you notice the posters of a smiling Hungarian-
American Jew, his arms around opposition politicians who brandish
wire cutters and have cut through a fence.

The man in question is George Soros, the billionaire investor and
philanthropist. He's not on any ballot, but his international renown and
funding of liberal causes has made him the chosen symbol, for Prime
Minister Viktor Orbán and his right-wing Fidesz Party, of all they
loathe: international speculators, sappers of nation and Christendom,
facilitators of mass migration.

As a young man, Orbán fought against Bolshevism. Western liberal democracy was the Promised Land. Now it has morphed into the
enemy. The West is the site of European cultural suicide, the place
where family, church, nation, and traditional notions of marriage and
gender go to die.

"The danger is threatening us from the West," Orbán, who has been
in power for eight years and is seemingly headed for re-election Sunday,

said in February. "This danger to us comes from politicians in Brussels, Berlin, and Paris."

To counter it, the Hungarian prime minister has established a template: Neutralize an independent judiciary. Subjugate much of the media. Demonize migrants. Create loyal new elites through crony capitalism. Energize a national narrative of victimhood and heroism through the manipulation of historical memory. Claim the "people's will" overrides constitutional checks and balances.

And, lo, the new Promised Land: competitive authoritarianism, a form of European single-party rule that retains a veneer of democracy while skewing the contest sufficiently to ensure it is likely to yield only one result.

There's no totalitarian secret police. Nobody disappears in the night. Foreign capital is welcome. Hungary is not unfree, but it's not free either. It's the new semi-closed hybrid of Orbán and Jarosław Kaczyński, the shadowy leader of the conservative governing Law and Justice Party in Poland, both of whom fought as youths for the liberty the West embodied.

Donald Trump's election was part of a worldwide nationalist and autocratic lurch. A vigorous counterrevolution against the liberal-democratic orthodoxy of diversity and multiculturalism is under way. The fact that Trump reflects, and reinforces, this broad movement, exactly a half century after the heady flowering of every liberty in 1968, suggests he will be much harder to dislodge than many liberals imagine. Orbán was the first European leader to back Trump during his campaign, and celebrated his victory as the end of "liberal non-democracy." Trump called Orbán "strong and brave" in a meeting with the Hungarian ambassador, according to the Hungarian magazine *Figyelő*.

The European nations most enamored of freedom—those released three decades ago from the withering grip of the Soviet empire—have transformed into those most skeptical that liberal democracy provides it. It's an extraordinary turn. The Brussels-based European Union (of which Hungary has been a member and financial beneficiary since 2004) and Chancellor Angela Merkel of Germany are viewed in Hungary with greater suspicion than Vladimir Putin. Poland, the most populous Central European state, has so embraced the Hungarian model that Kaczyński calls it the "example." The Czech Republic may not be far behind.

Orbán, who attended Oxford as a young man on a Soros-funded scholarship, has hailed "a new era" reflecting a popular desire for democracies that are not open. Adam Bodnar, Poland's embattled ombudsman in Warsaw, suggested to me, "Hungary has shown there's no need to introduce a typical authoritarian system. You can control what happens without it."

One of the politicians embraced by Soros in the election posters around Budapest is Bernadett Szél, a co-leader of the Green Party. She told me she has never met Soros. The image is a fake. According to Laura Silber, the spokeswoman for Soros's Open Society Foundations, it has been "doctored to make Soros's nose longer—right out of the Goebbels playbook."

Szél, who is trying to unite Hungary's chronically splintered opposition against Fidesz, said Orbán "is poisoning Hungary day by day." A member of the Parliament's National Security Committee, she faces a smear campaign from Fidesz politicians determined to oust her. She fears for her country. "Orbán," she told me, "is becoming a pharaoh who wants to adopt the Russian, Turkish, or Chinese model."

For such a project, Orbán needs enemies. Thousands of migrants, many fleeing the war in Syria, straggling through Hungary in the late summer of 2015, encamped for weeks at Budapest's main railway station, provided them. Merkel's decision to admit so many made of German *Willkommenskultur*, or welcoming culture, the "surrender" Orbán would define himself against. It was a pivotal European moment.

No universal human right to dignity, invoked by kale-eating Western liberals racked by colonial or war guilt, would be used to destroy Hungarian or Polish culture!

"Hungary First" is Orbán's election slogan. His relentless anti-immigrant campaign, including claims from a Cabinet minister that migrants and refugees would force Hungarians to eat insects, has produced a startling level of fear. Csaba Toth, a political scientist, told me, "Children in kindergarten have drawn Soros as the devil and migrants as evil figures who will take you away if you are not good."

One gray afternoon, I went out to Orbán's home village of Felcsút, population eighteen hundred, about an hour's drive west of Budapest. His simple white house has a cross on its gabled roof. Opposite the house, a spaceship has landed. It takes the form of a giant soccer stadium, complete with turrets and vaulted wooden beams that can accommodate more than twice the population of the village.

Orbán is passionate about soccer—and rewarding his cronies. Lőrinc Mészáros, the mayor of the village and a former pipe fitter, has virtually overnight become one of Hungary's richest men, the owner of several regional newspapers. In and around the stadium, where a couple of hundred people, including the prime minister, were watching a desultory match, I heard how Orbán brings jobs, how Hungary does not need immigrants who "rob and murder," how "1,000 percent he will win the election." Later, at the Mediterranean Café, I met András Vigh, a childhood friend of Orbán, who confessed to me, "We've never seen a migrant in our lives." No matter: "I watch TV and I know. I don't want any immigrants. Only an idiot would allow them in."

The other face of fear is venom. In homogeneous societies like Hungary and Poland, it has proved easy to stoke fury against the unknown "other." In October 2015, the month after the train-station ordeal, Kaczyński's Law and Justice Party swept to victory in Poland with an absolute majority. His blueprint would be the one Orbán has developed since taking office in 2010.

I visited Poland and Hungary regularly in the early 1990s to chronicle their extraordinary postcommunist transformation. Nowhere was the passion for the liberty and security the West seemed to offer stronger than in Poland, heroic vanguard of the liberation of Europe in 1989 through the Solidarity movement of workers and intellectuals. Nowhere today is the turn against Western liberal democracy more startling or seemingly perverse.

European Union funds—some ninety billion dollars between 2012 and 2016 alone—have fast-forwarded Polish modernization. (Hungary, with about a quarter of Poland's population of thirty-eight million, received close to thirty-three billion dollars in the same period.) After traveling from Hungary to Poland, I boarded the high-speed train from the capital, Warsaw, to Kraków. Gazing out, I was confronted with a tableau of rapid change: orange-vested laborers, boxcars painted a reassuring blue, new suburbs, a church spire above drab five-story communist-era apartment blocks, poplars and willows, storks' nests suspended in wintry branches, crumbling farm buildings.

Poland: obliterated from the map for more than a century; restored and transformed; killing field par excellence of the Nazis; home to a burning Catholic faith, the "Christ of nations" in a collective subconscious brimming with persecution mania.

Membership in NATO and the European Union, both attained by 2004, was supposed to confer normality and security. A market economy and the rule of law were intended to cement them. These objectives, through painful transformation, were reached.

So why, with the prize in hand, this nationalist, xenophobic stiffening, across Central Europe? The Polish economy, like the Hungarian, has been expanding briskly, attaining 4.6 percent growth last year, a rate Western Europe can only dream of.

Of course, growing inequality, perceptions of impunity, the arrogance of liberal elites, and the disruptions of globalization have played a role, just as they have in the United States and Britain. But something more is at work. Perhaps, I thought, the tumultuous kaleidoscope seen through the train window provided a clue.

For three decades, Poland, like Hungary, has been going somewhere: the destinations were NATO, the European Union, and a free market. Now that these are attained, a question arises: Was all the sacrifice, in this nation whose self-image is of heroes and martyrs, just for shopping malls and German cars? A burned-out generation has transformation fatigue. The point of comparison used to be communist gray. Now it's prosperous London and Berlin.

Kaczyński declares that immigrants carry "parasites and protozoa." He turns the 2010 death in a plane crash in Smolensk, Russia, of his twin brother, the former president Lech Kaczyński, into a Russian plot, condoned by the centrist, pro-European Civic Platform Party, which was then in power. He promises a "Fourth Republic," with a new Constitution, rid of Brussels and the lingering hand of communists co-opted by Civic Platform. It's not always clear what he means, but his conspiracy theories get the blood up. He has a project!

"In 1989, we all emigrated to the West," Karolina Wigura, a sociologist based in Warsaw, told me. "We were all going somewhere in our souls, and, as you know, emigration is not an easy process. And then, when we finally thought we'd done it, we saw all these new people coming into Europe, and we couldn't take the idea of immigrants, because that's what we felt we'd been."

Capitalism, in other words, was another country. The rallying cry throughout Central Europe in the early 1990s was "free-market democracy." Get the all-controlling state out; let the market in. Nobody stopped to ask whether the market and liberal democracy were necessarily eternal twins. Turns out they're not.

The "market" equaled globalization, good for the hyper-connected metropolis, less so for the hinterland. Poland and Hungary, too, have their Wisconsin and Ohio. Adam Bielan, a senator who is close to Kaczyński, told me that the difference in wages between his constituency in the provincial town of Radom and in Warsaw had doubled over the past dozen years.

The policy of Civic Platform, in power from 2007 to 2015, was "to concentrate European Union funds in the big cities," Bielan argued. The result: "A huge part of Poland was forgotten." These forgotten Poles voted overwhelmingly for Kaczyński, who has since rewarded them with a $150 monthly handout to all families with two or more children. If you don't want immigrants, the only way you can offset an aging population in Poland or Hungary is with babies.

Kaczyński has set about undermining democracy guaranteed by constitutional checks and balances, the very thing Poland craved after 1989 as insurance against tyranny. In the name of the people's will, using a false democratic mantle, he has taken relentless aim at what he once called "legal impossibilism"—the counterbalancing power vested in an independent constitutional judiciary. His ruling party has in effect commandeered the Constitutional Tribunal and the Supreme Court in a way that has led the Venice Commission, a panel of constitutional-law experts, to declare that Polish judicial independence is "at serious risk."

Marcin Matczak, a prominent Warsaw law professor, asked me: "What does this say about political transitions? It's the Supreme Court that rules if an election is valid or not. This feels like some kind of preparatory stage for worse."

Bolshevism, the cradle in which Orbán and Kaczyński were rocked, was an ideology bent on force-marching society toward some higher ideal. In fact, the reality, as the Polish poet Zbigniew Herbert put it in "The Monster of Mr. Cogito," was that it "poisons wells / destroys the structures of the mind / covers bread with mold." Something of this urge, it seems, remained in the two men. It was not enough for them to succumb to the permissiveness of the West. They needed a mission. They have decided to save Christendom, no less, whatever the damage to open societies.

Witold Waszczykowski, the former Polish foreign minister, has said Poland must be cured of the onslaught of those who believe history is headed inevitably toward "a new mixture of cultures and races, a world made up of cyclists and vegetarians, who only use renewable energy and who battle all signs of religion." He's Trump's kind of guy.

Of course, in this worldview, Muslims in Europe are a problem. Bielan, the senator close to Kaczyński, told me: "Integration has failed. I worked in Brussels and there were no-go zones. Poles don't want the social problems of France or Belgium. Why would we be more successful than France in this?"

On that basis, Poland has refused to take the seven thousand asylum seekers it agreed to absorb under a decision taken by European Union member states during the refugee crisis of 2015. Hungary and the Czech Republic have also refused. They have shown contempt for European solidarity in the name of racial and religious purity.

A mood of high nationalist righteousness has taken hold. Poland recently passed an absurd "death camp" law that makes it a crime to accuse "the Polish nation" of complicity in any "Nazi crimes committed by the Third Reich." Poles saved Jews; they also denounced and, in villages like Jedwabne, killed them. This by now is well known. It has become a crime in Poland to speak the truth.

Hungary and Poland are turning the clock back to Europe's darkest hours. Today they are all about erecting borders—real and imagined—against Islam, migrants and refugees, Jews, the European Union, the United Nations, Soros, and what they portray as a pluralistic international conspiracy. Hungary erected an actual barrier on its southern border following the refugee crisis of 2015, the fence Orbán portrays the opposition as wanting to cut.

It was precisely the measures taken to construct and preserve a homogeneous society that lay at the core of the most heinous crimes of the last century. The illiberal trend represents a rejection of the core postwar insight that borders should be dismantled to save Europe from its repetitive suicides. Ever-closer union meant ever-expanding peace.

Taken to its end point, the new Hungarian and Polish authoritarianism means danger. It is more dangerous because Trump's despot-coddling America has disappeared as a countervailing force. The president has ceased upholding the values that advance liberty.

In Warsaw last summer, Trump declared, "The fundamental question of our time is whether the West has the will to survive." He continued, "Do we have enough respect for our citizens to protect our borders?"

There was no criticism of Kaczyński or his illiberal steps. I was told the Polish government feels empowered by Trump.

Nor have Poland or Hungary felt remotely threatened by the European Union, whose censure of the countries' turn against liberal democracy has been prudent to the point of feebleness. The billions of dollars still going to Warsaw and Budapest from Brussels should be diverted elsewhere for now. The union rests, by treaty, on the principles of "democracy, equality, the rule of law and respect for human rights."

The democratic West needs to awaken from its slumber. The forgotten people of the post-1989 decades have spoken. They have embraced disruption at any cost, declaring "Enough!" to the economic prescriptions (mainly austerity) and the smug impunity of globalizing elites. Europe cannot open its doors to everyone. It needs a shared immigration policy that works, economic policies that offset rather than accentuate inequality, and a Brussels bureaucracy that delivers tangible results to a half-billion Europeans.

The worst is not inevitable. Orbán could yet lose (Fidesz suffered a surprising local-election defeat recently), but that is a long shot. Poland lags behind Hungary in the descent into authoritarianism. It is bigger, more diverse, and more hostile to Putin's Russia for historical reasons. It has a stronger civil society and retains a more vigorous independent media. These are important distinctions. They provide some hope.

But Europe's drift is ominous. "I have the weird sense this is the future—it feels like the transition to something new," Michael Ignatieff, the president of the Budapest-based and Soros-funded Central European University, told me of Orbán's ascendant illiberalism. The university, a symbol of academic freedom conceived to anchor Central Europe in the West by providing a liberal education, is under threat of closing by Orbán.

When I asked Zoltán Kovács, Orbán's spokesman, why the government uses anti-Semitic riffs against Soros, he said: "We're not riffing on his Jewishness. We're riffing on what he does as a speculator, spending dubious money for his cosmopolitan conception of the globe."

This is the new-old language of Europe today. Marcin Matczak, the law professor I met in Poland, told me: "The young take liberty for granted. They never had to fight for it."

THE INSANITY
AT THE GAZA FENCE

Another year, another Gaza conflict. Some Israelis call it "mowing the grass," to evoke the routine aspect of the flare-ups, a terrible phrase given the loss of life.

APRIL 20, 2018

When snipers shoot to kill civilians approaching a wall, there are disturbing echoes for anyone who has lived in Berlin. I lived in Berlin.

I have passed several times through the fence separating the first world of Israel from the rubble-strewn open-air prison of Gaza. It's a violent transition in a place of unreason. As usual, Israel overreaches, an eye for an eyelash, as the Oxford professor and former Israeli soldier Avi Shlaim once observed.

Israel has the right to defend its borders, but not to use lethal force against mainly unarmed protesters in the way that has already left thirty-five Palestinians dead and nearly a thousand injured. Overreaction is inherent to the existential threat Israel claims, but that is ever less persuasive. Israeli military dominance over the Palestinians is overwhelming, and Arab states have lost interest in the Palestinian cause.

Hamas, Israel claims, is using women and children as human shields for violent demonstrators who want to penetrate the fence and kill Israelis. The script is familiar: international investigations will follow, inconclusive outcomes, redoubled hatred.

Israel wins but loses. Israel haters, and Jew haters, have a field day. You know pornography when you see it. You know a disproportionate military response when you see it.

Gaza redux: the violence is inevitable. The Israeli-Palestinian status quo, so called, incubates bloodshed. It's important to look beyond the Gaza fence, symbol, like all fences, of failure. This is what happens when diplomacy dies, when compromise evaporates, when cynicism triumphs. Even President Trump has lost interest in his "ultimate deal" and sees North Korea shimmering.

Six former directors of Mossad, the Israeli intelligence agency, sounded the alarm a few weeks ago. When those most responsible for Israeli security say Israel's current course is self-defeating, it's worth paying attention.

Here's Tamir Pardo, Mossad chief from 2011 through 2015, speaking to the Israel daily *Yedioth Ahronoth*: "If the State of Israel doesn't decide what it wants, in the end there will be a single state between the sea and the Jordan. That is the end of the Zionist vision." To which Danny Yatom, director from 1996 to 1998, responds: "That's a country that will deteriorate into either an apartheid state or a non-Jewish state. If we continue to rule the territories, I see that as an existential danger. A state of that kind isn't the state that I fought for. There are some people who will say that we've done everything and that there isn't a partner, but that isn't true. There is a partner. Like it or not, the Palestinians and the people who represent them are the partners we need to engage with."

This is the conviction for which Prime Minister Yitzhak Rabin died, assassinated by an Israeli agent of the messianic fanaticism opposed to all territorial compromise that has steadily gained influence since 1967. There is no partner if you've chosen God over several million people you'd rather not see. But if you look, there is.

Palestinian belief in two-state compromise has also eroded over the past two decades. Increasingly, you may hear "occupation" used as a term to describe Israel's very existence, rather than the West Bank and Gaza, both occupied during the 1967 Six-Day War (Israel withdrew from Gaza in 2005 but maintains effective control through an air-and-sea blockade, among other measures).

The Friday Gaza marches are protests against the eleven-year-old blockade of Gaza but also focused on reigniting international interest in Palestinian claims of a right of return to homes they were driven from in 1948. There's no point mincing words: the right of return is flimsy code for the destruction of Israel as a Jewish state. It's consistent with the absolutist use of "occupation" as defining Israel itself and with the view that the sea is a pretty good place for Jews to end up.

Palestinians lost their homes after Arab armies declared war in 1948 on Israel, which had accepted United Nations Resolution 181 of 1947, calling for the establishment of two states of roughly equal size—one Jewish, one Arab—in British Mandate Palestine. The resolution was a compromise in which I still believe, not because it was pretty, but because it was and remains better than other options.

Intransigent Palestinians like to say they take the long view. Well, seventy years is a while, and Palestinians have been losing. Half the territory is now less than a quarter in any imaginable deal. I don't see why that trend would be reversed absent creative, unified, and pragmatic Palestinian leadership focused on a two-state future: laptops for kids rather than keys to lost olive groves.

The dead have died for nothing. Israel, through overreach, has placed itself in a morally indefensible noose, policing the lives of others.

Palestinian leaders have borne out Yeats's lines: "We had fed the heart on fantasies, / The heart's grown brutal from the fare."

Shabtai Shavit, another Mossad director, from 1989 to 1996, said: "Why are we living here? To have our grandchildren continue to fight wars? What is this insanity in which territory, land, is more important than human life?"

"THE CHRONICLES OF NAMBIA," OR WHY TRUMP KNOWS NOTHING OF AFRICA

My parents' country, South Africa, which they left because of apartheid, now offers some encouragement. Its democracy—younger and flimsier than America's—survived the deeply corrupt presidency of Jacob Zuma. If it did, that was due to the strength and independence of its judiciary, and a vigorous press, not the least the online *Daily Maverick*.

JUNE 10, 2018

CAPE TOWN—Trump has struggled with Africa. He twice alluded to a nonexistent country called "Nambia"—an apparent stab at Namibia—in addressing the United Nations last September, before he lumped the continent among the "shithole countries" early this year.

Other than that, give or take a flurry on the import of elephant tusks, the real Africa, continent of nearly 1.3 billion people, has scarcely impinged on Trump's "Chronicles of Nambia."

Here in South Africa, one of the continent's three largest economies, there is no United States ambassador eighteen months after the last one departed, and no sign of one being nominated. South Africans have taken note. Their country, scarcely mentioned by the president, sits at the bottom of a continent Trump disparages.

That's a pity. South African goings-on are instructive. The country has just emerged, its democracy shaken but intact, from nine years of plundering, corrupt rule by former President Jacob Zuma.

The ingredients of Zuma's methods will be familiar to Americans in the Trump era: policy as personal whim, contempt for democratic institutions and the rule of law, entanglements with Vladimir Putin, attacks on a free press, enrichment of pliant friends, and governance as an exercise in values-free narcissism.

Poor Zuma! Dethroned now, he insists he's cash-strapped, despite his systematic placing over many years of corrupt people who would do his whim at the top of state enterprises and government ministries. So penniless, he says, that he has no money to pay for his defense against fraud and racketeering charges that date back to an arms deal before he became president—and proceeded to turn the nation's highest public office into the scandal-ridden hub of a quest for private gain.

His successor, President Cyril Ramaphosa, who took office in February, has embarked on the arduous task of repairing the damage. Ramaphosa is everything Zuma was not: decent, skillful, at heart a constitutionalist. He's not untainted, and his mandate is not strong, but he's a serious, smart man who is determined to start over.

There's talk of "Ramaphoria." The president is seeking foreign investment, having declared South Africa open for business once again. Certainly, many South Africans feel a long nightmare has come to an end, even if the economy is contracting and unemployment is at 26.7 percent.

Geoff Budlender, a prominent lawyer who was deeply involved in the long struggle against apartheid, told me, "Terrible damage has been done." He spoke of "damaged institutions"—including a "broken police," troubled situations at the national tax agency and Treasury, and "captured state enterprises that are in deep trouble." Wherever he could, Zuma demanded not competence but loyalty, enriching business cronies like the now disgraced Gupta brothers who served his interests.

"The question with structural and institutional damage is how do you reverse it," Budlender said.

In 2020, or just possibly before that, or perhaps not until 2024, the United States is going to face a similar question in the aftermath of Trump. His unrelenting attacks on a free press, an independent judiciary, truth, decency, and America as a nation of laws will have taken their toll.

South Africa offers some encouragement. Its democracy—younger and flimsier than America's—survived a deeply corrupting presidency. I believe America, like South Africa, will survive the Zuma-Trump test of a democracy's essential character.

OF COURSE, IT COULD NOT HAPPEN HERE

The unimaginable should be imagined if it is not to be lived.

JUNE 29, 2018

PARIS—The German government of Chancellor Angela Merkel falls, torn apart by demands from her conservative interior minister, Horst Seehofer, that refugees already registered in another European Union state be thrown out of Germany.

The xenophobic Alternative for Germany, or AfD, enters a new nationalist governing coalition. The party's cry of "Take back our country and our *Volk!*" echoes through Berlin.

Congratulatory calls pour in from the nationalist leaders of Hungary, the Czech Republic, Poland, Italy, Austria—and the United States. The American ambassador to Germany tweets his approval.

European Union leaders, buckling before the anti-immigrant tide, opt for the establishment of large detention centers for all migrants. Asylum seekers whose claims are verified will be admitted, but economic migrants merely in search of a better future will be evicted.

Riots erupt in these vast walled compounds. Rapid triage proves impossible. Conditions fester. Matteo Salvini, the rightist Italian interior minister, declares that a disastrous mistake has been made. The detention centers should have been located in North Africa. He defends his orders to the Italian Coast Guard to ignore calls for help from ships filled with migrants, who, he says, may prove to be criminals and rapists.

The abduction of a Russian girl by Moroccan migrants at a Spanish beach resort causes an uproar. It turns out to be "fake news," the work of Russian cyber-geeks deployed for information warfare, but not before rightist leaders across the European Union have denounced the "foreign animals" holding "little Tatiana." Spain's fragile government collapses.

Germany, Italy, the Czech Republic, and Hungary announce that they are leaving the Schengen Area and will reintroduce border and passport controls. The free movement of people, a cornerstone of the European Union, collapses. President Trump congratulates Europe on "coming to its senses at last." His ambassador to Germany tweets a hymn to "rediscovered, strong nations."

President Trump, arriving in Brussels for a NATO summit, explodes at the sight of the vast new $1.3 billion NATO headquarters building— "a scandal, a monstrosity, an insult to ordinary Americans."

He declares that NATO is no longer an alliance; it's a cost center. The United States is paying too much. Why, he asks, are European armies not being used to round up "the immigrants who infest your countries and destroy your Christian cultures"?

Turning on his former friend President Emmanuel Macron, he denounces the French defense of a united Europe as "weak, weak." Asked about the Trump-Macron relationship, a spokesman for Macron responds, "As we say in France, '*Les grands amours finissent toujours mal*'—great loves always end badly."

The NATO summit proves more fractious than the recent G-7 summit in Canada. Trump rages and sulks. He pouts and pesters. He declares that, just as he has stopped joint United States military exercises with South Korea because they are a provocation to "my friend Kim Jong-un," so he has decided, after consultation with "my friend Vladimir Putin," to withdraw from NATO military exercises in Poland and the Baltics because such exercises are a "provocation to Russia."

A briefing paper prepared by his national-security adviser, John

Bolton, is leaked. It defines the president's strategic objective as "the destruction of the World Trade Organization, NATO, and the European Union." Much progress, it notes, has been made toward all three goals. "The liberal-democratic club is crumbling under the weight of its own decadence and political correctness."

President Putin, citing "crimes" against the Russian minority in Estonia, sends the Russian Army into Estonia, a NATO member. He insists that there has been no "invasion" but that ethnic Russians in Estonia have justifiably taken up arms.

Satellite imagery of Russian troops crossing the border is dismissed by Trump as "fake news." Leading Republicans unanimously support his position.

NATO fails to invoke Article 5, which says an attack against any one NATO member must be considered an attack against them all. Allied governments abandon Estonia to its fate.

NATO disbands. Putin proposes replacing it with the Alliance of Authoritarian and Reactionary States, or AARS. Trump says he finds the idea "interesting."

Britain leaves the carcass of the European Union. Germany, under its rightist coalition, announces it is giving up the euro and readopting the deutsche mark. The eurozone collapses. The American ambassador to Germany tweets his delight.

The European Union disbands. Its flag is lowered at the French-German border, where work on a high-tech wall flanked by banks of barbed wire has begun. Trump and Marine Le Pen, the French National Front leader, tweet their approval. Germany announces a strategic alliance with Russia. The United States Supreme Court rules, on "national security" grounds, that due process is not required before expelling undocumented immigrants. Mass deportations begin. Trump tweets that due process "is overrated."

It could not happen. Of course, it could not happen. Only a fool would believe for a moment that it could.

McCAIN AND A REQUIEM FOR
THE AMERICAN CENTURY

I always respected Senator John McCain, even when I disagreed
with him, as I often did. It was fitting that Trump did not attend the
ceremonies commemorating his passing.

AUGUST 31, 2018

DENVER—The services across the nation marking the passing of
Senator John McCain are also a requiem for the American century. He
lived through the zenith of postwar American power; believed, despite
setbacks, in America's unique capacity to forge a more open and democratic world; and held America's word as pledge in the cause of liberty.

These ideas seem quaint today, tired relics glibly discarded. Perhaps
that is why McCain's death has caused a moment of national reflection.
The world has changed. China has risen. American power is no longer
determinant. Flux is in the nature of things. But did the United States
of President Donald Trump really need to take a sledgehammer to its
values, its responsibilities, and the anchors of its prosperity?

It is fitting that Trump has been absent from the ceremonies. The
two men loathed each other more than death could overcome. Trump's
aim is the dismantlement of the world that gave McCain's life purpose:
the Atlantic Alliance, a rules-based international order, resolve toward
Vladimir Putin's Russia. Honor, decency, and duty were ideas around
which McCain built his life of service. They are concepts that have no
meaning for Trump, the bone-spur rich kid from Queens.

The president of the United States is persona non grata at services
that speak of bipartisanship, of American ideals, of self-sacrifice rather
than self-interest, of an American global commitment that goes beyond
"Pay up now!" Trump stands outside the American tradition.

In years past, I would watch McCain at the Munich Security Conference. The experience was never less than bracing. Beside him, others

seemed mealymouthed. He had known the extremes of human experience, lived in full. His voice contained that fullness. He was a man of conviction. He preferred to be wrong than to bend.

Torture over more than five years of captivity had imbued him with a humanity that transcended politics, even if did not dim his cantankerous bellicosity. He had bombed Vietnam in a losing war of confused aims and official obfuscation. He emerged unbowed in his belief in "the world's greatest republic, a nation of ideals, not blood and soil," as he put it in his farewell letter. McCain was obstinate, sometimes to the point of obtuseness.

America's many failures were as nothing beside American achievement. Stubbornness defined him in an age of finger-to-the-wind opportunism. As a spineless Republican Party folded into the Trump Party, McCain came to stand almost alone as a politician of principle. His party moved. He did not.

Nowhere was McCain greater than on the subject of torture, a practice for which Trump's sympathies are evident, and not only in his appointment of Gina Haspel—a woman deeply involved in the Bush administration's "enhanced interrogation" regime—to head the CIA. Here is McCain in 2014, responding to the Senate Intelligence Committee Report on CIA methods deployed in the aftermath of the 9/11 attacks:

> I know from personal experience that the abuse of prisoners will produce more bad than good intelligence. I know that victims of torture will offer intentionally misleading information if they think their captors will believe it. I know they will say whatever they think their torturers want them to say if they believe it will stop their suffering. Most of all, I know the use of torture compromises that which most distinguishes us from our enemies, our belief that all people, even captured enemies, possess basic human rights, which are protected by international conventions the U.S. not only joined, but for the most part authored.

An important voice for "basic human rights" is gone. Trump does not know what human rights are. That McCain voice could be erratic or impetuous, but it was never petty.

I disagreed with McCain about many things: his incorrigible itch to bomb Iran, his bizarre back-and-forth on Barack Obama's Affordable Care Act. He ran a comically disastrous campaign as the Republican candidate for the presidency in 2008. His choice of Sarah Palin as his running mate elevated the jingoistic idiocy that has become a Republican hallmark. It was a terrible mistake. The Straight Talk Express, as his bus was named in both his presidential campaigns, has degenerated a decade later into Trump's "tell-it like-it-is" Fox News spectacular.

I wish I could believe the outpouring of sympathy for McCain marks the moment when principle and bipartisanship will rise above lies and fracture in American politics. But I don't, at least not in the near term. The nationalist, nativist, xenophobic tide has not yet run its course. In many respects, McCain was a dinosaur.

That's because his words from 2017 are out of fashion: "To refuse the obligations of international leadership and our duty to remain 'the last best hope of earth' for the sake of some half-baked, spurious nationalism cooked up by people who would rather find scapegoats than solve problems is as unpatriotic as an attachment to any other tired dogma of the past that Americans consigned to the ash heap of history."

These words will resonate nonetheless, beyond "America First" and all that ash-heap-bound Trump drivel.

AN INJUDICIOUS MAN, UNFIT FOR THE SUPREME COURT

Why Brett M. Kavanaugh should not be serving on the Supreme Court.

SEPTEMBER 28, 2018

What America saw before the Senate Judiciary Committee was an injudicious man, an angry brat veering from fury to sniveling sobs, a judge so bereft of composure and proportion that it was difficult not to squirm. Brett Kavanaugh actually got teary over keeping a calendar because that's what his dad did. His performance was right out of Norman Rockwell with a touch of *Mad Men*.

This is what you get from the unexamined life, a product of white male privilege so unadulterated that, until a couple of weeks ago, Kavanaugh never had to ask himself what might have lurked, and may still linger, behind the football, the basketball, the weight-lifting, the workouts with a great high-school quarterback, the pro-golf tournaments with Dad, the rah-rah Renate-ribbing yearbook, the Yale fraternity, and the professed sexual abstinence until "many years" after high school.

"Sometimes I had too many beers," Kavanaugh said. "In some crowds, I was probably a little outwardly shy about my inexperience; tried to hide that," Kavanaugh also said. Christine Blasey Ford, his steady accuser, made a persuasive case that, in the summer of 1982, she paid the price for the teenage aggression and insecurity linking those two avowals.

Kavanaugh swears under oath that he never "sexually assaulted anyone." To entertain even the possibility of it would be to dismantle the entire edifice of his holier-than-thou life. He's the all-American jock, the model only child. For God's sake, he contingently, and a little presumptuously, hired four female law clerks to work with him at the Supreme Court, the first (prospective) justice to have "a group of all-women law clerks."

The words that resonate for me are the very words Kavanaugh used about his mother, Martha, the Maryland prosecutor and trial judge, whose trademark line was "Use your common sense. What rings true? What rings false?"

For my common sense, Mr. Kavanaugh "doth protest too much, methinks." Christine Blasey Ford rang true. I'll take her "100 percent" over his. She felt no need to yell. Nor did she hide behind a shield of repetition. She did not succumb to pathos ("I may never be able to coach again"). She spoke with a deliberation, balance, and humanity missing in the judge.

This was a job interview, not a criminal trial. The accusation against Kavanaugh—involving an incident thirty-six years ago in an undetermined location, uncorroborated by those present—would not currently stand up in a court of law. As a juror, with the available evidence, I could not say "beyond a reasonable doubt" that he committed this assault. (This, of course, is precisely the evidence that the FBI investigation that Kavanaugh evaded backing, and that Senator Jeff Flake has now decisively endorsed, might produce.)

But Kavanaugh's bleating about due process and presumption of innocence—his rage at a supposed "national disgrace"—misses the point. He failed the job interview. Who would want this spoiled man pieced together on a foundation of repressed anger and circumscribed privilege—this man who quite plausibly was the teenage drunk near-suffocating Christine Blasey Ford as he ground his body against hers, this man who may now have perjured himself—occupying a place for life on the highest court in the land?

I began this column by describing what America saw on Thursday. But it's not what all of America saw. Millions of Americans, including President Trump and Senator Lindsey Graham, saw something else: a despicable Democratic Party conspiracy against an innocent and upstanding middle-aged judge, the latest victim, along with his family, of gender politics, the #MeToo revolution, and an ascendant culture dictating that whatever women say must be true and whatever men say must be false.

The hearings were a Rorschach test for America's tribes. They saw what they wanted to see. For Kavanaugh's supporters, his rage was as good a primal scream for threatened white male privilege as may be imagined. No wonder Trump loved it.

A tribal confrontation is not conducive to the establishment of truth. That's why the FBI investigation is important. Despite Trump's best efforts to trivialize the everyday lie, facts matter.

Addressing the Democrats on the committee, Graham fumed: "You want this seat? I hope you never get it." But of course, as Democrats will never forget, Republicans stole a seat. Remember Merrick Garland? There is something so hypocritical in Republican outrage that it would be comical if the issue were not so grave.

It's hard to argue that America's tribal democracy is not dysfunctional these days, but still the United States is a democracy. Flake's eleventh-hour decision to demand a week's delay before a full Senate vote to allow the FBI investigation—a decision driven by conscience over Republican Party allegiance—is a small act of honor in a tawdry time. It can take a while for democracies to zigzag toward the truth.

Kavanaugh has revealed himself to be a man without measure, capable of frenzy, full of conspiratorial venom against Democrats. Justice would not be served by his presence on the Supreme Court.

AN INSIDIOUS AND CONTAGIOUS AMERICAN PRESIDENCY

Trump wants tribal allegiance from the Supreme Court. He went a long way toward securing it, to the lasting detriment of the American idea.

OCTOBER 5, 2018

Insidious is the man. Insidious is his pollution of the FBI, whose former director James Comey he fired after Comey refused to show "loyalty." Loyalty in this instance meant willingness to shelve, at Trump's demand, an investigation into dealings between his first national-security adviser, Michael Flynn, and Russia.

Now the FBI—given a week to investigate what happened thirty-six years ago between Brett Kavanaugh and Christine Blasey Ford—concludes an investigation on which the lives of our children and grandchildren may hinge in *less than a week*. It does so as Trump, speaking behind the seal of the president of the United States, unloads his bile on Dr. Blasey.

Contagious is the man. Contagious is Trump's view that judges should be agents of those who appoint them rather than the independent guarantors of America's constitutional democracy. Trump wants loyalty from Kavanaugh, too, and the angry, emotional testimony that the judge provided to the Senate Judiciary Committee carried this subliminal message: "I am one of yours." It was right out of the Trump playbook.

The Supreme Court is the ultimate arbiter of the rule of law. It was conceived as a critical part of the political system, not as just another venue for ordinary, ugly, polarized politics. Kavanaugh's confirmation would be the capstone to a shift in that direction. Courts were meant to be America's great levelers, not their great dividers and inciters.

"Kavanaugh's statements were so partisan and suggested so strongly an inability to be independent on any sort of issue salient to contemporary politics that his confirmation would put at serious risk the rule of law," Stephen Burbank, a professor at the University of Pennsylvania Law School, said. Imagine a Justice Kavanaugh on political gerrymandering.

It's worth remembering that Kavanaugh was reading a prepared statement when he said Dr. Blasey's allegations and a "long series of false, last-minute smears" were a "political hit" and "revenge on behalf of the Clintons." The charge was not extemporaneous. His *Wall Street Journal* mea culpa—"I might have been too emotional at times"—is unpersuasive.

Poisonous is the man. Poisonous is Trump's inability to abandon mob incitement as his mode of political operation. Meanness is how this man gets his kicks. Always was, always will be.

It has become axiomatic to regret the tribal division of the United States—the inability to build bridges or even hold conversations across ideological divides, the sharpening national fracture into algorithm-consolidated political silos—and, of course, the Kavanaugh hearings now constitute Exhibit A in this unraveling.

There's something pathetic about these laments. No call for civility or the capacity for civilized disagreement (the sign of any healthy society) has any weight when, from the highest office in the land, there emanates a stream of partisan vilification. The Oval Office either ennobles Americans or befouls them. There is no escape from the current poison, other than to vote Trump out.

Corrupting is the man. Corrupting is a presidency dedicated to the blurring of the line between truth and falsehood. False or misleading statements have issued from him several times a day. It's impossible to recall on Friday the lie that outraged you on Monday. The effect of this is to devalue truth. More and more Americans care little for the sacredness of facts. I see references, even in the nation's best newspapers, to the "reality-based press" or "fact-based journalism." What other kind is there?

In the end, the Kavanaugh hearings have been about the pursuit of truth—the truth of this Jekyll-and-Hyde man, the truth of whether he assaulted Dr. Blasey, the truth of his words. I believe he failed the test of truth in ways that disqualify him from confirmation.

But the meaning of honesty is not something Americans can agree on anymore. So the hearings have been about everything but that: white privilege, the #MeToo movement, and, of course, Donald Trump.

Corrosive is the man. Corrosive is the pollution of the FBI, which now seems about to be extended to the Supreme Court. Other pillars of the Republic, including a free press, are in Trump's sights. Behind the scattershot outbursts, there is a consistent pattern. It conforms to all we know about a president whose sympathies lie with the autocrats of the world, from Moscow to Manila, rather than with democratic leaders.

Free societies do not die overnight. The growth of a climate of intellectual fear is one sign of their weakening. So are the development of a personality cult, the stripping of meaning from language, and the spread of disorientation.

Infectious is the man. Infectious is Trump's hard work to bring the whole country down to his level. A spineless Republican Party folds into the Trump Party. Uncle Sam wants you in his indecent reality show. If, as now seems likely, Kavanaugh is confirmed, Trump will be confirmed; and the damage this president has done will look more irreparable in the age of the judge-agent.

THE BARBARIANS
ARE WITHIN

America is threatened to its core and only Americans are to blame.

OCTOBER 26, 2018

I have been reading J. M. Coetzee's novel *Waiting for the Barbarians*. It concerns a magistrate, a servant of Empire, stationed on a remote frontier, who watches with mounting indignation as fear of barbarian encroachment is used to justify a brutal and self-defeating imperial campaign of violence and torture. It is a portrait of an aging man, stung by his conscience, bewildered by his times.

In one passage, Coetzee writes: "Every year the lake-water grows a little more salty. There is a simple explanation—never mind what it is. The barbarians know this fact. At this very moment they are saying to themselves, 'Be patient, one of these days their crops will start withering from the salt, they will not be able to feed themselves, they will have to go.' That is what they are thinking. That they will outlast us."

Barbarians come in different guises. Coetzee's novel turns in part on the fact that the barbaric presence in his pages is the Empire, not the Empire's imagined enemies. It is of the nature of declining powers to imagine foes, to flail, to produce zealots, to embark on doomed wars, to flex the atrophying muscles of dominance. It is of the nature of life that imagined enemies, once provoked, turn into real ones.

On horseback, ragged mirages in the dust, Coetzee's barbarians do not really need to do anything. Hardly more than chimera, they suck the Empire into their labyrinth. This is because the Empire is dying, just as the magistrate is dying. He is an aging libertine with an agile mind and a love of knowledge—a speck, as he sees with unforgiving insistence, on history's tide. This is a novel about the desperation of mortality.

Surveying the American scene in the run-up to the midterm elections early next month, it is hard to escape that word: desperation. This time the barbarians are not shabby. They are well groomed, well heeled, loudmouthed; and they never heard a chord, or read a phrase, or saw a sensuous line on a canvas that caused them to pause in wonder.

These barbarians chose their moment well. The Empire Lite has not known a victory in far-flung wars in all the seventeen years since it was attacked. The millions who served at distant, tedious frontiers were scarcely recognized on their return. They trudged their trauma home in sullen silence.

They watched, these unacknowledged servants of the imperial Republic, as certainties evaporated and precariousness spread and words lost meaning and money rode roughshod over sacrifice. The mood in the Empire was restive, ripe for a self-declared savior ready to deploy the language of violence and identify scapegoats.

In due course, along came the barbarian savior, marching across the ramparts, through the gates of the capital, and declaring the rapt crowd to be the largest in recorded history. He had been chosen to blow up the whole place. He set about his task with vigor.

What can be said at this point about the self-styled savior? He is a man of fiendish energy and malicious intuitions who gets the blood up by appealing to the barbarian in us all. He says he wants to make the Empire great again, but all he really wants to do is to loot it on the way down. His Republican cronies enable him because their love of power blinds them to the contagion they propagate.

The barbarian savior loves to see a reporter body-slammed, to parade his ignorance, to strut his lies, to broadcast his bigotry, to empower rich Middle Eastern murderers, to humiliate a woman traumatized by sexual assault, to incite his followers to violence, to sap civilization, to toy with nuclear Armageddon as a distraction from his scam.

The barbarian game is clear: To blind Americans to the fact that the United States is a self-governing enterprise. To say government is evil, government is terrible, bad government is what Democrats do—so just leave it to us! In short, the objective is to *outlast us*, and to eviscerate the institutions that make us, us. But no! We Americans are self-governing, and in the face of malevolent and feckless and corrupt people, there are better options. That is what the vote on November 6 is about.

In Coetzee's novel, the magistrate encounters a zealous officer,

Colonel Joll, who has been dispatched to the frontier to crush the barbarians. Joll is a torturer, a man of implacable certainties, blinding "barbarian" prisoners, crushing their feet. The magistrate-narrator strives to
maintain a certain civility in his exchanges with Joll, but grows disgusted:
"Throughout a trying period he and I have managed to behave towards
each other like civilized people. All my life I have believed in civilized
behaviour; on this occasion, however, I cannot deny it, the memory
leaves me sick with myself."

There comes a moment, when the barbarian is within, to draw a
line, to say enough, to speak out, to make a stand whatever the cost. The
desperation of mortality can also yield the lucidity of courage.

AMOS OZ'S REBUKE
TO COWARDICE

I lost a good friend and a great writer and reflected on his passing
in a world where his values are threatened.

JANUARY 4, 2019

Napoleon is said to have remarked that if he had been killed in 1812,
as he entered Moscow in triumph, he would have gone down in history
as the greatest general who ever lived. Then came the retreat, the long
limp back to France, and unspeakable loss.

Good timing in death, as in any departure, is important. I have been
thinking about this in relation to the passing last month of Amos Oz, the
great Israeli novelist whom I counted as a friend. He was the conscience
of Israel, true to the founding ideals of the nation and to Judaism itself,
and he went as every idea he had stood for—peace, compromise, dignity, decency, and human rights—is being trampled in the Holy Land
and beyond.

Oz, at least, will be spared the spectacle of Benjamin Netanyahu, the Israeli prime minister, fawning over an American president, Donald Trump, whose notion of peace in the Middle East seems to be a dismissal of every Palestinian claim. He will be spared the littleness of the leaders of Israel and Palestine. He will be spared their cowardice. He will be spared the farce of Jared Kushner's ideas about peace, should they ever issue from His Languidness. History is spinning backward.

I would meet Oz at his Tel Aviv apartment. He was an early riser. His best working hours were between 5:30 and 8:30 a.m. "You have to work very hard for your readers not to note a single false note," he told me. "That is the business of three quarters of a million decisions." He told me, with that twinkling smile of his, about receiving a literary prize from China and telling a crowd in Beijing how honored he was because between them the Chinese and the Jews represented close to 20 percent of humanity.

He believed that Jews should laugh.

Scorning zealotry, he also believed Jews should never abandon contentious debate, the "intergenerational quizzing that ensures the passing of the torch," as he put it in *Jews and Words,* written with his daughter Fania Oz-Salzberger. He believed Jews need a homeland, Israel. His father, as a young man in Lithuania, endured the refrain: "Jews go home to Palestine." Now plenty of people scream, "Jews get out of Palestine." Enough said.

Or not quite enough said. Jews will be just fine in a binational state shared with the Palestinians! Jews will be just fine as anti-Semitism rises again! Jews will be just fine forgetting the millennia of persecution and insult in the diaspora! Jews will be just fine trusting those they have no cause to trust!

Oz, who fought in two wars, did not believe it. I do not believe it. As he once said to me of that most sacred of Palestinian principles, "The right of return is a euphemism for the liquidation of Israel."

At the same time, Oz was clear-eyed about the insidious corruption of Israel through more than a half century of the occupation of the West Bank. How it has gradually blinded Israelis to the humanity of millions of Palestinians. How it has made the oppression and humiliation of another people somehow acceptable. How it has ingrained habits of arrogance. How it has fed the rightward lurch that has buried in messianic nationalism the dream of a two-state peace and ensconced a leader, Netanyahu, who made it his foul business to bury Yitzhak Rabin's push for that peace.

Oz told me Netanyahu was a "coward," the anti-Rabin in his inability to have a big or generous thought.

"Building settlements in occupied territories was the single most grave error and sin in the history of modern Zionism, because it was based on a refusal to accept the simple fact that we are not alone in this country," Oz told me.

I once summed up Oz's political credo this way: "Two states, absolutely, are the only answer. Palestinians and other Arabs once treated Israel like a passing infection: If they scratched themselves hard enough it would go away. Israel treated Palestine as no more than 'the vicious invention of a Pan-Arabic propaganda machine.' These illusions have passed. Reality now compels a compromise—'and compromises are unhappy; there is no such thing as a happy compromise.'"

That was a few years ago. Today, it is harder to believe that "reality" compels a two-state compromise. Reality is pushing in another direction. Ethno-nationalist bigots are on the march.

In his masterpiece, *A Tale of Love and Darkness*, Oz described walking out early each morning into the desert near his home in Arad. "Now," he wrote, "you can hear the full depths of the desert silence. It isn't the quiet before the storm, or the silence of the end of the world, but a silence that only covers another, even deeper, silence."

That is how I imagine Oz now, inhaling the biblical silence— a silence that is also an admonition to the shrieking of the cowards who would call themselves leaders.

WHY I AM A EUROPEAN PATRIOT

I am a European patriot and an American patriot. I am from not one
place but several. The bond that binds the West is freedom—the cry
of revolutions on both sides of the Atlantic. There is no contradiction in my patriotisms. Patriotism is to nationalism as dignity is to
barbarism.

JANUARY 25, 2019

When I covered the war in Bosnia I got to know Nermin Tulić, a prominent Sarajevo actor. He had his legs blown off by a Serbian shell on
June 10, 1992.

He raged. He begged me not to look at his stumps. He wondered
how he had ever taken his wife, who was half Serb, in his arms. He told
me how he had wanted to die as he lay in the hospital and, on the floor
below, his wife gave birth to their second daughter.

Only his father's words gave him the will to live: "A child needs his
father even if he just sits in the corner."

I am a European patriot because I witnessed how nationalism could
turn a cosmopolitan European city into the place where Tulić lost his
legs. Nationalism, self-pitying and aggressive, seeks to change the present in the name of an illusory past in order to create a future vague in all
respects except its glory. Pregnant with violence, manipulating fear, it is
an exercise in mass delusion. I hate it with all my being.

As François Mitterrand, the former French president, observed
in 1995, prejudices must be conquered because the alternative is
nationalism—and "nationalism is war."

Almost a quarter century later, nationalism advances. The American
president declares: "You know what I am? I'm a nationalist. Okay? I'm a
nationalist." This is how dangerous words achieve banality.

From Hungary to France, from Poland to Britain, nationalists pour
scorn on the European Union and seek its unraveling.

I am a European patriot because I read the war diary of my uncle Bert Cohen of the Sixth South African Armored Division, Nineteenth Field Ambulance. He reached Italy's Monte Cassino on July 21, 1944. His diary entry:

> Poor Cassino, horror, wreck and desolation unbelievable, roads smashed and pitted, mines, booby traps and graves everywhere. Huge shell holes, craters filled with stagnant slime, smashed buildings, hardly outlines remaining, a silent sight of ghosts and shadows.
>
> Pictures should be taken of this monument to mankind's worst moments and circulated through every schoolroom in the world.

That was Europe not so very long ago. I would also send to every schoolroom a photo of Willy Brandt, the West German chancellor, on his knees in the Warsaw Ghetto in 1970 ("I did what people do when words fail them"); Mitterrand and Helmut Kohl, the French and German leaders, holding hands at Verdun in 1984 in the place where hundreds of thousands of their countrymen died fighting in 1916; Muslim refugees from the Bosnian town of Srebrenica, women and children, their menfolk executed by Serb nationalists, clamoring for help from United Nations forces in 1995.

Will anyone remember Europa? As the Polish poet Wisława Szymborska wrote of the aftermath of war: "Those who knew / what was going on here / must make way for / those who know little. / And less than little. / And finally as little as nothing."

European patriots do remember. They are multiplying in the face of danger. Writers including Milan Kundera, Elfriede Jelinek, Ian McEwan, Anne Applebaum, Salman Rushdie, Bernard-Henri Lévy, Herta Müller, Adam Michnik, and Orhan Pamuk have just published an important European manifesto, drafted by Lévy.

Europe, it declares, "has been abandoned by the two great allies who in the previous century twice saved it from suicide; one across the Channel and the other across the Atlantic. The continent is vulnerable to the increasingly brazen meddling of the occupant of the Kremlin. Europe as an idea is falling apart before our eyes. . . . We must now fight for the idea of Europe or see it perish beneath the waves of populism."

We must. European unity is a peace magnet. I am a European patriot for my children and grandchildren. It is they who will pay the price if the most beautiful postwar political idea dies.

"EVERYONE HERE KNOWS TRUMP HATES BROWN PEOPLE"

I visited El Paso and Ciudad Juárez and found the American and Mexican cities complementing each other in many ways. Trump had done his best to aggravate the immigration question, an issue no recent administration has been able to resolve, with his wall.

FEBRUARY 11, 2019

EL PASO—I have a suggestion for President Trump. Instead of fanning fear during your visit to this city on Monday night, stroll across the Paso del Norte Bridge into Ciudad Juárez. Join the seventy thousand people crossing four bridges who daily form the human tissue linking the United States and Mexico. They work, they study, they eat, they shop, all part of what Dee Margo, the mayor of El Paso, calls "one region, one culture."

I crossed the bridge. Things slow down, as they do when you move from the developed to the developing world. Secondhand clothes for sale hang on simple brightly painted homes, the poorest made of pallets and corrugated iron roofs. Juárez, home to many of the foreign-owned assembly plants known as *maquiladoras*, has a violent history and big social problems, but in the dusty streets and cafés serving steaming bowls of tripe-and-bean soup I discerned no tension.

"It's simple," Julián Cardona, a photographer, told me. "Everyone here knows Trump hates brown people. We call him 'Trompudo,' or 'Big Mouth.'"

From that mouth seeps the sinister specter of an "invasion." Thousands of active-duty troops are dispatched to the border. Concertina wire spreads. The government shutdown that ended on January 25 could be followed soon by Trump's declaration of a national emergency to build his wall. Presidential powers include the power to manufacture a threat where none exists.

"From my vantage point in El Paso there is no crisis," Margo, the mayor, told me. "You look south and you can't tell where El Paso merges into Juárez."

Bridges, in other words, trump walls.

At one of the shelters run by the nonprofit Annunciation House, I met Iris Galindo Maldonado, an undocumented forty-three-year-old woman from Guerrero State, in southwestern Mexico, who entered the United States on January 15 with her ten-year-old daughter to request asylum. Her husband was killed seven years ago by drug dealers angered by his refusal to cooperate with them. She said they have threatened her in turn for refusing to help them smuggle cocaine.

"I've already lived," she told me. "I hope the American authorities support me for my daughter, so she's not in danger, she's not menaced, and gets educated. I told her, even if we stay one week, two weeks, however long it is, use the opportunity to learn English. She's already in school, and I pray to God a lot."

Galindo has been processed by ICE, fitted with an ankle bracelet, and let go to face a long wait in American limbo, along with several hundred thousand others, before her day in immigration court. She has no family in the United States.

"Trump calls us killers, delinquents, and drug dealers," she told me. "In fact, that is exactly what we are fleeing from!"

Annunciation House took her in. Ruben Garcia, the director of the organization, says he is finding beds these days for more than two thousand people a week. If nothing else, Trump's rhetoric and policy swerves have helped feed chaos.

"For Trump, to be a refugee is to be a murderer and a rapist," Garcia told me. "This is what he ran on. He has a can of paint filled with a certain ideology and paints everything with it. To supporters of the wall, I ask: Is it time to take down the Statue of Liberty?"

Representative Veronica Escobar, the successor to Beto O'Rourke, now a possible Democratic presidential candidate, took me down to the spot, near a stretch of existing wall, where border agents detained an eight-year-old Guatemalan boy, Felipe Gómez Alonzo, in December. He later died in United States custody.

The spot is over the Rio Grande, in the United States, but just short of the wall, raising the question of the barrier's usefulness. That is a question the president has refused to address with any seriousness. His wall is much less about security than about macho symbolism—"a monument to bigotry," in Escobar's words.

I got talking to an agent who stopped us as we stepped south of the wall. He said agents in that area detained "three hundred bodies a day." He said the "bodies" were jumping the line. He said that, by the time their cases came before an immigration judge, "the bodies are somewhere else, so they get to stay." So, he concluded, "we really have no authority to enforce the law."

"Bodies," I noted, is a term generally used for dead people. Would it not be better to call them people or human beings, as this is what they are? The agent said he didn't mean that they are dead, but that "bodies" was the favored term.

I was subsequently advised not to read too much into this "law-enforcement vernacular." Border agents are under a lot of pressure. Their gestures of humanity—a birthday cake, a soccer ball—tend to go unrecorded. Still, if you talk about bodies you are liable to see bodies: that is to say, people stripped of their humanity, their agonizing choices, their humble ambitions, and their hopes. It is then easier to forget what we Americans are and where we came from.

When I walked back across the bridge, a United States passport-control officer pored over my passport for several minutes: the Iranian visa, the Iraqi visa, the Chinese visa, the Indian visa. She asked what I do, whether I'd crossed the bridge before, why I'd entered Mexico. She was hostile.

"This guy's from The New York Times," she said, turning to the agent next to her. "What should I do with him?"

He looked me over. "Let him go," he said. I thanked her for the warm welcome home. "Just doing my job," she said.

Trump's rhetoric is not innocuous.

JEREMY CORBYN'S
ANTI-SEMITIC LABOUR PARTY

The rise of anti-Semitism in Britain was evident in Jeremy Corbyn's Labour Party, and was a shameful stain on it.

FEBRUARY 28, 2019

LONDON—Europe's gathering Jewish question came into sharp focus this month when a British MP declared that she had come to the "sickening conclusion" that one of the country's two main political parties, Labour, is now "institutionally anti-Semitic."

Imagine, to gauge the import of this statement, Bernie Sanders suggesting the same thing of the Democrats.

Jew hatred has re-entered the European mainstream through a toxic amalgam of spillover from vilification of Israel, the return of the Jewish plutocrat as hated symbol of the 1 percent, and the resurgence of the Jewish "cosmopolitan" as the target of ascendant nationalists convinced a cabal of Jews runs the world.

The British politician was Luciana Berger, who is Jewish and has been MP for Liverpool and Wavertree since 2010. She has watched, with dismay, as Jeremy Corbyn has allowed a demonological view of Israel to foster Jew hatred in the Labour Party since taking over its leadership in 2015.

So, I asked in an interview, is Corbyn an anti-Semite? "Well," she said, "he's certainly been responsible for sharing platforms with anti-Semites and saying things that are highly offensive and anti-Semitic."

Corbyn, Berger suggested, has contrived to make British Jews different in some way, a process she called "othering." She's had to endure "pictures of Stars of David superimposed on my forehead, and my face imposed on a rat, or many rats. There are pornographic images, violent images, oversize features like a witch. You name it, they've done it." Nine months pregnant, the mother of a small child, she's faced death threats and has to take security measures "a lot more now than I did before."

Not all the anti-Semitic slurs have come from within the party, but the volume of attacks from the left has convinced Berger she had to quit Labour. "I didn't make that decision lightly," she told me, having always believed that Labour was Britain's antiracist party par excellence.

Corbyn, who has taken the party sharply leftward from the now reviled Blairite center, and whose anti-Zionism has long been apparent, has insisted, "I'm not an anti-Semite in any form." He has promised (and promised and promised) to rid the Labour Party of any such poison.

There's nothing anti-Semitic about sympathy for the Palestinian cause or support of Palestinian statehood or disdain for the rightist government of the Israeli prime minister, Benjamin Netanyahu, and its kick-the-can policies to prolong or eternize the occupation of the West Bank. That should be obvious.

But where anti-Zionism crosses into anti-Semitism should also be obvious: dehumanizing or demonizing Jews and propagating the myth of their sinister omnipotence; accusing Jews of double loyalties as a means to suggest their national belonging is of lesser worth; denying the Jewish people's right to self-determination; blaming through conflation all Jews for the policies of the Israeli government; pursuing the systematic "Nazification" of Israel; turning Zionism into a synonym of racism.

The denial of the millennial Jewish link to the Holy Land and the dismissal of the legal basis for the modern Jewish state in United Nations Resolution 181 of 1947 (Arab armies went to war against its Palestinian-Jewish territorial compromise and lost) as a means to argue for the abolition of the Jewish homeland and portray it as an immoral, colonial exercise in theft often flirts with anti-Semitism. It is at its most egregious when it issues from Europeans who seem to have forgotten where the Holocaust was perpetrated. Once in the gas chambers was enough for the Jews.

For Corbyn, who turns seventy this year, misunderstandings or imprecision explain incidents like his description of British Zionists as having "no sense of English irony"; or his inviting to Parliament a Palestinian Islamist who had suggested Jews were absent from the World

Trade Center on 9/11 ("I have on occasion appeared on platforms with people whose views I completely reject," Corbyn says); or his appearance in 2014 at a wreath-laying ceremony in Tunis that appears to have honored Palestinians associated with the 1972 Munich Olympics terrorist attack, which killed eleven Israelis.

(Corbyn has said that he was present but "not involved" in the wreath laying and that he attended out of a desire to see "a fitting memorial to everyone who has died in every terrorist incident everywhere.")

The semantic evasions and denials that Corbyn "just kind of trots out," in Berger's words, have not dented the persistence of the problem, to the point where she's had it: "Enough is enough."

Berger is not alone. Eight other Labour MPs have quit the party, mainly in protest at Corbyn's leftward lurch and rule by diktat. All but one of them, Ian Austin, who decried Labour's "culture" of anti-Semitism, have joined a new Independent Group, bolstered by three Conservative parliamentarians, in an attempt to rebuild the British political center.

The jolt to Labour seems to have galvanized the party to confront the seeping infiltration of anti-Semitism. Tom Watson, the deputy leader, has called on Corbyn to expel Labour members accused of anti-Semitism. They've tended to face mild reprimands, if that. John McDonnell, the shadow chancellor, said there'd been "a lot of listening but not enough action." Jon Lansman, a founder of the Momentum organization, which has supported Corbyn, now says there is "a major problem" with "hard-core anti-Semitic opinion." Where have these guys been in recent years, during what Pat McFadden, another Labour MP, described to me as "open season for the abuse of my Jewish colleagues"?

In a typical incident this week, a Labour MP who is a Corbyn ally, Chris Williamson, tried to express regret for saying the party had been "too apologetic" about anti-Semitism, only to claim in his "apology" that it is "often forgotten" how few cases of anti-Semitism there are. He has been suspended.

Under Corbyn, actions have usually lagged words. The party decided in 2016 that "Zio," an insult used by the Ku Klux Klan, was unacceptable. Its use persists as an abbreviation of Zionist, itself turned into a dirty word.

"I am very proud and very relaxed about the fact that I openly support the creation of the state of Israel and the right for the Jewish people to have a homeland," Berger said, noting that she's a Zionist but "others have sought to hijack the word" and "we know" what "language can inspire and what actions it can result in."

We do. This month, Yellow Vest protesters in Paris accosted Alain Finkielkraut, a leading French essayist and the son of an Auschwitz survivor. Their abuse included cries of "Back to Tel Aviv" and "France belongs to us." A Jewish cemetery was desecrated. Anti-Semitic incidents rose 74 percent in France in 2018.

The eternal Jewish ogre resurfaces—a convenient scapegoat for economic resentments, precariousness, fear, frustration, or Israel's oppression of Palestinians. Corbyn, wittingly or not, has fed this poison, as his party is now realizing. He has made an irrefutable case for Israel through Labour's abetting of revived European Jew-hatred.

The fundamental link between European anti-Semitism, annihilationist at its apogee, and the decision of Jews to embrace Zionism in the conviction that only a Jewish homeland could keep them safe is something contemporary European theorists of a demonic Israel prefer to forget. This amnesia is an additional reason that I, too, like Berger, am a proud Zionist.

A homeland for the Jewish people, which is what the state of Israel was created to be, can't be majority Palestinian. At the same time, a legitimate democracy can't deny rights to a national minority. Israel walks this fine line; in the fifty-two-year-old West Bank occupation, it tramples on it. That is why Israel needs a two-state solution. There is no other way to remain Jewish and democratic, no other way to escape the insidious moral corrosion of dominion.

I don't believe Jews would be just fine without Israel any more than I believe the moon is a balloon. To criticize Israel is imperative; to disavow it, for a Jew, a form of ahistorical folly.

TRUMP AND CONSCIENCE IN THE AGE OF DEMAGOGUES

I told the story of how a Jewish plumber's helper from Brooklyn, Isadore Greenbaum, tried to accost a Nazi during a rally of Hitler sympathizers at Madison Square Garden in 1939. He was reprimanded by a New York judge for putting people's lives at risk.

MARCH 22, 2019

His name is Isadore Greenbaum. He's a Jew, a plumber's helper from Brooklyn. He rushes onto the stage, beneath a portrait of George Washington flanked by swastikas. He tries to accost the Nazi who is denouncing the "Jewish-controlled press" and calling for a "white gentile-ruled" United States. Uniformed storm troopers beat him. Police officers drag him from the stage, pants ripped, arms raised in desperate entreaty. The mob howls in delight.

It's February 20, 1939. More than twenty thousand Nazi sympathizers are packed into Madison Square Garden as Greenbaum attempts to silence Fritz Kuhn, *Bundesführer* (so-called) of the German American Bund. Greenbaum has been enraged by Kuhn's demand that the country be delivered from Jewish clutches and "returned to the American people who founded it."

The twenty-six-year-old Jew is brought before a magistrate who, according to an account in this newspaper, tells him, "Innocent people might have been killed." To which Greenbaum retorts, "Do you realize that plenty of Jewish people might be killed with their persecution up there?"

"Plenty" is an inadequate word for six million, but that was 1939, and human beings tend not to imagine the unimaginable. The pale, dismayed face of the young Jewish boy, arms raised, being rounded up in the Warsaw Ghetto in 1943 is well known. Greenbaum's expression of terrorized anguish in New York City presages it.

All this is caught in Marshall Curry's remarkable Oscar-nominated documentary short, A *Night at the Garden*, composed of footage from the time. Attacks on the press; the take-back-our-country cry; hymns to the true American (or German): there's not much new, as Curry notes, about fascism.

History teaches that a people terrorized will generally comply, but there will always be a few exceptions.

Think the "Tank Man" of Tiananmen Square. Think Anton Schmid, the sergeant in Hitler's army who helped Jews in the Vilnius Ghetto and was executed in 1942. Think Ron Ridenhour, the helicopter gunner in Vietnam spurred by conscience to gather information that led to the official investigation into the My Lai massacre. Think Isadore Greenbaum. It is the essence of such gestures that they appear futile, yet have the power to redeem humanity.

Our age, too, is one of demagogues. What are we to make of our "ivory-gold colossus"—James Lasdun's phrase in his brilliant new novel of the #MeToo era, *Afternoon of a Faun*? This colossus, "at once menacing and cosmically aggrieved," who for two hours perorates before the Conservative Political Action Conference (only would-be or actual dictators afflicted with narcissistic disorders talk for that long) and declares: "I'm in love, and you're in love. We're all in love together."

Who, for President Trump, are his people in love? They are "our people." Now, "our people" are not synonymous with the American people. This president, unlike his predecessors, has never seen himself as the president of all Americans.

No, they are the CPAC crowd, his fans. They are the "tough people," the people who could make things "very bad" if necessary—police and military and bikers who, the president claimed in an interview with *Breitbart News* this month, support him. He needs people in his thrall, like that Madison Square Garden crowd. As Lasdun wrote, "Nothing short of dominion over the entire universe could compensate for the wrongs done to him."

The wrongs, that is, of journalists, judges, and Hollywood directors—anyone who thinks the president might just be a dangerous white nationalist charlatan. Why think that? Because Trump, from day one, has maligned brown people and Muslims; and, as president, he saw "very fine people on both sides" at the 2017 Charlottesville rally where white nationalists chanted "Jews will not replace us" and a woman who protested, Heather Heyer, was killed.

I am not suggesting Trump resembles Hitler. That should be obvious—but not so obvious that I will refrain from writing this column. The white nationalist mass murderer of Muslims in New Zealand was not out of his mind in seeing Trump as a symbol of "renewed white identity and common purpose." Trump's love affair is with revanchist white people who don't like the demographic look of the twenty-first century.

Throughout the world today, from Saudi Arabia to the Philippines, from Guatemala to North Korea, bad things happen because the Trump administration winks at them. The United States as moral guardian, however flawed, has vanished.

It's not that Trump could be dangerous. He is dangerous. People die because the worst leaders know they enjoy the American president's connivance. The debate on whether Trump is harmless, whether we should laugh away his grotesquerie, is misplaced. I have no doubt that the worst is yet to come. In his own mind, whatever the Mueller report contains, Trump cannot lose.

Greenbaum and his wife moved to southern California. A fisherman at Newport Pier, Greenbaum died in 1997. There was, as Philip Bump observed in *The Washington Post*, "a brief mention of his passing in the local news."

A CATHEDRAL
FOR A FRAGILE AGE

Notre-Dame burned. Paris, and the world, gazed in horror at the flames engulfing a cathedral that came to symbolize a generous faith.

APRIL 16, 2019

Kilometer Zero: Notre-Dame de Paris, the place from which distance in France is measured, the reference of a people, the starting point and end point, the "epicenter," as President Emmanuel Macron put it. That is why so many people, religious or not, were in tears as the great cathedral burned. A part of themselves, their bearings, was aflame.

Ransacked during the revolution in an anticlerical frenzy, restored and rebuilt during the nineteenth century after tempers cooled, site of imperial coronation, national liberation, and presidential funerals, Notre-Dame became the nation's soul, the place where France could reconcile its turbulent history, the monarchical and the republican, the religious and the secular.

The centuries proved ecumenical. Time made the cathedral everyone's, in France and beyond France. "A mine of memories," said Claire Illouz, an artist born and raised in Paris. "For us all."

What is Paris after all? Beauty. The horror of it lay in watching beauty burn, the delicate spire toppling into an inferno of eight-hundred-year-old beams. Here was as powerful an expression as exists of the sacred, going up in black smoke.

The loss of human life is terrible to behold, but the destruction of beauty may be no less so. In a time of anxiety, of ugliness and hatred and lies, the blaze felt ominous. "Beauty is truth, truth beauty," John Keats wrote, and that is "all ye need to know."

A friend in Paris, Sarah Cleveland, wrote to me: "It was strangely quiet and still, as if people were in a trance, watching the fire boil inside the shell of the cathedral walls, like a cauldron. The scene was solemn, reverent. Hopeless. It seemed impossible that something so monumental could be so fragile."

Civilization is fragile. Democracy is fragile, like that spire. It is impossible today, it is dangerous, to ignore that. When a universal reference goes up in smoke, an abyss opens up.

I remember the cool of the immense interior, now open to the sky, during the summer of 1976, the first summer I lived in Paris. There was a heat wave. Rivers were reduced to a trickle, fountains dry, stores emptied of bottled water. People sat in the pews, stunned. Some prayed. Children played. The young and the old, the innocent and the wise, were gathered. Blue light filtered through the magnificent stained-glass rose windows above the portals. The air smelt of stone and candle wax.

The holiness struck me as inclusive. Notre-Dame is a sanctuary, in a time when the American president spits on sanctuaries and has considered, as punishment, dumping poor migrants in those cities that dare to call themselves by that name.

The half-lit cathedral I first saw as a young man allowed for human error, like those revolutionaries after 1789 lopping the stone heads off biblical kings they mistakenly took to be French. In time the children playing in the transept would be mine. Two of them were born in Paris, city of gilt and gravel, its islands pointing their prows to the bridges, its arteries anchored by Notre-Dame; the cathedral always there across the Seine, reassuring, its façade as solemn as the twin bell towers, its flanks as fanciful as the flying buttresses and gargoyles, monumental from any angle whatsoever.

Our Lady of Paris is still there after the blaze, with her towers, roofless now. President Macron vowed to rebuild the cathedral. Money is pouring in. The French president was dignified, a reminder of the unifying power of dignity at a time when it has vanished from the White House.

Notre-Dame, Macron said, is "our history" and "our imaginary": a means, in other words, to remember and an inspiration to all who aspire for something transcendent, beyond self. The contribution of President Trump, for whom self is all, was to suggest sending "flying water tankers" to douse the cathedral. His advice was ignored.

Perhaps, for an American, the closest thing to Notre-Dame, in its power to represent the nation, is the Statue of Liberty, work of a French sculptor. A mist hung over the water the other day, with the magical result that the torch of liberty hovered in the air, apparently detached. Seeing it, I imagined Emma Lazarus's poem rewritten for the age of Trump:

> *Give me your despots, your rich,*
> *Your vulgar tax evaders yearning to flee,*
> *The depraved and debauched that itch*
> *To steal, I will make them free.*
> *Send these, the dishonorable, to watch*
> *How easy it is to corrupt like me.*

I don't recall French civilization feeling so important in my lifetime. It's what we have. There will be ugly polemics over the coming weeks, once the first shock passes, over who was responsible, how this disaster happened, what negligence was involved. But in those silent, reverent, hymn-singing crowds on the streets of Paris, I also saw the possibility of a French coming-together in the determination to rebuild—not only the cathedral, but also a nation shaken by the violence of the Yellow Vest movement and the social divisions it reflects. The story of Notre-Dame is a story of endurance and rebirth.

It is also a story of European civilization. Notre-Dame survived Hitler, just. Its fragility, now demonstrated, demands Europe's unity, too.

ROBERT MUELLER IN
THE AGE OF THE UNICORN

Of the Theranos scam and the political culture it reflected. Elizabeth Holmes's pinprick blood testing never worked. Yet she held the powerful in her thrall.

APRIL 19, 2019

"What about these notes?" President Donald Trump demands of Donald McGahn, then his White House counsel. "Why do you take notes? Lawyers don't take notes. I never had a lawyer who took notes."

Of all the hallucinogenic moments chronicled in Robert Mueller's report, this is one of the most dizzying. McGahn has been summoned to the White House in February 2018 because a livid Trump wants him to deny something truthful. McGahn explains that he can't "correct" an accurate report in *The Times* that the president had instructed him to have Mueller "fired." He takes notes because he's a "real lawyer."

In fact, McGahn, like many sucked into Trump's corrupting White House orbit, takes notes in the same way people try to get themselves inoculated when they enter a zone of contagion. He wants a contemporaneous record of the truth to protect himself and—God knows—the Republic against Trump's lies. He knows what an oath to uphold the Constitution means. If there is one overwhelming conclusion of the Mueller report it is that Trump, aka "boss man," holds the law and truth in utter contempt. That this is unsurprising only makes it more appalling.

"I've had a lot of great lawyers, like Roy Cohn," Trump tells McGahn. "He did not take notes." You don't take notes when you want no record of your dereliction. Of course, Cohn is Trump's role model: in New York, Cohn, McCarthyism's ruthless enforcer, was disbarred for misconduct including dishonesty and fraud.

The Mueller report won't move the political needle. Trump's tens of millions of supporters know all this. They knew he was a scam artist before they voted for him in 2016. One of the reasons the report is devastating is that its portrait of an iniquitous presidency once again begs a question of all Americans: How did we put this man in the Oval Office?

It's a question for everyone. To deflect responsibility is too easy. The mirror Trump holds up is to America in its entirety, from Hudson Yards to the death of Main Street, from the Kardashians to the opioid crisis, from the financiers doing the rigging to those left out or left behind, from callow Republicans to compromised Democrats.

The idea of America as a land of unbound self-invention is not new—F. Scott Fitzgerald captured that in *The Great Gatsby*. America is about forgetting; hence the extravagance of its creations. Still, Trump's self-invention is remarkable for its scale and depravity—the way he grasped how hyper-individualism, the money culture, simmering anger, and the collapse of the line between truth and falsehood could be channeled into a victorious presidential campaign. How, in short, he could become the orange icon of the Age of the Unicorn.

The great parable of our age is John Carreyrou's *Bad Blood*, a remarkable account of how a twenty-something Stanford dropout, Elizabeth Holmes, built a company called Theranos that fooled everyone with a supposedly transformational method to test blood. Holmes's pinprick testing that would do away with the hypodermic needle never worked. It was fakery.

There was no there there in Theranos, ever. There was only Holmes, with her strange baritone, parlaying zilch into a company once valued at an estimated nine billion dollars. She entranced a kind of American *Who's Who*—including George Shultz, Jim Mattis, and Henry Kissinger. Theranos was the ultimate "unicorn"—the term coined in 2013 by the venture capitalist Aileen Lee to describe the several dozen software start-ups launched since 2003 and valued at a billion dollars or more, companies that avoid the scrutiny of going public while raising vast sums.

Belief in the Theranos unicorn split families. Shultz clashed with his grandson Tyler Shultz, who became a whistle-blower after working at Theranos. It also crossed party lines: President Barack Obama appointed Holmes as a presidential ambassador for global entrepreneurship. Joe Biden called Theranos "the laboratory of the future."

Holmes spoke—with Chelsea Clinton beside her—at a 2016 fund-raiser for the Clinton campaign.

Myth and manipulation turned Holmes into a billionaire. She incarnated America's collective hallucination and corruption, its vertiginous loss of bearings.

Theranos collapsed thanks to Carreyrou's *Wall Street Journal* reporting. The Security and Exchange Commission charged Holmes with "massive fraud" (she settled), and the U.S. Attorney's Office for the Northern District of California indicted her on federal wire fraud and other charges.

So much for that unicorn. Brexit, another, endures for now.

The unicorn, let's recall, is a legendary creature believed over centuries to exert miraculous powers, particularly through its horn, which—as amulet or powdered—was thought to work as a prophylactic or antidote. Leonardo da Vinci wrote that only "fair maidens" could appease the unicorn's ferocity. The unicorn never existed. It was collective fantasy. That did not make belief in it less tenacious.

We now have a full accounting of the unicorn-in-chief's world. I fear he still has America in his thrall.

"HERE THERE IS NOTHING"

I told, in detail, the story of a single life, which has always seemed to me the most powerful way to tell a wider story. In this case, that of immigration across the Mexican border. After meeting Rigoberto Pablo in New Mexico, wearing an electronic ankle monitor affixed by Immigration and Customs Enforcement, I decided to travel to his home village.

MAY 10, 2019

VADO, New Mexico—Rigoberto Pablo ran out of hope. There was no work, no decent schooling for his children. Nothing in the dried-out streams, wilting coffee plants, and wafting sewage of his village in the western highlands of Guatemala gave him reason to think his family's suffering would end. So, late last year, he crossed the nearby Mexican border, U.S.A.-bound.

Three months later, in February, I met him in this small New Mexico town, a timid man with a gentle smile. Pablo, age thirty-seven, is in American limbo, like hundreds of thousands of migrants. Seated on a sofa in the home of his hosts, he reached down, turned up the hem of his pants, and revealed the electronic ankle monitor that Immigration and Customs Enforcement affixed when it released him. A green light confirmed he was being tracked. "If I take it off," he said, "they'll come after me."

His fourteen-year-old son, Alex, who crossed the border with his father on November 14 and is now in seventh grade at a nearby school, gazed at the device. His dad, he said, is "not a rapist or murderer. He wants to work and I want to study."

If only it were that simple. Rigoberto and Alex Pablo are part of a vast influx. Already, the 460,294 migrants apprehended at the southern border this year outnumber those for all of 2018. Since October, 1 percent of Guatemala's total population—more than 160,000 people—have crossed. Many are children. Almost a year after President Trump ended his cruel "zero tolerance" policy, which ripped kids from their parents, children, most from Central America, are still pouring in—some forty thousand in April alone, almost nine thousand of them unaccompanied by a parent. Last month Juan de León Gutiérrez, sixteen years old, became the third Guatemalan child to die in federal custody in five months. The others were seven and eight.

This situation is unconscionable. Americans of all political stripes should be able to agree on that. The United States has to reconcile being a nation of immigrants and a nation of laws.

Yet our immigration policy is mired in shameful congressional paralysis, with the great diversion of Trump's sea-to-shining-sea wall serving only to fire up his base and fan political differences. His policy zigzags, and his revolving-door appointments, and his threats (including the construction of a "contingency" detention center for migrants at Guantánamo Bay, Cuba) do nothing to address the root of the immigration crisis: the implosion of Central America.

"This crisis is about children, their safety, and the future of our region," said Kevin McAleenan, the acting secretary of homeland security, this month. Nothing he or Mark Morgan, Trump's nominee to head ICE, does will work until the collapse of the region is addressed.

Guatemala is led by a former TV star (sound familiar?) named Jimmy Morales, who ran in 2015 on a slogan of "Neither corrupt nor a thief." That is now a joke. He has tried to expel the International Commission Against Impunity in Guatemala, a United Nations–backed group. He wants to grant amnesty to the perpetrators of the 1980s genocide that killed hundreds of thousands of Guatemalans, most of them indigenous people like the Pablo family. Meanwhile, the state is failing to provide its people with basic food, health care, education, and protection from narco-violence.

Trump says he wants to punish Guatemala and its neighbors for not doing enough to stop the migrants. "No money goes there anymore," he said. But he has winked at Morales's corruption, emboldening him to trash the rule of law that is Guatemalans' only defense. State Department officers seethe at America's abandonment of its values, but political appointees overrule them. Morales keeps Trump happy in various ways. Guatemala moved its embassy in Israel to Jerusalem immediately after the United States did.

No wonder people like Pablo are fleeing. He is planning to petition for asylum, though gaining it will prove difficult; poverty alone isn't a justification. Nonetheless, the backlog in immigration court means he'll probably be able to remain for two to three years before his case is heard. In the meantime, he can't legally work. He's living with Aurelio and Maria Aranda, a family he met through the El Paso–based Border Network for Human Rights. His son is learning English, at least. Migrants bring children because it improves their chances of getting in, but also out of a fervid desire to give them a future.

Pablo told me about the hunger and fear on the weeklong road to the border. Meager rice and beans offered once a day. Being herded this way and that by coyotes—the smugglers he'd paid five thousand dollars in borrowed money. Running under a full moon, climbing eight-foot wire fences, passing babies beneath them and children over them, surrendering in the dawn to the United States Border Patrol.

He has no idea what will happen now. "My wife and three other children are back in the village," Pablo told me. "I miss them. My youngest son was sick. I could not afford the medicine."

The candor of his gaze was almost unbearable. I decided I had to go to his village of Aldea Las Guacamayas to see for myself what had propelled him northward.

It takes over nine hours to drive the roughly 220 miles from Guatemala City northwest to Pablo's home. Volcanic mountains soar, dense with vegetation, browned from lack of rain. Neglect is everywhere: subsiding hillside terraces are barren of cultivation, half-finished houses point rebar at the sky, unkempt shrines commemorate lives tipped over a precipice. Straight-backed indigenous women in bright fabric bestride this wounded landscape.

Guatemala is a beautiful, traumatized country, marked by centuries of white criollo racism toward the Mayans and other indigenous people. During the early 1980s, military-backed death squads rampaged through entire communities, justifying a scorched-earth policy on the spurious principle that "indigenous villages were the rivers in which the leftist guerrillas swam," as Edgar Gutiérrez, a former foreign minister, put it to me. Leftist Sandinistas had triumphed in Nicaragua. The United States, determined to prevent this from happening in Guatemala, supported the paramilitary marauders.

Some two hundred thousand people were killed, including forty thousand who disappeared. This was the Guatemalan genocide, an indelible wound. President Morales has encouraged the slogan "There was no genocide"—a tip of the hat to the military who support him. That Trump has embraced this government, given the past American military support that President Bill Clinton acknowledged as a "mistake," underscores this administration's contempt for human rights.

Pablo's wife, Candelaria Sales Garcia, greeted me outside the family's hillside shack, where a duck pecked at a watermelon rind and a little dog called Dollar slept in the shade. In the kitchen, a wood fire heated beans in blackened pots.

Sales is a woman with a broad smile that can't quite mask her obvious pain. Her husband and one son are gone to North America. Another son, nineteen-year-old Valdomero, struggles to find work. Her daughter, Gabriela, twelve, sits idle because her schoolteachers are no-shows. Her youngest, an eight-year-old named Leo, has a cheek swollen from an intractable infection.

"I said nothing to my husband, although he was leaving me behind here," she told me. "Because I knew that there is nothing here."

Nothing. I kept hearing the word. Nothing from the government, nothing to do—no water, no education, no health care, no jobs—"here there is nothing, nothing," Valdomero declared, sweeping a hand across the sunbaked landscape. The state hardly bothers to collect taxes—they represent a smaller percentage of gross national product than remittances—and does little with them.

Listening to this bright, bilingual young man (he and his family speak the Mam dialect and Spanish), knowing that their brown skins make them invisible to their government, I was reminded of my South African father's summation of why he could not stand apartheid and left: "The waste."

Valdomero does the work his father used to do. He unloads concrete building blocks from trucks. He stacks them. For a day of this, he says, he is paid about eight dollars: hardly enough to keep the family in tortillas. You do this and do this and do this—and then, one day, you have to get out.

As dusk fell, the young man suggested we take a walk up the mountain. It has changed since he was a child. The streams where he played and drank are gone. The birds are gone. So are the coffee trees. The mountainous amphitheater, visible from a ridge, is no longer verdant. For three or four years now, it has been dry and hot.

I have never been anywhere that conveyed such a palpable sense of the earth dying. President Trump thinks climate change is a joke. He should come here. He would understand another big migration-driver.

The only sign of development is a couple of spindly red-and-white telecommunication towers on the ridges. A basic phone is cheap, and Guatemalans pay as they go: the twenty-first century's bread and circuses for the masses.

The next morning, I drove into Mexico with Valdomero. White posts with an official stamp mark the frontier, but there is no control of any kind: no police, no customs or border agents, no barrier, nothing.

A Toyota Hilux roared up from the Mexican side but its driver, seeing a gringo, spun around. "Narcos," Valdomero said. We continued some fifteen miles into Mexico without being asked for a passport or papers.

Coffee, gasoline, corn, chickens, and coffee are openly smuggled back and forth on that road. So are people and drugs, mainly cocaine. Only a tiny fraction of the estimated fourteen hundred tons of cocaine transiting the country annually is interdicted. Congressmen, mayors, and police officers have been paid off by the cartels. Morales will soon be term-limited out; for the presidential election next month, his party has put forward a new candidate, Estuardo Galdámez, who recently posed for a photograph with a convicted drug trafficker.

Guatemala is sliding backward at an alarming rate. The passage from national trauma toward democratic decency is never easy. Here it began with the peace accords of 1996. For a dozen years now, democracy has been buttressed by the efforts of the International Commission Against Impunity in Guatemala, or CICIG, established through a treaty between the United Nations and Guatemala.

CICIG is central to Guatemala's efforts to establish an independent justice system. Morales's two predecessors were jailed on charges of corruption. The United States last month arrested and charged Mario Estrada, a presidential candidate close to Morales, with conspiracy to import cocaine. Morales himself is being investigated in Guatemala for campaign-finance irregularities, and his brother and son face fraud charges. Some of the country's richest families are being investigated for the illegal financing of Morales's political party.

Now President Morales has turned on CICIG, ordering its expulsion and unilaterally terminating its mission. He has banned Iván Velásquez, its head and a former Colombian prosecutor, from re-entering the country—all to scarcely a whimper from a Trump administration notoriously hostile to the United Nations and multilateralism.

Guatemala's Constitutional Court has ruled Morales's measures illegal. The president has said its judgment means nothing: so much for the rule of law. CICIG continues its work, with Velásquez leading it from abroad, but, stripped of any police protection for its personnel, the organization is "in intensive care," as one American official put it to me. When I visited its headquarters in Guatemala City, a ghostly air prevailed.

American support for CICIG had been critical. In 2013, Stephen Rapp, the State Department's ambassador at large for war crimes, visited the courtroom where Efraín Ríos Montt, the former dictator, was tried. Montt was convicted through the bravery of survivors and CICIG-backed prosecutors, though the verdict was later vacated on a technicality. The message could not have been clearer: the United States is resolute in its support of an independent judicial process and Guatemala's nascent rule of law.

No longer. Trump's America has gone AWOL.

"CICIG has mounted a system of terror where it persecutes those who think differently," Morales declared grotesquely to the United Nations General Assembly last September. Earlier that month, Secretary of State Mike Pompeo had tweeted, "We greatly appreciate Guatemala's efforts in counternarcotics and security." That was it.

The State Department, through its deputy spokesman but not Pompeo himself, has declared that the United States is "deeply concerned" about Morales's recent efforts to pass a bill that would grant amnesty to, and free, those convicted of gross human-rights violations during Guatemala's thirty-six-year civil war. But this mild protest was dismissed in Guatemala City as the murmurings of a third-tier bureaucrat—in effect, tacit authorization. The government operates on the basis that it has a green light from the White House.

Many in the State Department are troubled. One officer told me: "It's a strange and disturbing thing. The arguments we make to political appointees are not heard. We have a State Department that basically stood by while Jimmy Morales dismantled the mechanisms put in place to confront impunity."

Luis Arreaga, the United States ambassador in Guatemala, is a career diplomat who has tried to stand up for American principles. For this he has been dismissed in local media as an Obama holdover, called the "worst ambassador in the world," and accused of being both on George Soros's payroll (of course) and an agent of Cuba or Venezuela.

All this is consistent with an elaborate Guatemalan lobbying operation in Washington that has sought to portray CICIG as a bunch of Soros-backed liberal lefties. Several Republicans, including Representative Rick Crawford of Arkansas and Senator Mike Lee of Utah, have proved receptive.

In January, Crawford tweeted in support of the expulsion of CICIG, saying Guatemalans were "entitled to their own sovereignty." In March, Lee tweeted: "Free and fair elections of a nation's representatives, chosen by and for the people, is the foundation of republican government. Our friends in Guatemala should be able to exercise this right, free from foreign influence by the U.S. State Department."

This amounted to a thinly veiled attack on Arreaga, whom Guatemalan media have attempted to portray as backing the presidential candidacy of Thelma Aldana, a tough former attorney general behind several anticorruption cases. She now faces an arrest warrant for alleged embezzlement as Morales maneuvers desperately to block her candidacy. She has taken refuge in El Salvador.

In line with the nationalist playbook at work in Hungary and Poland, Morales has also gone after the independent judiciary relentlessly. Judges are regularly branded as "terrorists."

I went to see Gloria Porras, one of the five justices on the Constitutional Court, Guatemala's last bastion of the rule of law. She is a woman of great poise and dignity, under constant attack.

"Every time we uphold a case of corruption," she told me, they make it possible for "public money to be spent on the basic problems we have." The government says that public money is not sufficient for medicine, education, and roads. "I believe it is sufficient but not used in the right way," she said.

Porras and other colleagues have been threatened with removal from the court. This month there was a bomb threat that forced the court's evacuation. She looked at me with defiant pride.

"They assault my dignity," she said, "because I have zero tolerance for narcotics trafficking and I am independent in my positions. The traffic of drugs to the United States is, as musicians say, in crescendo. The traffic is tied to corruption. Whatever the risks, whatever the attacks, I will do my work. It is a question of legality. It is also a question of honor.

"Every time I make the right decision," she continued, "I contribute to the creation of hope that my country can change."

Every anticorruption decision by an independent justice, in other words, fosters a Guatemala where Pablo and his family do not have to leave in desperation, because they might just have a future.

Before I left Rigoberto Pablo's village, I spoke to his daughter, Gabriela. School had been canceled. She was bored and frustrated. "I want to go to America, I want to study there with my brother," she said. "And I want to see Papa."

No wall will stop the flow of migrants. No raging about rapists or threats to separate families will stop it. No racism against brown people or fear of demographic change in twenty-first-century America will stop it. A broken American immigration system certainly won't stop it. Not as long as Central Americans are desperate.

Trump doesn't believe in multilateral diplomacy. If he were serious, he would involve Guatemala, El Salvador, Honduras, and Mexico in diplomacy on practical steps. He would explore fair and efficient in-country asylum processing. He would stop talking about a wall and slashing foreign aid and start talking about Central American development, a possible Marshall Plan for the region. Mexican migration has declined as Mexican standards of living have risen. There's a lesson there, if Trump were interested.

He would pursue ways to make the Guatemalan-Mexican border something more than a joke, to combat corruption and narcotics trafficking, to fight impunity and establish the rule of law in Central America, to give Guatemalans some belief in their government, to empower the likes of Gloria Porras, to restore American values, to protect human rights, and to match migrants with jobs. And he would declare, "We cannot tolerate the death on our watch of ONE MORE child!"

The unique energy of America's churn is indivisible from the renewal new immigrants bring.

At the same time, if generosity breeds lawlessness, it defeats itself. Somewhere between those truths lie possible compromises on immigration that Republicans and Democrats could agree on—if Trump had not reduced politics to partisan war.

My journey to the border and on to Guatemala left me with a familiar feeling: Trump's America is betraying itself. What brought Rigoberto Pablo and his child here is an old and honorable idea of the United

States: "I came to this country to make money and to improve my life," he told me when we spoke this month. His ankle bracelet had been removed a few weeks before, and in August he will appear in court to apply for asylum. He is a decent, honest man with a decent, honest family. He deserves better than Jimmy Morales's lawlessness and Donald Trump's posturing.

REFLECTIONS ON THE GRADUATION OF MY DAUGHTER

I felt pride, joy, and the remorse of a too-often-absent father when my youngest child graduated from the University of Southern California.

MAY 17, 2019

LOS ANGELES—It's college-graduation month, time of reunions and reflections, an ending and a commencement, and as good a moment as any to take stock. To watch a child go out into the world is to know that there is no hiding from the real measure of your life.

If, as I did, you had a daughter graduating from the University of Southern California, you had to get used to the instant response—"How much did you pay to get her in?"—much as anyone plying my craft these days must grow accustomed to "Oh, yeah, fake news!"

USC has, of course, been Exhibit A in the college-admissions scandal, that squalid parable of a status-obsessed age. A number of very rich people saw no moral issue with paying millions of dollars to get their underperforming children through the side door into top schools. How, after all, could they attend a party without being able to let drop that Henry or Ella is now at Yale?

I am not going to expend any outrage on this. A lot of people are turning inward. There's so much noise, so much hysteria, so much hatred, so much pettiness, so much falseness, so much intolerance, so much that's stomach-turning—and all of it public! The only refuge is inwardness. Nobody can rob you of that.

It was the youngest of my four children who was graduating, so perhaps it was inevitable that I would find myself gripped by sobs. Tears flow freely in my family. Still, what was this? I felt time hurrying on, accelerating toward the exit. I felt pride in her achievement and joy in her radiance. I thought of the long and winding road from her birthplace in Paris to California. I remembered her at her bat mitzvah telling everyone she disagreed with God, and I thought of my parents, now gone, laughing at that. This baby of mine has never been one to sugarcoat her views.

There was something more to those tears: remorse. I could have been a better dad, more present, more patient, more understanding, less consumed by the next deadline. Yes, I could. It's not what school a child goes to that makes the difference, it's the amount of love a child receives that builds the surest foundation for happiness. Not for success, however that is measured, but for happiness.

Sure, I could have done worse, but that's no excuse. There's no point in taking stock unless it's unsparing; and there's no other way to change.

My three other children attended Yale, St. Olaf College, and Boston University. Believe me, there are a lot of good schools in America. I was in Lagos, Nigeria, on assignment when my oldest called me to say she'd gotten into Yale. She said she was going to think about it. "What?" I said. "Yes," she said, she wasn't sure; she might accept a place at Brown or elsewhere. I was outraged. How ridiculous that outrage now seems!

One of the pleasures of growing older is the shedding of ambition.

Times change. When I graduated from Oxford with a second-class degree, having gotten a scholarship to my high school and an Exhibition to Balliol College for academic excellence, my father called me into his office at Guy's Hospital in London. "This is the first time in life that you've failed," he said. He was referring to the fact that I had not gotten a first-class degree.

His verdict crushed me, but I have forgiven him. To be a parent is to fall short.

Jonathan Kellerman, a novelist and psychologist, was the commencement speaker at USC's Dornsife College of Letters, Arts and

Sciences, attended by my daughter. Kellerman, a USC alum, summed up the wisdom he'd gleaned from ingesting countless psychological tomes: "Be nice." That put me in mind of a line sometimes attributed to Plato: "Be kind, for everyone you meet is fighting a hard battle."

Life is a riddle whose only, imperfect solution is love. Love cheats time because it's passed along, refracted through the generations; and it's the reason, with all its illusions, that we're here in the first place. As Eudora Welty writes, "In the sense of our own transience may lie the one irreducible urgency telling us to do, to understand, to love."

All four of my children, whom I love beyond words, having traveled from as far afield as Ho Chi Minh City, in Vietnam, were there in the house we rented for a few days in Los Angeles, along with my ex-wife, whom I love, and her beloved parents, one of them a Holocaust survivor who got through the war in Poland in hiding after her mother had been ripped from her and taken to the gas chamber. Another slender thread: Kraków to L.A. by way of Brazil.

One memory above all: my four children at the kitchen counter doing something we all love—preparing food—with music playing, dancing, laughing, strong, together. It felt intense, beautiful; and it had something to do with my hard-earned capacity for remorse.

It's never too late to grow or to love.

STEVE BANNON IS A FAN OF ITALY'S DONALD TRUMP

Here was a look at the efforts of Steve Bannon in Italy to take the Trump phenomeon global.

MAY 18, 2019

MILAN—Italy is a political laboratory. During the Cold War, the question was whether the United States could keep the communists from power. Then Italy produced Silvio Berlusconi and scandal-ridden showman politics long before the United States elected Donald Trump. Now, on the eve of European Parliament elections likely to result in a rightist lurch, it has an anti-immigrant, populist government whose strongman, Matteo Salvini, known to his followers as "the Captain," is the Continent's most seductive exponent of the new illiberalism.

Steve Bannon, Trump's former chief strategist, has been close to Salvini for a while. That's no surprise. Bannon is the foremost theorist and propagator of the global nationalist, anti-establishment backlash. He's Trotsky to the populist international. He sensed the disease eating at Western democracies—a globalized elite's abandonment of the working class and the hinterland—before anyone. He spurred a revolt to make the invisible citizen visible and to save Western manufacturing jobs from what he calls the Chinese "totalitarian economic hegemon."

Now Bannon is crisscrossing Europe ahead of the elections, held Thursday through next Sunday. He's in Berlin one day, Paris the next. As he explained during several recent conversations and a meeting in New York, he believes that "Europe is six months to a year ahead of the United States on everything." As with Brexit's foreshadowing of Trump's election, a victory for the right in Europe "will energize our base for 2020." The notion of Wisconsin galvanized by Brussels may seem far-fetched, but, then, so did a President Trump.

Polls indicate that Salvini's League party, transformed from a northern secessionist movement into the national face of the xenophobic right, will get over 30 percent of the Italian vote, up from 6.2 percent in 2014. Anti-immigrant and Euroskeptic parties look set to make the greatest gains, taking as many as 35 percent of the seats in Parliament, which influences European Union policy for more than a half-billion people. In France, Marine Le Pen's nationalists are running neck-and-neck with President Emmanuel Macron's pro-Europe party. In Britain, Nigel Farage's new Brexit Party has leapt ahead of the center-right and center-left.

Salvini, whose party formed a government a year ago with the out-with-the-old-order Five Star Movement, is a central figure in this shift. The coalition buried mainstream parties. He is, Bannon told me, "the most important guy on the stage right now—he's charismatic, plainspoken, and he understands the machinery of government. His rallies are as intense as Trump's. Italy is the center of politics—a country that has embraced nationalism against globalism, shattered the stereotypes, blown past the old paradigm of left and right."

For all the upheaval, I found Italy intact, still tempering transactional modernity with humanity, still finding in beauty consolation for dysfunction. The new right has learned from the past. It does not disappear people. It does not do mass militarization. It's subtler. It scapegoats migrants, instills fear, glorifies an illusory past (what the Polish sociologist Zygmunt Bauman called "retrotopia"), exalts machismo, mocks do-gooder liberalism, and turns the angry drumbeat of social media into its hypnotic minute-by-minute mass rally.

Salvini, the suave savior, is everywhere other than in his interior minister's office at Rome's Viminale Palace. He's out at rallies or at the local café in his trademark blue "Italia" sweatshirt. He's at village fairs and conventions. He's posting on Facebook up to thirty times a day to his 3.7 million followers, more than any other European politician. (Macron has 2.6 million followers.) He's burnishing the profile of the tough young pol (he's forty-six) who keeps migrants out, loosens gun laws, brandishes a sniper rifle, and winks at fascism—all leavened with Mr. Nice Guy images of him sipping espresso or a Barolo.

His domination of the headlines is relentless. When, during my visit, a woman was gang-raped near Viterbo, his call for "chemical castration" of the perpetrators led the news cycle for twenty-four hours. Like Trump, he's a master of saying the unsayable to drown out the rest.

"I find Salvini repugnant, but he seems to have an incredible grip on society," Nathalie Tocci, the director of Italy's Institute of International Relations, told me. No wonder, then, that the European far right has chosen Milan for its big pre-election rally, bringing together Salvini, Le Pen, Jörg Meuthen of the Alternative for Germany party, and many other rightist figures.

"The European elections will be decisive for the future of our continent," Macron warned in a manifesto called "For European Renewal." That's probably an exaggeration, but none has ever felt this important, precisely because European integration, the foundation of postwar peace, and liberal democracy itself seem vulnerable. "Nationalist retrenchment offers nothing," Macron declared. The Brexit fiasco is

Exhibit A in that argument. Still, Macron's proposal for the creation of a "European Agency for the Protection of Democracies" speaks volumes about where we are.

A nationalist tide is still rising. "We need to mobilize," Bannon told me. "This is not an era of persuasion, it's an era of mobilization. People now move in tribes. Persuasion is highly overrated."

Bannon gives the impression of a man trying vainly to keep up with the intergalactic speed of his thoughts. Ideas cascade. He offered me a snap dissection of American politics. Blue-collar families were suckers. Their sons and daughters went off to die in unwon wars; their equity evaporated with the 2008 meltdown, destroyed by "financial weapons of mass destruction"; their jobs migrated to China. All that was needed was somebody to adopt a new vernacular, promise to stop "unlimited illegal immigration," and restore American greatness. His name was Trump. The rest is history.

In Europe, Bannon said, the backlash brew included several of these same factors. The "centralized government of Europe" and its austerity measures, uncontrolled immigration, and the sense of people in the provinces that they were "disposable" produced the Salvini phenomenon and its look-alikes across the Continent.

"In Macron's vision of a United States of Europe, Italy is South Carolina to France's North Carolina," Bannon told me. "But Italy wants to be Italy. It does not want to be South Carolina. The European Union has to be a union of nations."

The fact is, Italy *is* Italy, unmistakably so, with its high unemployment, stagnation, archaic public administration, and chasm between the prosperous north (which Salvini's League once wanted to turn into a secessionist state called Padania) and the southern Mezzogiorno. Salvini's coalition has done nothing to solve these problems even as it has demonized immigrants, attacked an independent judiciary, and extolled an "Italians first" nation.

A federal Europe remains a chimera, even if the euro crisis revealed the need for budgetary integration. Bannon's vision of Brussels bureaucrats devouring national identity for breakfast is largely a straw-man argument, useful for making the European Union the focus of all twenty-first-century angst.

The union has delivered peace and stability. It's the great miracle of the second half of the twentieth century; no miracle ever marketed itself so badly. It has also suffered from ideological exhaustion, remoteness, division, and the failure to agree on an effective shared immigration policy—opening the way for Salvini's salvos to hit home in a country that is the first stop for many African migrants.

Salvini grew up in Milan in a middle-class family, dropped out of university, joined the League in its early days in the 1990s, and was shaped by years working at Radio Padania, where he would listen to Italians' gripes. "What he heard was complaints about immigrants, Europe, the rich," Emanuele Fiano, a center-left parliamentarian, told me. "He's run with that and is now borderline dangerous."

The danger is not exit from the European Union—the government has come to its senses over that—or some fascist reincarnation. It's what Fabrizio Barca, a former minister for territorial cohesion, called the "Orbánization of the country," in a reference to Viktor Orbán, the right-wing Hungarian leader. In other words, insidious domination through the evisceration of independent checks and balances, leading Salvini to the kind of stranglehold on power enjoyed by Orbán (with a pat on the back from Trump) or by Vladimir Putin. "The European Union has been ineffective against Orbán," Barca noted. Worse, it has been feckless.

Another threat, as in Trump's United States, is of moral collapse. "I am not a Fascist but . . ." is a phrase increasingly heard in Italy, with some positive judgment on Mussolini to round off the sentence. Salvini, in the judgment of Claudio Gatti, whose book *The Demons of Salvini* was just published in Italian, is "post-Fascist"—he refines many of its methods for a twenty-first-century audience.

Barca told me that the abandonment of rural areas—the closing of small hospitals, marginal train lines, high schools—lay behind Salvini's rise. Almost 65 percent of Italian land and perhaps 25 percent of its population have been affected by these cuts. "Rural areas and the peripheries, the places where people feel like nobody, are home to the League and Five Star," he said. To the people there, Salvini declares: I will defend you. He does not offer a dream. He offers protection—mainly against the concocted threat of migrants, whose numbers were in fact plummeting before he took office because of an agreement reached with Libya.

The great task before the parties of the center-left and center-right that will most likely be battered in this election is to reconnect. They must restore a sense of recognition to the forgotten of globalization. Pedro Sánchez, the socialist Spanish prime minister, just won an important electoral victory after pushing through a 22 percent rise in the minimum wage, the largest in Spain in forty years. There's a lesson there. The nationalist backlash is powerful, but pro-European liberal sentiment is still stronger. If European elections feel more important, it's also because European identity is growing.

As for the curiously prescient Italian political laboratory, Bannon is investing in it. He's established an "Academy for the Judeo-Christian West" in a thirteenth-century monastery outside Rome. Its courses, he told me, will include "history, aesthetics, and just plain instruction in how to get stuff done, including facing up to pressure, mock TV interviews with someone from CNN or *The Guardian* ripping your face off."

Bannon described himself as an admirer of George Soros—"his methods, not his ideology"—and the way Soros had built up "cadres" throughout Europe. The monastery is the nationalist response to Soros's liberalism. There's a war of ideas going on in Italy and the United States. To shun the fight is to lose it. I am firmly in the liberal camp, but to win, it helps to know and strive to understand one's adversary.

THE LESSONS OF PARIS
AND THE VIOLENCE OF HOPE

I came to live in Paris for the first time in 1975–76 and never recovered. Here I examined why.

MAY 31, 2019

PARIS—To be a Francophile is a life sentence. It's not exactly a badge of honor, not a burden either, but a slightly illicit gift of ever-renewed pleasures.

How I love French realism, the shrug and the *"Bof"* that say this too will pass, even the Orange Man in the White House. It is not only in matters of the heart that the French are shockproof.

Paris has been important to me. It's where I came of age, escaping the damp clutches of Oxford to teach in a *lycée* beside the prison in the southern suburb of Fresnes. (Aaah, the whiff of garlic, sauvignon blanc, and Gitanes on the early-morning Métro.) It's where I started in journalism forty-two years ago. It's where I was freed by another language to reinvent myself and discovered that, despite appearances, I was an outsider. It's where I began to see that writing was not a choice but a need.

It's where I lived and loved and wandered and had two of my four children. It's where I returned from covering the Bosnian war—the hundred thousand dead, the 2.2 million displaced—and understood the moral abdication of the bystander and the moral imperative of engagement and decency, that word dear to Camus. It's where I felt the bond forged in the blood of France and the United States, and grasped the vigilance needed to safeguard the institutions that transformed and protected this Europe: NATO and the European Union. It's where I grappled with history and memory and understood, even before the Balkans, how distinct they are—and how vulnerable is the civilization Paris embodies.

The idea that nobody is above the law is what stands between civilization and barbarism. There's a reason the American president's oath is to the Constitution, not to the people (*das Volk*), who may become a mob.

The rightist wave rises still. But 2019 is also the year when the European Parliament election ceased to be a sideshow. Many Europeans, I feel here, have awoken to the need to preserve the great miracle of the second half of the twentieth century—that aspiration of the bloodied, that bastion of law, that European Union.

For a long time, over the course of my life, I watched liberty and democracy spread. The fall of the Berlin Wall and the wars of Yugoslavia's destruction were pivot points. They cemented, for me, the link between America and freedom, America and peace. Alone among nations, the United States could make me an insider overnight. That is why New York is my home.

I lived enough of the American century to feel it in my bones. That movie, however, has ended. History is not an argument leading to a logical conclusion, any more than human nature is a thing of black and white. History is flux and our natures conflicted. The specters of nationalism and xenophobia have stirred. It's time to recall that the quest for homogeneous societies led the twentieth century to its most unspeakable horrors.

The unimaginable can happen. In April, flames engulfed Notre-Dame. Democracy is fragile, like that toppled spire. The Jews of Germany have been advised not to wear kippas in public, to which the response of every member of the German government should be to don a yarmulke.

President Trump beckons us into the abyss of the hateful. The arc of his mind bends toward injustice. I wish I did not have to say this. I am a naturalized American with an outsized belief in my country's capacity for good—the blemished beneficence of American power.

Today, however, patriotism demands the defense of the Constitution, the rule of law, truth, freedom, human rights, and the planet itself against the ravages issuing from the Trump White House. Every day the American idea is sullied. Every day the distinction between truth and falsehood is undermined. I hear talk of fact-based journalism. What a ridiculous tautology!

Looking ahead to 2020, I feel uneasy. Americans are decent people. Trump authorized the forced separation of thousands of children from their parents. On that basis, the result of the presidential election should be a foregone conclusion.

But the old politics are dead. The post-1945 world is gone. The post–Cold War world is gone. Donald Trump is the most formidable exponent of the Age of Undoing. The incumbent always has an advantage. With a strong economy, that advantage is redoubled.

Pax Americana had a good run. It was eroding before Trump; he applied the coup de grâce. In this unquiet transition, Paris reassures me. It is a repository of our fantasies, a redoubt of hope, a source of courage.

Courage is needed today. It is a time to fight without relenting for the idea of Paris against the rise of nationalist bigotry.

When I was a young man in Paris, I learned by heart Guillaume Apollinaire's poem "Le Pont Mirabeau." I recall standing on the bridge and murmuring one line in particular—*"Comme la vie est lente, et comme l'Espérance est violente"*—"How slow life is, and how violent hope."

RICHARD HOLBROOKE AND A CERTAIN IDEA OF AMERICA

I watched Richard Holbrooke achieve the impossible and end the Bosnian war. More than one hundred thousand people had already been killed; another hundred thousand might have died. He was not easy. But he was always deeply serious in his belief in America's capacity to create a more free and more just world.

JUNE 14, 2019

On July 6, 1939, a couple of months before the outbreak of World War II, a young Polish Jewish immigrant named Abraham Dan Golbraich went before a judge and changed his name to Dan A. Holbrooke.

He was to be the father of Richard Holbrooke, a diplomat whose fierce talent ended a European war and whose life story has now been told in George Packer's remarkable book, *Our Man*. Of Golbraich's instant American reinvention, Packer observes: "What a great country!"

Richard Holbrooke believed this to his core. America could remake, redeem, and rescue, as it had his family. His conviction drove a quest to spread peace to the far corners of the earth. "America is always best," Holbrooke noted in a journal, "when it is true to its own values + ideals," advanced through "steady articulation and skillful pressure." The forty-eight-year arc of his experience from Vietnam to Afghanistan exposed America's failings but never dented this essential patriotism. Packer writes: "Human suffering didn't plunge him into psychological paralysis or philosophical despair. It drove him to furious action."

As a *New York Times* correspondent covering the Bosnian war in 1995, I saw the Holbrooke whirlwind up close. Every journalist then in Sarajevo knew that, with a hundred thousand people already killed in more than three years of fighting, the war could not be stopped. He stopped it.

The bullying theater was riveting, but, as always with Holbrooke, spectacle was also purpose. Another hundred thousand human beings may be alive today in the Balkans because of him. I will never forget it. Holbrooke deserved the Nobel Peace Prize, a slam-dunk case. Barack Obama, later his chilly nemesis, would win one just for existing.

By what strange process this achievement of Holbrooke's has been belittled—a review of Packer's book in *The New Republic* speaks of the "liberal legend," of how "he had solved the riddle of the Balkan Peninsula"—is a conundrum that says much about our times. This is an age of cynicism, of limited hope, of valueless posturing, in which American interventionism is ridiculed.

Holbrooke, raised on postwar optimism at the apogee of American power, perceived the world otherwise. The optimism extended into my generation. We saw the Berlin Wall fall about halfway through our lives and understood with visceral certainty how American values, resolutely defended, advance liberty, not least for about a hundred million Central Europeans.

This was no liberal legend. It was liberal conviction based on the experience of America's steady shaping of a more stable world. The

NATO bombing that led to Bosnian peace was successful interventionism. It saved countless lives; it also salvaged humanity in the sense that it was a belated response to the Serb-run concentration camps for Bosnian Muslims—a horror grasped by Holbrooke when he encountered brutalized survivors in 1992. Holbrooke always wanted to see for himself, a conspicuous virtue.

Interventionism's moral core is not some disposable adjunct. It's inextricable from the idea, now atrophied, of an improvable world in which certain inalienable rights exist and certain forms of evil—those bestial camps—must be confronted. That's the American idea. The Iraq war showed its fallibility but not its worthlessness. Holbrooke, as Packer writes, "believed that power brought responsibilities, and if we failed to face them the world's suffering would worsen."

Holbrooke could be a pompous, self-serving, ruthless, insinuating ass. He bumped an old couple, survivors of the Holocaust, off the official American bus to Auschwitz on the fiftieth anniversary of the liberation to secure a place for himself—what else do you need to know? He was a cheapskate. He slept with his best friend's wife. He was dismissive of colleagues. He was an absent father—"Daddy all gone," says his younger son, Anthony—and a man of "scattered cruelties." I introduced him to my ex-wife seven times; she did not matter to him and was therefore invisible. He barreled through life intent on becoming secretary of state, never turning his otherwise lucid gaze inward; and so he made the enemies who would frustrate that devouring, ultimately blinding and life-curtailing, ambition.

Packer's book makes clear how much of his subject's frenzy was compensatory, a masking device. Even as his family's story inspired him in ways he would not avow, Holbrooke expended immense psychological energy on suppressing that past. He expunged his father, who died young, and he suffered through the joke that the rumors he was half Jewish were only half true.

"He became the son of no one and nowhere—of himself, of America," Packer writes. Holbrooke avoided Israel-Palestine in his diplomacy, because it was a minefield that might demand inward reflection. The result is a paradox: a man passionate about America's vocation to save, yet burying the saved Polish Jew Golbraich, his father, inside him.

This was a strain. There is pathos in Holbrooke's words to Diane Sawyer, a longtime girlfriend between his three marriages: "I've had to fight like hell for everything I have, because for some reason people don't like me." Some reason? Holbrooke never considered that question worth exploring. So he veered from the high seriousness and idealism of his diplomacy to the self-defeating nakedness of his ambition.

"Try to separate the best from the worst—you can't," Packer writes. Holbrooke, so split, emerges as "almost great."

This is another unfashionable view in a time of shrieking certainties. The notion that people contain multitudes, not all of them pretty; that human nature is shifting; that the most talented American diplomat of the late twentieth century might also be a lousy husband and sometime jerk (or that, for example, a Trump supporter may be a decent, smart American), does not sit easily with all-out tribal warfare.

Nuance is so pallid. Holbrooke was the first American official to denounce the Khmer Rouge, a conspicuous moral stand. He ends up recommending that Cambodia's seat at the United Nations go to Pol Pot's faction because he concludes that America's national interest demands it—a conspicuous moral cave-in. To be a diplomat is to have to swallow hard and accept unsatisfactory outcomes that are better than the alternative. In this particular case, I think he swallowed too hard.

As Tony Lake, Bill Clinton's national-security adviser and a former friend whom Holbrooke alienated through his behavior, observed: "What Holbrooke wants attention for is what he's doing, not what he is. That's a very serious quality and it's his saving grace."

Lake and Holbrooke went to Vietnam in the 1960s "as innocents." Foreign Service officers, they wanted to make a difference. Disillusionment sets in. Holbrooke sees that America is fighting not communism but a Vietnamese quest for national liberation—an impossible war. He sees that "Reports lie, they lie." He sees "women crying over the torn bodies of their husbands," and would never forget the image. Like Lake, he carries "the stigma of being on the scene at America's first lost war," and, like Lake, he is driven to make amends over a lifetime.

It's not just Bosnians who were saved by Holbrooke's obsessions. Add to them the hundreds of thousands of Indochinese admitted as refugees to the United States by 1982 in part because of his urging; the millions of African victims of AIDS helped by his relentless efforts; the people of East Timor saved by the international force he helped hurry into Dili; the single journalist, David Rohde, freed by the Serbs in 1995 because Holbrooke kept insisting. Slobodan Milošević, the Serbian strongman, was astounded: "You would do all this for a journalist?" Yes, Holbrooke would.

Of all this, Obama and the people around him knew little and cared less. Holbrooke was windy; he droned on about Vietnam. Jake Sullivan, a senior official, was an exception, an admirer of Holbrooke, but even he saw Holbrooke "as a diplomat from a foreign country—the past."

As Obama's envoy to Pakistan and Afghanistan, the job he held when he collapsed and died from an aortic dissection in 2010, Holbrooke was repeatedly humiliated. The president went to Kabul without him. At the State Department, where higher floors denote seniority, Holbrooke ended up in a cramped office on the first floor. At one point, he defined his goal as "trying to get the Pakistani military to be incrementally less deceitful toward the United States."

Friends told him repeatedly to get out, leave it—abandon a fool's errand. He was willfully blind. He insisted that he could still make a difference, that Obama would soften; perhaps he could even realize his dream of a negotiation with the despised Taliban (of the ultimate necessity of that, he was right as usual); and maybe, somehow, in some unimaginable way, he would yet become secretary of state. At sixty-nine, he was dead.

Holbrooke had a lonely death—abandoned by his president, overtaken by his times, at a moment when his marriage to the author Kati Marton was under strain. In extremis, a doctor tells him to relax. "I can't relax. I'm in charge of Afghanistan and Pakistan," he says before going into the operating theater, never to awaken. Reading all this, I wept.

Marton did an extraordinary thing by giving Packer the intimate correspondence and other papers that made this masterpiece possible. I did not weep just for a friend but also for the America of hope and uplifting ambition that Holbrooke embodied, so entombed in tawdriness right now.

What a great country! Yes, America is, and will be once more, when the nightmare passes, as it must if Americans have half the stubborn resourcefulness and passionate idealism of Richard Holbrooke.

TRUMP'S INHUMANITY
BEFORE A VICTIM OF RAPE

In a conversation with Nadia Murad, a Yazidi woman who won the Nobel Prize in 2018, Trump revealed, again, the breathtaking extent of his ignorance and contempt.

JULY 26, 2019

Daniel Patrick Moynihan, the Harvard professor and four-term United States senator from New York, famously observed, "Everyone is entitled to his own opinion, but not to his own facts."

Today, everyone is entitled to his own facts, or their own facts, since even grammar has changed. The message from the Trump White House, and from Boris Johnson's rise to prime minister in Britain, is that facts don't matter. The bald-faced lie is perfectly acceptable, so long as it keeps you at the center of what passes today for attention. The important thing is to feed the machine. Shock is the best fodder. Social media die without outrage.

In the mid-1930s, a few years before World War II, Robert Musil, the author of *The Man Without Qualities*, wrote, "No culture can rest on a crooked relationship to truth." The political culture of both the United States and Britain is sick. It is unserious, crooked, and lethal. There is no honest way to dissociate the rise of Trump and Johnson from the societies that produced them.

The triumph of indecency is rampant. Choose your facts. The only blow Trump knows is the low one. As the gutter is to the stars, so is this president to dignity. Johnson does a grotesque Churchill number. Nobody cares. The wolves have it; the sheep, transfixed, shrug.

Indignation is finite. Power, the Italians say, wears out those who do not have it. That's Trump's credo. I confess to moments when anger refuses to be summoned by the latest Trump outrage, since, anyway, nobody can remember Friday what was so unconscionable Monday.

Still, I cannot forget Trump's recent treatment of Nadia Murad, a Yazidi woman who won the Nobel Peace Prize last year for her campaign to end mass rape in war. The Islamic State, or ISIS, forced Murad into sexual slavery when it overran Yazidi villages in northern Iraq in 2014. Murad lost her mother and six brothers, slaughtered by ISIS.

She now lives in Germany, and has been unable to return home, a point she made in her July 17 White House meeting with Trump. "We cannot go back if we cannot protect our dignity, our family," she said.

Trump sits there at his desk, an uncomprehending, unsympathetic, uninterested cardboard dummy. He looks straight ahead for much of the time, not at her, his chin jutting in his best effort at a Mussolini pose. He cannot heave his bulk from the chair for this brave young woman. He cannot look at her.

Every now and again, in a disdainful manner, he swivels his head toward her and other survivors of religious persecution. When Murad says, "They killed my mom, my six brothers," Trump responds: "Where are they now?"

Where are they now???

"They are in the mass graves in Sinjar," Murad says. She is poised and courageous throughout in her effort to communicate her story in the face of Trump's complete, blank indifference.

Why this extraordinary attitude from Trump? Well, at a guess, Murad is a woman, and she is brown, and he is incapable of empathy, and the Trump administration recently watered down a United Nations Security Council resolution on protecting victims of sexual violence in conflict.

At the mention of Sinjar, Trump's response is "I know the area very well, you're talking about. It's tough." Let's play how-well-does-President Trump know Sinjar? It's a wildly implausible game.

Toward the end of the exchange, Trump asks Murad about her Nobel Prize. "That's incredible," he says. "They gave it to you for what reason?"

"For what reason?" Murad asks, suppressing with difficulty her incredulity that nobody has briefed the president. Nobody can brief this president. It's pointless. He knows everything. "I made it clear to everyone that ISIS raped thousands of Yazidi women," she says.

"Oh, really?" says Trump. "Is that right?"

Yes, that's right. One reason this exchange marked me is that I found myself in 2015 in a Yazidi refugee camp in southeastern Turkey, interviewing a survivor named Anter Halef. In a corner sat his sixteen-year-old daughter, Feryal. She sobbed uncontrollably. I had seldom seen such grief etched on a young face. Life had been ripped from her before she began to live. There was no road back for her. Her eyes were empty vessels, left so by rape.

I have watched the Murad-Trump exchange several times. It is scary. This president is inhuman. Something is missing. In his boundless self-absorption, he is capable of anything.

I am grateful to Brian Stelter of CNN for recalling this month the words of Edward R. Murrow in 1954 in response to Senator Joseph McCarthy's attempt to provoke public frenzy at supposed communist infiltration of American life. "We cannot defend freedom abroad by deserting it at home," Murrow says.

Of McCarthy, Murrow observes: "He didn't create this situation of fear; he merely exploited it—and rather successfully. Cassius was right. 'The fault, dear Brutus, is not in our stars, but in ourselves.'"

And then: "Good night and good luck."

LOST AND FOUND
IN HEMINGWAY'S SPAIN

I got lost without water in the mountains of Spain, was eyed by two vultures, but was not yet ready to satisfy their appetite.

NOVEMBER 29, 2019

Earlier this year, I got lost while hiking in the Sierra de Guadarrama, which rises to almost eight thousand feet in central Spain. It had been a grueling day under the September sun. The trail, scattered with boulders, was longer and steeper than expected. What had been described as a gentle glide along a ridge after a tough initial ascent proved unrelenting.

About seven hours in, I fell behind my two friends. I was following stone mounds, or cairns, not the clearest indicators in this case. False guides, they pulled me deeper into the mountains.

This was not a sudden realization but a growing unease that culminated in an admission: lost. Lost as in: every human being has vanished. Lost as in: I have to slow my heartbeat. Lost as in: there are perhaps two more hours of daylight, my lips are dry, and I'm out of water. Lost and small in a sierra suddenly vast and threatening.

The stupidest decisions can seem natural enough. For the three of us to separate, for our remaining water to be with my friends, even to undertake this trail without adequate information, was lunacy. Yet it seemed like harmless lunacy—until the mountains rebuked me.

I had no water but did have a faint bar of reception on my dying cell phone. All I managed to communicate to my friend was two words— "I'm lost"—before we lost each other again. I looked around. I'd been descending, several hundred feet. I needed to climb again, get around the rocky outcrop above me, to be more visible. In the direction I'd been heading lay only wild terrain and jagged peaks.

Adrenaline is the most exhausting form of energy. Fear is a survival instinct as long as panic does not supplant it. I climbed without feeling the effort, leaping from boulder to boulder, but growing more parched. Far below me the switchbacks of a forest track appeared. No visible way to reach it.

Don't fall or twist an ankle. Don't trust that rock with your weight, misjudge the depth of the juniper thicket, or turn in circles. How and at what point does extreme thirst affect the mind? Don't panic. Think.

Then I saw the birds, two of them. They were looking at me. Hulking and black, they were perched side by side on a rock like bloated chess pieces. No, they were not looking at me, they were *eyeing* me.

In Spain, I like to read Hemingway's short stories. I had just reread one of the great tales of a dying man, "The Snows of Kilimanjaro": "The cot the man lay on was in the wide shade of a mimosa tree and as he looked out past the shade onto the glare of the plain there were three of the big birds squatted obscenely, while in the sky a dozen more sailed, making quick-moving shadows as they passed."

I was headed toward the birds. Every fiber in me rebelled against their intent. How hideous in their appetite the vultures looked. I heard Harry, in his rage, dismissing his lover in the story: "'Don't be silly. I'm dying now. Ask those bastards.' He looked over to where the huge, filthy birds sat, their naked heads sunk in the hunched feathers."

Yes, naked heads, that was right. Naked-beaked, they sat in judgment on my life. The record was mixed. There were things I still needed to set right. For that I had to be found. I had to set a course and stick to it, build and not destroy, find a path to the light. The only way out was through.

There was Harry, dying in Africa, unable to love the woman who loved him, hurting her instead, full of bile. "It was not her fault that when he went to her he was already over." Dying from the inside. "He had destroyed his talent by not using it, by betrayals of himself and what he believed in. . . ."

As I approached the birds, one launched itself into the air, its massive wings casting long shadows. I shuddered. Climbing and plunging, I pressed on, until at last I saw a man on a ridge, far off and faint, but not so faint that he could not serve as my marker.

A small group came into view, farther down the ridge. I waved. They waved. I saw a helicopter circling in the sky. How strange, I thought, not connecting it to me as my savior-bird. And now I saw a path out. My thirst was overwhelming, until I found myself surrounded by fellow hikers—generous, worried Spaniards—and I drank.

They told me my friends were looking for me farther up. They asked if I could climb. I said I was sorry, but no. I looked up the trail and everything converged: the helicopter landing, my friends gesturing, the rescue crew clambering out the chopper, the straight-backed Spanish man who'd given me water climbing toward them.

There were hugs. I boarded the chopper and collapsed in sobs. For my friends, who felt terrible and had managed to contact the rescue service; for this good Spanish crew, who would ask for nothing; for my foolish disrespect of the mountains; for the gift of life; for my children; for love.

As the helicopter climbed I looked back toward the wilderness. There were three birds now, circling. I'd eluded them. I'd set a direction and held to it. I'd been found. I felt thankful.

I thought of another Hemingway short story, "Hills Like White Elephants," which I'd once read out loud, to meet this response: "I don't think I've ever read a short story about a couple arguing."

She and I were very happy then. That's what couples do, sometimes: quarrel. They survive or not, but, irrespective of their fate, the white elephants of eternity are always out there, much bigger than we are, and the only way to see them clearly, to defy loss, to feel the vibration of the infinite, is to love and to create.

Of Harry, Hemingway writes: "Now he would never write the things that he had saved to write until he knew enough to write them well."

TWO DEATHS AND MY LIFE

Of Sonny Mehta, a great publisher, and Ward Just, a great journalist and writer, and their impact on my life.

JANUARY 10, 2020

Samuel Beckett, when asked one beautiful spring morning whether such a day did not make him glad to be alive, responded, "I wouldn't go as far as that." Life is a predicament, death the elephant at the horizon that looms larger as the years pass.

Still, life is what we have. To give less than everything to it is dereliction. In the end its wonder is unimaginable without the presence of death. As the dew dispels, the mist dissolves, and the sap rises on a morning such as the one that did not quite win over Beckett, the energy of life is unmistakable. That is what put us here in the first place.

Great souls resemble the elements in their immensity. They absorb everything—pain, injustice, insult, folly—and give back decency and kindness. They are not born of a piece. They come into being through unflinching confrontation with life's spears. They reach quiet. Discipline is the backbone of graciousness. Stoicism is the other face of wounds. In the most beautiful smile, painful knowledge hovers.

Midwinter is not what prompted these reflections, although when a freezing wind whips off the East River all thoughts turn to refuge. No, the death in quick succession of two friends was the catalyst. They were older than me. But they were not old enough and not so distant in age that their memento mori feel less than urgent.

Sonny Mehta, who died last month at the age of seventy-seven, would caress the books he loved. For them he lived. He guided Alfred A. Knopf through more than three decades of rapid change. He was a complete publisher, eclectic in his tastes, ferocious in his will, guided by a mission to bring the finest books to Knopf and publish them only once editing had honed them to irreproachable form. Yet he wanted to be remembered above all as a reader.

I knew Sonny for three decades. He published my last two books. His civility never wavered. The twinkle in his eye never faded. His friendship was constant. Whiskey and a cigarette and the meandering conversation that went with them were more his thing than the treadmill. He was a beautiful man.

How so? In his gentleness that contained wisdom, in his diffidence that contained enthusiasm, in his discretion that contained curiosity. You had to listen carefully, for he spoke softly, to the clues he offered. His long marriage to his wife, Gita, brought to my mind, in its respectfulness and vitality, Rilke's phrase about love as protecting the solitude of the other.

A child of India, brown-skinned in what was, when he started, the white preserve of British publishing, was once asked if he was perhaps seeking a job in the stockroom, Mehta never stooped to unkindness. His writers knew they had come home. He commanded the unswerving loyalty of the likes of Michael Ondaatje, Kazuo Ishiguro, Germaine Greer, and Julian Barnes. "I feel that my heart has been ripped out," Jon Segal, his longtime colleague at Knopf, told me.

When Mehta's father, a diplomat, died in Vienna, Mehta found in his desk a folder with every article ever published about him. The pride of his father, who had never complimented his son, was evident. Remote fathers: vast subject. Hearing this story, I understood more of my friend's elegant stoicism.

Earlier in December, Ward Just, a journalist who turned to fiction, a great *Washington Post* correspondent in Vietnam who became a great novelist, died at the age of eighty-four. Like Mehta, he was a lover of Scotch. I had not seen much of Just since we became friends in Berlin twenty years ago, but his death hit me hard. I recalled him saying to me back then: "I was useless for journalism after Vietnam. I knew I was not going to do any better work."

Just probed the delusions of people and nations, and the damage they suffer. His prose was understated. In *A Dangerous Friend*, one character observes, "I have always believed that a mountainous ego resulted from an absence of conscience." And that was before His Neediness seized the Oval Office.

As with Mehta, Just's prodding was subtle, his smile contained sorrows, his wisdom was hard-earned, his constant humor wry. Wounded by a grenade blast in 1966, winched to safety by a chopper, he later wrote, as quoted in his *Washington Post* obituary: "When you got there, you said instinctively, I made it. And over and over again, Jesus Christ."

I can hear my friend saying that, stress on the "Christ." Life hangs by a thread. Pay attention to its ephemeral gifts. Of Truman Schockley, dead at nineteen in Vietnam, Just wrote in 1967: "Smoking a Lucky Strike and staring off into the mountains, Schockley died with a sniper's bullet through the heart and stopped breathing before the cigarette stopped burning."

Now, there's a perfect sentence that might even have persuaded Beckett. Spring passes. Truth distilled does not.

REQUIEM FOR A DREAM

Brexit feels like a self-amputation, a fiasco reflecting a changed world.

JANUARY 31, 2020

I have covered many stories that marked me over the past forty years, in war zones and outside them, but none that has affected me as personally as Britain's exit from the European Union. Brexit Day, now upon us, feels like the end of hope, a moral collapse, a self-amputation that will make the country where I grew up poorer in every sense.

Poorer materially, of course, but above all poorer in its shriveled soul, divorced from its neighborhood, internally fractured, smaller, meaner, more insular, more alone, no longer a protagonist in the great miracle of the postwar years—Europe's journey toward borderless peace and union. Britain, in a fit of deluded jingoism, has opted for littleness.

The fiasco was captured this week when that pompous and pitiful British nationalist, Nigel Farage, waved a miniature Union Jack in the European Parliament as he bid farewell and was cut off by the vice president of the Parliament, Mairead McGuinness. "Put your flags away, you're leaving, and take them with you," she said.

Farage looked like a sheepish schoolboy caught breaking rules. He blushed. An Irish woman from a country uplifted by European Union membership reprimanding the new breed of little-England male as he exits history in pursuit of an illusion: the symbolism was perfect. "Hip, hip hooray!" Farage's flag-waving Brexit Party cohorts chanted. Save me, please, for I shall weep.

Speaking of symbolism, the fact that President Trump has been a fulsome supporter of this folly is apt. An ahistorical, amoral American leader cheering on a British abdication sums up the end of an era. The world was rebuilt after 1945 on something of more substance than British-American lies and bloviation; it took resolve. The torch has passed. To whom exactly is unclear, perhaps to a country slow to contain a plague.

Brexit belongs to this era in one quintessential way. It is an act of the imagination, inspired by an imaginary past, carried along by misdirected grievances, borne aloft by an imaginary future. The age of impunity is also the age of illusion turbocharged by social media.

Inequality, poor infrastructure, low investment, inadequate schools are real British problems, but the take-back-your-country transference of blame for them onto "Brussels bureaucrats" proved that the imagination now overwhelms reality. Truth withers. The mob roars.

Yes, Britain was undefeated in World War II and helped liberate Europe. But it could do so only with its allies; and it was precisely to secure what it is now turning its back on: a free Europe offering its people the "simple joys and hopes which make life worth living." Those are Churchill's words in 1946 in a speech that also contained this phrase: "We must build a kind of United States of Europe." Unbowed Britain was once consequential Britain; no longer.

I used the word "abdication" advisedly. Europe needs the great tradition of British liberalism at a moment when Hungary and Poland have veered toward nationalism and, across the Continent, xenophobic hatred is resurgent. It is perverse for Britain to try to look away. Europe is part of Britain. Visit the great Norman monasteries in England and tell me this is not so. The British dead who lie in the Continent's soil having given their lives for its liberty tell the same story of interlaced fate from a different perspective.

To be so orphaned is painful. The forty-seven years of British membership cover the entire arc of my adult life. Europa was our dream. I covered Anwar Sadat, the Egyptian president, speaking to the European Parliament about hope and peace in 1981, eight months before his assassination. So much for dreams.

Yet they persist, for otherwise life is unlivable. I wandered from Brussels to Rome to Paris to Berlin to London, and everywhere I lived I experienced some iteration of Europe's beauty, as a physical thing, as a cultural bond, and as a transformative idea.

The sensation was most acute in Germany, where the idea of the union was the most effective escape from postwar shame and the rubble of 1945, a form of atonement. But it was ubiquitous, the guarantor of our deliverance and the symbol of our capacity to reinvent the world and even make it better.

Every European country, through the goal of ever-closer union, changed itself. They grew richer, no small thing. But they also reframed their self-image.

Italy and Spain left Mussolini and Franco behind to become stable, prosperous democracies. France found its tortuous way to truth after the humiliations and predations of Vichy and discovered a European avenue to express once more its universal message of human rights founded on human dignity.

Central European countries stabilized their escape from the deadening Soviet imperium to which Yalta had confined them. Britain ceased equating Europe with scourges like intellectuals, rabies, and garlic, as it had in my childhood. The British economy surged. Britain had given up its colonies and found a new identity in association with Europe, or so it seemed, flickeringly.

Then I lived in Sarajevo, covering the Bosnian war, and I saw, in inert bodies torn by shrapnel, and in history revived as galvanizing myth of might and conquest, the horror from which the European Union had saved my generation. It had laid bad history to rest. That was enough to make me forever a European patriot.

But not enough for the British a quarter century later. In the words of my friend Ed Vulliamy, who also covered that war, Britain has become a country "that boards cheap flights for stag outings to piss all over Kraków."

Hip, hip hooray!

A bunch of flag-waving fantasists, at the wrong end of actuarial tables, have robbed British youth of the Europe they embrace. They will be looking on as 450 million Europeans across the way forge their fate. Their automatic right to live and work anywhere from Lisbon to Stockholm will be lost.

I've lost a limb; more than a limb, my heart. Europe helped Britain grow bigger and more open and more prosperous. Now it will shrink. Another suffering friend, Patrick Wintour, the diplomatic editor of *The Guardian*, sent me these lines of Auden:

> *In the nightmare of the dark*
> *All the dogs of Europe bark,*
> *And the living nations wait,*
> *Each sequestered in its hate;*
>
> *Intellectual disgrace*
> *Stares from every human face,*
> *And the seas of pity lie*
> *Locked and frozen in each eye.*

A better epitaph for the aborted story of Britain in Europe and the tragedy of a disoriented nation's willful infliction of enduring self-harm is impossible to imagine.

A SILENT SPRING
IS SAYING SOMETHING

In New York City, as COVID-19 struck, my world shrank to a few blocks in Brooklyn. Everyone's world was upended. A silent spring. Do things differently at the other end of the scourge, some mystic voice murmured, do them more equitably, more ecologically, with greater respect for the environment, or you will be smitten again.

MARCH 27, 2020

This is the silent spring. The planet has gone quiet, so quiet you can almost hear it whirling around the sun, feel its smallness, picture for once the loneliness and fleetingness of being alive.

This is the spring of fears. A scratchy throat, a sniffle, and the mind races. I see a single rat ambling around at dusk on Front Street in Brooklyn, a garbage bag ripped open by a dog, and experience an apocalyptic vision of vermin and filth.

Scattered masked pedestrians on empty streets look like the survivors of a neutron bomb. A pathogen about one-thousandth the width of a human hair, the spiky-crowned new coronavirus, has upended civilization and unleashed the imagination.

From my window, gazing across the East River, I see a car pass now and then on FDR Drive. The volume of traffic reminds me of standing on the Malecón, the seafront promenade in Havana, a dozen years ago and watching a couple of cars a minute pass. But that was Cuba and those were finned fifties beauties!

It is time of total reset. In France, there's a Web site to indicate to people the one-kilometer radius from their homes in which they are permitted to exercise. That's one measure of everyone's shrunken worlds.

Yet to write, to read, to cook, to reflect in silence, to walk the dog (until it braces its legs against moving because it's walked too much), to adapt to a single space, to forsake the frenetic, to contemplate a stilled world, may be to open a space for individual growth. Something has shifted. The earth has struck back. Exacting breathlessness, it has asserted its demand to breathe.

From animal to human the virus jumps, as if to demonstrate the indivisibility of life and death on a small planet. The technology perfected for the rich to globalize their advantages has also created the perfect mechanism for globalizing the panic that sends portfolios into a free fall.

Do things differently at the other end of this scourge, some mystic voice murmurs, do them more equitably, more ecologically, with greater respect for the environment, or you will be smitten again. Next time the Internet will collapse. The passage from real world to virtual world to no world will then be complete.

It is not easy to resist such thoughts, and perhaps they should not be resisted, for that would be to learn nothing.

Speaking of rats, Camus's *The Plague* is out of stock on Amazon, as the world awakens to the novel's eternal reminder "that the plague bacillus never dies or vanishes entirely, that it can remain dormant for dozens of years in furniture or clothing, that it waits patiently in bedrooms, cellars, trunks, handkerchiefs and old papers, and that perhaps the day will come when, for the instruction or misfortune of mankind, the plague will rouse its rats and send them to die in some well-contented city."

The book was published in 1947, two years after the political plague of fascism had been vanquished with the loss of tens of millions of lives. Camus's warning was political. The virus returns as inevitably as the psychotic leader with mesmeric mythmaking talents.

In an election year, it has been impossible to witness the mixture of total incompetence, devouring egotism, and eerie inhumanity with which President Trump has responded to the COVID-19 pandemic and not fear some form of corona-coup. Panic and disorientation are precisely the elements on which the would-be dictator feasts. The danger of an American autocratic lurch in 2020 is as great as the virus itself.

This is Trump's world now: scattered, incoherent, unscientific, nationalist. Not a word of compassion does he have for America's stricken Italian ally (instead, the United States quietly asks Italy for nasal swabs flown into Memphis by the U.S. Air Force). Not a word from a United Nations Security Council bereft of American leadership. Not a word of plain simple decency, the quality Camus most prized. In their place, neediness, pettiness, and boastfulness. The only index Trump comprehends is the Dow.

I have experienced physical shock in recent weeks watching leaders like Angela Merkel in Germany, Justin Trudeau in Canada, and Emmanuel Macron in France speak about the pandemic. We Americans do not grasp how insidiously Trump has accustomed us to malignancy. A germophobe, he has spread the germ of untruth.

That self-satisfied, nasal, and plaintive presidential voice has become a norm. And so merely to hear a sane, caring, scientific response to the virus from other leaders is riveting and reorienting.

The mother of all crises has met the ne plus ultra of presidential ineptitude. "We have it totally under control," the president says in January. "One day—it's like a miracle—it will disappear," is the refrain in February. "I don't take responsibility at all," Trump declares in March. He has a good "feeling" about malaria drugs whose efficacy against the virus is untested. He is all over the place on China. And now, against widespread medical advice, and the protests of desperate governors, he wants the United States "opened up and just raring to go by Easter," in a couple of weeks.

I don't blame Trump entirely for America's unpreparedness. The American health-care system has long been a colossal study in waste. But I do blame Trump for wasting a couple of months in denialism that reminded me of Thabo Mbeki and his criminal dismissal of AIDS in South Africa. I blame him for then leaving state and local governments to fend for themselves, mobilizing federal resources belatedly, weakly, and inconsistently. I blame him for the small-minded America First obsession that made it impossible for him to learn from other countries.

I blame Trump for the fact that my son-in-law, a physician on the front line at Grady Memorial Hospital in Atlanta, was for weeks unable to test his patients or himself for infection and still faces shortages. I blame him for the disappearance from view of the Centers for Disease Control and Prevention, America's foremost agency for fighting infectious disease, now forced to kowtow to Trump's ego. In this president's view, the limelight exists for him alone.

The lessons are in plain view. The countries that have fared best are those that have been fastest to test, track, and isolate areas of infection, giving them a good idea of the size of the outbreak and the best means to flatten the curve of its spread. Look at South Korea or Germany.

Trump's United States lost a couple of months. It then tried, in the absence of any detailed data, to quarantine everyone. That works in Wuhan and a surveillance state but not in a nation of individualists wedded to the idea of self-sufficiency. The test-isolate-track moment was lost. The results have been predictably poor. The economy went into a nosedive that, a two-trillion-dollar stimulus package notwithstanding, could lead to a depression. Many more could die destitute.

Polls say Trump's popularity has edged up a little since the virus struck. The best way to think of that is: He's still a singularly unpopular wartime president. He is beatable. So is the virus, if America puts its shoulder to the wheel with seriousness of purpose.

In this silent spring, the forsythia has bloomed and the magnolia buds are bursting. Nature, as Rachel Carson chronicled in her *Silent Spring*, published fifty-eight years ago, is telling us something.

THERE IS NO WAY OUT
BUT THROUGH

The pandemic has taught an unsuspecting generation what it is to be swept away by the gale of history.

APRIL 3, 2020

My sister, Jenny Walden, who lives in London, has been passing lockdown time going through old slides of my father's, discovered last year. Every now and then she sends me a grainy or mildewed photograph, a message in a bottle from across the ocean. The pandemic has prompted a universal time of reflection. The past, more present, is the new field of exploration, absent movement.

There we are, my sister and I, still in the cocoon of innocence, happy, curious, with my mother mainly, my father occasionally, my grandparents. Everyone but us in the photographs is now dead. My parents, all those South African aunts and uncles, that world, gone.

The dead feel much closer now, along with all those things they lived, the Depression, the war, confinement. Ships drift around the world with unwanted people, like the Jewish refugees aboard the MS *St. Louis* on its voyage of the damned on the eve of World War II.

The virus teaches something forgotten, what it is like to be swept away by the gale of history, what it is to have every assumption collapse, what is precious in each single contemplated breath.

It is said the camera never lies. But behind those smiles in my dad's slides lay family tragedy. When I researched my grandparents' history in Lithuania and gazed at photographs of the Jewish life there that would be extinguished, I recall thinking: *You, sir, are doomed—and you on the wagon, and you with a hand on your horse's withers.* Roland Barthes observed that in every old photograph lurks catastrophe.

Yet I feel more connection than catastrophe. To my family, to everyone out there looking backward and inward, sifting memories, adjusting priorities. Less is more. Old recipes revived, old purses reopened and redolent of a grandmother's apartment, old rhythms of life in a small radius rediscovered.

It's the end of an era. The virus kills—to what degree is still unclear. It also screams: You must change your life.

The world that emerges from this cannot resemble the old. If this plague that cares not a whit for the class or status of its victims cannot teach solidarity over individualistic excess, nothing will. If this continent-hopping pathogen cannot demonstrate the precarious interconnectedness of the planet, nothing will. Unlike 9/11, the assault is universal.

Yet the two most powerful men on earth, President Xi Jinping of China and President Trump, have responded with petty national interest that has cost myriad lives. They have failed the world, a superpower debacle.

China covered up the initial coronavirus outbreak in December for several weeks and then tried to divert attention from its biological

Chernobyl through trumpeting its success in containing the illness (the numbers remain dubious), offering international assistance (some in the form of defective masks and tests), and propagating the wild conspiracy theory that the plague did not start in Wuhan but was cooked up in an American military lab and delivered by the United States team attending the Military World Games in Wuhan last October.

The lesson is not, as China would have it, that despotic regimes deal more effectively with disaster but that they incubate the fear that made it impossible for doctors and authorities in Wuhan to communicate rapidly the scale of the threat. A series of tweets last month from the Chinese Embassy in France lauding China's and Asia's superior response to the virus thanks to the "sense of community and citizenship that Western democracies lack" was grotesque. Li Wenliang, who died in February, and Ai Fen, who appears to have disappeared, are the whistle-blower doctors of Wuhan whom humanity must never forget.

Trump tweeted on March 29, as Americans died, "President Trump is a ratings hit." His daily COVID-19 reality TV show, which he called his "coronavirus updates," had "an astounding number" of viewers, "more akin to the viewership for a popular prime-time sitcom."

If you want a quick definition of obscenity, that's it. This is the mentality, or, rather, the mental affliction, that compounded the Chinese cover-up with a Trump-authored American confabulation that lost another six weeks in dismissal of the pandemic as a hoax.

The world is leaderless. Every country for itself. Swirling in lies and rumors. Schoolyard petulance, like Mike Pompeo, the worst American secretary of state in a long time, insisting on calling this coronavirus "the Wuhan virus." This is Trump's world, and Xi's.

It is hard now, here in New York—everywhere, really. Reading the numbers. Trying to make sense of them. Seeing the triage tents and portable morgues. Watching small businesses close. The millions suddenly without jobs. The people dying alone, without their loved ones, because of the risk of infection. Discarded blue and white latex gloves on a street. Insomnia. Choppers over the city at night. The Zoom gatherings that console but also recall that touch is beyond technology. The way people veer away from a passerby, the coronavirus swerve. The sirens. The silence that makes the sirens louder.

All this has happened before, not quite like this, but yes. My sister's photographs are also a memento mori. And the world has come through. Because of people like Craig Smith, the surgeon-in-chief at NewYork–Presbyterian Columbia Hospital who wrote of COVID-19 patients in a moving dispatch to his medical troops, "They survive because we don't give up."

It's coming apart. Take care of it. *We don't give up.* We are connected to one another and to generations past and future. There are no strangers here.

COME BACK, NEW YORK, ALL IS FORGIVEN

Every now and again, a column, like this one, goes viral. It came to me all of a piece, its lilt in my head as I woke up. I wrote it out in a couple of hours. I forgave New York City everything if only it would return.

APRIL 10, 2020

I forgive you, New York. I forgive you your snarl, your aggression, your hustle and hassle. I forgive you La Guardia and your summer stench of uncollected garbage. I forgive you no cabs in the rain. I forgive you the crusty, deceptive puddles of slush at curbside. I even forgive you the Mets and no place to park and delivery trucks in the bike lane.

All is forgiven if you will only return: the subway soliloquies of the homeless, the trains that never come, the trains that stop in the middle of the tunnel, the traffic, the garbage trucks blocking cross streets, the jackhammering of construction, the hiss of smoke from a manhole cover, the idling stretch-limo SUVs, the drone of a million air-conditioning units, the drivers leaning on horns, the city hum that never ceases, until it did.

I forgive you. I forgive you now and forever. How could I ever begrudge you your restlessness, your relentlessness, your lip, your effrontery, your appraising glance, your pushiness, your impatience, your disregard for social niceties, when I knew all along that your great secret was that an extreme degree of ambition coexists in your streets with the empathy every New Yorker feels for a fellow New Yorker?

Only come back and all is pardoned: the tourists meandering in the theater district, your roads pitted with potholes, your crazy prices, your dinner parties ending at nine-thirty because tomorrow is another New York day and there's money to be made, your awful basketball, your restaurants that have a table—maybe—in a couple of months, your overcrowded sidewalks, your iPhone addicts gathered at the exit of a subway station, your way of never, ever relenting until you turn every one of your workers into a zombie by nightfall.

I forgive you the rats—yes, even the rats—and I'll throw in the roaches. The swelter of August, forgiven. The icy winter winds off the Hudson and the East River, forgiven. The impossibility of getting across town, forgiven. I forgive you the crowds, the craziness, the cruelty, the cursing, the complaining customers, the impatient merchants, and the most uncomfortable cabs in the world.

I forgive you your kale salads, your restaurants that sell only oatmeal, your trends. I forgive you your street preachers, your sanctimonious parents who drone on about their children's schools. I forgive you Macy's during the Christmas season and Times Square always. I forgive you your ticket-holder lines, your throngs blocking out the paintings at MoMA, your rush-hour subways crammed with humanity. I forgive you the holding of subway doors, your drunks peeing and puking on the street.

I forgive you Penn Station. I forgive you the Port Authority, yes, even that! I forgive you the brutal division of haves and have-nots. I forgive you the bus to the cabs at La Guardia-in-construction and the recording that tries to persuade you that the bus is really great news.

Look, I'll pardon the madness of having AirTrain JFK start in Queens rather than Manhattan. I forgive you the whiff of urine on a Sunday morning, the broken glass in Central Park, and the way you persuade people that saying, "I may have a window next month," is okay behavior.

I forgive you for driving me crazy at times, for making me want to scream, "Get me out of here!" I forgive you everything without exception if you will only promise to reappear.

Please, do not be proud. I know, we cursed you with irresponsible abandon. Forgive us, as I forgive you. We did not imagine the silence that could fall, the sirens that would fill the night, the sick and the dying, the doctors laboring on the tenth circle of the inferno, the ghostliness of shuttered stores, the empty skies, the canceled events, the post-apocalypse latex gloves scattered here and there. We took you too much for granted. Yes, forgive us for not giving daily praise for the miracle of New York.

I know I did not thank you enough for those clear winter mornings, for that dive I love on West Twenty-sixth, for your tolerance, for your open arms, for the sun glinting on the Empire State Building, for your ampleness, for New York Noodletown, for your secrets slowly revealed, for your endlessness, for your boldness, for your churn, for the Met Cloisters, for your humanity, for your wit, for Coney Island, for the water towers, for the Staten Island Ferry being free, for banking over the city into La Guardia or JFK and seeing you and thinking this is home, for taking me in as no other city ever could.

Being a New Yorker, I was in a hurry. I was forgetful. You get that. Please forgive me. Please forgive us all. I'll throw in the pigeons. Forgive you for every one of those awful birds. Just come back, just return, please. I know we can make a deal.

DESPOTISM AND DEMOCRACY IN THE AGE OF THE VIRUS

The pandemic ushers in, and reflects, a changed world.

APRIL 24, 2020

The first major crisis of the post-American world is ugly and is going to get worse. A pandemic required a pan-planet reaction. Instead it found Pangloss in the White House, blowing smoke and insisting, as disaster loomed, that it was still the best of all possible worlds in America.

"There's not been even a hint of an aspiration of American leadership," Carl Bildt, the former Swedish prime minister, told me. "That is fundamentally new."

It is. The world's American reference point has vanished. The prize for greatest disappearing act of the coronavirus crisis goes to Mike Pompeo, the American secretary of state.

Into the global vacuum has stepped, well, nobody. No number of flag-waving Chinese officials disembarking from planes onto European soil with offers of masks and ventilators can obscure the fact that all this began with a biological Chernobyl in Wuhan, covered up for weeks as a result of the terror that is the currency of dictatorships.

The Asian powers that have emerged best from this disaster are the medium-sized democracies of South Korea and Taiwan. The great competition of despots and democrats for the upper hand in the twenty-first century is still open.

The Great Depression that began in 1929 produced two distinct results on either side of the Atlantic. In the United States, it led, beginning in 1933, to Roosevelt's New Deal. In Europe, it led to Hitler's rise to power in the same year, the spread of fascism, and eventually devastation on an unimaginable scale.

This time, as the coronavirus stops production and leaves more than twenty-six million Americans newly unemployed while in Europe it causes salaries to be "nationalized," in the words of Emmanuel Macron, the French president, the effects of an economic collapse not seen in almost a century may be flipped.

Donald Trump's United States, which the German magazine *Der Spiegel* now calls "the American patient," is ripe for an authoritarian lurch.

Awash in Trump's lies, battered by the virus, buried in incompetence, lacerated by division, and ruled by a lunatic unbound, the country approaches an election in November whose theft, subversion, and even postponement are credible scenarios. Nothing in Trump's psyche allows him to conceive of defeat, his family's prospects out of power are dim, and crisis is the perfect pretext for a power grab. War—and this pandemic has similarities to one—fosters "executive aggrandizement," as James Madison warned.

Trump embodies the personal and societal collapse he is so skilled in exploiting. Insult the press. Discredit independent judges. Remove the checks. Upend the balances. Abolish truth. Pocket the system step by step. Mainline Lysol. Dictatorship 101.

Europe is a different story. Its division between the prosperous North and the poorer South sharpened by the pandemic, and its fracture line between the democracies of Western Europe and the illiberal or authoritarian systems of Poland and Hungary further exposed, the Continent faces a severe test of its capacity for unity and solidarity. It has underperformed, but I would not write it off.

The initial European reaction to the pandemic was weak—Lombardy will not soon forget its abandonment—and the European Union's response to the March 30 assertion of near-total autocratic power by the Hungarian leader, Viktor Orbán, was pathetic, equivalent to appeasement.

For the union to commit to providing billions of dollars in aid to Hungary through the Corona Response Investment Initiative on the very day Orbán began ruling by decree for an indefinite period was "mad, bad, and dangerous," as Jacques Rupnik, a French political scientist, told me. Orbán is a politician Trump admires.

But in Angela Merkel, the German chancellor, Europe has again discovered a leader inspiring in her candor and sanity and steadiness. Cometh the hour, cometh the woman.

European societies, with their buffering welfare states that are covering the wages of laid-off workers and providing universal health care, are better prepared than the United States for a disaster on this scale. Governments and the European Central Bank have now mobilized massive resources.

Macron, in an interview with the *Financial Times*, has made the argument that the virus should ultimately reinforce multilateralism and herald the return of the "human" over the "economic"—or, roughly interpreted, European solidarity over American unfettered capitalism.

Certainly, the underpaid first responders, garbage collectors, farmworkers, truckers, supermarket cashiers, delivery people, and the rest who have kept people alive and fed while the affluent took to the hills or the beaches have delivered a powerful lesson in the need for greater equity and a different form of globalization. People suffocate from COVID-19. They may also suffocate one day, as Macron pointed out, from an overheated, overexploited planet. Whether the lesson will be heeded through a radical rebalancing, both personal and corporate, is another story.

What is clear is that if the European Union does not stand up for liberal-democratic values, those values will be orphaned in the menacing world of Trump, Putin, and Xi Jinping.

I said the great twenty-first-century democracy-dictatorship battle is far from over. Emergencies serve autocrats but can also demonstrate the failings of their systems and provoke radical rethinking.

The pivotal date in the struggle is now November 3. If Trump wins, assuming the election is held, and Pangloss continues his assault on truth, the Merkel-Macron democratic camp will struggle. If Joe Biden, the presumptive Democratic nominee, wins, the United States will not recover an American-led world, because that world is gone forever, but the return of American decency and principle will make an enormous difference. To begin with, autocrats will no longer have an American carte blanche.

"The virus is attacking an incoherent, deglobalized world," Bildt said. "And as long as that is the case, the virus wins."

NO RETURN TO
"THE OLD DISPENSATION"

The deepest question posed by the pandemic is whether there can be any return to "the old dispensation," in T. S. Eliot's phrase. The agony could constitute a revelation, or even some redemption, or it may merely prove to be a costly interruption.

MAY 8, 2020

In T. S. Eliot's "The Journey of the Magi," the three wise kings, having witnessed the birth of Christ at the end of a long and difficult journey, return home to find themselves "no longer at ease here, in the old dispensation."

Back in "our places," the kings are troubled. They feel they are in the presence of "an alien people clutching their gods." Yet they left their kingdoms not so long ago. What has transpired to estrange them so from all that was once familiar? How can they question the very worlds they shaped?

The narrator, one of the kings, is led to speculate on what they have seen in Bethlehem during their journey: "I had seen birth and death, / But had thought they were different; this Birth was / Hard and bitter agony for us, like Death, our death."

The birth of Christ is also the death of their pagan worlds. There is no going back to "the old dispensation." There is return only in the physical sense. To live as they once lived has become impossible. They no longer see their fellows before them. They see strangers with idols.

I have been thinking of this short poem because perhaps the deepest question posed by the pandemic is whether there can be any return to the "old dispensation." This "agony" could constitute a revelation, or even a redemption, or it may merely be a costly interruption.

Having witnessed the unimaginable, having been on this journey into an unfamiliar world of silence and stillness and death, having been obliged to change unquestioned habits, will humanity simply return to its former ways if that proves possible?

To bet against the human tendency to relapse into old bad habits is foolish. Tragedy tends to foster expressions of idealistic unity that prove fleeting. Remember September 11.

The history of greed, venality, stupidity, cruelty, and violence is long, because that part of human nature is ineradicable. As the twentieth century demonstrated, it is better to bet on a liberal society's capacity to temper these flaws and iniquities than on a utopia's false promise to eradicate them. Those promises end being written in blood.

In a provocative BBC podcast, Zia Haider Rahman, a British novelist, alludes to Eliot's poem and concludes that people will no doubt return to the old dispensation, more or less, "and in short order." They will do so, he suggests, for the simple reason that no alternative is within easy reach.

"What," he asks, "can possibly slow the monster of modernity?"

The monster that has given global corporations the ascendancy over individuals and created, in an advanced society like Britain, a situation where the life expectancy of the elderly has been falling and the infant mortality rate rising.

This is the same monster, turbocharged by technology, that in the United States has produced fast-growing inequality, diminishing class mobility, growing precariousness in the workplace, and broad social fracture. The coronavirus, attacking those most vulnerable above all, has had a field day in this America, just as Donald Trump had one promising to "Make America Great Again."

"American carnage," it turns out, was not Donald Trump's Inaugural Day description of the country's recent past, but his prediction for the country under his rule.

Of course, globalization also ushered hundreds of millions of people from poverty and opened myriad possibilities for human advancement. But cycles of history run their course. By 2008, it was clear that the world economic system was seriously skewed. Bailed out, it staggered on until now, accompanied by growing anger in Western societies. The rise of autocrats has been a direct reflection of their ability to exploit popular frustrations with anonymous global forces.

The virus is a searchlight that lays everything bare. All the grotesque needed, to be revealed as such, was for time to stop. How quickly the world greens and new life stirs when the trains, planes, and automobiles fall silent. What the frenetic "old dispensation" was doing to the fragile environmental health of the planet is right there in plain sight.

I agree with Rahman that change will be hard. It always is. But a lot of people, in this quieted world, have experienced some transforming miracle, such as that brought on for the Magi by an infant in a stable on a bed of straw. They have heard Rilke's admonition in the last line of "Archaic Torso of Apollo:" "You must change your life."

Perhaps "rebalancing" is a useful word, because attempts at wholesale reinvention, like those utopias, tend to end badly. From consumption to contemplation, from global to local, from outward to inward, from aggression to compassion, from stranger to guest, from frenzy to stillness, from carbon to green.

My life has been uneventful these past weeks; it has also been richer. I've been thinking about children and the virus, this invisible thing that upended their lives, closed schools and playgrounds, ended playdates, introduced them to Zoom. How they draw the hideous red spiky-headed pathogen with spindly legs and downturned mouth. How they advise their furry animals they cannot leave the dollhouse today "because of the virus." How they ascribe cancellations of their activities to "the virus." How they will put a mask on stuffed animals, because of the virus, and how they want to be told fairy tales, to be distracted from the virus.

For them, and for this vulnerable planet, and more than thirty-three million newly unemployed Americans, it is worth trying to ensure that "the old dispensation" yields to something new, something more balanced, born of a strange revelation.

THE MASKED VERSUS
THE UNMASKED

The virus, far from uniting America, aggravated its tribalism.

MAY 15, 2020

Back in the other world, before all was stilled, Scott Lacy, a neighbor in Colorado would tell me it was time for liberals to "gun up." The other side was armed, he argued, and would stop at nothing. What would we tell our grandchildren when Ivanka Trump took office as the forty-sixth president of the United States in 2025 and term limits were abolished? That we tried words, all manner of them, he scoffed, but they had the rifles.

I waved him away. American democracy was not Hungarian democracy, now dead. Its checks and balances were resilient. Too many guns are an American scourge. No, he insisted, you will see by June 2020. Civil war, or something like it, is coming. Gun up, dude, before it's too late.

My neighbor did not predict the uniforms of America's warring factions. How masks would become normative in Democratic strongholds like Telluride or Ridgway but be scorned in Colorado Trump country as the giveaway dress of the liberal egghead terrorized by the virus. The responsible crowd, with face half hidden, confronting the unmasked live-free-or-die crowd across the vastness and fracture of an unled country.

Once again, in this frayed Republic, there is scant middle ground. The virus is Godzilla destroying all before it. The virus is a myth, get over it. Biking onto the Manhattan Bridge, I pass a new piece of graffiti: "Bezos made the virus."

Nobody foresaw what a pathogen about one-thousandth the width of an eyelash could trigger in a society where truth itself has been obliterated by President Trump, day after lying day. If he could deny the *visible*, like the number of people at his inauguration, imagine what he could do with the *invisible*. Or don't imagine it, just look around.

Trump, in a tweet last month, urges his tens of millions of followers to "LIBERATE" Virginia from the lockdown and "save your great 2nd Amendment," which is "under siege." Or, roughly translated, grab your guns while you can to fight the liberal virus conspiracy, just the latest attempt after climate change and all the rest to emasculate America.

His Languidness, Jared Kushner, the president's son-in-law and go-to person for every known problem on the planet, is asked by *Time* magazine whether he is willing to commit to the holding of the November 3 election. "I'm not sure I can commit one way or the other, but right now that's the plan," he says.

Good to know. Right now, there's a plan to hold an election. *Gun up, dude, before it's too late.*

For Trump, this disaster is no more than a deep state conspiracy, like the Mueller investigation or the impeachment proceedings. All of it: the virus death toll, surely inflated by officials as a means to defeat him; the dented Dow; the highest unemployment numbers since the Great Depression; the collapse of his "spectacular" economy; the dire scientific predictions of the consequences of premature economic reopening. It's all about him, because everything is.

Followers of QAnon, a far-right conspiracy movement, provide fodder for the president's paranoia, as reported by my colleagues Matthew Rosenberg and Jim Rutenberg. I hear that the letter "Q" now appears on T-shirts at far-right protests in Germany. Signs at a recent demonstration in Stuttgart listed the "worst dictators" in history: Bill Gates followed by Angela Merkel and, down the list, Hitler.

Some German protesters wear yellow stars. They claim that Anne Frank would have been among them, protesting the "corona dictatorship" that unnecessarily shut down Europe's largest economy. Christian Drosten, a top German virologist with a popular podcast, receives death threats, like Anthony Fauci, America's top infectious-disease expert. History, science, truth, the Enlightenment are under siege. Anything could happen in America between now and November.

I mean, anything. This month, Trump's Department of Justice

dropped charges against former national security adviser Michael Flynn, who had twice pleaded guilty to lying to federal investigators in the Russia inquiry. A more flagrant demonstration of Trump's political cronies at the Department of Justice, led by Attorney General William Barr, bending to the president's diktat rather than fulfilling their oath to the Constitution, is hard to imagine. No wonder more than two thousand former Department of Justice officials have called in a letter for Barr's resignation. He is a disgrace.

So much for those resilient checks and balances I lauded to my Colorado neighbor.

Back then, in the bygone era, he wrote to me: "No wonder Republicans are laughing at us. The billionaire politicians have complete control (besides the military at this point), no oversight, and most of their constituents are armed, some heavily, and ready to defend them. Roll over and die? What the hell? Time to even things up. To save this country. Hopefully, guns will always be a deterrent, but they may be our last hope to save this country. Time to gun up, liberals!"

If you prefer, think of "gun up" as get real, get tough, get registered, get mobilized, get implacable, and vote Trump out. Or you may just want to go down to the range.

PRESIDENT TRUMP
IS A DOUGHNUT

On living with a president whose false or misleading statements never ceased cascading from his pursed lips.

MAY 29, 2020

In a much-loved children's story, "The Doughnuts" by Robert McCloskey, a boy, Homer Price, is left alone in his uncle Ulysses's luncheonette, where a newfangled doughnut machine has been installed. As he puts the final touches to it, Homer sets the machine in motion and finds he cannot stop doughnuts "comin', an' a comin', an' a comin'."

Trump resembles that doughnut machine in the Centerburg, Ohio, luncheonette, unable to stop lies from coming out of his pursed mouth at giddying velocity. There is a hole in the middle of everything the president says.

In their new book, *Donald Trump and His Assault on Truth*, Glenn Kessler, Salvador Rizzo, and Meg Kelly of *The Washington Post* clock the number of false or misleading statements from Trump at 16,241 in his first three years in office, or fifteen a day.

There were six such falsehoods a day in 2017, nearly sixteen in 2018, and more than twenty-two in 2019. The mercury in the presidential mendacity meter is rising; so is the extent to which Americans are inured to Trump's lying. Trump-speak, the fact checkers write, is a "constant stream of exaggerated, invented, boastful, purposely outrageous, spiteful, inconsistent, dubious and false claims."

This leads us to the most critical question for American democracy: Will President Trump concede if he is defeated by Joe Biden in the November election? Or, put another way, can a liar accept a truth incompatible with his devouring ego? The need to pose these questions reflects the depth of the national nightmare.

That Trump will spread disinformation over the coming months on an unprecedented scale is a given. But to some degree, that's politics. The evidence that he will also encourage voter intimidation and suppression efforts is compelling. His attacks on the integrity of mail voting are relentless. That makes a lot of sense if he is planning to declare a state of emergency in battleground states and ban polling places from opening.

He has amplified baseless claims of voter fraud in the same states. That makes a lot of sense if he is planning to declare the election was rigged and he won't leave the White House. Hell, he even declared the election he won in 2016 was rigged.

In a piece this week on doomsday-scenario planners mapping out responses to some form of Trump putsch, my colleague Reid J. Epstein suggested one possibility: "A week before the election, Attorney General William P. Barr announces a criminal investigation into the Demo-cratic presidential nominee, Joseph R. Biden Jr."

Not implausible. Barr is Trump's hired gun. He is to justice what a hit man is to due process.

Of late, Trump has turned to "horrifying lies." That's how the wid-ower of Lori Klausutis, who died almost twenty years ago in the Florida office of Joe Scarborough, then a Republican congressman and now an MSNBC news host, has described Trump's recent slandering of Scar-borough. In tweets, Trump has called Scarborough a "psycho" and asks if he may have gotten "away with murder."

The facts—that Scarborough was in Washington and that the police found no evidence of foul play—make no difference to the conspiracy-theorist-in-chief.

Now, after his avalanche of lies, Trump has signed an executive order trying to curtail Twitter's legal protections in retaliation for its append-ing fact-checking labels to two of his tweets about mail-in ballots. Oh, the audacity of Twitter in suggesting that Trump's accuracy should be checked! Attempted interference, Trump claims, in the 2020 election! The president's mantra owes much to Cosa Nostra: Threaten, threaten, threaten, and to heck with legality.

Tell me, are you inclined to trust a president who this week retweeted a video from an account called "Cowboys for Trump" in which the speaker starts by saying, "The only good Democrat is a dead Democrat"? The speaker then says he's not speaking literally—affording Trump plausible deniability as, with an eye to November, he winks to his gunned-up Second Amendment cohort.

Or the president who, in response to growing protests over the death in police custody in Minneapolis of George Floyd, an African Ameri-can, tweets, "when the looting starts, the shooting starts"? Trump's tweet violated company rules on glorifying violence, Twitter said.

Trump is a coward. Perhaps, if Biden wins, the president will skulk out of the White House like the little boy he is who never grew into a man. And the nightmare will be over. I don't think so. The chances are growing that Trump will not concede in the event of a Biden victory, that he may encourage violence and use the fear and division spread by the virus to extend autocratic power.

Trump is a doughnut. There is a hole in the middle of him where honesty, humanity, decency, morality, and dignity never formed. He has done incalculable damage. Kessler and his colleagues quote Jonathan Swift: "As the vilest writer hath his readers, so the greatest liar hath his believers: and it often happens, that if a lie be believed only for an hour, it hath done its work." Three and a half years of Trump lies have done their work.

In "The Doughnuts," before the machine goes haywire, a wealthy woman loses the diamond bracelet she took off to mix the doughnut batter. Homer has a fine idea! To offer a hundred dollars to anyone who finds the bracelet. The excess doughnuts get bought and devoured; the bracelet is found inside one.

Behind this oversized, sticky, misshapen doughnut of a president, the hard diamond of recoverable truth lurks. To seize it, and save the Republic, requires the certain knowledge that Trump will stop at nothing between now and November 3.

"GET YOUR KNEE OFF OUR NECKS"

The knee on George Floyd's neck and all it says about America.

JUNE 5, 2020

Get your knee off our necks.

Marcus Delespinasse, weary-eyed, stands on Broadway in the late afternoon. "The culture of America," he tells me after I approached him on the street, "is that it's okay to treat Blacks this way. That cop knew George Floyd would not make it. He still kept his knee there."

Yes, Derek Chauvin, who has been charged with second-degree murder, kept his knee on Floyd's neck for almost nine minutes. A powerful white man asphyxiating a powerless Black man, a scene with a long American history, part of the nation's iconography. Chauvin was a *training officer* for the other cops at the scene. His blithe expression said, "Watch me kill."

"Get your knee off our necks," is the Reverend Al Sharpton's phrase for the uprising of 2020. The "knee" has been there for a while. It was in the Constitution's three-fifths clause, which set the census value of a slave at 60 percent of a free human being's. The "knee" is slavery and Jim Crow and lynching and segregation in schools and transportation and neighborhoods and on and on and on through all the inflections of systemic state oppression of African Americans that allowed Chauvin to believe he had the right as a white man to do what he did.

"Being Black in America should not be a death sentence," Jacob Frey, the mayor of Minneapolis, the liberal city where Floyd was killed, said. He had to say that more than a half century after the civil-rights movement. Think about it.

Get your knee off our necks.

Aged fifty-two and unemployed, Delespinasse is Black. I feel despair as I write that sentence. So-and-so is white. So-and-so is Black. All those parentheses running through copy, the refrain of failure. To explain what exactly? America's societal fracture; America's original sin; America's shame that life, liberty, and the pursuit of happiness have never been equally afforded its citizens. I might have written: "Aged fifty-two and unemployed, Delespinasse is a human being." The likes of Chauvin still cannot see that.

"You look at that video and think, That could be me, or my cousin, or my uncle," Delespinasse tells me. "Police have impunity. No wonder young people are enraged. That cop with his knee resting there sums up the savageness of white apathy."

Delespinasse looks out with those weary eyes on a ghostly New York. First the hum-and-honking of the city gave way to pandemic-induced silence interspersed with ambulance sirens. Now, after the looting, the sound of New York is the screeching of electric saws cutting plywood to board up broken windows, and the rumbling bursts of electric screwdrivers fixing the panels in place. This is the audio of a great city's disaster. This is the audio of a virus that sharpened the inequities of American dysfunction.

Get your knee off our necks.

There is no right to pillage and burn in the United States. But human beings will react to entrenched state violence—in extreme cases a license to kill—which is what Black Americans have confronted for centuries. All that is needed for rebellion against relentless oppression is a spark. What happens to a dream deferred? asked Langston Hughes. "Does it explode?"

The savageness of white apathy: a striking phrase, and sometimes it is worse than apathy. Consider Amy Cooper, that highly educated white woman caught on video in Central Park. She found herself saying she would tell the police there is "an African American man threatening my life." Because a Black man, Christian Cooper (no relation), an avid birder, had properly asked her to leash her dog.

Those impulses are what President Trump, a racist who launched his successful campaign in 2015 by calling Mexicans entering the country "rapists," plays on. Violence and division are his elements. He has no other. Hence his recent threat to deploy the military to quash "domestic terror," his repeated talk of "domination," his encouragement to violence couched in endless references to Second Amendment rights, and his tweeting support for Senator Tom Cotton, a prominent Republican, who called in a tweet for the deployment of "10th Mountain, 82nd Airborne, 1st Cav, 3rd Infantry—whatever it takes to restore order."

Whatever it takes to do what? To stop the lawbreakers and looters, Trump and Cotton would say with breathtaking disingenuousness. The military is not needed for that.

No, the point would be this: to assert with a great show of force, after the slow-motion murder of George Floyd by a white police officer, that the oppressive system that produced this act is not about to change and armed white male power in America is inviolable. That is Trump's fundamental credo. His Bible-brandishing, American Gothic portrait this week outside St. John's Episcopal Church in Washington is one of the most disturbing portraits of psychopathic self-importance seen since 1933.

Get your knee off our necks—and American democracy.

Trump was widely dismissed in 2015. He was dismissed in 2016, for that matter, until he won. A fringe loony, he would burn out. Turned out tens of millions of Americans thought like him.

Cotton followed up on his tweet with his now infamous send-in-the-troops op-ed in *The New York Times*. The piece was wrong, repugnant, mistimed, and flawed. It was also extremely relevant and very dangerous to ignore. I prefer to read it and vote with rage than experience again, in November, the consequences of complacent liberal ignorance.

THE OUTCRY OVER
"BOTH SIDES" JOURNALISM

An op-ed by Senator Tom Cotton entitled "Send In the Troops" provoked an uproar at *The New York Times*. The piece, while offensive, reflected the views of millions of Americans. It had its place in the name of open debate. If "Resistance" equals Cancel Culture, it does not liberate, it closes minds.

JUNE 12, 2020

I have never believed much in the notion of journalistic "objectivity." We all bring our individual sensibilities to bear on what we write. Great journalism involves the head and the heart, the lucidity to think and the passion to feel, the two in balance.

If you have lived a privileged white life, as I have, you can and must make the effort to understand what it is to have lived an oppressed Black life, to know what it's like to walk into a building and be asked if you are the help, to see the police not as protector but as threat, to know that some view your life as cheap.

In all the places I have worked, from South Africa, where I had spent my infancy, to Nigeria, to Brazil, I have tried to do that, writing stories about injustice and the ravages of misery. But I cannot inhabit the minds of the subjects of those pieces, however hard I have tried.

If I have always been skeptical of objectivity, I have always believed in fairness. That is to say, in the attempt to speak to people on both sides of a question, to report your way to some approximation of the truth by filtering diverse views.

That is what distinguishes a journalist. Heading toward the storm in the opposite direction from the crowd, seeking understanding by being there, in Jerusalem and Gaza, in Tehran and Washington, in Cape Town and Khayelitsha. Bearing witness involves looking into the eye of strangers whose lives and ideas seem irreconcilable.

When, in Sarajevo, I covered the war in Bosnia and watched lives blown away daily by indiscriminate Serb shelling, I made the effort to cross the lines to speak to the nationalist leaders who had twisted Serbian victimhood into a license for mass murder of Bosnian Muslims.

General Ratko Mladić and Radovan Karadžić, both since convicted of genocide by an international court, were delirious in the belief that the Muslims were the old Ottoman Turk enemy, that the Serbs were victims, not perpetrators. History, I learned, can illuminate but also blind.

These men were heinous. Should I have spoken to them? I thought the quest for understanding demanded it. I don't think I was objective. My goal was to describe evil.

Today, a quarter century later, journalists inhabit a historical fault line. There is a movement in people's minds. The *ancien régime* is crumbling, and when that happens there are decapitations.

The Times recently published an op-ed by Senator Tom Cotton calling for the deployment of troops to quell civil unrest as demonstrators took to the streets, enraged by the killing of George Floyd, a Black man, by a white police officer. The piece was odious; the editorial process behind it, flawed. A staff outcry ensued, driven in part by the view that the article was directly threatening, especially to African American journalists. This led to the ousting of James Bennet, the former editorial-page editor, and to the paper saying, after some back-and-forth, that publishing the piece was a mistake.

Cotton's dangerous views are supported by millions of Americans, including Trump. If he is not publishable—and, in the current climate, I believe that, even flawlessly executed, his op-ed would have provoked fury at *The Times*—then an old liberal journalistic consensus is waning. That is ominous.

Speaking of truth, I was Bennet's boss when he covered the Second Intifada with extraordinary bravery and aplomb, risking his life on a regular basis. He was mine until a few days ago. He is a man of exceptional honor and decency, humanity and sensitivity—a thoughtful, progressive, nuanced, open-minded colleague for over two decades, "journalistic integrity" personified. This is a terrible loss.

I also recognize another truth: that the Floyd killing illustrated that racism in the United States is systemic, and white-dominated American newsrooms are ill-equipped to deal with this reality, because only more diversity can capture multiple perspectives.

"LET FREEDOM RING" FROM GEORGIA

I visited Kentucky in 2016 and concluded Trump would likely win. I visited Georgia in the summer of 2020 and concluded he would likely lose. The momentum lay with Metro Atlanta, where Black rage over police killings had intensified determination to get out the vote.

JUNE 26, 2020

ATLANTA—This, an old saying goes, is "the city too busy to hate," one of the few places in America where enlightened leaders, Black and white, chose prosperity over prejudice and a large Black middle class emerged decades ago. Birthplace of Martin Luther King, Jr., cradle of the civil-rights movement, Atlanta, with its gleaming towers and porch swings, was an American exception. The city managed racial conflict through compromise. It was the Black mecca. Or so the story went.

James Forman, Jr., a Pulitzer Prize–winning professor at Yale Law School, and the son of the prominent civil-rights activist James Forman, Sr., recalled how, at age twelve, he moved from New York to Atlanta because "my mother, as a divorced white woman raising Black children, wanted us surrounded by Black success. She wanted my brother and me to open the paper every day and see Black people making decisions." That was the 1970s. Every Atlanta mayor since 1974 has been Black.

Yet now the city is an epicenter of America's double meltdown: over racial injustice and over the coronavirus that has hit marginalized African Americans particularly hard. This is the home of the Centers for Disease Control and Prevention, which went AWOL on the virus. This is where a young Black man, Rayshard Brooks, was killed on June 12 by a white police officer.

Over the course of a two-week stay, I encountered swirling fury over the Brooks killing; a primary-election debacle that, by design or Republican dereliction, included hours-long waits in polling stations in predominantly Black counties; and a protest march on the State Capitol where a banner saying "Legalize being Black" conveyed the rampant ire.

What became of the dream of Atlanta? It was always a progressive enclave surrounded by reactionary forces. If City Hall was the nexus of racial cooperation, the State Capitol was the nexus of segregation, now and forever. Perhaps things were never quite as good as they seemed. African Americans remained disproportionately poor and vulnerable. When Atlanta hosted the 1996 Olympics, Georgia's flag was still, in essence, the Confederate flag.

Progress on race issues is not resolution of race issues. Not in Atlanta, not anywhere, as Derek Chauvin's white knee on George Floyd's Black neck demonstrated. Police brutality, mass Black incarceration, poor education, redlining of neighborhoods all told a story so routine as to be invisible: A Black life is worth less than a white life in America. That idea is woven into the psyches even of people loath to admit it.

The Floyd detonation was long in the making. With its large African American population, about a third of the electorate, Georgia was bound to feel the reverberations. Democrats have not won Georgia, with its sixteen electoral votes, since 1992, and Donald Trump had a clear victory here in 2016. Now several polls suggest Joe Biden is leading by a small margin (and is considering driving home his ascendancy here by choosing either Stacey Abrams or the Atlanta mayor, Keisha

Lance Bottoms, as his running mate). This is the COVID-Floyd election, and Georgia has become a bellwether.

The narrow 2018 defeat of Abrams, campaigning to become the nation's first Black female governor, showed how demographic shifts have changed Georgia. The metropolitan-rural political and cultural chasm, evident across the nation, is particularly acute here. Fast-growing Metro Atlanta, with its diverse Democratic-leaning population, faces a hinterland where, for many white rural Georgians, Trump is still the tough, straight-talking dude the country needs. The vote will be close. If Trump loses Georgia to Biden, he likely loses everything. But that's still a big "if."

The bungled June 9 primary has sharpened fears of voter suppression in a state where the governor, Brian Kemp, is Republican and the House and Senate Republican-controlled. "We never thought we'd be talking about voting rights a half century on from the civil-rights movement," Andrea Young, the executive director of the ACLU of Georgia, told me. "The dysfunction is distressing ahead of what will be a highly contested general election, the most important of our lifetimes. We believed in America's promise, not a George Wallace presidency."

That promise has generally proved illusory when it comes to race. Throughout American history, white cruelty in keeping Blacks down has been matched only by white ingenuity in finding new ways to do so. Trump is part of that tradition. He has doubled down of late on the same images of lawless Blacks that sustained Jim Crow.

Forman "toggles back and forth," as he put it, on the question of how much has changed between the time his father was arrested, beaten, and held incommunicado by the L.A. police in the 1950s and his eleven-year-old son insisting, today, on joining the countrywide uprising against racial injustice.

"I have never seen anything like this in my lifetime," Forman told me. "I have many white friends with whom I have tried to raise issues of racial inequality and injustice. But it was never front and center in their lives. Now they bring it up nonstop. Perhaps it's like when people saw the images of police attack dogs being set on Black children in Birmingham in 1963. You know, 'I can't believe that!' Maybe this is how that felt."

"Like Emmett Till in the casket, the Floyd image made clear no Black person is safe," Carol Anderson, a professor here at Emory University and author of *White Rage*, told me.

The question, of course, is whether this awakening can achieve what even the civil-rights movement could not: the full humanization of Black Americans. "It has been said that the opposite of criminalization is humanization," said Jonathan Rapping, an Atlanta defense attorney who has focused on providing equal justice for marginalized communities.

In other words, when will America awaken to the fact that Rayshard Brooks was a human being, in full, who should not have ended up dead because he dozed off in his car in the drive-through lane of an Atlanta Wendy's?

I have watched the video too often. Brooks groggy in his parked car on June 12. The initially amiable forty-one-minute encounter between Brooks and officers, including Garrett Rolfe. Brooks's reasonable offer to lock his car and walk to his sister's place. The tussle when Rolfe abruptly moves to make a DUI arrest and handcuff Brooks. A Taser grabbed by Brooks from an officer. Brooks running. Turning and firing the Taser toward Rolfe, who responds with two bullets into Brooks's back.

"What I see is a shooting that was unnecessary," Sam Starks, a Black Atlanta lawyer, told me. "Park the car. Lock it. Take that person home. Brooks was on probation. He is terrified. He knows the cage he's headed for."

Unarmed, Brooks was no threat to anyone. His car was stationary. He would not be dead if he was white. He would be at his sister's place.

Having served a one-year sentence for credit-card fraud, Brooks was in the maw of a system that condemns young Black lives long after the cell. A poor Black man's chances of finding work on probation resemble a snowball's chances of surviving hell.

In an interview in February with Reconnect, a company that works to combat mass incarceration and recidivism, Brooks, twenty-seven, said: "I just feel like some of the system could look at us like individuals. We do have lives. It's just a mistake we made." A mistake is not a reason to be treated "as if we are animals."

Ahmaud Arbery, twenty-five, another young Black man killed in Georgia this year, was hunted down like an animal on February 23 as he jogged through Satilla Shores, near Brunswick, a coastal neighborhood of pleasant bungalows beneath live oaks garlanded with Spanish moss.

Gregory McMichael, sixty-four, and his son Travis McMichael, thirty-four, both white, grabbed a revolver and a shotgun, piled into their pickup truck, and pursued Arbery—convinced, they told the police, that he looked like a suspect in recent break-ins. In a video that took months to emerge, Travis is seen shooting Arbery dead at point-blank range as they tussle over his shotgun in the bright sunlight.

So, on the one hand, a dead Black man, Arbery, and two white men with guns who walk away. On the other, a young Black man, Brooks, dozing in a car, and police try to arrest him, and he ends up dead.

A growing outcry—driven by social media, a groundbreaking article in April by my colleague Richard Fausset, and at last the release in early May of the incriminating video—led to the McMichaels' arrest on May 7. It took seventy-four days. The video had been in the possession of the police from day one.

Three days after the Brooks killing, on an unseasonably cool Georgia morning, I joined a protest in downtown Atlanta. "We are done dyin'," a banner proclaimed. A large crowd, mostly young, of every hue, milled around. I fell into conversation with Justin Brock, a white professional skateboarder, who had brought along his seven-year-old son, Jasper.

"We need education reforms," he told me. "We need to teach the terrible things we did to make this country. They are known and hidden at the same time."

Brock looked hard at me. "I want to show my son the world and what actually goes on."

Jamal Harrison Bryant, a pastor, grabbed a microphone. "This is not a moment, it's a movement," he said. Cheers echoed around the still-ghostly pandemic-hit city.

"We're sick and tired of every week having a different hashtag for innocent Black lives," he continued. "We're sick and tired of them finding money for Georgia Tech but finding no money for Morehouse and Spelman."

Catherine Quashie, a Black woman, was standing next to me. Bryant is her pastor. She told me it took her two hours and forty-seven minutes to vote in Stonecrest, a city southeast of Atlanta. I heard stories of seven-hour waits in Fulton County. In upscale Buckhead, voters were in and out in ten minutes. "The encouraging thing," Quashie said, "is, nobody left the line."

Most of her family is in Europe. "They keep asking me: 'WHAT IS GOING ON IN AMERICA?'"

When I leave the demonstration, I drive southeast out of Atlanta toward Arbery's hometown, Brunswick, five hours away, on the Atlantic Ocean, across God's country, where nobody wears a mask.

Roger Johnson runs a fruit stand near McRae, in an area famous for its sweet Vidalia onions and, of course, Georgia peaches. His daughter, Taylor, helps out. "This is the Bible Belt," Johnson tells me. "Twelve churches between here and the interstate." He's a stocky, friendly guy with a mustache, a belly, and narrow, shrewd eyes. A sign outside says TOMATOES and ONIONS in red and blue letters, with Trump's name at the top.

So why, I ask, do you like the president? "Because he doesn't take any crap. Because he cannot be bought by other pols. Because he's not a career politician. He might stretch the truth a little, but don't we all? And it's the news that stretches it a lot."

Those knowing eyes look me over. Watermelons, Johnson advises, are a little mushy if they give a dull thud when tapped. "Should be like knocking on a door," he says. Noted. "People work hard for what they got," he continues. "They should not face looting."

I like this man. I disagree with him on just about everything. I was a foreign correspondent much of my life. This, for a New Yorker, is foreign soil. It's interesting, if unfashionable, to consider everything from a different angle, to imagine your way into a stranger's life, to have conversations that involve more than the quest for the wittiest expression of agreement on Trump's perfidy.

What about the killing of George Floyd? "They arrested and charged the officer who did that, and the other three standing there like dummies also need to be prosecuted," Johnson says. "But that's no reason to tear up stores."

Jerome Wilson, a Black vet, strides in, wearing a Twenty-fifth Infantry Division red cap. He's from Jesup, seventy miles down the road, and likes the fruit here enough to make the journey. He tells me about being in military uniform, about to be deployed to Vietnam, and having to enter the bus taking him to Fort Benning through the back door.

"I was going to fight for my country, maybe die, and I was only good enough for the back doors," he says.

It's not true that nothing has changed. Many things have, for the better, in the great fight for racial justice. It's just the essence that has not changed. Wilson and Johnson stand there, arm in arm, a Black man and a white man, friends. That, too, is America, perhaps especially the South, ever ready to surprise you when you write it off.

Morris Selph, Johnson's father-in-law, put up the Trump sign. Selph tells me he's "had more brag on that sign than people condemning it." Seated on a plastic chair at roadside, red-faced and bearded, he says he likes Trump a lot.

"Business went up. Toughest president I've ever seen. He's the Energizer Bunny. Ain't nobody going to knock him down."

Trump's lies are viewed here as straight talk. His detention of child migrants in camps at the border is a stand for law and order. His toughness is a remedy for moral decay. "In schools here they still paddle," Selph says approvingly.

"He's a redneck," Taylor, twenty, says with a smile.

Her mother, Elsie Johnson, trained as an accountant. "What Trump sees is not people, but numbers. He can't see people at all," she says. "China, pay more! But people, no. Maybe that helps him make the tough decisions. He toots his own horn, but I think he's looking out for America."

Away into the distance, green and undulating, America unfurls. Loggers haul timber. Stores advertise guns and ammo. Pawnshops abound. Outside a church a sign proclaims: "Hell is real. Hell is hot. Jesus is coming. Ready or not."

This is Trump country, even if Trump doesn't know which way is up in the Bible. Georgia was flattened by the Union Army in the Civil War, much of Atlanta burned to the ground. This humiliation has never been entirely digested by many white Georgians. Defiance simmers below the surface of Southern gentility. The lost cause of the Confederacy has a tenacious hold; and that cause comes down to white dominion, Trump's leitmotif.

Ahmaud Arbery was quiet, polite, and unassuming, friends and family told me. He was killed a couple of miles from his home, a white bungalow with blue shutters that now has a FOR SALE sign outside. In the house opposite, Jenifer Bolin fumes. "Citizen's arrest, my ass! They were racists."

If Arbery was not forgotten, if the McMichaels were indicted this week by a grand jury for felony murder, if #IRunWithMaud has become a global hashtag signifying the fight against racism, it is thanks in part to Jason Vaughn, a force of nature who as a football coach at Brunswick High School coached Arbery.

I met Vaughn at a Mexican joint. The case, long dead in the water, had troubled him from the outset. The whole thing was a fiasco: white connections and impunity denying justice in the good old way of the Deep South. With the help of his brother, a lawyer, Vaughn pressed to get the police report and also helped start a Facebook page to coordinate pressure.

"The wheels on the bus of justice turn slowly," Vaughn told me. "But this bus had no wheels until we got engaged. A football coach should not have to study law and policing to bring this about."

Four years ago, I traveled to Kentucky and came away with the clear impression a Trump victory was likely. It was in the air, a heady excitement. Today the Trump balloon feels deflated; his old race-baiting, anti-elite, anti-science lines are tired. He still has a hard core of support. The biggest mistake for Democrats would be to think he cannot win. Still, I came away from Georgia thinking the energy is with the people who want Trump out, and his defeat is more likely than not.

The response to the killing of Arbery and Brooks has been remarkable. The Georgia Legislature this week passed a hate-crime bill that Governor Kemp says he intends to sign into law. Georgia was one of only four states holding out against such legislation.

In Atlanta, recent months have shown that, for all its Black professionals and power, the city is as much in need of reform as any other. "As a public defender, you would not know white people are breaking any laws," Rapping, the defense attorney, told me. "Like every city, Atlanta has been shaped by a four-hundred-year-old narrative that says Black or brown people don't matter."

The system that turns Black kids into case numbers, that holds young Black men in cells for months pretrial because they cannot put up money bonds, that prosecutes for smoking marijuana, has to change. It's a form of violence, and it breeds violence. "Law and order" is no answer.

Every weekend, Georgians in their ever-growing diversity—interracial couples, people in hijabs, gay couples—swarm over Stone Mountain, whose North Face is carved with bas-reliefs of Confederate generals. It's as if a new Georgia, defying its racist past, is heeding King's 1963 "I Have a Dream" speech, in which he said, "Let freedom ring from Stone Mountain of Georgia!"

One day, I went to Decatur, a city in the Metro Atlanta sprawl, to see a Confederate monument, a thirty-foot obelisk engraved with tributes to the "loyalty and truth" of men "who held fast to the faith as it was given by the fathers of the Republic." Graffiti—"No justice, No Peace"; "Black Lives Matter"—had been scrawled all over it. A few days later, on a judge's order, it was gone, hoisted out by a crane. This is not the election, or the country, it was before Ahmaud Arbery and George Floyd and Rayshard Brooks.

Andrea Young, the ACLU director, is the daughter of Andrew Young, an Atlanta mayor, United Nations ambassador, and civil-rights icon. I asked her if there was reason to hope that this moment could accomplish what that movement could not.

"Nobody has believed more in the promise and mythology of America than Blacks," she told me. "We have believed all people were created equal, fought over generations for the truth of the statement. The fact I am here means I am descended from people who, even enslaved, did not give up hope. To do so now would be a betrayal."

LAST TESTAMENT OF
MAURICE THE ROOSTER

Maurice became the most famous rooster in France. When he died,
I imagined his last message to humanity.

JUNE 26, 2020

Meanwhile, in other news, Maurice, the most famous rooster in France,
is dead.

I know, there's been a lot to think about. Keeping six feet apart, losing jobs, living in rectangular Zoom boxes, learning new unhappy forms
of greeting, dealing with bored children, making payroll, getting used to
the deprivations of a virtual life. It's not been easy to separate the wheat
from the chaff, as Maurice might have put it.

The crowing *coq* from Oléron, a small island off France's western
coast, became a national hero last year when he and his owner were
sued by second-home neighbors who wanted Maurice removed for
making too much noise and waking them up on their vacation.

A great French fight pitting rural tradition and *terroir* (that ineffable
mix of soil, sun, and moisture that define a place and a person's imme-
morial connection to it) against tourism and modernity was engaged.

This was a case of deep France versus globalization, heritage versus
holidays, the rooted chicken-owner versus the rootless urban-dweller,
a parable of our times. A cockerel in a culture war is a formidable thing.

About 140,000 people signed a petition supporting a rooster's right
to make a noise. (The crowing Gallic *coq* is of course an eternal symbol of France.) Last September, a judge ruled in Maurice's favor and his
lawyer, Julien Papineau, pronounced a great truth: "This rooster was not
being unbearable. He was just being himself."

Now Maurice is no more. Perhaps the stress got to him. Corinne
Fesseau, his owner, announced last week that he had died in May of

coryza—a respiratory infection common to chickens—and she had buried him in her garden. She waited to divulge the news because France was in crisis and "COVID-19 was more important than my cockerel."

Maurice, whom my colleague Adam Nossiter memorably described as "a cantankerous fowl with a magnificent puffed-out coat," was six years old. Fesseau offered this epitaph: "Maurice was an emblem, a symbol of rural life, and a hero."

She did not allude to Maurice's last will and testament, but a neighbor in Saint-Pierre-d'Oléron, where the rooster lived and died, sent it along to me:

> I am not a hero. That's an overused word. I spoke my own truth. I did what came naturally to me. Many things change but the essential things do not.
>
> The sun sets. The sun rises. Shaking my wattles, raising my head, I had to greet the morning. I could never resist, and why should I have? I had to crow. This was my particular joy, my particular thing. Each of us has one. Honor it.
>
> I am sorry to have caused a fuss. I never wanted to annoy anyone. Those neighbors from Limoges, with their busy city lives, I know they wanted their peace. They had been saving for their summer vacation. Perhaps what they missed is that a sound, like my crowing or a ship's foghorn or a train whistle, may form part of the peace of a place.
>
> A little more patience, a little less agitation, never did any harm. I never went anywhere, and I was happy. There's more to a coop than meets the eye. There's more to any place if you look long enough.
>
> I was content to have three hens as companions. They kept me busy. Contentment, for me, was being attuned to the rhythms and cycles of life. The chicken and the egg.
>
> This is a strange season to be ending my days on this small planet. Human beings, so restless, seem fearful. I hear there is a virus. I am not sure exactly what the virus is. I think the virus is many things. It always lurks, and it will pass, and some other scourge will appear. Keep your eye on the sunrise.
>
> My countrymen are angry. What else is new? It's always too much or too little in France but, my God, what a country of boundless pleasures!

Bastille Day is coming along. Off with their heads, out with the old, in with the new! We French are revolution specialists. The world needs a good revolution now and then.

Even if everything changes so that everything can stay the same. Cultivate your garden. That never disappoints.

I will miss Corinne. I will miss strutting about. I will miss puffing out my plumage and making heads turn (yes, I admit it, I noticed that). I will miss emptying my lungs in the dawn, such a perfect feeling. I will miss the little familiar sounds that offer comfort.

I bequeath the one thousand euros the judge awarded me to the establishment of an online (yes!) audio museum of rural sounds. Lest this hectic world forget.

May peace spread across the earth, but please do not confuse peace with silence.

Maurice the Rooster

We live in earnest, sensitive, and literal times, so I had better specify that I made that up. There's a lot to be said for make-believe. Especially when you are living in a socially distanced box.

THE MOST DANGEROUS
PHASE OF TRUMP'S RULE

Foreboding as the 2020 election approached. Trump, in his own mind, could not lose. He was therefore prepared to do anything, even destroy American democracy, to secure "victory."

JULY 10, 2020

PARIS—Think of postwar European institutions as an elaborate shield against fascism. The European Union diluting nationalist identity; the welfare state cushioning the social divisions dictators may exploit;

NATO transforming the United States into a European power and the ultimate protector of democracy against totalitarian ideologies.

This was Europe's collective response to its double suicide in the first half of the twentieth century. It was not just Germany that had to resurrect itself from the rubble of "zero hour" in 1945, but the whole continent. Europeans owed it to the myriad corpses beneath their every step to build societies and institutions that were fascism-proof.

No wonder President Trump, whose dictatorial inclinations are as hard to suppress as Dr. Strangelove's Nazi salute, hates these European institutions so much. His itch is to undermine, or even destroy, them. "I'm a nationalist," he once said. Yes, he is—flags, military flyovers, walls, monuments, and all, in exaltation of "the greatest, most exceptional, and most virtuous nation in the history of the world," as he put it on July 4.

Since arriving in France, I've heard a couple of French people describe Trump as "funny." For Europeans, the novelty of America's showman has worn off. He's a loudmouth. He's a fool. These observations have emerged from societies that have settled their painful scores with history and found a middling security. The United States, however, has not. In fact, I think Trump has just entered the most dangerous phase of his presidency.

It is important to see Trump in historical context. The country he took over had been through a seesawing quarter century of trauma. First the giddy all-powerful interlude after the disappearance of the Soviet Union, with its temptations of hubris. Then the disorienting shock of September 11, which shattered the idea of America-the-inviolable and propelled the nation into its wars without victory. Then the Great Recession, with its indelible lesson that, as Leonard Cohen put it in his song "Everbody Knows," "the poor stay poor, the rich get rich." Then the fact, irrefutable with the rise of China, of America's relative decline, a development Barack Obama, the first Black president, opted to manage with cool realism.

All this provided the perfect context for "a clumsy, lurching and undiscriminating American nationalism that would boomerang upon itself," as Jacob Heilbrunn described it in his tribute to Owen Harries, the Australian foreign-policy intellectual, who predicted such a fate after September 11.

Trump, masterful media-manipulator, is the vehicle of that nationalism. He exploited a pervasive sense of American humiliation. It was out there, in search of a voice. Trump is not funny. He is fiendish.

Nationalism is not fascism but is a necessary component of it. Both seek to change the present in the name of an illusory past in order to create a future vague in all respects except its glory.

One of the core characteristics of fascism is nostalgia, a pining for a culture of masculinity and monumentalism, evident in Hitler's Nazi Party and the architecture it embraced for the thousand-year Reich. Trump's nostalgia is for some unidentified moment of American greatness, when white male property-owners ruled alone, the nation's global dominance was unchallenged, women stayed home, and gender was not 360. By choosing to speak at Mount Rushmore on the eve of Independence Day, Trump attempted to inscribe his nationalism in a monumental narrative of American heroism. It was straight from the autocratic playbook.

Another central characteristic of nationalism and fascism is their need to define themselves against an enemy. Trump has chosen his: China, designated as the culprit for the coronavirus debacle (and the scapegoat behind which the president can hide his own equal responsibility); and the "angry mobs" he alluded to at Mount Rushmore who constitute, Trump said, a new "far-left fascism that demands absolute allegiance."

It is Trump who demands "absolute allegiance"—look at his trembling Cabinet—and whose nationalism is fascist-tinged. He has turned an uprising against racial injustice after the killing of George Floyd into a pretext to lash out against "criminal" mobs.

There have been excesses among the protests. It is always better to try to contextualize history than to excise it. Cancel culture is inimical to free speech. But the overarching threat the United States faces in the run-up to the November 3 election is from Trump.

The fascism in the air is on the far right of the political spectrum. If Trump could identify national humiliation as his ace in the hole in 2016, he can also seize the potential of the coronavirus pandemic to muddy the waters and stir pervasive fear.

Last month, Trump tweeted: "RIGGED 2020 ELECTION: MILLIONS

OF MAIL-IN BALLOTS WILL BE PRINTED BY FOREIGN COUNTRIES, AND OTHERS. IT WILL BE THE SCANDAL OF OUR TIMES!" Of course, that foreign country would be China.

Trump is preparing the ground to contest any loss to Joe Biden and remain president, aided, no doubt, by Attorney General William Barr's Justice Department. I know, it's unthinkable. So was the Reichstag fire. Europeans, like Americans, should focus on just how unfunny Trump is.

THE TENACITY OF THE FRANCO-AMERICAN IDEAL

France, America, and the world's freedom, as the two nations' contributions to emancipation are questioned.

JULY 17, 2020

PARIS—Perhaps the root of the mutual fascination that binds France and the United States is that each sees itself as an idea, a model of some kind for the rest of the world. This is an immodest but tenacious notion, bound up with the founding articles and myths of both republics. No other countries make such claims for the universality of their virtue.

These are now unfashionable ideas, having their roots in the white patriarchal societies of the late eighteenth century. Beware of fashion. It may overcorrect. I will try to explain.

In France, the Declaration of the Rights of Man and of the Citizen, adopted in 1789 as the expression of the ideals of the French Revolution, states in its first article: "Men are born and remain free and equal in rights." The declaration defines these natural rights as "liberty, property, security, and resistance against oppression," and says that liberty "consists of doing anything which does not harm others."

Thirteen years earlier, in its Declaration of Independence, the United States set out certain "self-evident" truths: "that all men are created equal, that they are endowed by their Creator with certain unalienable Rights, that among these are Life, Liberty and the pursuit of Happiness." The right to govern stemmed "from the consent of the governed." Over the ensuing fifteen years, these ideas were enshrined in the United States Constitution and Bill of Rights.

France and the United States were intertwined as political allies, but also as twinned sources of Enlightenment principles. Thomas Jefferson, a slave owner, influenced the formulation of the French declaration and was an author of America's founding laws.

The revolutions were sweeping. There was nothing "self-evident" about them. Out with monarchy, in with "We the people." Out with divine right, in with human rights. Out with rule by edict, in with the separation of powers and the rule of law. So, falteringly, began the liberal-democratic experiment, now under attack.

The experiment was as flawed as Jefferson himself. All men are created equal. Sounds good, but what about women? (A Declaration of the Rights of Woman and the Female Citizen was written in France in 1791 by the French feminist Olympe de Gouges.) And what of Black slaves, their value set in the Constitution at 60 percent of a free human being? Let's rephrase the sentence: All white male property-owners are created equal. Not much of a ring to it, but has the merit of accuracy.

And what of France, trading in slaves well into the nineteenth century, ushering Jews to emancipation through the principles of the revolution only to contribute to their mass murder during World War II, fighting a savage colonial war in Algeria between 1954 and 1962?

So, a cry goes up. These pretensions of embodying ennobling ideals for humankind were false, reflecting no more than the narrow worldview of eighteenth-century white males whose talk of equal rights was shot through with exploitative hypocrisy.

The perfect becomes the enemy of the good. In an age of absolutist moral certainty, the most conspicuous feature of humankind—its fallibility—becomes unpardonable. Can a slave owner be celebrated for penning a liberating sentence? How can a progressive socialist French president, François Mitterrand, have been an official of the Vichy regime? Because the second-most conspicuous feature of human beings is their contradictory natures.

"I don't think any people enjoys rooting around in the unpleasant parts of their past," Robert Paxton, a prominent American historian whose groundbreaking work helped bring France to a full understanding of the crimes of the Vichy regime, told me. "Denial is often ineradicable. I think on the whole the French came out of it quicker than we did."

It took more than a half century, until 1995, for France, in the person of President Jacques Chirac, to acknowledge that the French state, and not some handful of misguided Vichy operatives, had "committed the irreparable" in sending some seventy-six thousand French and foreign Jews to their deaths. It was more than a half century after France left Algeria that Emmanuel Macron, while a candidate for the French presidency in 2017, called the French colonization of Algeria "a crime against humanity" and later, as president, acknowledged French "atrocities."

The United States has never formally apologized for slavery. President Clinton, in Africa more than two decades ago, managed to say that "we were wrong" to have "received the fruits of the slave trade." That was all he could muster.

Now, in the midst of another push to overcome America's original sin, would be a good moment for such an apology.

That, after all, is what democracies like France and the United States are capable of: continuous adjustment, improvement, recognition of past mistakes, atonement, progress toward their ideals. If they are, it is thanks in large part to the flawed brilliance of the architects, direct or indirect, of the two republics.

We can and should acknowledge their flaws without denigrating their achievement in spreading the ideas of liberty, free expression, and the rule of law across the face of the earth. The words that issued from Paris and Philadelphia between 1776 and 1791 have served the cause of freedom, even if they were the product of minds and cultures foreign to the Great Awokening of recent years, whose own chief flaw may prove to be self-righteous intolerance.

FIGHTING THE VIRUS IN
TRUMP'S PLAGUE

I came down with COVID-19 in Paris, before the vaccine.

SEPTEMBER 4, 2020

PARIS—A friend of mine opened her closet the other day and felt she was gazing at the clothes of a dead person. They belonged to the *world of yesterday*. She had no use for them in the age of the coronavirus. It was like looking at her grandmother's clothes after she died.

Everyone is jolted these days in such ways. I assumed I would not get COVID-19 if I took basic precautions. Now I have COVID-19. My head feels like a cabbage. Aches swirl down my arms and legs. So, please, dear reader, grant me a little indulgence this once.

My symptoms began Thursday, August 27, a sharp prickling in my throat, from nothing. A cabdriver said, "You are coughing, sir." I said, I know, I am sorry, I am trying not to cough.

I am in a Paris apartment I have rented for a couple of weeks. On the bookshelves my eyes fell on a copy of Stefan Zweig's *The World of Yesterday*, written in Brazil before he and his wife, Charlotte Altmann, committed suicide in 1942. A Viennese Jew born into an empire that no longer existed, his books burned in a Europe reduced to barbarism, Zweig wrote: "All the livid steeds of the Apocalypse have stormed through my life."

A day later, my symptoms worsened. I had a fever of 101. Hot flushes and shivers alternated. My mind swirled. So this is it. The plague that stopped the world. I was more curious than afraid. It's hard to shed the reflexes of a life lived as an observer.

Since the pandemic started, I have wondered, like everybody, how to live. "Stay safe" is no guide to a life worth living. Surrender to fear and it's over. My most powerful memories and experiences involved risk.

When you quit, you're done. Yet now an invisible enemy demanded prudence.

For more than three months, I scarcely moved from my Brooklyn neighborhood. I mourned New York. I tried to get used to the end of conviviality and the way "coronavirus" slips from the tongues of my five grandchildren, aged two to six.

I tried and failed. Still, we have to get on with it, show up. That's life's first admonition. I drove to Georgia, did some reporting, and wrote. I came to Europe to look and listen.

Zweig's book fell open at this: "I have seen the great mass ideologies grow and spread before my eyes—Fascism in Italy, National Socialism in Germany, Bolshevism in Russia, and above all else that pestilence of pestilences, nationalism, which has poisoned the flower of our European culture."

My president, Donald Trump, is a proud *nationalist*. He embraces its mythology of violence as he flirts with cataclysm. Jump! he says. How high? says his Cabinet. He's ready to fight his battles down to the last sucker. If he goes down, it will be in flames.

The virus is deadly serious but plays games. A little relief to tempt you into activity—then it smites you with a cudgel. I felt better last weekend until I tried a peach tart. It's eerie to experience texture without taste. A Coke with ice and lemon was no more than fizz. My body was a stranger. It was out there somewhere, fighting. The fight demanded all its energy. There was nothing left for me.

I stared at the walls. I thought, My world is gone. More than half a life lived in the Cold War, who cares about that any longer, or the values it bequeathed. A phrase of Albert Camus came back to me: "The most incorrigible vice being that of an ignorance that fancies it knows everything and therefore claims for itself the right to kill."

For three hours, I lined up for a free coronavirus test. A medic told me the swab in my nostrils would be "disagreeable but not painful." She then stabbed my brain with what looked like a narrow brochette stick.

My test result, received two days later, was "positive." I knew it would be, but, still, reading the lab result was hard. I am not sure why. Perhaps the certain knowledge that a virus is inside you that could kill you. But, then, so many things can, and death is life's one certainty—and we don't stop the world. We try to make life better.

The plague is back. In fact, as Camus observed, it never goes away. It is waiting to exploit stupidity. Trump wants violence. Do not give it to him. Turn the other cheek. Be stoical. Be the person who stops the tank by standing there.

I am hunkered down. My survival chances are still better than those of an opposition leader in the Russia of Trump's buddy. My daughter and her husband, both doctors, say I have a moderate case. I think I picked it up in a crowded Paris bar, watching a soccer match. But then soccer has saved me more than once, as when a shared love of Didier Drogba, the former Chelsea striker, caused an Iraqi border guard to allow me across the border into Kuwait.

The epigraph to Zweig's book is a quote from Shakespeare's *Cymbeline:* "And meet the time as it seeks us."

I will still try to do that. We must all fight, in the way my body is fighting now with every ounce of its strength to see off the enemy within, if the orange face of the plague is not to devour us all.

TRUMP'S CORONA CORONATION

How January 6, 2021, was a disaster foretold.

SEPTEMBER 25, 2020

"There won't be a transfer, frankly. There will be a continuation." That's President Putin—I'm sorry, I mean President Trump—declining to assure Americans of a peaceful transfer of power after the November election. Does it get any clearer than that?

Trump, in the fog of a pandemic, has opted for chaos. If he can generate enough, he figures, the election results can be disputed, and a post-Ginsburg Supreme Court will hand him victory. "The only way we're going to lose this election is if the election is rigged," he says.

If it looks like a duck, swims like a duck, and quacks like a duck, then it probably is a duck. The duck is called a Trump power grab.

Oh, we've heard it all these past forty-four months, Trump is a harmless buffoon, he is inconsequential, the adults in the room have him by the cojones. Yes, and we know from twentieth-century history that raving loudmouths, lunatic clowns, and cunning actors never do real damage, right? Wake up!

It's not easy. My city, New York, feels semi-anesthetized. Madison Avenue, midmorning on a Monday, is ghostly. People are dazed. They're so done with the virus. What they would most like to know is what they can't know, which is how far through this nightmare are we? Halfway? More? Or, God help us, less?

And what exactly is the nightmare? Trump tramples on science, turns it into a political tool, and so the plague becomes a double one in which the death of more than two hundred thousand Americans and the death of reason fuse. A terrible foreboding takes hold. Meaning has succumbed to fever. We are trapped in a Zoom box inside four walls in cities with moats around them and the drawbridges pulled up. The Great Calamity is upon us.

The calamity has many elements. Trump makes repeated and baseless claims that mail-in balloting will result in rampant voter fraud and an election stolen by the Democrats. He offers hymns to violence. Predicts "citizen militias," calls an assault on a journalist "a beautiful sight," condemns protesters as "domestic terrorists." He explores using the Insurrection Act and the military to suppress disorder. To an impossible defeat, the Great Leader intimates, the only response is violent resistance in the name of his *continuation.*

Trump's Republican Party is servile. It is conspiratorial. Senator Mitch McConnell, his zealous functionary of indecent hypocrisy, reacts to the death of Justice Ruth Bader Ginsburg by racing to install a conservative replacement. "O most wicked speed," as Hamlet put it. No need even to attempt to disguise the purpose. Vice President Mike Pence suggests a new justice—Trump is said to be nominating Judge Amy Coney

Barrett—must be seated to decide "election issues" that may arise "in the days following the election."

Hamlet again: "The time is out of joint." What is the scream gathering in tightened lungs? It is the death of language. Trump's incessant lies do that, strip words of sense. The virus does that, too, creating hideous neologisms. To see someone is now to have an "in-person" or "live" meeting. This has become a privilege. Think about it.

Look at children, now in "pods" or "cohorts," subject to "synchronous" classes that involve having a teacher there in real time (either in person or on video), and the less desirable "asynchronous" classes, meaning a prerecorded video or some posted assignment. This is Orwell territory.

Or look at the Skid Rows forming as businesses close and tourism dies, and try to consider a terrible thought—that a tribal America is so incapable of constructive debate that even a coherent response to a pandemic became impossible, and masks are turned into a political statement.

And still the scream will not be released from lungs under constant scrutiny because it is all too much to bear. The pathogen hyperinflates anxiety, 1930s-style.

A friend, a naturalized American like me, writes from Austria: "I am baffled. I am shattered. I question my entire belief system, my trust in America, my darling adoptive country: Was I too naïve? Too idealistic? Too young? Too stupid? The hardest part for me to understand is not the one lunatic, not the one certifiably, wickedly twisted mind, but all of his enablers, all of his supporters. Who are they? How are so many of them even possible?"

They are possible because America First nationalism is a heady drug for a nation past the zenith of its power, battered by forever wars and economic precariousness. They are possible because the Great Leader says your ugliest demons are in fact your greatest assets. Just look at me!

"It's a rigged election. It's the only way we're going to lose," Trump says. A pliant judiciary, a press he calls the "enemy of the people" tamed, a personal militia, a miraculous vaccine by November: he wants it all for his continuation. He's got his son Donald Trump, Jr., claiming Democrats "will add millions of fraudulent votes that can cancel your vote and overturn the election." The disease runs in the family, you see. They want a corona coronation.

The time is out of joint. Wake up! See the duck for what it is. Vote. Register and vote. The Great Calamity is upon us.

TRUMP'S LAST STAND FOR WHITE AMERICA

To look at America on the eve of the 2020 election was to see a free country on the brink.

We face a choice between a true renewal and a warped fantasy of the past.

OCTOBER 16, 2020

Less than twenty days. It has been a long, hard road to this election. I see fearful faces, those of tormented migrants at the Mexican border, and hate-filled faces, those of the white nationalists in Charlottesville chanting, "Jews will not replace us."

Donald Trump has been all about the fear of replacement, or, as it's sometimes called, "the great replacement." His has been the stand—I am tempted to say the last stand—of whites against nonwhites.

Of America First nationalists against migrants; of straight people against LGBTQ people; of the gunned-up against the unarmed. Of Trump against all those he believes would *replace* the likes of him.

All means have been used—lies, brutality, incitement. But fear has been Trump's main weapon. Fear, which depends on pitting one group against another, is the currency of the Trump presidency. It is therefore no surprise that the America that is about to vote is probably more fractured than at any time since the Vietnam War.

Change can be frightening, which is what the great-replacement conspiracy theory of Renaud Camus, a French writer, hinges on. Camus warns grotesquely of a "genocide by substitution," the replacement of a white French and European order by Muslim hordes in a plot orchestrated by cosmopolitan elites. In Trump's case, read: a white American order replaced by brown Mexican rapists and Black pillagers.

France is worried about Muslims from North Africa. Germans were once so worried about Jews replacing them that they killed six million of them. In a world of mass migration, fear rages: some idea of the nation will be diluted or lost!

America is particularly susceptible to fear today because the world has changed in unsettling ways. Power has migrated eastward to Asia. America's recent wars have been unwon. By mid-century, non-Hispanic whites will constitute less than 50 percent of the population.

It is frightening to see an industry disappear, like coal in Kentucky. Trump understood that he could be the voice of that fear. He would build a wall to keep those brown people out!

He is an impostor. He puffs out his chest, Mussolini-style, but he is a bone-spur coward. A narrow ramp makes his limbs tremble. He is good at getting the blood up. He is good at undoing. He is not good at getting anything constructive done.

Less than twenty days.

America will decide whether to opt for the future or burrow self-destructively into some warped fantasy of the past. It will decide whether to reinvent itself again or turn mean and further inward.

As Edward R. Murrow remarked, "We cannot defend freedom abroad by deserting it at home."

That was in 1954, at the height of McCarthyism. For Senator Joseph McCarthy, the danger to the Republic came from communist infiltration of American life. The real danger came from his obsessions. From the purges and blacklists that branded countless Americans as un-American.

Murrow, a great journalist, stood up to McCarthy.

Donald Trump does business the McCarthy way. He deals in specters: immigrants, and Muslims, and brown people, and Black people, and LGBTQ people.

As with McCarthy, however, the real danger comes from Trump's obsessions, not from these imagined enemies.

American freedom is in decline. The freedom to think, because thought depends on truth. The freedom to dissent, because Trump believes he has "the right to do whatever I want as president." The freedom to breathe, because Trumpism—its nepotism, its cozying to dictators, its incessant volume—is suffocating.

The freedom inextricable from the American idea that I, a naturalized American, hold sacred with an unreasonable ardor.

No, we cannot defend freedom abroad by deserting it at home. We can only defend those who trample human dignity and human rights. As Trump has done with cavalier abandon.

Is it unreasonable to see renewal in a seventy-seven-year-old man, Joe Biden? No. We live in the real world, where the perfect cannot be the enemy of the good. Indecency demands the restoration of decency. That's ground zero of this election. The choice was starkly evident in the televised town-hall events Thursday, as Trump spouted wild far-right conspiracy theories while Biden had the self-deprecating honesty to say that if he lost it could suggest he's "a lousy candidate." Biden is not a lousy candidate; he is a good man, a brave man. I doff my hat to any parent who survives with such dignity the loss of two of his four children.

Of McCarthy, Murrow observed: "He didn't create this situation of fear; he merely exploited it—and rather successfully. Cassius was right. 'The fault, dear Brutus, is not in our stars, but in ourselves.'"

The fault is in ourselves. Time for Americans to look in the mirror—and realize their America is irreplaceable if it is lost.

FREEDOM AS THE
MUZZLE OF A GLOCK

I visited Rifle, Colorado, and was thrown out of the Shooters Grill restaurant, where at the time the waitresses all packed heat. The restaurant was closed in 2022, when the landlord refused to renew the lease. It was run by Lauren Boebert, a hard-right Republican, who would be elected to Congress in November 2020. She says, "Our country is on the line." She's all about American freedom—up to a point. I was apparently not free to talk to people who think differently.

OCTOBER 30, 2020

RIFLE, Colorado—At the Shooters Grill, whose waitresses pack heat, I found Gary Nichols enjoying a burger. A man with bright-blue eyes and a shock of gray hair, he got right to the point.

"Trump has my vote," he told me. "I'll go with whoever supports my beliefs and my freedom."

For Nichols, an investigator in the sheriff's office in nearby Moffat County, where he's worked for more than thirty-five years, the Second Amendment is "probably top of the lot." The right to carry a gun "is just a basic freedom," he argued. "It's about individual choice, self-thinking, not having the government think for us, the right to protect ourselves."

Look, Nichols said, "this is how we started. People came here, out to the West. They worked hard, helped their neighbor. America was not about government interference. It was about doing the right thing. Biden and Harris are way to the left of what I consider good for America. They're always putting America down. I believe in this country."

There you have it. The soul of America is on the ballot Tuesday, any way you look at it.

For Joe Biden and the Democrats, the election is about rescuing American democracy and restoring decency in a nation dragged into the mire by President Trump's lies, self-obsession, racism, and creeping autocracy. It's about firing a corrupt charlatan who has sullied the Oval Office and sown the violence that could well erupt after the vote.

For the Trump Party, still known for some reason as the Republican Party, it's about preserving American self-reliance—the God-fearing, straight-talking, and gun-toting heart of the frontier—against Biden's politically correct socialist takeover. It's about the unbridled spirit of the land of the free, where no pandemic should shutter business.

These two Americas often live in proximity. Rifle, a small conservative ranching town, is a little more than an hour's drive from the Democratic stronghold of Aspen, where the "Aspenites," as they are known here, hold festivals on the state of the world. But they might as well be on different planets, so impossible has dialogue become.

Trump, a multimillionaire from Queens, has exploited this division with astute cynicism. He does not know which way is up with a Bible, could not shoot an elk if it stood in front of him on Fifth Avenue, and has no idea what morality means. Yet he has become the hero of millions of upstanding, churchgoing rural Americans like Nichols, who grew up with guns and have never had it easy. The president's political heist defines demagogy in the digital age.

I put this to Nichols. Sure, he told me, Trump says things that make him cringe. "If he were a member of my congregation, I'd probably go over and talk to him." But that's small stuff. Trump, he said, "stands against abortion, kept us out of wars, brought industry back, defended the Second Amendment, and is big on fossil fuel. We cannot go solar overnight."

I looked around the restaurant. Waitresses with guns holstered on their hips. A cardboard cutout of Trump with a red MAGA hat. Signs saying, "We Don't Call 911, We Use Colt." And "Smith & Wesson Spoken Here." And "Keep Calm and Carry." And "God, Guns, Trump." And "Don't Tread on Me." Copies of the Constitution and the Declaration of Independence.

The Shooters Grill is the creation of Lauren Boebert, a thirty-three-year-old hard-right Republican who, as my colleague Carl Hulse observed, has something of the combative flourishes of Sarah Palin. Boebert, who did not respond to a request for an interview, beat Representative Scott Tipton, the five-term Republican in Colorado's Third Congressional District, to win her way into the general election. Despite several brushes with the law—including a citation for disorderly conduct and a recent cease-and-desist order for allowing indoor dining despite quarantine restrictions—she's in a tight race against Diane Mitsch Bush, the Democratic candidate.

Colorado has been losing its swing-state status as an influx of immigrants and young people has settled in the more urban and liberal Front Range, east of the Rockies. That, combined with Trump fatigue, has nudged the state into what looks like secure blue territory. But Boebert's outspoken campaign, symbolized by the Glock 26 on her hip, has resonated.

It's that soul thing. "We are in a battle for the heart and soul of our country," she likes to say—a Biden-through-the-glass-darkly riff. Or, "Our country is on the line." For Boebert, a mother of four boys, who quit high school her senior year before earning a GED certificate, her hardscrabble battle to make it defines the can-do American spirit Democrats want to stifle.

"Hell, no, you're not," she famously declared when Beto O'Rourke, then a Democratic presidential candidate, said, "Hell, yes, we are going to take your AR-15, your AK-47."

Boebert is backed by Lanny and Jonilyn Hall, two "1,000 percent" Trump supporters, who were also lunching at the Shooters Grill. They moved west from what Lanny called "the communist state of Washington, D.C." He has grown his blond hair long and won't cut it until the "propaganda bull" of the virus is over. "It's my COVID rebellion," he told me. As for Biden, "If he wins, he'll open borders and give immigrants everything we worked for."

Jonilyn Hall, who drives a school bus, loves Trump because he "has done a lot for the vets," and her father, who will turn one hundred next month, fought in World War II. "Our country is special," she told me, "and with the Democrats we'll lose that Constitution." She worries about violence after the election. "There is going to be chaos," she said, "and those Democrats and liberals will be to blame."

Everyone I spoke to in Rifle agreed that the election would not go smoothly. Tamara Degler, the owner of the Crescent Moon Spiritual Goods store and a former nurse, told me, "Protests? Violence? Yes, for certain." She called Trump "a high-vibration person sent to guide us through this time."

It's Trump, of course, who has done everything he can to stir doubt and violence around the election. He will not go easily. But in the world of Rifle, it's Black Lives Matter pillagers who have created this America pregnant with tumult.

As I was talking to the Halls, one of those gun-holstered waitresses approached me to say she had spoken to Boebert, who did not want me interviewing people in her restaurant. I stepped outside and carried on the conversation there.

When I went back to my table, she approached me again to say Boebert wanted me out of the restaurant. Period. On what grounds? "She just wants you out."

So much for "freedom," Boebert's slogan on her campaign posters. So much for freedom of expression and the freedom to talk to people who think differently. So much for the freedom of the press and that free American "spirit."

That's what freedom may look like in a second Trump term: more the my-way-or-the-highway muzzle of a Glock than the liberty enshrined by the Constitution and the rule of law.

THE PEOPLE VERSUS
DONALD TRUMP

In a democracy, every vote is counted and each vote counts. But Trump, a bully born on third base, could not play by the rules of the game and accept the sanctity of the electoral process and the law.

NOVEMBER 6, 2020

The night is darkest before the dawn.

To see that child-man charlatan in the White House spouting lies yet again, asserting without a trace of evidence, "If you count the legal vote I easily win," claiming, "I won Pennsylvania by a lot," and Michigan and Georgia, too, was to be reminded of the American nightmare of these past four years that the American people seem to have brought to an end.

It was a nightmare in which truth died, decency was trampled, science was flouted, division was fanned, and the American idea was desecrated, as President Trump wheedled his way into the minds of every American with an insidious cascade of self-obsessed posturing and manipulative untruth.

In a democracy, a beautiful idea for which so much blood has been shed over the centuries, every vote is counted and each vote counts. That is what happened in 2016, when President Trump won Michigan by 0.2 percentage points, Pennsylvania by 0.7, and Wisconsin by 0.8. What goes around comes around. The difference in 2020 is that the child-man cannot accept having his treat snatched away. A bully born on third base cannot play by the rules of the game and accept the sanctity of the electoral process and the law.

As I write, it appears that Joe Biden will be the forty-sixth president of the United States.

There may be recounts. There will be legal challenges. But Trump's attempted coup against democracy, for it is no less than that, will be resisted. The United States is far bigger than this little man.

It seems almost churlish to pick apart Trump's arguments, which in fact reflect no more than the hysteria of a narcissist for whom the phrase "You're fired!" is unbearable. He cannot seem to distinguish between voting after the election, which would be illegal, and the process of receiving and counting votes cast in a timely manner. Or, rather, he can make that distinction, but only when it comes to Arizona, where he hopes the ballots still being counted will reverse Biden's lead.

Trump has another mental problem. He cannot, it seems, distinguish between a snapshot of a moment—when, for example, he was ahead of Biden by several hundred thousand votes in Georgia and Pennsylvania on election night—and the eventual result after all votes are counted. He keeps bleating that he "won" and that some vast conspiracy by the media and a corrupt Democratic Party machine has mysteriously "whittled down" his triumph until it takes on the hideous hue of defeat. Another name for "whittling" is counting the votes.

Such desperation—the antics of the sandbox transposed to the Oval Office—is excruciating to watch, not least because it is so predictable.

Throughout his life, when in a tight corner, having stiffed his contractors or ushered his businesses to the brink of bankruptcy, Trump has responded with lawsuits, lies, and threats. His method was simple:

attack, attack, attack. It often worked. But until now, he has not faced the will of the American people in the opposing corner.

An attempted coup against democracy, I said. For months now, Trump has been peddling the notion that, as he put it in July, "mail-in ballots will lead to massive electoral fraud and a rigged 2020 election." He has returned to the theme relentlessly, without any evidence that mail ballots lead to fraud. This was the groundwork for a power grab.

Now it is Biden's moment, on the eve of his seventy-eighth birthday. The moment of a man with a deep respect for America's institutions, its alliances, and the rule of law. The moment of a man who reached out to all Americans during the campaign. The moment of a man who became the Democratic nominee as people turned to safe hands to confront the coronavirus and now, it seems, will be asked to heal a wounded nation. The moment of a man who came to a gift for empathy through the devastating loss of his first wife and two of his four children. The moment of an American who understands that you cannot sculpt from rotten wood, and so every democracy requires the foundation of truth.

Trump's last-ditch incitement of his vast tribe—composed of tens of millions of Americans—will cast a shadow across an eventual Biden presidency. The battles of today will not quickly abate. But the restoration of sanity to the highest office in the land is the prerequisite for the rebuilding that must now begin. As Martin Luther King, Jr., put it, "The arc of the moral universe is long, but it bends toward justice."

I think now particularly of Georgia, where a Biden victory would be the first by a Democratic candidate in almost three decades. With its large African American population, and its sharp division between diverse, fast-growing Metro Atlanta and a mainly white conservative hinterland, Georgia was a bellwether of a changing America reeling from a pandemic and racial tension.

" 'Let Freedom Ring' from Georgia" was the headline on a column I wrote from there in June, predicting a Trump defeat.

Democracy is messy but stubborn. It is the system that best enshrines the human desire to be free. This massive American vote has been many things—bitter and ugly among them—but above all, it has been a beautiful testament to the power of each, single ballot in the world's oldest democracy.

AU REVOIR BUT NOT ADIEU

My last column. It was not easy to go, but timing is everything. I'd had a good run, and Paris beckoned. There comes a moment to pass the baton to the next generation.

NOVEMBER 14, 2020

When I was a younger man, a quarter century ago, I clambered into the armored Land Rover provided by this newspaper to cover the Bosnian war. It was, at the best of times, an unbalanced vehicle. At the worst, it would shudder as if possessed. I was headed from Sarajevo back to Paris to see my third child born. There was no other way home. The airport, under fire from Serbian artillery, was closed.

Over Mount Igman, out of range of those Serbian guns, on the paved highway to Split, I exhaled. The blast from a shell as I walked through the old town had blown me off my feet a few days earlier. Now I was out of suffocating Sarajevo, home free. Until the steering wheel, spinning in my hands, lost all connection to the wheels. I was helpless. The car slalomed across the oncoming lane, tumbled several feet down an embankment, flipped over and over across a field, to settle at last on its side. The first thing I saw was a small red ax. To smash the bulletproof windows.

If, unlike several dear colleagues, I walked away from the war, it was to say something. Otherwise, life was wasted breath. Something about crazed nationalism, how it giddies people with myth, how it gets their blood up building walls, how it births loony ideas like turning the east-west crossroads of Sarajevo into an ethnically pure Serbian preserve, how its endpoint may be a hundred thousand dead or more in the rubble and the ashes. How it quashes tolerance, destroys civilization, enables dictators, and devours freedom.

To say something, also, to my four children, whose lives I was lucky to see unfold, about engagement in the great causes of the world, about the pursuit of justice, about what Supreme Court Justice Oliver Wendell Holmes called "the bitter cup of heroism," and about his advice to wear the "heart out after the unattainable."

Life is a struggle but we must seize it, for hope is the last to die. I like the spirit of Shakespeare's Henry V: "We would not seek a battle, as we are; / Nor, as we are, we say we will not shun it."

This, dear readers, is goodbye, my last column for *The New York Times*. I have tried to defend the causes I believe in—freedom, decency, pluralism, the importance of dissent in an open society, above all. Uniformity of thought is the death of thought. It paves the road to hell.

I've learned a lesson or two. I can say, after more than a dozen years, that the best columns write themselves. They come, all of a piece, fully formed, a gift from some deep place. They enfold the subject just so, like a halter on a horse's face.

Such inspiration is rare. Most columns resemble exquisite torture. Having an idea is not something you can order up, like breakfast. The battle between form and subject is ferocious. Eight hundred words constitute a rigid carapace resistant to descriptive writing and narrative.

Lincoln did all right with 272 words at Gettysburg. When the cutting began, I tried to console myself with that. But shed no tears for the columnist's lot. I always wanted to witness what I wrote about. Armchair pontification too often turns to bloviation. Travel the world, see desperation in the eye of a raped Yazidi girl or a refugee dumped by Australia in Papua New Guinea, and battle to render the unimaginable in a few words. Brevity is a bitter stimulant to pithiness.

It is hard to go at this moment. I did not expect the lessons of Bosnia to come home to the United States of Donald Trump's "America First" nationalism. Because each vote still counts, because no state has seceded yet, because a "gunned-up" population has not taken up those guns, the country I love appears to be emerging from the Trump nightmare. It is not yet free of the tentacles of his derangement. To beat back the defeated president's ongoing assault on truth, the rule of law, and the institutions of democracy has been the absolute moral imperative of our times.

The American idea freed me, a British Jew from the land of "trembling Israelites," as it has freed countless others in various ways. Naturalization is a rite of passage to responsibility. "Life, Liberty and the pursuit of Happiness" depend on the engagement of citizens. The fight to defend America's openness, renewal, and unity against Trump's walls, retrogression, and fracture is inseparable from the struggle to save the world from the creeping autocracy of the twenty-first century. On lies is tyranny built.

But to everything there is a season. I have tried not only to say what I think but also to reveal who I am. That work is done. You know me, unfiltered, for better or worse. Wisdom is also knowing when to go. Persist too long and, like all those armies bent on reaching Moscow, you may face the Russian winter.

Nobody ever told me what subject to choose, much less what to say about it. "You write and you are free," a Saudi friend once said in Jeddah. He could scarcely imagine to what degree. Free and solitary, like a runner on the beach in the early morning at low tide. Such freedom is rare.

The thing is to use it. To listen through the silences for a clue. To see the intersection of personal and national psyches, the richest point of journalistic inquiry. To marry the head and the heart. To make a difference. To know, and it's enough, that a column saved a life. To suggest, in the name of a child's innocent gaze, that putting food on the table beats an eye for an eye, for then, soon enough, everyone is blind. To hold power to account.

Having spent my infancy in South Africa, grown up and been educated in England, and then, after a peripatetic life as a foreign correspondent, found my home in New York (the place that took me in), I have been concerned with belonging.

It could scarcely be otherwise. From Lithuania to Johannesburg, from South Africa to Israel and Britain, from London to New York, my family has been on the move since the 1890s. Trees have roots. Jews have legs. Displacement is hard. A new land is also the loss of the old. The mental toll, as on my intermittently suicidal late mother, may be severe.

Exclusion precludes belonging. I learned that young. The beach at Muizenberg, near Cape Town, was full of white people. The surf leapt. Bathers frolicked. Blacks waded into the filthy harbor at Kalk

Bay. They slept in concrete-floored outbuildings with little windows like baleful eyes.

But I stray into descriptive writing, anathema to the columnist. Suffice to say Bosnia redoubled the lessons of South Africa. Racism is a close cousin to nationalism, as America has been reminded. They both depend on scapegoating or persecuting "the other."

There is no place, on this small, interconnected, vulnerable, depleted planet, for the ideologies that took tens of millions of lives in the twentieth century. So, dear readers, fight on for an American democracy freed at last of racism, for a borderless federal Europe, and for a sustainable world.

I am off to head our bureau in Paris, the city I miraculously reached after that Land Rover somersaulted, the city where I started in journalism more than forty years ago. I may even indulge in some narrative writing, possibly also a good meal, conceivably a decent glass of wine. I will set opinion aside, as I did in Bosnia, where everyone knew what I thought, for we are human after all.

I hope this is au revoir, not adieu. And muchibus thankibus, as Joyce put it in *Ulysses*, for bearing with me down the years. It's the voyage that counts, they say, but so does the ever-flickering destination, that promised land where the unquenchable quest of every human being to be free and live with dignity is honored and safeguarded in perpetuity.

ACKNOWLEDGMENTS

A column for *The New York Times* comes with remarkable freedom. Over a dozen years I was never asked where I planned to go or what I intended to say. "You write and you are free," a Saudi friend once said to me in Jeddah. That about summed it up.

For this gift, I wish to thank Arthur Ochs Sulzberger Jr., A. G. Sulzberger, Andy Rosenthal, Katie Kingsbury, Stephen Dunbar-Johnson, and, for his wisdom, camaraderie, and example over two decades, James Bennet. For their deft editing and wise counsel, my thanks go to Serge Schmemann, Brian Zittel, Jim Dao, Linda Cohn, Nick Fox, and Honor Jones. I was blessed with wonderful assistants in Tariro Mzezewa, Rosie Goldensohn, and Alexandra Petri. My fellow columnists Maureen Dowd, Tom Friedman, Nick Kristof, Gail Collins, and Bret Stephens were terrific companions-in-arms. For a leave that allowed me to complete this book, I am grateful to Michael Slackman, Jim Yardley, and Kirk Krauetler. Deep thanks, also, to Jeff Roth, caretaker of the *New York Times* "morgue," for his research.

Conversations with countless friends and colleagues informed this work. Among them are Daphne Anglès, Jan Benzel, David Bernstein, Richard Bernstein, Sandra Breka, Gahl Burt, Paola Ceccarelli, Kyle Crichton, François Delattre, William Drozdiak, Salam Fayyad, Dexter Filkins, Robert Fox, Ruth Franklin, Claudio Gatti, Jas Gawronski, Rick Goldstone, Stephen Heintz, Warren Hoge, John Huey, Martin Indyk, Duncan Irving, Walid Jumblatt, Joe Kahn, David Kirkpatrick, Scott Lacy, Susan Lacy, James Lasdun, Alex Levac, Kati Marton, James McAuley, Lawrie Mifflin, Constantine Normanby, George Packer, Jane Perlez, Jeffrey Price, Sally Quinn, Sigrid Rausing, Alan Riding, John Rielly, Roxana Saberi, Karim Sadjadpour, Stefan Schmitz, Janny Scott,

Nick Taylor, Goran Tocilovac, Ozgur Ulusoy, Paolo Valentino, Nick van Praag, Scott Veale, Ed Vulliamy, Robin Walden, Alex Ward, Bruce Weber, Jon Wells, Kael Weston, Patrick Wintour, and Robert Worth.

To the late Amos Oz, Bob Silvers, and Daniel Wolf I feel a particular debt of gratitude. They cast light, still.

I am lucky to have in Amanda Urban an extraordinary agent whose tireless, creative support for my work now extends over three decades. In Paris, Léontine Gallois did important research and fact-checking. At Knopf, I wish to thank Sarah Perrin and Ellen Feldman for their superb professionalism. My heartfelt thanks go to my editor, Jonathan Segal, a patient sage. Jon, armed with the sharpest pencil in the West, improves any sentence.

My children know by now the demands a book makes. I am lucky that, generally speaking, they can now laugh at their dad's absences. My deep, ever-renewed gratitude and love to Jessica, Dan, Blaise, and Adele. Also to my grandchildren Claudia, Max, Lenny, Will, Raphael, and Mathias, who make it impossible to be anything but hopeful about this century, evidence to the contrary notwithstanding.

Sarah Cleveland, my beloved, inspired me. She understood the reasons for this voyage, helped me always to see, and to find the words for what I had seen. Before her nurturing of this book, her eye on the natural world, and her uncanny ability to see every shooting star I tip my hat in wonder.

INDEX

A NOTE ABOUT THE AUTHOR

ROGER COHEN has worked for *The New York Times* for thirty-three years, as a foreign correspondent, foreign editor, and columnist. He is currently the paper's Paris bureau chief. Before joining *The Times*, he was a correspondent for Reuters and *The Wall Street Journal.* His previous books include *Hearts Grown Brutal*, a story of the Bosnian war, and *The Girl from Human Street*, an account of his Jewish family's wanderings and tribulations. His work, as both correspondent and columnist, has been recognized with several prizes. Raised in Britain and South Africa, he is a naturalized American.

A NOTE ON THE TYPE

This book was set in Electra, a typeface designed for Linotype
by the renowned type designer W. A. Dwiggins (1880–1956).
Electra is a fluid typeface, avoiding the contrasts of thick and
thin strokes that are prevalent in most modern typefaces.

Typeset by Scribe, Philadelphia, Pennsylvania
Printed and bound by Berryville Graphics, Berryville, Virginia
Designed by Jo Anne Metsch